Imagining the Gallery

Imagining the Gallery

THE SOCIAL BODY OF BRITISH ROMANTICISM

Christopher Rovee

STANFORD UNIVERSITY PRESS

Stanford, California 2006

Stanford University Press
Stanford, California

Library of Congress Cataloging-in-Publication Data

Rovee, Christopher Kent.
Imagining the gallery : the social body of British Romanticism / Christopher Rovee.
p. cm.
Originally presented as the author's thesis (doctoral—Princeton Univ.) under the title Imaging the gallery: aesthetic democracy in British romanticism, 2002.
Includes bibliographical references and index.
ISBN 0-8047-5124-2 (cloth : alk. paper)
1. English literature—19th century—History and criticism. 2. English literature—18th century—History and criticism. 3. Art and literature—England—History—19th century. 4. Portrait painting, English. 5. Romanticism—Great Britain. 6. Portraits in literature. I. Title.
PR457.R68 2006
820.9'145—dc22 2005032998

Printed in the United States of America on acid-free, archival-quality paper

Original Printing 2006
Last figure below indicates year of this printing:
15 14 13 12 11 10 09 08 07 06

Typeset at Stanford University Press in 10/13 Minion

To my parents

CAROLYN ROVEE-COLLIER

and

GEORGE COLLIER

Contents

Acknowledgments xi

Introduction 1

1. The Many Bodies of Edmund Burke 47

2. Everybody's Shakespeare 75

3. Painting Sorrow 105

4. Monsters, Marbles, and Miniatures 130

5. The Look of a Poet: Wordsworth 150

Epilogue 183

Notes 195

Index 237

Figures

1. John Chubb, *George Beale, merchant*, ca. 1797 9
2. Detail from title page to Thomas Hobbes's *Leviathan*, 1651 12
3. William Hogarth, *Heads of Six of Hogarth's Servants*, ca. 1750–55 14
4. John Kay, *Hieroglyphic Portrait of Buonaparte*, 1814 17
5. James Gillray, *The French Invasion: or John Bull, bombarding the Bum-Boats*, 1793 18
6. *George the Fourth, King of Great Britain and Ireland*, from J. P. Hemm, *Portraits of the Royal Family in Penmanship*, 1831 20
7. *His Royal Highness the Duke of York*, from J. P. Hemm, *Portraits of the Royal Family in Penmanship*, 1831 21
8. *George Taylor*, from J. Caulfield, *Portraits, Memoirs, and Characters, of Remarkable Persons*, 1819–20 27
9. *Blind Granny* (portrait and facing page), from J. Caulfield, *Portraits, Memoirs, and Characters, of Remarkable Persons*, 1819–20 28
10. *William Friday*, from John Thomas Smith, *Vagabondiana; or, Anecdotes of Mendicant Wanderers Through the Streets of London*, 1817 30
11. E. F. Burney [J. H. Ramberg?], *The Royal Academy Exhibition of 1784: The Great Room, East Wall*, 1784 35
12. Pietro Martini, after J. H. Ramberg, *The Exhibition of the Royal Academy, 1787*, 1787 36
13. Detail from Pietro Martini, after J. H. Ramberg, *The Exhibition of the Royal Academy, 1787*, 1787 37
14. Anonymous [Attributed to Frederick George Byron], *Frontispiece to Reflections on the French Revolution*, 1790 51
15. James Gillray, *Two Pair of Portraits*, 1798 54
16. Lucas Cranach the Elder, *Lucretia*, ca. 1533 64

17. Sir Joshua Reynolds, *Admiral Viscount Keppel*, ca. 1780 68
18. William Humphreys, *Who's in Fault? (Nobody) a view off Ushant*, 1779 69
19. Sir Joshua Reynolds, *Commodore Augustus Keppel*, ca. 1752–53 70
20. Luigi Schiavonetti, engraving after Sir Joshua Reynolds, *Midsummer Night's Dream*, 2.2. *The Dramatic Works of Shakspeare*, 1802 83
21. J. P. Simon, after John Opie, *Winter's Tale*, 2.3 92
22. Francesco Bartolozzi, after William Hamilton, *Winter's Tale*, 2.3. *The Dramatic Works of Shakspeare*, 1802 94
23. Joseph Collyer, engraving after William Hamilton, *Winter's Tale*, 4.4. *The Dramatic Works of Shakspeare*, 1802 95
24. James Fittler, after Francis Wheatley, *Winter's Tale*, 4.4 97
25. Samuel Middiman, after Joseph Wright, *Winter's Tale*, 3.3 98
26. Robert Thew, after William Hamilton, *Winter's Tale*, 5.3 101
27. James Gillray, *The Monster broke loose; a Peep into the Shakespeare Gallery*, 1791 102
28. Frontispiece to Volume II, Charlotte Smith, *Elegiac Sonnets*, 1797 110
29. Engraving to illustrate "Sonnet IV. To the Moon," *Elegiac Sonnets*, 1797 112
30. Engraving to illustrate "Sonnet XII. Written on the Sea Shore.—October, 1784," *Elegiac Sonnets*, 1797 116
31. Engraving to illustrate "Sonnet XXVI. To the River Arun," *Elegiac Sonnets*, 1797 118
32. Sir Joshua Reynolds, *Lady Elizabeth Delmé and Her Children*, 1777–79 128
33. Henry William Pickersgill, *William Wordsworth*, 1833 153
34. W. H. Watt, engraving after Henry William Pickersgill, 1835. Frontispiece to Volume I of *The Poetical Works of William Wordsworth*, 1843 155
35. Benjamin Robert Haydon, *Wordsworth on Helvellyn*, 1842 169
36. Sir George Hayter, *The House of Commons, 1833*, 1833–43 184
37. Thomas Rowlandson, *The House of Commons*, from R. Ackermann, *The Microcosm of London*, 1808 187

Acknowledgments

Many friends, colleagues, teachers, and students have supported me in the writing of this book, and it is a pleasure to thank them here. The readings, suggestions, and consistent encouragement of Starry Schor and Susan Wolfson shaped this study, not just in its early stages but even in its concluding ones, many years down the line. Jay Fliegelman was profoundly giving of his time and wisdom, and he continues to be a fountain of insight regarding my central arguments. Insightful, scrupulous, and energetic comments by William Galperin and Judith Pascoe helped make this a far better book than it otherwise would have been. Several people offered challenging and generous close readings, sometimes of a chapter, sometimes of the whole book; for this I am grateful to John Bender, Marshall Brown, Pamela Fletcher, Erik Gray, James A. W. Heffernan, Seth Lerer, Herbert Lindenberger, Andrea Lunsford, Stephen Orgel, Charles Ryskamp, Abraham Stoll, Anne Wallace, and Alex Woloch. Three anonymous readers also provided valuable input on sections of the argument. For stimulating conversations and timely interventions, I am obliged to Mark Allison, Jeff Dolven, Diana Fuss, Claudia Johnson, Rob Kaufman, Daniel Novak, Morton Paley, Peter Simonsen, Charles Tung, Blakey Vermeule, and James Vernon. It was a pleasure to work with so magnanimous and encouraging an editor as Norris Pope. Lucy Newlyn will be surprised to know how far her influence, dating from the book's prehistory, has stretched.

Yvonne Töpfer, Javanni Munguia-Brown, Jacey Davis, Monica Canas, and Chen-Chen Lu have, between them, provided the best and surest childcare a parent could want—and with it the peace of mind needed to write. The recipient of their attentions has kept me remarkably sane these last five years: thank you, Julian, for your powers. To Denise Gigante I owe more than an acknowledgment can express. This book could not have done without her exacting and oft-repeated readings any more than its author could do without her love and friendship.

Stanford University's English Department, along with the School of Humanities and Science, provided a much-needed subvention to cover the cost of image reproductions. For facilitating this, I wish to thank my former and current chairs, Robert Polhemus and Ramón Saldívar, as well as my dean, Iain Johnstone. A short-term fellowship at the Harry Ransom Humanities Research Center allowed me to gather materials essential for completing this study. Additional financial assistance was provided by Stanford University's Vice Provost for Undergraduate Education, the Donald and Mary Hyde Foundation, and Princeton University's Graduate School. The staff at Stanford University's Department of Special Collections has been extraordinarily helpful and cheerful to boot; I especially wish to thank John Mustain and Polly Armstrong. I am also grateful to the staffs at the Harry Ransom Humanities Research Center; the National Portrait Gallery, London; and the Princeton University Department of Rare Books. Cyndy Brown, Jacob Doty, Maia Krause, Ivan Ortiz, and Eliza Ridgeway helped me put the final product together. Versions of chapters two and four were first published, respectively, in *Studies in Romanticism* (v. 41, no. 4, Winter 2002, Copyright the Trustees of Boston University) and *Studies in the Novel* (v. 36, no. 2, Summer 2004, Copyright 2004 by the University of North Texas). A portion of chapter five appeared in *Literature Compass* (Blackwell Publishing, Inc.). I thank these publishers for kindly allowing me to include this material.

My dedication reflects feelings of incredible good fortune, ever on the increase, in having been raised by Carolyn Rovee-Collier and George Collier.

Imagining the Gallery

Introduction

> Human beings can . . . embrace their village, or valley, with a single glance; the same with the court, or the city (especially early on, when cities are small and have walls); or even the universe—a starry sky, after all, is not a bad image of it. But the nation-state? "Where" is it? What does it look like? How can one *see* it?
>
> —Franco Moretti

> The spectacle is not a collection of images, but a social relation among people, mediated by images.
>
> —Guy Debord

In *Pride and Prejudice*, Miss Bingley goads Darcy by talking of his "supposed marriage" to a daughter of the local gentry: "Do let the portraits of your uncle and aunt Philips be placed in the gallery at Pemberley," she says; "Put them next to your great uncle the judge. They are in the same profession, you know; only in different lines."[1] Imagining a gallery in which portraits of Elizabeth Bennet's relations hang alongside portraits of Darcy's ancestors, Miss Bingley highlights a distinction based not on heritage but on wealth: for all his power, Darcy's great uncle was a commoner, not an aristocrat.[2] By insinuating that the Bennets don't belong in the gallery at Pemberley, she affirms her self-importance and naturalizes her own status as a member of Britain's new economic elite. Her allusion to the family pictures is a pointed one, for in galleries like the one at Pemberley ancestral portraits conventionally articulate the continuity of family and of nation. They are a material correlative to what Edmund Burke calls the "*entailed* inheritance derived to us from our forefathers"; they show the march of generations in a glance. Essential elements in a visual display of wealth and power, the ageless faces of the illustrious dead epitomize the symbolism of the private gallery, which was to instruct members of the public of their transitory place within what Burke calls the nation's "permanent body."[3]

Miss Bingley, eyeing a merger with ancient descent, asserts her rightful place in that permanent body. By contrast, Elizabeth Bennet encounters Darcy's family pictures on rather different terms. Standing before the awesome image of Pemberley's master, surrounded by the materiel of dominance, Elizabeth indulges her preference for a smaller, more intimate scale of representation:

> In the gallery there were many family portraits, but they could have little to fix the attention of a stranger. Elizabeth walked on in quest of the only face whose features would be known to her. At last it arrested her—and she beheld a striking resemblance of Mr. Darcy, with such a smile over the face, as she remembered to have sometimes seen, when he looked at her. She stood several minutes before the picture in earnest contemplation, and returned to it again before they quitted the gallery. Mrs. Reynolds informed them, that it had been taken in his father's life time.
>
> There was certainly at this moment, in Elizabeth's mind, a more gentle sensation towards the original, than she had ever felt in the height of their acquaintance. The commendation bestowed on him by Mrs. Reynolds was of no trifling nature. What praise is more valuable than the praise of an intelligent servant? As a brother, a landlord, a master, she considered how many people's happiness were in his guardianship!—How much of pleasure or pain it was in his power to bestow!—How much of good or evil must be done by him! Every idea that had been brought forward by the housekeeper was favourable to his character, and as she stood before the canvas, on which he was represented, and fixed his eyes upon herself, she thought of his regard with a deeper sentiment of gratitude than it had ever raised before; she remembered its warmth, and softened its impropriety of expression. (263–4)

What might have been a scene of instruction in familial and national heritage proves, instead, a scene of desire. Elizabeth hardly looks at Darcy's picture, let alone those of his ancestors. Recognizing more than ever his place within the social power structure, she simultaneously reduces the impact of his image to the memory of a smile, the echo of a recent conversation. The grand portrait becomes an occasion for Elizabeth to look inward, to fix her attention on the portrait's "original" as it hangs in the gallery of her mind. In a jarring, uncanny sentence, Austen in effect has Elizabeth bring the picture to life: "She stood before the canvas, on which he was represented, and fixed his eyes upon herself." Imagining herself as the object of his gaze issuing from the portrait, Elizabeth—who had initially been "arrested" by it—becomes an active participant in the commerce of looks.

Her energetic contemplation carries a profound ideological charge. A century earlier, Richard Steele had poked fun at a vain nobleman who spoiled the sublime effect of his ancestral portraits by noting the changing of fashion from one age to the next—thus missing the point of the aristocratic family gallery, which is not to observe alteration but to celebrate permanence.[4] In a less satirical vein, Austen's heroine, though impressed by Darcy's heritage and the responsibilities it entails, actively subordinates his public character to a private one. She concentrates significantly on "the only face whose features would be known to her," dislocating the portrait from its place in a succession of family pictures. In lieu of an abstract, permanent body, she contemplates a real one: a face whose features she knows. Disregarding the portrait's symbolic value, Elizabeth treats it not as an instrument of cultural control but as a sentimental object, capable of being fitted to her own desires.

But those desires are famously ambiguous, and no matter how assertively Elizabeth narrows her view to the portrait (and its original), it is impossible to parse out "love" from her recognition of a social context in which Darcy is, like his picture, larger than life. Mr. and Mrs. Gardiner can laugh off the "flaming character" (271) given him by the aptly named Mrs. Reynolds (evoking Sir Joshua, England's premier portrait painter), but for Elizabeth the praise confirms even as it incites her deepest wishes, be they romantic (for Darcy) or material (to become mistress of Pemberley). The practical consequence of such a fantasy is foreseen by Miss Bingley when she teasingly imagines a gallery in which the gentry and the ruling elite hang side by side—a proposition that registers the subversive potential of the love-plot of *Pride and Prejudice*, where marriage and the assorted material desires that assist it erode the genealogical stability pictured on the walls of the gallery.

Imagining a Social Body

Miss Bingley describes the portrait gallery as people at the beginning of the nineteenth century were beginning to experience it, as two things simultaneously: an institution invested with the authority of the past, and a representative space that could put on view the face of the present.[5] This book explores these competing conceptions of national representation and the commerce between them. Building on Benedict Anderson's influential argument that a nation, like any other community, is fundamentally an imagined entity, it will be my contention that in the years roughly separating two major events in national representation of Britain—the opening of the Royal Academy in 1768 and the passage of the First Reform Bill in 1832—the encounter with portraiture involved and instantiated the imagining of a British social body. Central to this argument is the fact that the dominant site for portraiture around 1800 was neither so insular nor so explicitly visual as the traditional family gallery. Portraiture flourished, instead, as a flexible discourse spanning the visual and verbal divide, whose myriad incarnations manifested a pressure to remake the nation in the image of the private individual. By the time Noel Desenfans published the first proposal for a National Portrait Gallery in 1799, the encounter with portraiture had long served as a prompt to a many-times-repeated act of imagination by which British people saw their country. In lieu of the ancestral gallery, the public art exhibition represented the "family" of the nation; its textual equivalent, the volume of print-portraits, allowed private individuals in private spaces to visualize a range of social bodies organized by private interests; political discourse unfolded as a series of character sketches; poems, novels, and histories incorporated portraits as subjects, plot devices, and organizational templates; and those cultural figureheads, authors, self-advertised through portraits even as their fictional characters found extratextual life in them. The charged encounter between Austen's gentry daughter and Darcy's grand-style portrait may be the most famous literary instance of portraiture, but it only hints at a more far-reaching phenemenon.

Across media and in various cultural locations, portraiture fixed, within the national imaginary, the face of the British nation as a diverse set of particulars. But in this, it was neither strictly progressive nor conservative. Rather, portraiture went both ways at once. At its most grandiose, as in the elite canvases by Joshua Reynolds and Thomas Lawrence, it embodied the mixing of mercantile and propertied classes that is the special hallmark of British industrialism. At its simplest, as in the engravings of working-class individuals often circulated in portrait books, it proffered a plain and radically inclusive social body. This political versatility originated in the eighteenth century, I suggest, in the disagreement between a populist, Hogarthian, representationalist aesthetics, and an elite, Shaftesburian, idealizing aesthetics—a disagreement that becomes especially fraught in an age when the increased social inclusivity of cultural institutions such as the gallery, the theater, and the novel, is offset by an ongoing lack of middle-class political representation. A private gallery in an estate like Pemberley, for instance, would have been open to certain members of the public only as a concession to a shifting cultural order in which the British elite was attempting to reassert authority. By presenting its own purchases of art as a national asset, Linda Colley argues, the aristocracy made their own private property "in some magical and intangible way *the people's property also*."[6] This phantasmatic merger between the aristocracy and the people was nurtured in the gallery's public space. When one considers the discontinuity between the expanded bourgeois influence on display there, and the actual political situation in the Commons—a relationship that seems to have been inversely proportionate—it becomes possible to conceive of the gallery in the terms provided by sociologist Georg Simmel, as a space of play that bears a similar relation to the political as "that of the work of art to reality." Donning what Simmel calls "the impersonal freedom of a mask," the spectators at an exhibition might be said to be "element[s] in a group that is held together *formally*"—

the apparent "democracy of sociability" enabled by its being "an *artificial* world."[7] In this sense, exhibition culture resembles what Bruce Robbins refers to as a "phantom public sphere" in which the relocation of civic virtue to "the domain of culture" is purely symbolic, entailing no reciprocal effect in the political domain.[8]

Not that the public gallery, as a type of this phantom public sphere, was an absolutely inclusive space, or that it was even advertised as such. The elitism of exhibition culture was clear enough in the Royal Academy's practice of charging a fee, in its President's own words, "to prevent the Rooms being filled by improper Persons."[9] An entrance fee may have been a not-unexpected strategy to preserve the exclusivity of a high-cultural space endorsed by the king himself. However, when the Society of Arts mandated a one-shilling fee to keep the "vulgar crowds" out of its 1762 show, the dissident Signboards Exhibition, presenting work more attuned to Londoners' everyday experience of art, attracted the participation of artists like William Hogarth.[10] These shows, meanwhile, jockeyed for the attention of art consumers along with overtly entrepreneurial galleries such as Boydell's Shakespeare Gallery (1789–1805) and Macklin's Gallery of the Poets (1788–97), high-end galleries that were themselves pressured by the spectacles at Sadler's Wells or by the mimetic likenesses in Madame Tussaud's Wax Museum. Aesthetic theory was inseparable from politics: at the Royal Academy, which encouraged elite history painting based on Continental models, engravers—mere copyists, in academic ideology—were not admitted; at the Society of Arts, which provided a space for a more naturalistic aesthetic considered native to England, they were. At the Shakespeare Gallery, the involvement of middle-class buyers seemed downright revolutionary, one commentator declaring that "the spirit of the People" had "accomplished a revolution . . . in Taste."[11] Yet when it went defunct in 1805, its space in Pall Mall was taken over by the British Institution for Promoting the Fine Arts in the United Kingdom, where the centrality of Continental paintings borrowed from country-house collections allowed the ruling elite "to influence the development of British art."[12] Through the endorsement of a distinct aesthetic and the active involvement or exclusion of classes of persons, each gallery became a site of national representation, which instantiated a particular, imaginary vision of the British social body.[13]

The emergence of the public exhibition did signal a trend toward social inclusion in the eighteenth-century culture of art, which the flourishing popularity of portraiture seemed to literalize. The Georgian-era exhibition was typically overrun with portraits; even at the Royal Academy, which in its official rhetoric had subordinated the private interests embodied in portraiture to the public claims of historical composition, portraits constituted nearly 50 percent of all paintings on display. "Portrait! Portrait! Portrait!!!! intrudes on every side," complained a reviewer of the 1817 show, "while history, poetry, fiction, fade before the overwhelming invader."[14] England had long been a bastion of portrait painting, stretching back through Van Dyck's searching portraits of the seventeenth-century nobility to Nicholas Hilliard's luminous Elizabethan miniatures. Jonathan Richardson, the preeminent art theorist of the early eighteenth century, called it "the best school for face-painting now in the world."[15] By century's end, however, the art had been radically democratized. Competition meant a going rate of about five guineas; on the low end of the market likenesses could be had for as little as a few shillings. One nobleman reflected that, prior to the eighteenth century, only "those who were of great families, or remarkable for their actions in the service of their country" would have "presented themselves to a painter," whereas now "every body almost who can afford twenty pounds, has the portraits of himself, wife and children painted."[16] As a result, spectators at art exhibits often found themselves surrounded by the faces of everyday Brits—often found *themselves* represented, as it were, in paintings of individuals more or less *like* them. The effect of everydayness was enhanced, around the turn of the century, as exhibition catalogues more frequently listed the names of sitters.[17] As the serious frown of a "Mrs. Smith," or the beaming sincerity of "Child of Rev. Beasley" mirrored the spectator's own life back to him or her, the gallery became a place where the middle classes achieved unprecedented—and quite literal—visibility.

But while the gallery was a kind of virtual House of Commons in these years, the image projected there of bourgeois economic and cultural power was strikingly far removed from political reality. "It was precisely the years between the American Declaration of Independence and the introduction of the Great Reform Bill," writes David Cannadine, "which saw the landowners of England, Wales, Scotland and Ireland become more rich, more powerful, more status-conscious and more unified."[18] Even as portraiture was enabling the middle classes to model themselves as owners of property and as possessors of art, the aristocracy was expanding its political power in stunning fashion. In 1785—a year in which, Marcia Pointon notes, nearly 40 percent of exhibits at the Royal Academy were portraits (as opposed to only 15 percent that were history paintings, battle scenes, or literary subjects)—140 peers and 120 commoners influenced the return of three-quarters of the lower house.[19] A "sense of common values" (and, more often than not, common ancestry) helped create "one of the most exclusive ruling elites in human history," and, in the words of the eminent historian John Cannon, made the opening of Parliament essentially "a family reunion for many members."[20] The situation was little altered by 1820, when 222 MPs, fully one-third of the House of Commons, were related to peerage, leading the radical William Cobbett to decry "one house filled wholly with landowners, and the other four-fifths filled with their relatives."[21] Unlike the gallery, a site of middle-class influence and visibility, the Commons "was increasingly representing only the patricians."[22]

This account might seem to posit exhibition culture as an oppositional political space. It was not. Instead, it was replete with hierarchical values. To conceive of oneself as a participant in it was, in essence, to imagine one's own special place within the gallery. For all its progressive potential, exhibition culture provided a prominent public space where the middle class could mimic high social status and even achieve it. While allegorical portraiture, to cite one example, allowed individuals to pose in ennobling classical drapery, this fluidity of character also turned the appearance of status into an object of aspiration and a sign of prestige. In *Romanticism and Realism* (1984), Charles Rosen and Henri Zerner cite the "assault on the hierarchy of genres" and the disappearing distinction between "high" and "low" art as central achievements of romanticism.[23] But this distinction, far from disappearing, seems rather to operate differently—more subtly, but just as effectively—as a more fluid system than one grounded in the certainties of property.

But neither was the gallery a purely ideological space where virtual representation simply forestalled the achievement of an extended franchise. There was nothing monolithic about the social body that took shape in various cultural locations. For Wordsworth in book seven of *The Prelude*, the "waxwork" at Madame Tussaud's and the foreigners populating the London streets represented a "parliament of monsters."[24] For the satirist John Wolcot, writing under his pen name Peter Pindar, an equally monstrous social body was to be found on the walls of the Royal Academy: in *Odes to the Royal Academicians*, his poetic critiques of the annual exhibitions, he demands, "How dare ye fill the room with such *pollution*?"[25] One person's social "*pollution*," of course, is another's social realism—as was evident in the West Country town of Bridgwater, where an amateur artist named John Chubb captured an assortment of working men in intimate and unpretentious watercolor portraits (figure 1). With subjects including a printer and bookbinder, a barber, a merchant, and a schoolmaster, Chubb, a wine-merchant's son with a hand in radical politics, gave a face to the social reality around him.[26] On the other hand, the portraits by Thomas Lawrence, "painter laureate to the British upper classes" (and the artist most synonymous with the romantic style), projected the image of the period perhaps most familiar to readers today: that of a self-consciously powerful nobility whose ranks were being swelled by the "peerage mania" of the nouveaux riches.[27]

The diversity of portraiture is most apparent in romantic print culture. A handful of titles will indicate the dizzying array of imagined galleries, each of which instantiated a particular social body. There was *The Scottish Gallery; or, Portraits of Eminent Persons of Scotland* (1797), and *Vagabondiana; or, Anecdotes of Mendicant Wanderers Through the Streets of London* (1817); *Portrait Gallery of Distinguished Females* (1833), and *Portrait Gallery of Distinguished Poets* (1833); John Charnock's *Biographia Navalis; or, Lives and Characters of Officers of the Navy of Great Britain* (1794), and *Portraits of Fops; or Portraits of the Foppish Character*, by "Frederick Foppling" (1811). Every profession, every class, every type, it seemed, had its gallery. Even trees had a place in this medley of cultural representations: *Sylva Britannica; or Portraits of Forest-Trees*, in fact, proved so popular in its ornate, large-scale printing of 1826 that a second, cheaper edition appeared four years later.[28]

By finding in visual culture an index of the massive reimagining of the national community that took place in romantic Britain, *Imagining the Gallery* approaches portraiture for its symbolic and social valences, instead of what is signified in a given portrait. My main concern is with its ideological investments, though my analyses take up a broader confluence of conceptual debate, involving matters such as realism, ekphrasis, privacy, authorship, and genius. Such methodological eclecticism is necessary to capture the wide range of portrait representations in the period and to understand its pervasiveness as a political idea. Yet my primary disciplinary commitment is to a formalism that acknowledges the importance of history and politics, as both a *condition* and an *object* of form.[29] Form is at issue in the shape of the books that people read in the nineteenth century, from the large-scale novels that Henry James would call "large loose baggy monsters" to the selective assemblages of the textual portrait gallery; in the ways poets and painters sculpt language and images so as to mystify and/or vitalize their political meanings; and (speaking as broadly as possible) in how the British social body, glimpsed partially in mass-exhibited and often mass-produced portraits, gets reimagined as an object of representation and of collective fantasy.[30]

This study reflects a recent shift in visual-verbal enquiry, away from comparative models that have tended to distinguish and produce hierarchies of media, and toward an archaeology of shared cultural assumptions that span the pictorial and the verbal.[31] Conventionally evoked as "the abstract of the personal" (Coleridge's description of "a very good portrait") or as reinforcement for the myth of the poet (Byron's celebrity portraits; the haunting death-mask

FIG. 1. John Chubb, *George Beale, merchant*, c. 1797. (Blake Museum, Bridgwater, UK)

of Keats), portraiture is revealed here to be a major conceptual category, a prevalent metaphor, and a ubiquitous form of print culture.[32] In an age when epic poetry gets written as extended self-portraiture; when the prestige of the novel is measured by its "galleries" of characters; and when political debate unfolds as a contest between rhetorical portraits, literary portraiture joins the sublime of landscape as an essential visual-verbal category.[33] As a result, portrait poems, which elaborate an affective response to small private objects, accrue a new centrality in a field long reliant for its visual cues on the natural sublime; landscape, the pictorial signifier of property ownership, gives way to portraits that conjure a performative and more inclusive image of Britishness; and the exhibition gallery displaces the mountaintop as a source of national imagery. The shift to portraiture is particularly suited to the literary history that has been excavated in recent decades, to include readers as well as writers, periodicals as well as poems, culture as well as imagination, women as well as men.

Allegories of State

Gallery originates as an architectural term: "A covered space for walking in, partly open at the side, or having the roof supported by pillars; a piazza, portico, colonnade" (*OED* 1). Suffused with the idea of ownership, it assumes social valences in the exhibition room or the museum, those prestigious homes for art that help to demarcate a select conception of the public. But it also slips from the architectural to the social, referring not just to the public viewing area of the theater (where the lower classes gathered for plays, operas, and other urban spectacles); the senatorial chamber; or, by the late nineteenth century, the sporting match, but to the people sitting and standing there. As both the location and the signifier of "the people," *gallery* embeds processes of exclusion and selection that are central to the project of defining a social body under bourgeois capitalism. This is nowhere so apparent as in the so-called Stranger's Gallery of Parliament, where to this day the public may witness political debate—and may also be asked to leave by any member who wishes to have the galleries cleared.[34]

That a person present in the parliamentary gallery could be deemed "strange" by his or her own representative body is a remnant of a past era of closed proceedings, yet the persistence of the terminology calls attention to the contest to define who belongs in the public gallery, be it devoted to art exhibition or to political debate. The word's suppleness of reference, its simultaneous reference to place and person, or to "people" and "elite," is primarily the product of the eighteenth century.[35] It signals the fluctuation of the British social body at a time when, according to John Barrell, "the division of labour had so occluded the perspectives of its members that none of them, or almost none, could grasp the 'idea' of the public."[36] Despite institutional efforts such as that of the Royal Academy, founded in 1768 in part to help reimagine a public, the idea of a singular, unified social body was increasingly phantasmatic. In its place, instead, was a multiplicity of social bodies consisting of private individuals motivated by their own private interests.[37]

Efforts to imagine a social body as more private, particular, and multiple dovetail with the failure of its large-scale embodiment. In his influential account of the rise of the novel, Ian Watt describes how "the unified world picture of the Middle Ages" gave way to a very different picture, "a developing but unplanned aggregate of particular individuals having particular experiences at particular times and at particular places."[38] Such extreme social multiplicity, coupled with the parliamentary prerogatives institutionalized in 1688, meant that the body politic could no longer be viably expressed as a lone, authoritative figure, as in the frontispiece to Hobbes's *Leviathan* (figure 2). At the end of the seventeenth century, the body politic, the king's "second body," was understood as primary; the executive, Locke made clear, derived his authority from and was subordinate to the supremacy of Parliament. Pierre Manent explains that, as "the natural place for national representation" came to be seen as "the legislative body," the king's "meaning and legitimacy" fell into question.[39] The king so powerfully evoked as an all-subsuming body would no more do as a national portrait than would Lawrence's intimate depiction, a century and a half later, of the dashing Prince Regent—a portrait that emphatically refuses the Regent's representative status in favor of a more private idiom. (In *Vanity Fair*, Becky Sharp would buy herself a copy of such a portrait—"in which the best of monarchs is represented in a frock-coat with a fur collar, and breeches and silk stockings, simpering on a sofa from under his curly brown wig"—showing just how far the royal image had fallen under the spell of consumer desire.[40]) The effort to present the royal family of George III as so many plain English folk, nowhere more apparent than in James Gillray's *Temperance enjoying a Frugal Meal*, is traceable to the Lockean belief that political legitimacy itself is a function of the people. It was less important that the king *embody* his people than that he *be like* his people.[41] This dispersal of authority, from an absolute (royal) center to a diversity of people and places, is reflected by a significant terminological shift. In the early nineteenth century, Mary Poovey writes, "social body" gained currency as a more flexible metaphor than "body politic." It could refer to Britain as an organic whole or to subsets of that whole, including an increasingly visible and economically vital one: the laboring poor.[42] No longer

FIG. 2. Detail from title page to Thomas Hobbes's *Leviathan*, 1651. (Courtesy of the Division of Rare and Manuscript Collections, Cornell University Library)

containable by a sovereign body, the image of the nation became an idealized projection onto the many representative spaces where bodies (and their representations) were assembled: the corridors of the art exhibition, the tables of coffeehouses, the pages of periodicals, the galleries of the theater, the floor of the Lower House at St. Stephen's. The symbolic shift was from an illusionary executive body to a plurality of social bodies, Watt's aggregate of "particular individuals having particular experiences at particular times and at particular places."

But even these were subject to idealization. Through much of the eighteenth century, according to Peter Stallybrass and Allon White, "the great labour of bourgeois culture" was to maintain the cleanliness and good order of the public spaces to which it laid claim, so as to generate "a sublimated public body without smells, without coarse laughter, without organs, separate from the Court and Church on the one hand and the market square, alehouse, street and fairground on the other."[43] This observation, while acknowledging the significance of place in helping to define a public body, also shows the persistent understanding of the corporate state. So, too, does much late-century iconography in which heterogeneity is essential to the metaphor: for instance, the revival of "Britannia" as an idealized, feminine, and domestic national image, which was enabled by the publication of countless novels, conduct manuals, and political tracts by and about women; and the ubiquity of "John Bull," the prototypical Englishman of the 1790s commonly understood as a metaphor for public opinion over and against state interests.[44] The de-emphasis of the king's body as an all-consuming representative space may be one expression of the neoclassical suspicion of allegory—the (Hobbesian) "image of one body incorporating others [being] the goal, so to speak, of allegorical expression"—but clearly, even the smaller and more multiple concept of the social body that took root in the legislative state had a strong allegorical tendency.[45]

As representative authority shifted from the body of the king to a multiplicity of locations where particular images of a social body could be glimpsed, the demographics of these spaces *as well as the aesthetic programs they endorsed* became matters of critical importance in reimagining the corporate nation. The art displays in London's first hospital for foundling children, the limited-access Royal Academy shows, and the bourgeois playgrounds at Vauxhall Gardens each implied a certain composition for the social body, and so too did the aesthetic associated with each site. Blake's incisive annotations of Reynolds's *Discourses*—"This whole Book," he writes, "was Written to serve Political Purposes"—reflect the struggle involved in aesthetic questions that seem relatively benign from today's vantage-point.[46] The main point of contention was between a particularist aesthetic that leaned toward referential realism, and a generalizing aesthetic that sought to idealize. The conflict has one of its earliest expressions in the dialogue that opens Part Two of Mandeville's *Fable of the Bees.* When a man of taste, Cleomenes, criticizes the particularity of a Dutch painting of the Nativity ("what a Fool the Fellow was to draw Hay and Straw and Cattle, and a Rack as well as a Manger"), a woman named Fulvia defends the painting's realism: "Sure nothing can be more like the Head of an Ox than that there. A Picture pleases me best when the Art in such a manner deceives my eye, that without making any Allowances, I can imagine that I see the Thing in reality." Cleomenes retorts that "Great Masters don't paint for the common People, but for Persons of refin'd Understanding." He gains support from a fellow man of taste, Horatio, whose language barely conceals class valences: "In a Country Stable, Madam, there is nothing but Filth and Nastiness, or vile abject things not fit to be seen, at least not capable of entertaining Persons of Quality." Summarizing the academic aesthetic, Cleomenes asserts that "It is not Nature, but . . . *la belle Nature,* that is to be represented; all Things that are abject, low, pitiful and mean, are carefully to be avoided, and kept out of Sight; because to

FIG. 3. William Hogarth, *Heads of Six of Hogarth's Servants*, c. 1750–55. (Copyright Tate, London, 2004)

Men of the true Taste they are as offensive as Things that are shocking, and really nasty." But Fulvia is adamant: "The *Dutch* Picture in the next Room has nothing that is offensive: but an *Augean* Stable, even before *Hercules* had cleaned it, would be less shocking to me than those fluted Pillars; for no body can please my eye that affronts my Understanding."[47]

Throughout the century, a view of art that privileged classical, idealized forms, associated with "Persons of Quality," contended with realistic representations associated with "the common People" and deemed by elite men of taste as "abject things not fit to be seen." Hogarth was often at the center of such arguments.[48] His so-called "Britophil" campaign was waged against Shaftesburian men of taste who preferred classical and Continental models of composition to native ones, and his *Analysis of Beauty* (1753) championed "variety in unity" over the supremacy of a central focal point.[49] Hogarth's aesthetics required active effort on the part of the viewer: it was not at all inimical to beauty for "lights and shades [to be] scattered about in little spots"—the consequence of such an effect being that "the eye is constantly disturbed, and the mind is uneasy, especially if you are eager to understand every object in the composition."[50] His insistence on representing English life in its abundant detail, and his refusal to idealize away "Filth and Nastiness" drew the opprobrium of artists and commentators who followed academic precepts. "Mr. Hogarth's painting . . . corresponds too closely to the objects it represents," Andre Rouquet complained, while James Barry, who championed the Aristotelian "probable impossible" over "the unfledged, debased notions of mechanical dabblers," censured his attention to the "trifling particulars of familiar life." "Hogarth is often so raw, and uninformed," Barry wrote, "as hardly to deserve the name of an artist."[51] While these men probably had in mind Hogarth's progresses, they could just as easily have been thinking of paintings such as the one depicting Hogarth's servants (figure 3): six unidealized working-class faces joined on one canvas, a glimpse of plain reality.

The split between the academic (Shaftesburian, generalizing, ideal) and the anti-academic (Hogarthian, particularizing, familiar), crystallized in the Mandevillian dialogue, was given fresh life, as Paulson explains, in conflicts within the St. Martin's Lane Academy in the 1730s and 40s—conflicts subsequently inherited by painters including Barry, Richard Wilson, and Benjamin West (on the academic side) and Johan Zoffany, George Stubbs, and Thomas Rowlandson (in the Hogarthian line).[52] This is an admittedly schematic division, and it should be noted that these groupings do not hold in strict political terms: Barry's civic humanism, for example, was inflected by Irish radical sympathies, while Rowlandson, for all his playfulness, often simply winks at established codes of decorum. Nevertheless, the schematism does help to explain the tradition of eighteenth-century art as romantic writers encountered it. One of its more famous distillations is the pair of contrasting portraits of Sarah Siddons painted by Thomas Gainsborough and by Reynolds. Gainsborough's *Mrs. Siddons* (1785) is plain, straightforward, elegant. Refusing outside reference, it remains, in the words of one commentator, "entirely unsullied by anything so elevated as an idea."[53] Gainsborough's famous complaint when he was painting the portrait—"Damn the nose, there's no end to it!"—has even led Paulson to read it as "a series of long slightly downward tilting ovals that parallel the shape of the famous nose." It was a high-concept Hogarthian joke: "To get Mrs. Siddons's nose into a formal scheme, Gainsborough simply made her all noses."[54] Conversely, Reynolds's *Mrs. Siddons as the Tragic Muse* (1784) is a consummately ideal portrait, enmeshed in the trappings of prestige. The image of the actress sitting on a throne, her features distilled and perfected (most notably her famously large nose, here shortened and softened), is densely allusive: it refers to texts, paintings, sculptures, myths—to anything, that is, but Siddons herself.

This idealizing aesthetic, which Reynolds championed in his *Discourses* to the Royal Academy, attracted vigorous responses from the romantics. "To Generalize is to be an Idiot," Blake wrote in his withering annotations of the *Discourses*; "To Particularize is the Alone Distinction of Merit." Hazlitt, in his essay "On Certain Inconsistencies in Sir Joshua Reynolds's Discourses," also advocated an aesthetics of particularity: "The greatest grandeur may coexist with the most perfect, nay with a microscopic accuracy of detail."[55] In their anti-Reynoldsian stances, writers like Blake and Hazlitt invested particulars with renewed value. If, for Blake, this value was finally intellectual and not empirical, in Hazlitt's writings (as I discuss in chapter four), the politics implied in an aesthetics of particularity are directed toward the idea of an inclusive social body. The politics had always been there, Barrell observes, in the frequent use of the adjective *servile* to describe *imitation* in civic humanist discourse, which implies that art is liberal only when freed from servility to the real.[56] But these class politics emerge forcefully amid post-Napoleonic debates over parliamentary representation, when questions about the particularity and inclusiveness of the British social body are as charged as ever.

I have suggested that the fiction of a singular body politic became difficult to support in an age of commerce, legislative authority, and increasingly visible social division, and that a range of more inclusive social bodies were imaged or implied in art spaces and artistic debates. These related trends merged together in visual allegories of state that appeared in romantic print culture. In these representations, an emphasis on the *detail* undercuts the fiction of a unified body politic. The Scottish artist John Kay, for instance, published in 1814 what he called a "hieroglyphic Portrait of Buonaparte" (figure 4), in which the French leader's body is constituted by a grotesque symbolism described in the picture's caption:

> The French Eagle crouching forms the *capeau en militaire.*
> The Red Sea represents his *throat* illustrative of his drowning armies.
> The *visage* is formed of carcases of the unhappy victims to his cruel ambition.
> The *hand* is judiciously placed as the epaulet drawing the Rhenish Confederacy under the flimsy symbol of the cob-web.
> The *spider* is a symbolic emblem of the vigilance of the Allies.

The grotesquerie that is Napoleon literalizes the violence intrinsic in the allegory of state. If the frontispiece to *Leviathan* represented King Charles's body as constituted by a passive and silent crowd, Napoleon's is constituted by death.

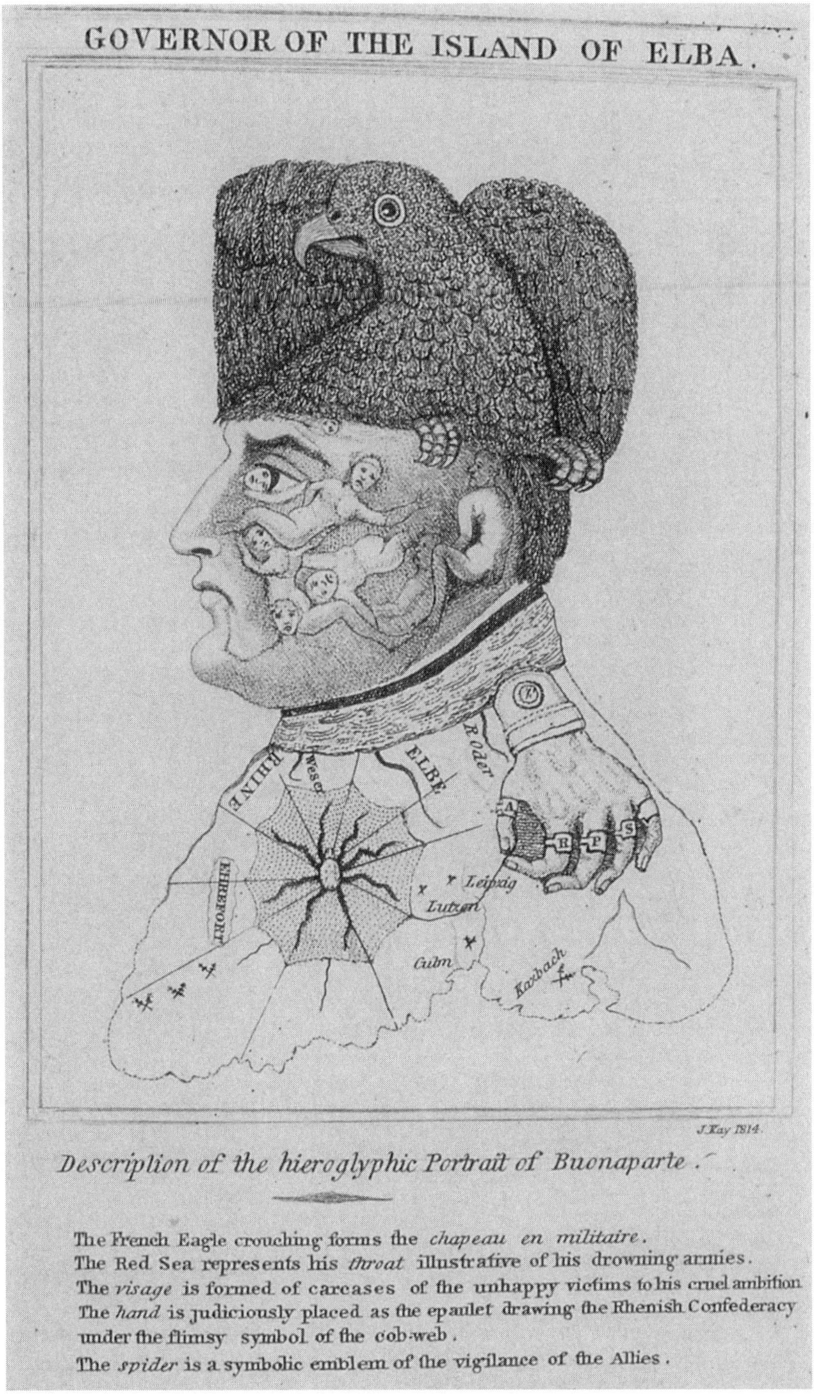
GOVERNOR OF THE ISLAND OF ELBA.
RHINE
Weser
ELBE
R Oder
Culm
J. Kay 1814.
Description of the hieroglyphic Portrait of Buonaparte.
The French Eagle crouching forms the *chapeau en militaire*.
The Red Sea represents his *throat* illustrative of his drowning armies.
The *visage* is formed of carcases of the unhappy victims to his cruel ambition
The *hand* is judiciously placed as the epaulet drawing the Rhenish Confederacy
under the flimsy symbol of the cob-web.
The *spider* is a symbolic emblem of the vigilance of the Allies.

FIG. 4. John Kay, *Hieroglyphic Portrait of Buonaparte*, 1814. (The Huntington Library, San Marino, California)

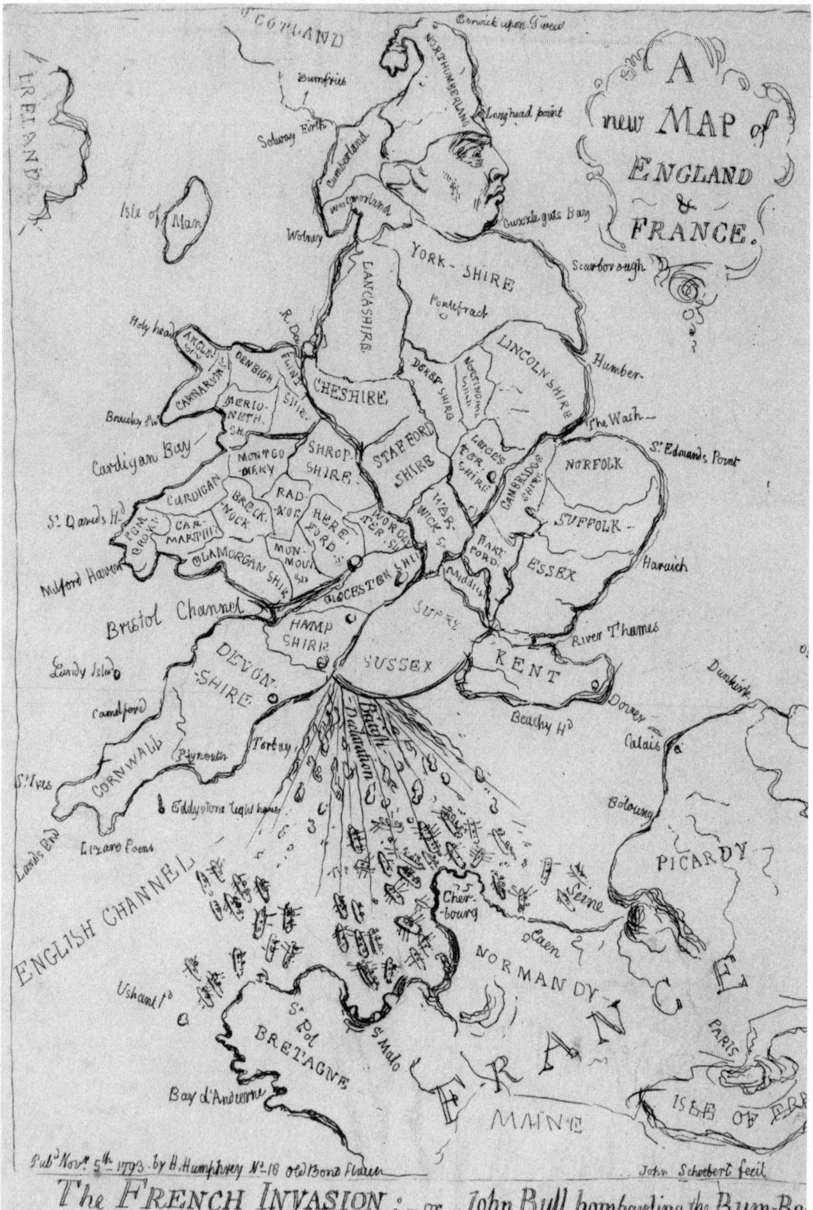

FIG. 5. James Gillray, *The French Invasion: or John Bull, bombarding the Bum-Boats*, 1793. (Courtesy of Department of Special Collections, Stanford University Libraries)

The "carcases" that swim, fetus-like, in his face, even compose his visible eye. Leadership is presented not as a unidirectional consumption of the people by the head, but as a circular dynamic. Leaders are made by their subjects (and by their treatment of those subjects); the grisly detail subverts the monolith's power.

A similar print, Gillray's *The French Invasion: or John Bull, bombarding the Bum-Boats*, is even more pointed in debunking the image of the unified social body (figure 5). Gillray's subject is the wartime impulse toward national unification, though like Kay he is more concerned with the costs involved. The convergence of landscape, portraiture, and history, a generic union characteristic of romantic aesthetics, here takes absurdly concrete form: George III *is* Britain. For this reason, the image has been called "deeply conservative": seldom "had the fusion of monarch and kingdom been so explicitly expressed in art," writes Colley; "George III is shown as being in the most intimate sense possible entirely at one with England and Wales . . . they give him shape, but he gives them identity."[57]

The print seems to me, however, to depict the violent wrenching of social multeity into national unity—and thus to portray the social face of Hogarthian aesthetics. I read it as engaged, rather directly, with that well-known description of the state as a body: Menenius Agrippa's fable of the belly, presented in Livy and retold in Shakespeare's *Coriolanus*. The fable, which is addressed to plebeians rioting against the patricians, describes an agreement between the stomach (senate) and the hands and feet (the common people). Just as the belly nourishes and makes possible the existence of the hands and feet, the argument goes, so too the work of the other parts should benefit the stomach. As allegory the fable figures a precarious unity, for the stomach, in order to provide nourishment, must also digest what it consumes. Gillray envisions the logical conclusion: the expulsion of the labor of the people in the cause of national unity. Equating the King's body as much as possible with the land of Britain (and by extension with the ruling elite that owns the land), he gives form to the processing, digesting, and defecation of the common people in the direction of France. Gillray's images, of course, are notoriously resistant to a specific ideology, yet he seems here vigorously to deny the unity of a national imagery by visualizing at whose cost such unity is achieved. Transforming the image of the king-as-nation into a functioning organism, he posits the body politic as a fantasy of oneness given the lie by the many particulars that make it work.

At the end of the period, the reversal of the dominant, Hobbesian image appears in J. P. Hemm's *Portraits of the Royal Family in Penmanship*, an elegant book-form gallery published in flat folio in 1831.[58] Though not at all overtly,

FIG. 6. *George the Fourth, King of Great Britain and Ireland*, from J. P. Hemm, *Portraits of the Royal Family in Penmanship*, 1831. (Courtesy of Department of Special Collections, Stanford University Libraries)

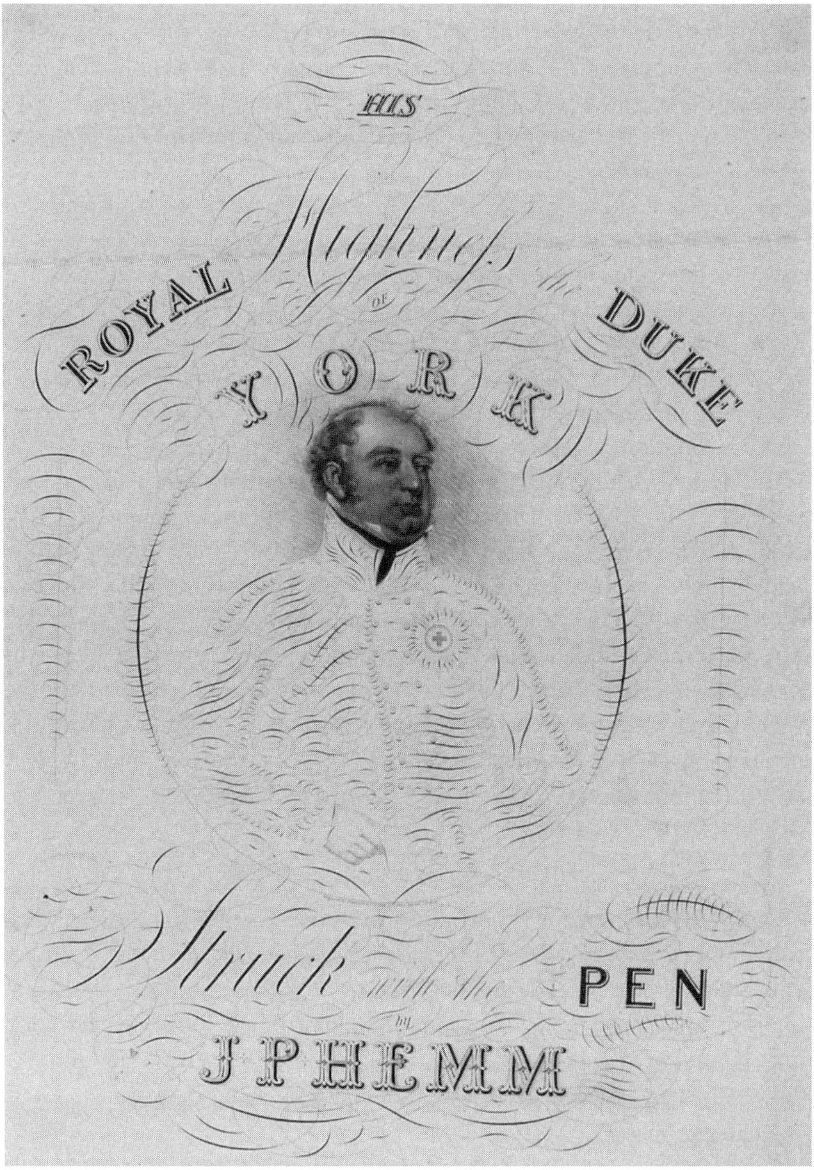

FIG. 7. *His Royal Highness the Duke of York*, from J. P. Hemm, *Portraits of the Royal Family in Penmanship*, 1831. (Courtesy of Department of Special Collections, Stanford University Libraries)

Hemm's project is underwritten by a bourgeois politics of representation. This series of eight portraits—stunning images that sometimes seem like doodling run amok—transmits royal bodies as objets d'art. Here George IV, to whom the volume is dedicated, becomes an elaborately wrought text, his exquisitely engraved head, hands, and feet "stuffed" (like Thomas Paine's royal bird) with the artist's florid strokes (figure 6). The king is dismembered by penmanship; his extremities float in textual space, connected only by wayward ink. The medium itself is significant, as the pen-swipes reflect the dandyism of George IV and reduce the idea of monarchy to a mere style, a superfluity bordering on camp.[59]

Marketed to an audience of connoisseurs, Hemm's "national portraits" oddly suited a culture where economic power belonged to the middle classes. They imagine the figurehead of nation and government as a work of art produced by political subjects on an inclusive canvas. Summarizing the force with which producers and consumers supersede the royal subject, the Duke of York's portrait is said to be "STRUCK with the PEN of J. P. Hemm" (figure 7). Unlike Hobbes's frontispiece, in which the dominant king subsumes and controls the bodies of his royal subjects, here the royal body is not just constituted, but even (potentially) disciplined by representation. "To be a subject" in the Machiavellian state, Gordon Teskey argues, "is to be vulnerable at every moment to an inscrutable violence on which the power of the state depends utterly."[60] The reverse of such a view could hardly be more explicit than in Hemm's portraits in penmanship, where the violence is performed (I intend the word in all its senses) on the royal body.

Distinguishing Class and Genre

Given the involvement of portraiture in the project of imagining a national community, it is no surprise that the language used to talk about it was suffused with political reference. The pun on "hanging" was common. At the conclusion of his pamphlet *Two Pair of Portraits* (1788), John Horne Tooke cites his verbal portraits of Lord Holland and Lord Chatham, and their sons Fox and Pitt:

> You have here been presented with four portraits (merely an assemblage of known indisputable facts.)
>
> 1st *Question.* Which two of them will you chuse to hang up in your cabinets; the PITTS or the FOXES?
>
> 2nd *Question.* Where, on your consciences, should the other two be hanged?[61]

Likewise Wolcot, citing the "pollution" on the walls of the London art shows, demands of the Royal Academicians: "Will Justice say, while thus ye *hang* / So sad and villainous a gang, / *Yourselves* should not be led to *execution*?"[62] Wordplay was coupled with a strenuous metaphorics of foreign invasion. One reviewer quoted earlier describes portraiture as an "overwhelming invader" at the Royal Academy shows. Another, lamenting that the larger pictures are "garnished round the edges with faces like a turbot with smelts," says that "along the top of Mr. West's Treaty between the Grand Mogul and Lord Clive, there are six or eight portraits a-row, resembling a battalion, or at least a grenadier company in line."[63] Non-aristocratic portraits are like foreign armies. Having vanquished France, it seems, the British public had a new enemy: the image of its own self.

The specific worry was that portraiture, a genre low in academic prestige, was raiding the borders of epic history painting and usurping its cultural authority. This concern was rooted in the struggle to define a social body, for the boundary said to be separating history painting and portraiture, so hotly contested throughout the romantic period, also implied a *class* boundary. Within the eighteenth-century hierarchy of genres, history painting held the elite position; through its allusiveness, it addressed an audience of classically educated, property-owning men. Portraiture, on the other hand, was seen to be a smug, middle-class art, the foil and usurper of history painting's righteous kingdom. It was the art world's answer to the phenomenon of "Terramania," by which the new moneyed classes bought up property, not inheriting but paying their way into a propertied identity.[64] Conceptually dependent not on property but on propriety, portraits revealed class as a performance. Against the stable notion of the propertied man, the fluid fashionings of individual identity enabled by portraiture mimicked the fluctuations of capital.

If this view of the genres sounds overly schematic, it is because the debate was less about generic difference than about class distinction. As history and portraiture bled into one another with increasing frequency, their *symbolic* valences became all-important—hence the overblown rhetoric they provoked. "This kind of work," writes Barry of portraiture, "is indeed made with paint, &c. spread upon wood or canvas; . . . but in all the higher respects it comes as far short of the art of Raffaelle, and the other great historical painters, as Homer and Milton are from little occasional versifiers; or Hippocrates, Harvey, and Boerhaave, from dentists and corn-cutters."[65] In the Shakespeare Gallery catalogue of 1790, John Boydell reveals the enduring influence of a strict generic hierarchy: "The abilities of our best Artists is chiefly employed in painting Portraits of those who, in less than half a century, will be lost in oblivion—While the noblest part of the Art—HISTORICAL PAINTING—is much neglected."[66] Unlike Barry, who writes as a history painter championing his genre of choice, Boydell is an entrepreneur invested in social hierarchy. Marketing Shakespearean history paintings to the middle classes, he implicitly reinforces an aristocratic cultural prerogative while acknowledging an economy of cultural goods in which consumers vie for distinction.[67]

In practice, portraiture and historical composition were becoming less easily distinguishable from one another. As far back as the 1720s, imported history painting was being downsized for a "diminished bourgeois world" in the form of the family piece.[68] Throughout the century, portraits drew on the high historical while historical subjects incorporated portraits. Even Barry, the arch-antiportraitist, in 1776 painted Edmund Burke as Ulysses leading his nation out of the state of nature in *Portraits of Barry and Burke in the Characters of Ulysses and a Companion*. Later, his series of historical panels (1777–83) for the Society of Arts included the sweeping *Commerce, or the Triumph of the Thames*, which was distinguished by a portrait of Dr. Charles Burney playing his harpsichord among the ocean waves, as well as a climactic panel, *The Distribution of the Premiums in the Society of Arts*, that was actually a 150-square-foot group portrait including portraits of Samuel Johnson, John Hunter, and Edmund Burke. Barry's *Account* of these panels ironically reveals how little the hyperbolic emphasis on generic hierarchy reflected artistic practice. Having raved that portraits can only "fill up for the moment the little minds of the thoughtless rabble" he adds, shortly after, that it was his "original intention to bring in a much greater number of portraits, as we have many other illustrious living characters, whose likeness posterity will enquire after."[69]

Generic slippage was not limited to artistic practice. History *writers*, following the success of James Granger's *Biographical History of England* (1759), incorporated portraits both literally, as textual ornamentations or supplements, and conceptually, by describing the past as a series of biographical moments. Robert Jephson's *Roman Portraits* (1794), a multimedia historical poem of over 3000 lines, interspersed brief poetic descriptions of characters in Roman history with visual portraits: images of Caesar and Cicero are engraved after paintings by Rubens, Mark Antony's image is taken from an ancient gem, Cleopatra's from a coin in Dr. Hunter's Museum. The rise of portrait-biography extended this trend. Hazlitt, a one-time painter, subtitled his *Spirit of the Age* (1825) "Contemporary Portraits," and elsewhere used portraiture as a template for character criticism: "The character of Henry VIII is drawn with great truth and spirit," he wrote; "It is like a very disagreeable portrait, sketched by the hand of a master." Later in the nineteenth century, Thomas Carlyle articulated a theory of history based not on "protocols, state papers, controversies and abstractions of men," but on "direct inspection and embodiment." "The bygone ages of the world were actually filled by living men," he explained; "Not abstractions were they, not diagrams and theorems; but men, in buff or other coats and breeches, with colour in their cheeks, with passions in their stomach, and the idioms, features and vitalities of very men."[70]

The tendency to view portraits as an epistemology, a source of historical knowledge, even influenced children's pedagogy. Jephson advertised his *Roman Portraits* as not only "the best vehicle to communicate early knowledge, but to rouse young faculties to the further pursuit of such subjects," and called for similar, portrait-based representations of British history (xxiii). If the novels of Scott would soon provide one kind of response, so too would educational games such as *Historical Pastime* (1828), in which British history was taught as a series of portraits that players traversed—Queen Elizabeth, Shakespeare, Newton—on a providential march to the centerpiece, a meticulous hand-colored engraving of George IV. Likewise in *The Mirror of Truth* (1811), a game of moral instruction published by John Wallis's Juvenile Repository, biographical portraits illustrated a range of virtues, from "Conjugal Fidelity" to "Filial Love." Each of the forty-five miniature pictures on this game's playing surface was keyed to an historical anecdote—brief portraits of virtue such as the story of Regulus, the Roman general put "to death amidst tortures too horrible to relate" in the disinterested service of his country, or the tale of "Volney Becker," a twelve-year-old who lost his life plucking his father from the jaws of a shark. Instructional books, staking out the ground of the personal, also blurred the difference between history and portraiture. *Scripture Female Portraits* (1820), a series of poems about the Bible's virtuous women, in its dedication encouraged girl-readers to

> read the sacred volume, dearest maid,
> There see in shining characters pourtray'd
> A train of female worthies—let each be
> A pattern, and a stimulus to thee.[71]

Even a youthful audience, it seems, was trained by the exhibition hall to transform the reading of typographical characters into the viewing of personified ones. With a comparable logic, the didactic biography *A Mother's Portrait* (1823) billed itself as a "familiar and faithful sketch" taken soon after its subject's death "for the study of her children." The book begins in unnerving fashion by telling how the author's friend, his wife having breathed her last in the family's easy chair, "calmly sketched the portrait of her corpse." This prompts the author's declaration of his wish to bequeath to his children "a portrait of [their mother's] *character* rather than her *countenance*." "For our moral portrait to be faithfully sketched," he writes, "the artist must . . . follow us home," a formulation that recalls Maria Edgeworth's claim in her preface to *Castle Rackrent* (1800) that private history is as important as public history.[72] *A Mother's Por-*

trait has for its frontispiece an image of the devoted father reading to four daughters, nicely delineating how a portrait, even (or perhaps especially) a verbal one, could be made to serve a particular ideology.

As commonly as history and portraiture were brought together across a range of genre, forms, and media, the continued assertion of their difference suggests the intensity of their symbolic valences. "History" and "portrait" were class signifiers, and yet their significance was coming to seem increasingly arbitrary. In portraits, some people donned classical drapery, parading their upward mobility as a natural aspect of their identity, as in Reynolds's idealized portrait of the Montgomery sisters, *Three Ladies adorning a Term of Hymen* (1773). Others posed in the shabby garb of the poor, flaunting their distance from poverty by reducing it to a mere style, as in John Hoppner's *Mrs. Sheridan and her Son* (1797), in which the mother poses as a farmwife fetching water while carrying her son on her back. This seeming breakdown in the system of generic and class signifiers is nowhere so apparent as in the proliferation of published galleries of "curious" or "remarkable" characters in the period. In bringing working-class individuals into public visibility through portraiture, these galleries posed explicit challenges to the existing order of representation.[73]

The most well known of these was James Caulfield's *Portraits, Memoirs, and Characters, of Remarkable Persons* (1794), a pre-Dickensian gallery of eccentrics that purported to tell British history through figures who typically went unrepresented. Through engraved portraits paired with brief memoirs, criminals, beggars, and freaks served here as embodiments of the years 1688–1760, a period described in the preface as "the most eventful in the annals of British history."[74] Included are marginal figures such as the pugilist George Taylor, alias George the Barber; and the London streetwalker known as "Blind Granny" (figures 8–9). Barrell has recently argued that at the end of the eighteenth century the representation of the rural poor as comic gave way to a more sober and serious imagery—a strategy, he writes, "at once more repressive and more concerned to solicit our benevolence."[75] His point is that the poor had to be presented in this way so as not to be a threat. More comic representations such as those by Thomas Rowlandson expressed potentially disruptive energies that were contained in the sober portrayals by Francis Wheatley. One could certainly make the case that print galleries such as Caulfield's fit this model. George Taylor—to quote Barrell's description of Wheatley's 1796 watercolor, *Returning from the Fields*—possesses "a degree of refinement obviously inappropriate to [his] social position, and well understood at the time to be an idealisation, but a necessary one, for a less idealised image of the poor would of course be that much less a model of how the poor should be" (18). But a key difference is entailed by

FIG. 8. *George Taylor*, from J. Caulfield, *Portraits, Memoirs, and Characters, of Remarkable Persons*, 1819–20. (Courtesy of Department of Special Collections, Stanford University Libraries)

the transmedia form of Caulfield's gallery. For in the *verbal* portraits that accompany the engravings, the comic reemerges, mobilizing the energies that Barrell deems disruptive. George Taylor's "remarkable judgment in the cross-buttock fall," for instance, is said by some to lack "that necessary ingredient of a boxer, called a *good bottom*" (4: 207–8); and Blind Granny is remembered as having annoyed pedestrians by "licking her blind eye with her tongue, which was of a most enormous length and thickness" (1: 108). The engraved portraits

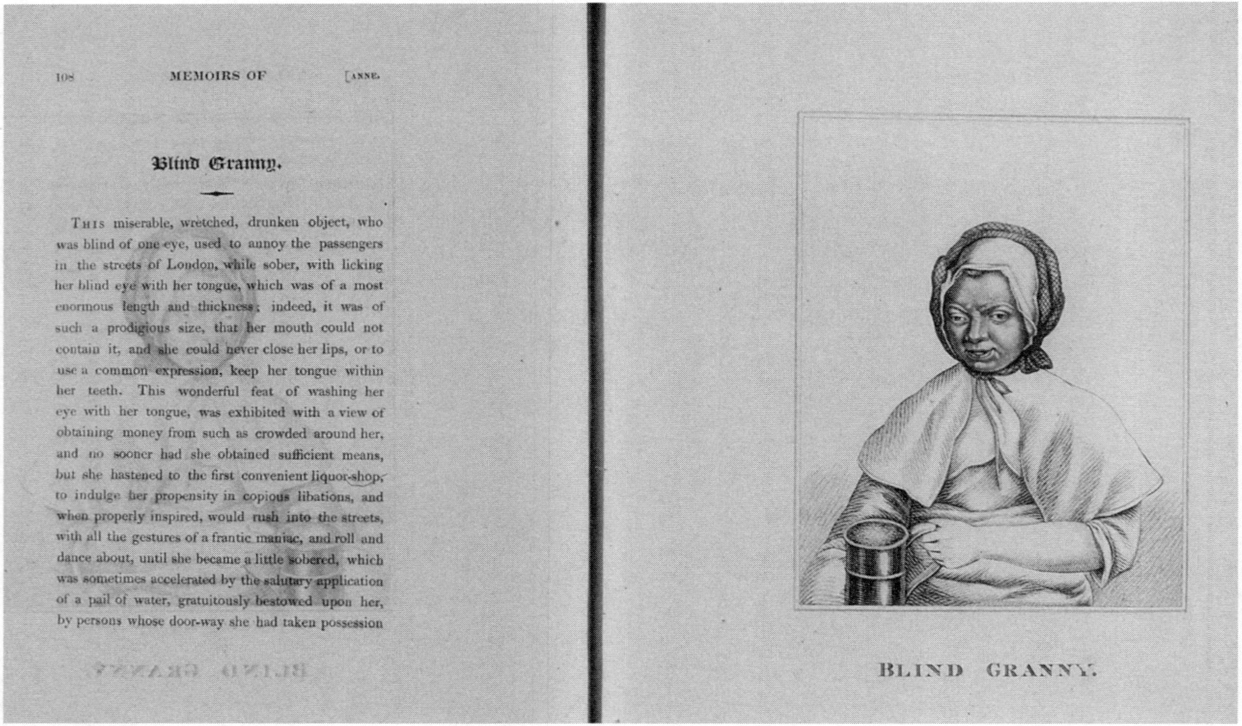

108 MEMOIRS OF [ANNE.

Blind Granny.

THIS miserable, wretched, drunken object, who was blind of one eye, used to annoy the passengers in the streets of London, while sober, with licking her blind eye with her tongue, which was of a most enormous length and thickness; indeed, it was of such a prodigious size, that her mouth could not contain it, and she could never close her lips, or to use a common expression, keep her tongue within her teeth. This wonderful feat of washing her eye with her tongue, was exhibited with a view of obtaining money from such as crowded around her, and no sooner had she obtained sufficient means, but she hastened to the first convenient liquor-shop, to indulge her propensity in copious libations, and when properly inspired, would rush into the streets, with all the gestures of a frantic maniac, and roll and dance about, until she became a little sobered, which was sometimes accelerated by the salutary application of a pail of water, gratuitously bestowed upon her, by persons whose door-way she had taken possession

BLIND GRANNY.

FIG. 9. *Blind Granny* (portrait and facing page), from J. Caulfield, *Portraits, Memoirs, and Characters, of Remarkable Persons,* 1819–20. (Courtesy of Department of Special Collections, Stanford University Libraries)

may seem incongruously noble, but the text enacts a Hogarthian impulse that resists idealization. Caulfield's verbal and visual portrait pairings, in their expression of a subculture as well as their fondness for play, attest not only the survival of an anti-academic aesthetic, but its significance in breaking down the class signifiers associated with history and portraiture.[76]

John Thomas Smith's 1817 gallery, *Vagabondiana*, also imagines a rather different social body than the one on display in the bourgeois art show. In his preface, Smith quotes from Granger's *Biographical History of England* to describe his project in political terms:

> I began with monarchs, and have ended with ballad-singers, chimney-sweepers, and beggars. But they that fill the highest and the lowest classes of human life, seem, in many respects, to be more nearly allied than even themselves imagine. A skilful anatomist would find little or no difference, in dissecting the body of a king and that of the meanest of his subjects.

Anatomizing the social body with an eye to capturing its overlooked details, Smith (notwithstanding his frequently patronizing tone) anticipates Henry Mayhew's sociological studies of *London Labour and the London Poor* in the 1850s. Offering, for instance, a description of the "simpler, whose business it is to gather and supply the city-markets with physical herbs," Smith then points to "such an innocent instance of rustic simplicity [as] William Friday, whose portrait is exhibited in the following plate." Readers, having been directed to the gracious woodcut (figure 10), return to the description to learn about the diverse, hands-on work that William Friday performs: "This man starts from Croydon, with champignons, mushrooms, &c. and is alternately snail-picker, leech-bather, and viper-catcher."[77] Such detail has as its forerunner the ennobling rusticity of Wordsworth, who describes a nature that can "breathe / Grandeur upon the very humblest face / Of human life" (*Prelude* 13: 286–7)—and whose own gallery of rustics, *Lyrical Ballads*, is an extension of a Hogarthian strain.

To recall Hogarth's influence in romantic-period discussions of portraiture is to access a powerful alternative to the Reynoldsian vision of the social body. Hazlitt, recollecting the directness of Titian's portraits—"There is that exact resemblance of individual nature which is always new and always interesting, because you cannot carry away a mental abstraction of it, and you must recur to the object to revive it in its full force and integrity"—embraces an aesthetics of particularity opposed to the Reynoldsian "general air" in both its aesthetic and its political valences.[78] A type of what William Galperin has called "the romantic visible," this particularist aesthetic—which was marketed by entrepreneurs

FIG. 10. *William Friday*, from John Thomas Smith, *Vagabondiana; or, Anecdotes of Mendicant Wanderers Through the Streets of London*, 1817. (Harry Ransom Humanities Research Center, The University of Texas at Austin)

like John Boydell (as I discuss in chapter two) and incorporated as political argument in such novels as *Frankenstein* (discussed in chapter four)—offered an early instance of a complex, detail-oriented realism.[79] When, across the Channel, Gustav Courbet famously aligned realistic representation with progressive politics, calling himself "not only a Socialist, but a democrat and a Republican as well: in a word, a supporter of the whole Revolution, and, above all, a Realist, that is to say a sincere lover of genuine truth," he inferred that the "democratization of the image" served as an index of social transformation.[80] Indeed, by 1847 *Punch* could make the everydayness of portraiture a target for satire, suggesting that portraits would soon be "reproduced in pats of butter"—a socially expansive notion of representation officially codified (if not actuated) by the First Reform Bill.[81]

But the path to Reform had been anything but straightforward, a fact that is reflected in the politics of romantic-era portraiture. Hogarth's aesthetic legacy resisted reduction to a popular radicalism or easy alignment with notions of representative presence—its ideological complexity was intrinsic to portraiture itself. That portraits often appeared at moments of national crisis suggests as much. In 1793, when revolutionary anxieties were exacerbated by the start of war with France, Henry Bromley's *Catalogue of Engraved British Portraits* reasserted social distinction with a "just discrimination" of the faces of "persons of eminence."[82] Six years later, as Napoleon crossed the Alps, the connoisseur Noel Desenfans published his proposal for a national portrait gallery that would "transmit to posterity, the Portraits of the most distinguished characters of England, Scotland and Ireland."[83] In the aftermath of Peterloo in 1819, Caulfield reissued his gallery of eccentrics; a year later, with the furor over Queen Caroline's trial for adultery imperiling the government, the British Institution exhibited 183 portraits in a show titled "Distinguished Persons in the History and Literature of the United Kingdom."[84] And in the early 1830s, when parliamentary reforms officially cut ties with the aristocratic past, published portrait galleries clutched onto the vestiges of tradition: John Burke's 1833 paean to aristocratic ancestry, *Portrait Gallery of Distinguished Females*, came complete with genealogies to validate the "worth" of the "beauties" it portrayed—a thinly veiled homage to the ideal of property.[85]

Galleries of the nobility, in particular, demonstrate the nationalizing influence of portraiture. Considering the relative novelty of the landowning class of the nineteenth century (much of the ruling elite had bought its way into power since the eighteenth century), galleries of the nobility silently fused *ancien* with *nouveau*.[86] They presented the image of a single, unified British elite as if it were representative of the nation. As a reviewer wrote of William Jerdan's *National*

Portrait Gallery of Illustrious Personages (1830–34), "We think this delightful publication well worthy of its name, *National*."[87] In *Bleak House*, Dickens made fun of the trend, citing a book called "The Divinities of Albion, or Galaxy Gallery of British Beauty" as a "truly national work" that represented "ladies of title and fashion in every variety of smirk that art, combined with capital, is capable of producing."[88] The political upshot of this merger between art and capital is clear enough in the satirical *Portraits of the Spruggins Family* (1829), by "Richard Sucklethumkin Spruggins." A send-up of the whole genre, the Spruggins gallery assails aristocratic excess in a cumulative portrait of vanity, triviality, and public uselessness.[89] Citing "the present important political crisis," the book's dedication sarcastically notes the public's "feverish interest [in] the opinions professed by the nobility"; it is hoped that "the world may not merely become acquainted with the characters and opinions of our forefathers, but may actually be enabled to draw their own conclusions, by studying the expressions of their countenances and the formation of their heads." As this satire lays bare, the national gallery-in-a-book was often simply the reformed machinery of patrilinear succession; it did the work once done by the country house.

Genre, Representation, Ekphrasis

Benedict Anderson has argued that print capitalism, and especially newspapers, enabled the bourgeoisie "to visualize in a general way the existence of thousands and thousands like themselves." But the many, particular portraits—painted or engraved, visual or verbal—that dominated public culture around 1800 enabled an even more literal visualization of the national community.[90] The displays of portraits at the Royal Academy; the sketching of character portraits in novels; and the textual portrait galleries that infiltrated people's living spaces and occupied their leisure time all reveal a preoccupation with an imagery of the social body. The phenomenon is visible in Wordsworth's attempt "to give a picture of a man" in "Michael"; Coleridge's description of Shakespeare's plays as "a splendid picture gallery"; and Hazlitt's assertion that Van Dyck's portrait of a mother's affection represents "an English face." Franco Moretti's pointed series of questions about the idea of the nation—"What does it look like? How can one *see* it? . . . [V]illage, court, city, valley, universe can all be visually represented—in paintings, for instance: but the nation-state?"—are all reflected in the romantics' unrelenting concern with how, precisely, to imagine the gallery.[91]

The literary form that, with portraiture, did the most to expand social representation in nineteenth-century culture was the novel. A socially inclusive textual space, the novel took up the humbler scale of everyday life, turning its gaze away from extraordinary universal figures and toward unremarkable English men and women. Tobias Smollett intuited this shift in focus as a pictorial problem at the outset of his comic novel, *Ferdinand Count Fathom* (1753). Finding in the form of the novel a principle of decentralized harmony in which each individual is absorbed within a wider social canvas, he calls it a "large diffused picture" where the various "characters of life" are "disposed in different groupes, and exhibited in various attitudes, for the purposes of an uniform plan . . . to which every individual figure is subservient." But a tension inheres in the painting metaphor, as Smollett recognizes. In theory the novel may subordinate individuals to the social tableau, but in practice it functions more like a portrait: "This plan cannot be executed with propriety, probability or success," he adds, "without a principal personage to attract the attention, unite the incidents, unwind the clue of the labyrinth, and at last close the scene by virtue of his own importance."[92] Smollett's metaphor indicates the novel's peculiarly pictorial arrangement of characters: the entire work may comprise a gallery filled with portraits, but one portrait in particular—that of the hero—would serve as the centerpiece.

The representative sociality of the novel was viewed with suspicion by writers such as Wordsworth, who in book seven of *The Prelude* describes an unnerving multiplication of people, storylines, and pictorial foci that mirrors the explosion of representation one finds in an art show or novel. His xenophobic account of street life considers an expanding social body in terms of actual, proliferating bodies—an urban "face to face—/ Face after face" where too much language and too much commerce squeeze out imagination. Confronting a blind beggar—"this unmoving Man, / His fixed face, and sightless eyes" (*Prelude* 7: 621–2)—Wordsworth encounters what seems to him a pure image, a portrait that cannot return his gaze. The human undergoes a pictorial reduction to seemingly inanimate bodies suspended between life and death, stillness and movement. Watt's description of the shift from a "unified world picture" to a more dispersed model grounded in particulars becomes, for Wordsworth, a low urban spectacle, a "parliament of monsters" (7: 692).

In rejecting social realism's excess of detail as formal monstrosity, Wordsworth echoes writers on aesthetics and politics who sought to organize an unwieldy mass of individuals into a formal ideal. In 1790, Reynolds wrote disparagingly of the masses:

> A hundred thousand near-sighted men, that see only what is just before them, make no equivalent to one man whose view extends to the whole horizon round him, though we may safely acknowledge at the same time that like the real near-sighted

> men, they see and comprehend as distinctly what is within the focus of their sight as accurately (I will allow sometimes more accurately) than the others. Though a man may see his way in the management of his own affairs, within his own little circle, with the greatest acuteness and sagacity, such habits give him no pretensions to set up for a politician.[93]

Reynolds's use of the word "safely" signals the danger he felt in the perceptive capacities of working men, a danger quickly subsumed into an idealized vision of a body politic in which one person stands in for the many.[94] The opposition between the body of the state and the innumerable bodies that exist within it—between the "one man whose view extends to the whole horizon" and the "hundred thousand near-sighted men" said to "see only what is just before them"—is distilled in what Alex Woloch has described as "the character-system" of the novel. Arguing that major characters, those beacons of bourgeois morality with whom readers invariably identify, gain their appeal and grace at the expense of the many minor characters who cede narrative space to them, Woloch presents this formal struggle as a version of the political: the character-system is a canvas upon which is figured "the competing pull of inequality and democracy."[95] Between the opposing imperatives to represent the expansive body of the public and to explore the depth of the private individuals who comprise that body, the novel actuates a brutal competition for a limited amount of narrative attention. Despite its potential bagginess, as an imagined gallery that stakes a claim to a reader's attention, the novel—like the Commons and the exhibition hall—has a fixed amount of space.

Whether imagined or real, the walls enclosing these representative spaces framed a carefully organized social body. Just as Smollett preserves a remnant of the epic by centralizing a hero, so too the hanging of paintings could quite literally center a certain kind of (tasteful, well-off) viewer. As a detailed drawing of the East Wall at the 1784 Academy reveals, the arrangement of paintings gave physical form to the eighteenth-century hierarchy of genres (figure 11). Large paintings were placed high on the walls to enhance viewers' sightlines, with the most prestigious work often in the principal position, while smaller paintings, except when used to fill space in the upper corners, generally hung low. The effect of this arrangement was to organize spectators according to their tastes. Those viewers interested in—and possessing the cultural apparatus to understand—the larger, more prestigious historical compositions would have to move toward the center of the room in order to view them properly, while viewers with a taste for small landscapes, genre scenes, and portraits could only gain an unobstructed view by moving to the room's margins. This process is illustrated by Pietro Martini's engraving after J. H. Ramberg's *The Ex-*

FIG. 11. E. F. Burney [J. H. Ramberg?], *The Royal Academy Exhibition of 1784: The Great Room, East Wall*, 1784. (Copyright The Trustees of the British Museum)

hibition of the Royal Academy, 1787 (figure 12), in which the authoritative figure of the Prince of Wales occupies a principal position, while the middle classes stand in obscurity on the side of the room.[96]

But these arrangements also made possible other, more disruptive effects. For if the more prestigious works held pride of place, they also existed in remarkable detachment from the life of the exhibition. Works categorized as lower in the academic hierarchy were hung lower on the walls, and yet this placement could also nourish an intimacy between painting and viewer, as is evident in the print below, where the spectators most deeply engaged with art are those women (at the far right-hand side) straining to view the miniatures (figure 13). Although they were the least elite form of art on display, miniatures were experienced up close and intensely. Being moved to the corner of the room actually brought one closer to art. Recognizing this entails seeing the hierarchies of prestige that seem to characterize this scene as rather tenuous. The infant reaching out toward one of the pictures as if it were a toy, or the con-

FIG. 12. Pietro Martini, after J. H. Ramberg, *The Exhibition of the Royal Academy, 1787*, 1787. (Copyright The Trustees of the British Museum)

FIG. 13. Detail from Pietro Martini, after J. H. Ramberg, *The Exhibition of the Royal Academy, 1787*, 1787. (Copyright The Trustees of the British Museum)

noisseur in the foreground gazing at this same group of women as if they themselves were art objects, show the neat orderliness of the social body giving way to primal or sexual energies that can be disruptive.[97] Such was the funhouse mirror of consumption. History painting may have been the genre of the ruling elite, but it was also estranged from the transactions—both visual and economic—that were the lifeblood of the marketplace for art.

The habit of aligning artistic and literary hierarchies of genre has led many to observe the affinities between novels and portraits, a relationship explored in more detail in chapters one and four. Relatively little attention has been paid to the nexus of poetry—especially romantic poetry—and portraiture. But especially at a time when the literary status of the personal was on the rise, the affective (if not generic or formal) resemblance between portraiture and the lyric deserves consideration. Studies of romantic poetry in its relation to the visual arts have clung to a traditional preference for the visionary over the visible, and for the enfranchised imagination over "servile" mimesis. This critical predilection, which shares origins with the romantic attitude toward portraiture, is an essential part of the political dialectic of representation under discussion. Consider Guido Reni's sixteenth-century depiction of Beatrice Cenci, described in Shelley's Preface to *The Cenci*. Shelley conveys the image's expressive intensity: "In the whole mien there is a simplicity and dignity which united with her exquisite loveliness and deep sorrow are inexpressibly pathetic. Beatrice Cenci appears to have been one of those rare persons in whom energy and gentleness dwell together without destroying one another." Shelley is fascinated by Reni's painting, in which he sees a real person, a figure existing in clear opposition to the "cold impersonations of [his] own mind," a woman whose "nature was simple and profound."[98] Theresa Kelley's argument that the romantics infused the cold figures of allegory with human warmth and pathos finds an exemplary site in Shelley's elaboration of this picture.[99] But Shelley himself, as Kelley shows, no sooner asserts the expressive power of the portrait than he allegorizes it away, making Beatrice Cenci's image "the mask and the mantle" of her sufferings—a movement toward abstraction reflected in the play itself.[100] He subordinates the local effects (and affects) of portraiture to the mystifying power of figuration.

This reflects a general pattern. The romantic tendency is not to represent particular portraits but to reveal something about the mind that perceives and creates them. "Wordsworth is obviously not interested in presenting the ideal portrait of a leech gatherer," writes Carol Christ, "but in demonstrating the way the mind can renew itself from such a sight."[101] Likewise in his "Essay On Love" (1818), Shelley tropes romantic sympathy as an idealized "miniature . . . of our entire self," thus rarefying the most commercial mode of portraiture, miniature painting, as "not only the portrait of our external being, but an assemblage of the minutest particulars of which our nature is composed."[102] That same year Coleridge would downplay the mimetic aspect of portraiture in favor of an imagined likeness: "It is not the likeness for actual comparison, but for recollection." Claiming the value of the portrait for nourishing personal affection, Coleridge goes on to remark how the pressure of reality strains this attempt at abstraction:

> The likeness of a very good portrait is not always recognized; because some persons never abstract, and amongst these are especially to be numbered the near relations and friends of the subject, in consequence of the constant pressure and check exercised on their minds by the actual presence of the original.[103]

To abstract, for Coleridge, is to shift from the material and sensible to the immaterial and ideational: it is, as he describes in *Biographia Literaria*, to "*love the purity of the idea*."[104] Recognizing a likeness requires that the viewer possess a mental portrait irreducible to line and color. Like Shelley's idealized, inward "likeness," Coleridge's portrait is not a fixed outline but a flickering essence that tells more about the beholder of the portrait than about the portrait itself.

This view was echoed in the *London Magazine*. An essay "On the Diversity of Opinions with regard to Likenesses in Portraits" (1822) opened by acknowledging that the parts of a face "are questions of geometry, determinable with as much precision as the width of the Thames," only to continue in a more Coleridgean vein:

> The fact is, that eyes, nose, and mouth are among the least important marks from which many persons derive their impressions of certain faces. . . . In countenances with which we are very familiar, we often perceive a variety of minute and indefinable casts of expression, many hints and shadows of meaning, spirit, or affection. . . . These deep secrets, these intimacies of the countenance, if I may call them so, have nothing to do with its grosser attributes, as a thing of eyes, nose, and other features . . . they are inseparably blended with all our thoughts and knowledge of an individual, and we consider them indispensable in any portrait that assumes to be a just representation.[105]

Perhaps in response to the blossoming culture of portraiture, the notion that the face reserves more than it reveals, that it holds "deep secrets" not readable by strangers, presented an attractive, and attractively *private*, alternative. Against the popular physiognomical theories of Lavater, which encouraged a faith in the expressive capacity of portraiture, the belief in "intimacies of the countenance" set personal relations over and above mass-cultural encounters.[106]

The conception of portraiture as an image in and of the mind constitutes a tradition of romantic ekphrasis.[107] Classic instances, such as Wordsworth's "Elegiac Stanzas Suggested by a Picture of Peele Castle," Keats's "Ode on a Grecian

Urn," and Shelley's "On the Medusa of Leonardo in the Florentine Gallery," transform the subject depicted into a focus for poetic imagination. Like the museum, whose purpose, as James A. W. Heffernan argues, is to "preserve the history embedded in works of art and to protect those works *from* history, from the ravages of time," romantic ekphrasis resituates the art object in a museum of words.[108] But while mental imaging has long been familiar to readers of romanticism, closer attention to such representations yields an understanding of romantic interiority as engaged with, rather than denying, the cultural objects that give it shape. As cultural artifacts, portraits insist upon a contextualized approach. For if Keats's "Ode on a Grecian Urn" and Shelley's "Ozymandias" turn objets d'art into texts for meditation, portraits confront the beholder with faces of friends, relations, or public figures. How different from Keats's "unravish'd bride," for example, is Anna Aikin's description of her brother's portrait, which assumes an overwhelming physical presence:

> O! should fate in some disastrous day,—
> Avert it Heaven!—the living form decay;
> Hide, hide, ye pitying friends, the mimic light,
> Veil, veil the image from my tortured sight;
> The shadow of past joys I could not bear,
> Nor would it speak of comfort, but despair.[109]

Whereas at the end of "Tintern Abbey" Wordsworth would leave the picture of his mind to the peaceful "mansion" of his sister's memory, Aikin finds no comparable solace in her brother's image. Keats's urn reveals how art is elevated and made meaningful through language; portraits, by contrast, generate an affective intensity that is difficult to transcend. Samuel Johnson defends their usefulness in "quickening the affections of the absent and continuing the presence of the dead," and yet, for this very reason, portraits can prove vexing to the romantic subject by challenging the distancing imagination.[110] It is striking that Keats, agonized by the sufferings of his brother, should find himself "beset by images" of Tom's face: "I am obliged to write, and plunge into abstract images to ease myself of his countenance."[111] The image of the face is overwhelmingly painful; unable to abstract it, Keats can only seek distraction from it. Portraits may have been an art of the bourgeoisie, but as images of relations they also held in reserve a power far more immediate than the figures on the Grecian urn, itself a (literally unfamiliar) "foster-child of silence and slow time."

In 1821, the *Magazine of the Fine Arts* celebrated portraiture as the art of "the absent lover—the affectionate orphan—the desolate widow," and in this we sense how nostalgia, particularly in alliance with a romantic myth of personal development, helped to contain portraiture's affective charge.[112] The emphasis on affect and its containment as nostalgia clarifies the special quality of romantic portrait poems. In a typically romantic reversal, Thomas Campbell describes portraiture in memorial terms as a "serenely silent art" that could "give us back the dead."[113] The portrait instantiates depth, making memory and even the death of a loved one the occasion for an experience of subjective presence. This is a far cry from Andrew Marvell's use of the portrait in "The Picture of Little T.C. in a Prospect of Flowers" (pub. 1681), where the emphasis is on innocence and a pending Fall:

> See with what simplicity
> This nymph begins her golden days!
> . . . .
> Yet this is she whose chaster laws
> The wanton Love shall one day fear,
> And under her command severe,
> See his bow broke and ensigns torn.
> . . . .
> . . . O young beauty of the woods,
> Whom nature courts with fruits and flowers,
> Gather the flowers, but spare the buds,
> Lest Flora, angry at thy crime
> To kill her infants in their prime,
> Do quickly make the example yours;
>   And ere we see,
> Nip in the blossom all our hopes and thee.[114]

The girl's portrait symbolizes mortality, female innocence and its loss—that is, it symbolizes any number of abstract ideas that cluster around the figure of the child, but not the child herself. For Campbell, the portrait turns back the clock on death; for Marvell it *is* death—always already a memento mori, destined to outlive its subject.

But in romanticism, death is often refigured at the level of individual development. Hazlitt, the period's foremost art critic, captures this when he remembers his first visit to the Louvre. Unable to revisit the gallery during the Napoleonic Wars, the paintings exist for him, like Dorothy Wordsworth for William, "from youth to age; the stay, the guide, and anchor of [his] purest thoughts." Likewise "the portrait of a man in black, by Titian," confirms for Hazlitt the sense of deep subjectivity that comes from experiencing the self-in-time: "It is still; . . . it does not turn its head, but it looks towards you to ask, whether you recognise it or not? It was there to meet me, after an interval of years, as if I had parted with it the instant before. Its keen, steadfast glance staggered me like a blow. It was the same—I was altered!"[115]

Portrait poems by Robert Southey and Felicia Hemans develop this idea in different ways. In Southey's "On My Own Miniature Picture, Taken at Two Years of Age," portraiture is an emblem of memory and a sign of past identity. Where one expects a sonnet, Southey gives an extended blank verse meditation that begins in medias res:

> And I was once like this! that glowing cheek
> Was mine, those pleasure-sparkling eyes; that brow
> Smooth as the level lake, when not a breeze
> Dies o'er the sleeping surface! . . . Twenty years
> Have wrought strange alteration![116]

Southey's incredulous opening anticipates Wordsworth's inability to "paint / What then I was," providing a source for the picture language of "Tintern Abbey." Seeing his past self, not in a "dear, dear sister" but in this "dearly prized . . . miniature" (line 6), Southey apostrophizes it: "Young Robert! for thine eye was quick to speak / Each opening feeling" (lines 18–19). The inward orientation of Southey's lyric portrait is echoed by Hemans, but with a difference, in "To My Own Portrait":

> How is it that before mine eyes,
> While gazing on thy mien,
> All my past years of life arise,
> As in a mirror seen?
> What spell within thee hath been shrined,
> To image back my own deep mind?[117]

Where Southey gestures toward subjective depth by invoking a past image as a visible sign of maturation, Hemans finds her "deep mind"—indeed, her entire history—imaged in her adult portrait. Southey's portrait enforces the pastness of the past; Hemans's does not just bring back the past, it revives the dead: "Such power is thine!—they come, the dead, / From the grave's bondage free" (lines 13–14). The memories that flood her take the form of an abstracted mimesis ("as in a mirror seen"). This is quite unlike the material proliferation of her engraved image in British culture, which led her to comment, "There is something absolutely frightful in this multiplication of one's self to *infinity*."[118] Ultimately, the portrait evokes the disjuncture between multiple, material selves—the numerous "Mrs. Hemans" in circulation—and the auratic serenity of this particular picture, the psychological depth of the self it presents:

> To see *thee* calm, while powers thus deep—
> Affection—Memory—Grief—
> Pass o'er my soul as winds that sweep
> O'er a frail aspen-leaf! (lines 31–4)

Southey and Hemans reveal poetic imperatives quite different from the more famous Victorian inheritor of the romantic portrait poem, the dramatic monologue. Rejecting nostalgia and depth, Browning's psychological portraits, for instance, show real experience leading to a knack for realistic painting: "That's the very man!" says Fra Lippo Lippi, declaring his aesthetic preferences,

> Look at the boy who stoops to pat the dog!
> That woman's like the Prior's niece who comes
> To care about his asthma: it's the life![119]

Browning's realism, in described portraits and through a portrait of the self, provides the means for communicating an unidealized everydayness—caring about a Prior's asthma; patting a dog. Conversely, Hazlitt, Southey, and Hemans all encounter portraiture as the experience of an idealized self-in-time. The portrait, contained by nostalgia, is an externalized emblem of the self.

The following chapters examine a set of specific convergences of the visual and the verbal across a broad spectrum of concerns: the personal nature of national discourse, the trumping of genius by mechanical reproduction, the gender dynamics of sentimentality, and the politics of realism, to name a few. I treat a range of texts to discover the scope and significance of the shared culture of text and portrait. Each chapter develops a different facet of portraiture: the political use of the "character sketch"; the way portraiture shapes how people read; the relation between portrait miniatures and sonnets; novelistic representations of portraits as barometers of an emerging theory of the novel; and the network of author portraits and poems about portraits that give a face to romanticism in the later part of the period.

My study begins by examining the cultural milieu of the 1790s, when the public art exhibition emerged as a metaphor for a more inclusive national ideal and as a site where that ideal was enacted. Chapter one reads *Reflections on the Revolution in France* (1790) in dialogue with the most prestigious statement of Enlightenment aesthetics, Reynolds's *Discourses on Art* (1769–90), to elucidate how Burke's verbal portraiture assists the transition from sublime patriarchal authority to participatory sentimental ideologies. His verbal iconography of Marie Antoinette typifies an age in which the ideological force of portraiture, visual as well as verbal, comes to dwell in affect. The language of the *Reflections*, suffused with *portrait moral* as a mode of political discourse, stages a conflict between establishment aesthetics and an anti-academic tradition.

Burke's attempt to define the nation as a propertied patriarchy unravels in his rhetorical gallery of portraits; conversely, London's premiere exhibition hall of the 1790s, the Boydell Shakespeare Gallery, was conceptually founded on such instability. Chapter two reads the Shakespeare Gallery as a site where generic boundaries are actively reconfigured to produce a public exhibition space that could be marketed as national. A for-profit experiment in cultural representation, the Shakespeare Gallery took the insular family gallery to the public, even as it rejected bourgeois portraiture as a focus for its nationalism. Yet, as I show through the Gallery artists' interpretations of *The Winter's Tale*, the painters themselves resolved these contradictions by relaying history painting as a visual semiotic of particularity and private virtue, often rejecting outright the academic bias at the theoretical heart of the project.

My third chapter moves from macrocosmic endeavors at national representation to microcosmic exercises in self-presentation. Tracing the cult of the miniature in the poetics of the lyric, I argue that Charlotte Smith's *Elegiac Sonnets* (1784–1800) achieves a public voice in the theatricalization of privacy associated with portrait miniatures. In a canny performance that advertises the self-reflexivity of women's sentimental poetry, Smith evokes portraits as public metaphors of political exclusion and as the endeared private objects of a poet who is also a mother. Her poetic self limns the border between covert and displayed, drawing it into a matrilineal inheritance of private sorrows, in contrast to the ancestral portrait galleries binding the nation to its patriarchal past.

The last two chapters of this study explore the widespread concern with extending portraiture's "democracy" into political practice. Treatments of Mary Shelley and the later Wordsworth anticipate the splintering of the romantic-period discourse of portraiture into, on the one hand, a representational realism that takes seriously the political promise of particularity, and on the other, an aestheticism that universalizes the individual's intensely felt encounter with art. Chapter four illuminates Mary Shelley's challenge to the establishment aesthetic of Reynolds and demonstrates the persistence of a Hogarthian counter-tradition. Reading *Frankenstein* (1818) and its representation of portraiture alongside contemporaneous debates about the Elgin Marbles, I explore the theory of realism that gets figured through Shelley's Creature: a composite of bodies from indiscriminate social classes that reflects what was widely discussed as the democratic aesthetic of the marbles.

Politics encounters the marketplace directly in my final chapter, on Wordsworth's late-career involvement with portraiture, which propels him into the Victorian marketplace. In a series of portrait poems written in the 1830s, Wordsworth tacitly asserts the original aura of his lyrics as a response to post-Reform literary culture. In his ekphrastic encounters with portraiture, the later Wordsworth turns sharply away from the discourse's (overtly) political meanings in celebrating the uniqueness of the revelatory encounter—a prototypically Wordsworthian finessing that renders politics at a second remove. Yet, even as he uses the genre of the portrait poem to safeguard the aura of his poetry, the scores of portraits for which he sits market that aura to middle-class readers. The contradictory meanings of portraiture are revealed in this visionary poet who becomes, late in life, obsessed with his own visibility.

The Victorian Wordsworth offers a fitting conclusion for a study that, in describing the romantic aftermath of the quarrel between a universalizing humanism and a populist aesthetics of the detail, offers a prehistory of Victorian realism and, especially, of the rise of photography, from a political orientation.[120] What some have called "the triumph of art for the public" and others "the vulgarization of art" is everywhere observable at the frame of the Victorian portrait: in portrait-publications such as Kenny Meadows's *Heads of the People; or, Portraits of the English* (1840–41), in Mayhew's working-class sociological portraits supplemented by actual engravings, in Browning's poem-portraits of eccentric individuals, in Dickens's "vivid pictures . . . fixed for ever like little twinkling miniatures painted on snuff-box lids," and in the unprecedented reproduction made possible by photography.[121]

But as I discuss in my epilogue, even after 1832 the gallery as a physical, textual, or purely imaginary space remained a location for fiction. For many, the 1832 bill was merely a concession by the elite to stave off revolution (with the evolution of Reform from within taking another thirty-odd years). It had a distinctly aesthetic quality, offering a beautifully symmetric image of the nation far removed from a meaningful extension of the franchise. After Reform, the Commons remained inhabited not by the people but by their shadows; the radical task was to transform shadow into reality.[122] The success of that effort is best left to a study of Victorian modes of representation. What most interests me here are the shadows of representation that emerge in the late eighteenth and early nineteenth centuries. *Imagining the Gallery* tells a story of familiarity and strangeness: the seeming localization of nation into an apparently more inclusive social body, as against the enduring alienation of the self from its representative political body. By illuminating this contradiction, it reveals as types of the Stranger's Gallery many of the representative spaces of early democratic culture, from the novel, to the viewing area at Parliament, to the floor of the Royal Academy.

CHAPTER ONE

The Many Bodies of Edmund Burke

His Pourtraits remind the Spectator of the Invention of History.
—Edmund Burke, "Character of Sir Joshua Reynolds"

In 1790, Sir Joshua Reynolds—son of a tradesman, President of the Royal Academy of Art, and portrait painter to Britain's elite—flipped over the manuscript of what was to be his final discourse to the Academy and wrote sardonically in the voice of "the ignorant (which are always the majority)."[1] "Destroy every trace that remains of ancient taste," Reynolds's imaginary John Bull exclaims; "Let us pull the whole fabric down at once, root it up even to its foundation. Let us begin the art again upon this solid ground of nature and of reason . . . [in] the glory of stepping forth in this great work of reformation, and endeavouring to rescue the world from the worse than barbarous tyranny of prejudice, and restore the sovereignty of reason."[2] What has come to be known as the "Ironic Discourse" belies the image of the complaisant portrait painter for whom political opinions were bad business practice.[3] Its withering sarcasm is as surprising as it is revealing of a man whose allegiances were notoriously difficult to pin down—who once dined with Burke and his nemesis Warren Hastings on consecutive days, and who fooled even his friend and biographer, James Northcote, into saying that "politics never amused him nor ever employed his thoughts for a moment."[4] In its Burkean hyperbole, the Ironic Discourse releases Reynolds's personality even as it recasts his canonical aesthetics politically as a defense of tradition, custom, and prejudice, and as a rejection of "*newly-hatched unfledged* opinions" (*Discourses*, 269).

It is tempting to infer that Reynolds owes this outspokenly counterrevolutionary politics to his close friend Burke, author of a far more public counterrevolutionary text of 1790.[5] That artistic tradition for Reynolds was certainly every bit the entailed inheritance that liberty was for Burke is apparent in the Ironic Discourse, which shares with *Reflections on the Revolution in France* not just a general stance but specific figures and emphases: drapery, prejudice, genius. But if Burke was Reynolds's primary political influence (particularly after the death of Samuel Johnson in 1784), it is equally plausible to understand Burke as espousing a Reynoldsian politics. Burke's central configurations—the "pleasing illusion" of the "lovely" state, the idea of the British nation as an extended aristocratic family, and the celebrated portrait of Marie Antoinette as a heroine in distress—all owe something to Reynolds, a friend he described as "a profound and penetrating Philosopher."[6] To acknowledge this is not to say that Reynolds was a closet reactionary or that he was instrumental (or even necessary) to Burke's political development; it is simply to recognize the politics of aesthetics in general, and of Reynolds's theory and practice of painting in particular. Long before Burke's *Reflections*, Reynolds conveyed to his friend Edmond Malone "his contempt of those 'Adam-wits,' who set at nought the accumulated wisdom of ages, and on all occasions are desirous of beginning the world anew."[7] The Burkean vehemence might remind us that "Reynolds's doctrine and Reynolds's art," as E. H. Gombrich writes, "represent the conservative programme in the true meaning of the word."[8] Here I wish to suggest that, for all its generative impact, the *Reflections* emerges in dialogue with Reynolds's *Discourses* and in a wider cultural context in which metaphors of painting did serious work in helping to reimagine the British social body.

Concerns about political access featured prominently in the *Discourses*. Reynolds's theory of painting embedded crucial questions about the social power structure: was the public for art an exclusive group of property-owning men for whom beauty was a moral quality indistinguishable from public spirit? Or was it a public of male and female consumers, driven by their private interests, for whom beauty was a bodily trait? At the end of the eighteenth century, John Barrell has argued, the latter was increasingly the case, with the traditional civic humanist position becoming more and more attenuated as a consequence. He locates a parallel turn in Reynolds's *Discourses*, away from an idea of art that addresses "a 'universal' republic of taste constituted on the uniformity of human nature" and toward "an art which would address itself to a national community, a nation state, different in character from other states"—to a Britain, constituted by its unique history and customs, that Burke would celebrate in the *Reflections*.[9] "Men's minds must be prepared to receive what is new to them," Reynolds proposes in the seventh discourse of 1776; "Reformation is a work of time" (141). Yet he also describes a strikingly democratic process of "imitation" or "borrowing": "No man need be ashamed of copying the antients: their works are considered as a magazine of common property, always open to the public, whence every man has a right to take what materials he pleases; and if he has the art of using them, they are supposed to become to all intents and purposes his own property" (107). In this formulation, the recourse to history guards against change, and the practice of appropriation helps to preserve a proper hierarchy. He may hint that the unrefined part of the population cannot make these determinations, but nevertheless, far from demarcating an unchangeable and inaccessible sphere of taste, Reynoldsian history ultimately promotes an aesthetic (and, by extension, social) mobility.[10] His elitism is, on the face of it, accessible.

These matters become particularly charged around questions of gender. For Reynolds, class and gender were the language of elevation, as he sought to raise portraiture from the effeminate sphere of bourgeois representation by investing it with the "manly, noble, and dignified manner" of history painting (153). He claimed that by "descend[ing] lower"—into portraiture—an artist could "bring into the lower sphere of art a grandeur of composition and character, that will raise and ennoble his works far above their natural rank" (52). What we might understand as the social mobility of allegory was especially concentrated in Reynolds's female portraits.[11] Cloaking female subjects in classical drapery and posing male subjects in attitudes drawn from classical sculpture or from Italian Renaissance art, Reynolds offered an aesthetic model for social mobility and prescribed the elevation of portraiture into the masculine province of history. Through the enhancement of what he called a "more manly, noble, and dignified manner," his Grand Style conferred on a private, consumer-oriented genre all the qualities of a public-spirited civic humanism. By the time of his death the *General Evening Post* could declare: "His very portraits are indeed Historic, or rather perhaps Epic."[12]

The same sense of generic (and hence ideological) slippage underlies the nuances of the Burkean position. If Reynolds's "Historical Style" is an important model for his friend, it also bequeathes the instability often associated with a Burke perched (in Isaac Kramnick's words) "between his identification with what might be called the aristocratic personality on the one hand, and the bourgeois personality on the other."[13] Like the *Discourses*, which walk a fine line between promoting civic art and encouraging an elevated kind of private portraiture, Burke's political writings of the 1790s revive a civic humanist rhetoric of civic virtue *through* a more modern vocabulary of sentimental self-interest. This in part explains why he has often been seen as a figure caught between "two seemingly opposite positions: the defender of a hierarchical establishment, and the market liberal."[14] The Burke problem, as C. B. McPherson describes this conundrum, might just as well be called "the Reynolds Problem," for just as the painter responded to economic necessities by investing bourgeois portraiture with the cultural authority of history painting, Burke turns to "paintings" of "character" as the medium of a new civic order. "It is indeed very difficult happily to excite the passions, and draw the characters of men," he wrote; "But our nature leads us more directly to such paintings than to the invention of a story."[15] Burke's verbal portraits, Stephen Browne avers, weave "into the fabric of history the multicolored threads of human agency and personality"; but as rhetorical devices that crystallize his political positions, they also operate intertextually to help him ground a masculine ideal in emotive private behavior.[16] Personal emotion goes public, with erotic interest doubling as national interest. In attempting to reconcile two distinct discourses—civic humanism with its ethos of disinterested public service, and sentimental ideology with its ethical basis in private behavior and individual affect—Burke limns a political theory out of character and passion, in verbal portraits that figure, in miniature, a social body in transition.

The Burke Gallery

From the very beginning, Burke's *Reflections on the Revolution in France* was perceived in pictorial terms. The satirical frenzy it unleashed began on November 2, 1790, just one day after its appearance, with an anonymous print from the radical publishing house of William Holland (figure 14). The print figures its rhetoric in terms of society portraiture: Burke, artist and beholder, under Cupid's influence, bows to his "delightful vision" of Marie Antoinette. By posing Burke as an enthusiastic fop, the caricaturist implies that portraiture—and especially Burke's rhetorical portraiture—has a prurient aspect. Disinterested aesthetic appreciation, the image suggests, is never far from sliding into erotic self-interest: by the "fixing of an inquisitive eye on beauty," as Hazlitt would put it, "the [portrait] painter may chance to slide into the lover."[17] It was a danger Burke himself had acknowledged in his 1757 *Philosophical Enquiry into the Origin of Our Ideas of the Sublime and Beautiful*, where the man who beholds beauty is said to be "softened, relaxed, enervated, dissolved, melted away by pleasure." The print of Burke as a painter-lover reminds us that portraiture in the late eighteenth century carries a dual value: it is associated not only with the disinterested perception of "personal *beauty*" (and the exaltation of the man who beholds it), but also with an erotic dimension driven by private interest.[18]

Charges of sexual equivocation, perversity, or self-interest adhered to the author of *Reflections*. From Mary Wollstonecraft's contemporary argument that Burke's "pretty flights" reveal a "pampered sensibility," to Kramnick's recent claim that his "preoccupation with naked women" signals a "serious confusion

FIG. 14. Anonymous [Attributed to Frederick George Byron], *Frontispiece to Reflections on the French Revolution*, November 2, 1790. (Copyright The Trustees of the British Museum)

and doubt about his sexual identity," commentators have always shown an acute sensitivity to the effects of Burke's masculine spectatorship.[19] This pattern is no doubt underwritten by the profoundly visual emphasis of the *Reflections*, apparent even in the title, which gives the appearance that it is the work of an eyewitness on the scene in Paris, rather than of a correspondent from across the Channel composing largely on the basis of hearsay and rumor.[20] By presenting himself as a spectator, Burke provoked responses ranging from Thomas Paine's ridicule of his "horrid paintings," to Joel Barlow's complaint that he "paints ideal murders," to Wollstonecraft's accusation that he describes events in Paris "without having troubled [himself] to clean [his] palette"—a clever wordplay that signals the impurity of Burke's *palate* in calling attention to the bodily basis of his rhetorical art.[21] The specific, material contexts for these artistic metaphors, however, have gone unremarked; refocusing these contexts, I suggest, reveals how Burke mobilizes the domestic portrait genre to catalyze the major concerns of his late writings. "Characters" were Burke's descriptive stock-in-trade, and in the charged revolutionary context of the 1790s, he hawked them like cheap reprinted broadsides to sell his readers on the counterrevolution. What people have taken to be Burke's narrative skill in turning history into story depends, in fact, on his ability to reroute story through character, so that history is translated as a series of set-piece portraits. Whether opposing the awe-inspiring "face of the kingdom of France" to what he calls the "*facies hippocratica*" (the death's head) of the infant republic (131, 185), or evoking beauty-in-distress in his rhetorical portraits of Marie Antoinette, Burke shapes contemporary political reality as a *musée imaginaire*, a phantasmatic gallery of portraits.[22]

His recourse to portraiture is yet another instance of what Frans de Bruyn observes as Burke's "persistent weaving of literary forms into his political discourse." In this case, however, Burke's "realization of content or ideas at the level of form" depends less on the forms of literary culture than on those of print culture.[23] The gallery of political portraits was a prominent book form in the late eighteenth century, one that reflected the pervasiveness of portraiture as a concept; even as Burke composed his *Reflections*, the London translation of Mirabeau's *Gallery of Portraits of the National Assembly* appeared in print, its verbal descriptions of French politicians laid out like an exhibition catalogue.[24] Another such gallery, *Sketches from Nature, in High Preservation* (1779)—which ran through almost two dozen editions—developed the fiction that each of its subjects (primarily members of Parliament) was a painter. Politicians were disguised as "noble artists . . . activated with no other view, than to rescue Great Britain from the imputation of inferiority to her neighbors in Italy, on the subject of excellence in painting."[25] At once a catalogue for a phantom exhibition and a gallery of portraits in its own right, *Sketches from Nature*, by presenting politics as art, gave concrete form to the Burkean view of aesthetic political representation. Burke himself is represented as a portrait painter whose "expression of features borders too much on the ludicrous." This judgment, taken from *Sketches'* commentary on an imaginary painting titled *Cicero declaiming against civil Commotions*, introduces a passage in which the painter is also the painting's subject: "The Painter has done too much for him, and Nature too little, for he has neither the dignity or height sufficient to recommend him in the character he has assumed. To speak impartially, the artist has made him what Cicero might, not what Cicero should have been." In saying that Cicero, as represented by this painting, lacks "the dignity or height" for the position "he has assumed," the commentator takes a not-so-subtle dig at Burke's own middle-class, Irish background. This is echoed in the commentary on Burke's other painting, *Longinus*, which is said to "have a roughness not truly suitable to the frown of antiquity" (45–46). These catalogue entries do more than simply declare how out of keeping Burke's background is with his parliamentary status. They also characterize his rhetorical style as one that makes his subjects into something more than they are. The author even implies a relation between the two criticisms, for if Burke's rendering of overblown characters is given here as a function of low origins, such a lack of gravitas is also said to originate his style. A Burkean painting, like Burke himself, is a portrait bordering "on the ludicrous."

As an example like this shows, both conservative and progressive programs sought to incorporate portraiture as a rhetorical tool. Yet anyone who would do so was left susceptible to damaging slippages in signification. James Gillray's *Two Pair of Portraits* (figure 15), published in the *Antijacobin Review and Magazine* of 1798, rehearses its doubleness. In it, Gillray illustrates the argument of John Horne Tooke's pamphlet of the same title, which had used contrasting verbal sketches of Lord Holland and Lord Chatham, and their sons Fox and Pitt, to argue the government's case in the Westminster elections of 1788. Yet in the background, a broadside linking "The Art of Political Painting" with "the most celebrated Jacobin Professors" reveals the political reverse.[26] Reformers extended the paradox, often exploiting the hierarchical valences of portraiture to suit their political objectives. For example, in *State Trials for High Treason* (1794), an ostensibly objective account of the 1794 treason trials, portraits were used to capitalize on the market for sentimental images. While boasting of its effort to present "the most minute and accurate detail of every proceeding," the book incorporated heroicized images of the accused as frontispieces that solicited the sympathies of readers. Another Gillray cartoon lampoons such slip-

FIG. 15. James Gillray, *Two Pair of Portraits*, 1798. (Copyright The Trustees of the British Museum)

pages in verbal as well as visual portraiture: *Notorious Characters*, a response to the *Public Characters* series of published character sketches, played on the ability to manipulate portraits even as it revealed the fine line separating caricature and portraiture.

What does it mean to "sketch" character in the late eighteenth century? We have observed the novel's provision of imaginary, socially inclusive space, and how this is reflected in visual metaphors for the novelist's art. When Jane Austen describes her narrative canvas in terms of miniature painting as a "little bit (two Inches wide) of Ivory," or shows Emma "publishing" (and distorting) character through private sketching, she suggests how novels, as galleries of portraits, are stocked by a writer's ability to apprehend personality as a near-physical quantity.[27] Similarly for Frances Burney, whom Burke would accuse of "sitting for characters," portraits functioned as keepsakes of character, object-like transcripts of a total personality. In a letter, Burney brings her own special skill (and obvious relish) in rendering "character" to a verbal portrait of one Mr. Musgrave:

> We have now a new character added to our set, and one of no small diversion,—Mr. Musgrave, an Irish gentleman of fortune, and a member of the Irish Parliament. He is tall, thin, and agreeable in his face and figure; is reckoned a good scholar, has travelled, and been very well educated. His manners are impetuous and abrupt; his language is high-flown and hyperbolical; his sentiments are romantic and tender; his heart is warm and generous; his head hot and wrong! And the whole of his conversation is a mixture the most uncommon, of knowledge and triteness, simplicity and fury, literature and folly!
>
> Keep this character in your mind, and contradictory as it seems, I will give you, from time to time, such specimens as shall remind you of each of these epithets.[28]

Burney's portrait summons the multiple eighteenth-century connotations of the term "character," which (among other things) signified "a graphic sign or symbol" (*OED* I.2); the "face or features . . . personal appearance" (I. 10); and, bridging both of these, "A description . . . of a person's qualities" (I. 14.a). Tony Tanner writes that, "since we cannot literally internalise another person, it is at all times extremely important what particular picture or portrait of that person we carry with us"; Burney, enjoining Crisp to "keep this character in [his] mind," figures character as a transportable quantity, personality as a verbal sketch that readers might store away for future reference.[29] The perception of character as something swiftly apprehended in the act of reading originates, Peter Brooks suggests, in the seventeenth-century use of *portrait moral* to represent character. As "a formal and traditional set-piece of rhetoric" that novelists use "for the presentation of character," *portrait moral* reflects a positivist attitude to personality, "repos[ing] on the belief that all the important characteristics of a person can be apprehended and can be expressed in language."[30] Just as character blossomed as an increasingly complex quality in the novel of the late eighteenth and early nineteenth centuries, *portrait moral* persisted in the frequent use of the personal sketch to crystallize and characterize political positions.

Burke was no exception to this trend. In 1774 his *Speech on Taxation* dazzled listeners with its series of character sketches, which included a celebrated characterization of Lord Chatham.[31] He had long played at sketching character in more private contexts: on the first anniversary of his marriage, for instance, he gave Jane Burke a short prose portrait titled "The Character of ———" (leaving her to supply the blank), in which he catalogued her physical, mental, and social attributes. "If such a person as I would describe really exists," he wrote, "she must be far superior to my description: and such as I must love too well to be able to paint as I ought."[32] But the thoroughness with which Burke engages portraiture in his later writings, particularly in *Reflections*, is unusually vexed. He evokes an older ideal of portraiture as a literally conservative art that keeps alive the spirit of the past, even as he activates that ideal in a Whig context. Of Burke's well-known description of the nation as a family, J. G. A. Pocock stresses that Burke's family is based not on shared blood but on a shared submission to law: "We have made the state a family; but have we not done so by constituting it a family in the sense in which a family is a relation in law?"[33] Nation, in this reading, is an institution that codifies an imagined relationship among private families. The metaphor of portraiture lurks behind this formulation, at once hinting at national intimacy and serving to qualify it. The key passage is the famous one in which Burke describes the nation's "choice of inheritance"; he seems here to resurrect and safeguard an older idea of ancestral portraiture: "Working after the pattern of nature, we receive, we hold, we transmit our government and our privileges, in the same manner in which we enjoy and transmit our property and our lives." Property itself, the privileges and values that constitute the national inheritance, takes the form of portraiture: the body politic has a "frame of polity" and assumes "the image of a relation in blood." But the insistence on metaphor here is resounding: the state is not a relation in blood but an *image of* one; not a body politic but a *frame of* polity. Against an essentialist model of a social body connected by blood, portraiture helps Burke to assert a social body with a purely institutional and aesthetic existence. Ancestral "heads" assume signal importance, not as the nation proper, but as the material correlative to the "*entailed inheritance* derived to us from our forefathers" (33).

Pursuing his description of the state as an aesthetic object, Burke turns to personification in order to figure the national inheritance as a portrait. In giving an inventory of the belongings that define the British nation as a family, he paints the explicitly masculine face of "liberty": "Our liberty . . . carries an imposing and majestic aspect. It has a pedigree and illustrating ancestors. It has its bearings and its ensigns armorial. It has its gallery of portraits; its monumental inscriptions; its records, evidences, and titles. We procure reverence to our civil institutions on the principle upon which nature teaches us to revere individual men; on account of their age; and on account of those from whom they are descended" (34–35). Burke's portrait of liberty may be "imposing and majestic," but it is also intimate and domestic. It takes the form of the "conversation piece" (or "family-piece"), a type of group portrait that flourished among the landed gentry and featured a detailed depiction of the objects owned by its sitters. Here "liberty" is a man of property ensconced in personal possessions. These consist of an amalgam of verbal and visual signifiers: not only writings (inscriptions, records, titles) but also paintings ("its gallery of portraits"). Unlike in France, where "Liberty" figured as an aloof goddess, Burke's "Liberty" is a landowning Brit, defined by belongings that preserve a vital connection with the past.

The most valued of these belongings is his ancestry. Signifying a national, patrimonial inheritance, the faces gazing from Burke's hallowed ancestral wall at once represent the state's "permanent body" and its "transitory parts." They are the unexchangeable, unexportable, "unbought grace of life" (75): like the English constitution, they simply are.[34] Beneath their watchful eyes, Burke writes, a "manly freedom" is acted out "as if in the presence of canonized forefathers" (35, 34). Hazlitt would later observe that in an ancestral gallery "we live in time past, and seem identified with the permanent form of things"; it is this sense of permanence that is so important to Burke.[35] The men's and women's bodies that stand for a national heritage he renders visibly within a grandiose and patriarchal conception of the state.

In their clarity and sobriety—these are "*illustrating* ancestors" (*OED* 8: "To clear [the head or brain]")—these iconic forebears render a national face characterized by order. In this, they emphatically contrast the cluttered illustrations of caricature, those "loaded portraits" whose truth claims, Lynch writes, depend on crass exaggeration and "physiognomical unruliness."[36] Burke himself was hardly averse to verbal caricature; he in fact revels in descriptions that show the influence of print satire, never more effectively than in his description, in *Letter to a Noble Lord*, of the Duke of Bedford as a series of animals, which I discuss below. In the *Reflections*, we are presented not just the absurd figure of Richard Price but also a France, once represented by Marie Antoinette "glittering like the morning-star" (75), as an *enfant terrible* whose diseased face is marked "with the symptoms of death": "the *facies Hippocratica* forms the character of its physiognomy, and the prognostic of its fate" (185). The opposition between "lovely" monarchy and ugly republic is thus rendered as a contrast between portrait and caricature—between an idealizing art that "ennoble[s] the character of the countenance . . . at the expense of the likeness," and a mimetic style that, in its tendency to particularize, verges on grotesquerie.[37] Nobility is Burke's general standard.

Burke turns to idealizing portraiture as an art immune to the vicissitudes of history and to the negative mobility of caricature, but he has to contend with the fact that, by century's end, portraits of all kinds were property not just in the galleries of estates but also in the marketplace. Not even family pictures were sacred—witness Charles Surface, in Sheridan's *School for Scandal*, exuberantly selling off the portraits of his relatives, "all stiff and awkward as the originals."[38] Burke's tacit opposition between the gravitas of the masculine portrait gallery and the unruliness of caricature signals a desire to emphasize distinctions, so that family pictures can once again be made to seem prestigious, like "the unbought grace of life." Hence Burke's description of Francophone radical discourse as "illicit bottoms": "the counterfeit wares which some persons, by a double fraud, export . . . in illicit bottoms, as raw commodities of British growth though wholly alien to our soil" (25–26). Though his principal reference is to smuggling ships, Burke's word choice signals his association of foreign trade and foreign revolution with the erotic, and specifically with sodomy. Unlike the illustrious heads of property-owning Englishmen, the debased, foreign, and vaguely pornographic "bottoms" figure an entailment that is transitory, not permanent; French, not British.

Given the significance he attaches to a continuous and insular pattern of property transmission, it is clear why, for Burke, "illicit bottoms" (and the nonreproductive sexuality they imply) are the antithesis to the virile "liberty" imaged in the "gallery of portraits." This metaphor applies, also, to Burke's concern for legitimate value (alternatively represented by kingship, bullion, flesh and blood, manly feelings) and its susceptibility to commodity culture and its extreme form: paper credit.[39] In France, as Burke discerns, *assignats* sent the reproduced face of the king into nationwide circulation. In the first three years of their distribution, most *assignats* bore one of three miniaturized profiles of Louis XVI. These likenesses are particularly shocking today for their prefiguration of what was to become another widely disseminated image: the beheaded king. The distribution of the king's diminutive face encapsulates the revolution's dispersal of authority. The dangers of circulation were that one could be undone by one's own portrait—the very portrait that declared one's sovereignty—as exemplified by the story of the king's secret escape being foiled at the Austrian border by a postal worker who recognized him by his likeness on a *Louis* coin. The "aura" of an authentic portraiture evaporated with the conveyance of the king's head into these "heads of incumbrance" (Burke's term for *assignats*; 240). What Walter Benjamin calls the "tremendous shattering of tradition" resulting from the elimination of aura is, in this case, extreme: Louis's engraved image was first leveled with the revolutionary "writing" constitutive of monetary authority, then reprinted and passed through the hands and pockets of Frenchmen everywhere. Finally, in a brutal endgame, its presence on *assignats* served as model for numerous caricatures and historical sketches that portrayed the king's head, in profile, torn from his body.[40]

That portraiture could be a barometer of social change is evident enough in Burke's story of the French Revolution: on one side the family gallery, the symbolic center of a nation grounded in laws of patrilinear inheritance, and on the other a French republic defined by a paper currency that had exposed the ultimate image of masculine authority, the king's head, to the possibility of symbolic castration.[41] Portraiture was an unstable genre, its boundaries dissolving from both above and below, but Burke seeks out a middle ground, where portraiture mobilizes the conflicting claims of noble history and "low" caricature and puts them to counterrevolutionary ends. In his most famous set piece, his portrait of Marie Antoinette as a Roman matron, he envisages a polity whose values are propertied but whose membership depends on a refined aesthetic sense, whereby a man realizes (in Addison's words) "a kind of property in everything he sees."[42] Submission to the "gallery of portraits" of "canonized forefathers," as we shall now see, is replaced by a consensual, affective response to the "lovely" state in "decent drapery"—a conception of the state that achieves formal realization in Burke's verbal portraiture.

A Roman Matron

When Burke declares that "to make us love our country, our country ought to be lovely" (78), he implies that the state should be imaginable as a woman, whose likeness could encourage feelings of "love, veneration, admiration, or attachment" (77). The purple passages of the *Reflections* model such a notion by generating an image of feminine distress to encourage the virtue of Britain's masculine ruling elite. Although these sections, more than any other, have occupied commentators since their first appearance, their pictorial quality, and especially their engagement with the meanings of portraiture as promulgated by Reynolds, deserve special attention.[43] By attending to the status of these descriptions as verbal paintings—and specifically as portraits—we are able to perceive a Burke working to reconcile two worldviews. If "Burke offers," according to Kramnick, "nothing less than a pivotal insight into that great turning point in our history—the transformation from the aristocratic to the bourgeois world," it is *portraiture*, in all its paradox, that shows him attempting to join an older, civic ideal with the consumerist (erotic, self-interested) ethos of a bourgeois order.[44]

Burke's rhapsodies about the beautiful state are themselves deeply indebted to the Reynoldsian theory and practice of portrait painting. Renowned for producing "lovely" images of his female sitters, Reynolds promoted a style that could rise "above all singular forms, local customs, particularities, and details of every kind," so as to attain "that central form . . . from which all deviation is a deformity" (*Discourses*, 44, 45). The "central form" was a composite of all the beautiful specimens of humankind, and thus no single portrait could possibly represent it except by a process of extreme idealization. To achieve this in his portraits, Reynolds painted "at the greatest possible distance from [his] sitter," often even working from a mirror.[45] His use of classical drapery enhanced the effect. Personal deformity was big business for the portraitist, whose job was to camouflage it. William Pulteney, first Earl of Bath, described going to Reynolds's studio "to mend my sickly look." Another commentator, describing the Reynoldsian vogue, wrote that a portrait painter "commits to canvass the exact pig's-head of a certain nobleman without offence, and copies out the eyes of the lovely countess as much to her satisfaction as her glass. 'Who is that?' you ask—pointing to the head of a man, or a woman, or a child.' 'That is Mr. Varnish,' you hear, and there can be no further question." As Hazlitt would write, "The finest lady in the land is as fond of sitting to a favourite artist as of seating herself before her looking-glass, and the more so, as the glass in this case is sensible of her charms, and does all it can to fix or heighten them."[46] The pleasures of sitting for one's picture depended on the painter's skill in highlighting some qualities while concealing others.

Burke's verbal portraiture works in a similar way, but on the wider scale of the national body. His elegy for the "lovely" state concedes the artifice for its political work and laments the tearing off of "decent drapery." He thereby renders the revolutionary moment as a contrast between universals and particulars—between a grand and a mimetic style:

> All the pleasing illusions, which made power gentle, and obedience liberal, which harmonized the different shades of life, and which, by a bland assimilation, incorporated into politics the sentiments which beautify and soften private society, are to be dissolved by this new conquering empire of light and reason. All the decent drapery of life is to be rudely torn off. All the superadded ideas, furnished from the wardrobe of a moral imagination, which the heart owns, and the understanding ratifies, as necessary to cover the defects of our naked shivering nature, and to raise it to dignity in our own estimation, are to be exploded as a ridiculous, absurd, and antiquated fashion. (77)

The emphasis on veils, wardrobes, and drapery reveals Burke's fear that too much transparency—unaccessorized, indecent bodies—would interfere with the universal submission to the semi-divine aspect of authority. Clothes preserve social bonds by concealing the deformities that mark differences among individuals; they protect authority by covering up the ugly actualities that incite displeasure in viewers. For Reynolds and Burke both, the central form is a fiction, a fabrication "from the wardrobe of a moral imagination" whereby kings and queens are prevented from appearing as mere men and women. "In recognizing the central form of the body," Barrell argues, "we recognise at once ourselves, each other, and the resemblance of us all; and this experience of recognition is the ground of social affiliation. The bodies represented to us by the central form are public bodies, and they enable us to see that we are members of the body of the public."[47] The integrity of the social body requires that the queen be an asocial body: ideal, unapproachable, even inhuman. The only way to ensure her representativeness, *even her safety*, is to keep the particularities or "defects" concealed by her "decent drapery" from being exposed for all to see. This exposure, Burke argues, is what the French republic has undertaken: it has eradicated the queen's (and the nation's) idealized "central form" and replaced it with a minute particular, subject to private interpretation.

Marie Antoinette had already been compromised by unauthorized public portraiture long before the debacle of October 1789. Images that focused on her excessive or even deviant sexuality were a cottage industry in France. The circulation of counterfeit memoirs, speculative biographies, and fictionalized letters was abetted by licentious engravings that portrayed a queen wracked with insatiable cravings. Endlessly reproducible and easily marketable, her royal figure succumbed to a plethora of erotic representations fit for a hungry public. Jacques Revel implies an analogy between this fictional circulation of "Marie Antoinette" and the paper currency produced by the revolution: "[These pamphlets] created a paper queen that, early on, in fact well before the revolution, gradually replaced the 'real' queen, until the latter was completely eclipsed."[48] The inflationary logic is apparent: as her paper existence (her "many bodies," in Lynn Hunt's words) proliferated, it sapped her status as a venerable sovereign. The many bodies of Marie Antoinette, all too often bereft of "decent drapery," prepared for her execution by desacralizing her in the eyes of the public. For the execution itself she was undraped of all noble signs and adornments—including her wig.[49]

And yet Burke, who laments this desacralizing process, participates in it as well. Pictorial moments such as the "almost naked" queen fleeing her bedchamber, kneeling "at the feet of a king and husband," and the ruffians ravaging her empty bed, supply images for readers to contemplate and for caricaturists to reproduce. Against Reynolds's complaint that the tame exactitude of Dutch painting produces "no violent desire of seeing any more," Burke arouses a hunger for more images.[50] Visual metaphors like the bayonets and poniards thrust into the queen's bed and the "sharp antidote" concealed in her bosom reveal Burke as paradoxically drawn to the very abandonment that threatens his image of the "lovely" state. He was certainly aware of the public's craving for such images: "I knew, indeed," he admits in the *Reflections*, "that the sufferings of monarchs make a delicious repast to some sort of palates" (72)—like Wollstonecraft, using the wordplay to confuse art and appetite, representation with tastelessness. And yet, in Tom Furniss's words, Burke "whet[s] the appetite he condemns," defending the queen while reproducing a male desire that requires her hypersexuality.[51]

But if desire is often inseparable from narrative (especially at this moment in the history of the British novel), Burke's sensationalism emerges from his concentration on character rather than event: "We are more naturally led to imitate the exertions of character and passion," he claimed, "than to observe and describe a series of events."[52] This might seem a surprising thing for him to say, given how liberally he turns history into story, yet Burke consistently turns to the static portrait as a way of heightening his story's effect. He frames his description of the October Days by famously invoking the female personification, "history"—a metaphor made visual three paragraphs later when he depicts radical upheaval as a failed attempt at history painting: "A groupe of regicide and sacrilegious slaughter, was indeed boldly sketched, but it was only sketched. It unhappily was left unfinished, in this great history-piece of the massacre of innocents. What hardy pencil of a great master, from the school of the rights of men, will finish it, is to be seen hereafter" (73). History painting is the artistic manifestation of the *ancien régime*, and Burke's metaphor signals a failed usurpation in the aesthetic as well as political domain. The republicans, he mocks, take art too literally: they attempt to act out a "great history-piece," to represent it too fully and completely; they have no taste for the indeterminate. Having noted their failure, Burke ironically undertakes to "finish" the picture with his own "hardy pencil." Shifting the scene from the broadly "historical" to the narrowly defined, he transfigures the unfinished "groupe of regicide and sacrilegious slaughter" into a sequence of images focused on the French queen, a sequence that culminates in a highly wrought portrait informed by Reynolds's theory of the Grand Style:

> I hear, and I rejoice to hear, that the great lady . . . has borne that day (one is interested that beings made for suffering should suffer well) and that she bears all succeeding days, that she bears the imprisonment of her husband, and her own captivity, and the exile of her friends, and the insulting adulation of addresses, and the whole weight of her accumulated wrongs, with a serene patience, in a manner suited

> to her rank and race, and becoming the offspring of a sovereign distinguished for her piety and her courage; that like her she has lofty sentiments; that she feels with the dignity of a Roman matron; that in the last extremity she will save herself from the last disgrace, and that if she must fall, she will fall by no ignoble hand. (75)

In Reynolds's formulation, the portrait painter who "wishes to dignify" his female subject "will not paint her in a modern dress, the familiarity of which alone is sufficient to destroy all dignity . . . [but rather] dresses his figure something with the general air of the antique for the sake of dignity" (*Discourses*, 140). Burke's self-consciously "antique" portrait of Marie Antoinette similarly embraces the idea that the superaddition of a "more manly" dignity would raise portraiture along a gendered academic hierarchy. He turns the male gaze into a gentlemanly vision. In this dehistoricizing and thus depoliticizing tactic, to make Marie Antoinette "timeless" is to remove her from and to immunize her against historically determinate detractions. Terms such as "great," "lofty," "courage," and "dignity" infuse the portrait with classical virtues. The effort to shift attention away from the queen's body and toward her character is apparent from the outset of the portrait, which tellingly begins with the ear, not the eye: "I hear," not "I see." But portraiture inevitably preserves an erotic dimension, and when Burke adds that the queen carries "the sharp antidote against disgrace concealed in that bosom," he draws as much attention to her body as to her fortitude (76). He thus draws a link between the exposure of the female form he has rhetorically exploited, and the disembodied loftiness of the Grand Style. Ethical behavior finds a basis in male heterosexuality; public virtue no longer demands disinterestedness.

In his treatment of Reynolds's female portraiture, Robert W. Jones writes that "the action of looking at women could not be reconciled with the civic demand that public art should prompt worthy action; indeed, it might all too easily encourage desire."[53] Since the male spectator cannot possess (self-interested) sexual desires *and* public virtue, an erotic appeal cannot coexist with a civic appeal. Yet Burke wants, at the least, to imply a patrician audience for whom historical composition represents the best artistic vehicle for depicting civic virtue. It is in this context that the figure of the "Roman matron" assumes special significance. Marie Antoinette, as painted by Burke, manifests the dignity of Lucretia, the model here, who conceals a knife in her garments and ends her life after her rape by Sextus Tarquinius.[54] Although Marie Antoinette's "sharp antidote" is primly identified by E. J. Payne's Victorian edition as poison, it also suggests the dagger that Old Master paintings consistently render as a substitute for the Tarquin's crime.[55] Burke's portrait of the Roman matron therefore draws upon potent historical meanings that tacitly meet the requirements of a prop-

FIG. 16. Lucas Cranach the Elder, *Lucretia*, c.1533. (Staatliche Museen zu Berlin - Gemäldegallery; Photo: Jörg Peter Anders)

erly civic art. Historically, Lucretia's rape represents the pretext for the revolutionary foundation of the Roman Republic, and most sources emphasize her unique power to inspire men to virtuous action. In Dio Cassius's account, she urges, "Do you, if you are men and care for your children, avenge me, free yourselves, and show the tyrants what manner of men you are"; in Livy, Brutus derides his fellow Romans as effeminate and exhorts them to avenge her rape with their swords, "as befitted men and Romans."[56] If the story of Lucretia, as Ian Donaldson tells us, "is essentially about the need to behave like *men*," it is continuous with Burke's appeal to a patrician class figured as the nation: "a nation of gallant men . . . a nation of men of honour and of cavaliers" (76). As Lucretia symbolizes violated Rome, Marie Antoinette embodies the *ancien régime*, as Burke invests his portrait of her with the grandeur of a pictorial tradition.

But even this proves a problematic gesture, for that pictorial tradition was one in which, Donaldson shows, "nearly all Lucretias have been nude" (with thematic as well as erotic effect). Lucas Cranach the Elder, in many of his thirty-five portrayals of Lucretia, veils her in transparency to evoke the spectator's violation of her body (figure 16).[57] Burke's own turn to "history" to dignify his salacious representation, then, could be seen as actually prolonging his imaginative exposure of the queen's body. Even his embrace of the elite cultural values associated with Renaissance painting becomes further evidence, not just of the disruptiveness implicit in all forms of portraiture, but also of Burke's shifting of propertied values toward what Claudia Johnson calls "heteroerotic sentimentality," by which "politeness [is] always erotic."[58]

Burke's presentation of the French queen as an all-too-bodily embodiment of the dignity of rank shows portraiture encoding the imaginary and the mimetic alike: it appeals both to the civic virtue of a patrician viewer and to the erotic desires of a male spectator. Through portraiture, which facilitates the representation of institutions by persons, he equates the affective discourse of sentimentality with the older, civic humanist code of public virtue—and in fact attempts to preserve the latter by adapting it to the former. Burke makes ethics a function of erotics: virtuous behavior is manly behavior. But in making this claim *pictorially*, Burke solicits problematic meanings, for the rhetoric of portraiture actually reproduces the crisis of civic masculinity that he laments.

Speaking Pictures: *A Letter to a Noble Lord*

I turn in conclusion from the female portraiture of *Reflections* to the male portraiture in *A Letter to a Noble Lord* (1796), in order to emphasize again how Burkean portraiture discloses the shifting conception of the British social body. Like its more famous precursor, Burke's late conservative tract employs a syntax of anxiety about the feminization of state authority. Written amid charges that he had encouraged the bloody events he foretold, it aggressively vindicates his public career and counterrevolutionary politics. In the earlier text, Burke had attempted to translate an erotic appeal into a civic one so as to adapt older codes to a bourgeois age. Here portraiture similarly provokes male sentiment, only to put it in the service of a nostalgia for an older brand of sociability.

Burke constructs *Letter to a Noble Lord* as a series of opposing portraits, the central opposition being that between himself and the man who had attacked his pension in the House of Lords, the Duke of Bedford. Vindicating his career, Burke writes of himself as if he were the aspiring hero of a middle-class novel:

> I was not, like his Grace of Bedford, swaddled and rocked and dandled into a legislator: "*Nitor in adversum*" is the motto for a man like me. . . . At every step of my progress in life (for in every step was I traversed and opposed) and at every turnpike I met, I was obliged to show my passport, and again and again to prove my sole title to the honor of being useful to my country, by a proof that I was not wholly unacquainted with its laws and the whole system of its interests both abroad and at home. Otherwise, no rank, no toleration even, for me. I had no arts, but manly arts. On them I have stood, and, please God, . . . to the last gasp will I stand.[59]

Signaling an ambivalence about the hereditary privileges he seemingly had endorsed in the *Reflections*, Burke draws a sharp contrast with Bedford: "My merits, whatever they are, are original and personal; his are derivative" (38). The embodiment of meritocracy, industry, and upward mobility, Burke presents himself as the opposite of Bedford, the great aristocrat, and he does so in an idiom that owes a debt to visual satire: "The Duke of Bedford is the leviathan among all the creatures of the crown. He tumbles about his unwieldy bulk, he plays and frolics in the ocean of the royal bounty. Huge as he is, and whilst 'he lies floating many a rood' he is still a creature. His ribs, his fins, his whalebone, his blubber, the very spiracles through which he spouts a torrent of brine against his origin, and covers me all over with the spray, everything of him and about him is from the throne" (37). Picturing Bedford as a gigantic, blubbery whale, Burke recalls (so as to reject) the Hobbesian distrust of human nature. Never content with a single blow, Burke offers additional images of his prey, transforming Bedford first into a mouse ("that little long-tailed animal that has been long the game of the grave, demure, insidious, spring-nailed, velvet-pawed, green-eyed philosophers") and, finally: "like the print of the poor ox that we see in the shop-windows at Charing Cross, alive as he is, and thinking no harm in the world, he is divided into rumps, and sirloins, and briskets, and into all sorts of pieces for roasting, boiling, and stewing" (62–63, 69). Such diction indicates a conscious debt to print satire: here he is less a portraitist than a serial caricaturist.

And yet, against this "odious and detestable picture" (as the conservative *Monthly Review* called the composite sketch), Burke poses yet another figure: his friend and the Duke of Bedford's uncle, the naval hero Lord Keppel. It is no coincidence that Burke's rhetorical portraiture joins with an actual Reynolds portrait in carrying the *Letter*'s peroration:

> It was but the other day, that on putting in order some things which had been brought here on my taking leave of London for ever, I looked over a number of fine portraits, most of them of persons now dead, but whose society, in my better days, made this a proud and happy place. Amongst these was the picture of Lord Keppel. It was painted by an artist worthy of the subject, the excellent friend of us both, with whom we lived for many years without a moment of coldness, of peevishness, of jealousy, or of jar, to the day of our final separation.
>
> I ever looked on Lord Keppel as one of the greatest and best men of his age; and I loved and cultivated him accordingly. He was much in my heart, and I believe I was in his to the very last beat. It was after his trial at Portsmouth that he gave me this picture. With what zeal and anxious affection I attended him through that his agony of glory; what part, my son, in early flush and enthusiasm of his virtue and the pious passion with which he attached himself to all my connexions, with what prodigality we both squandered ourselves in courting almost every sort of enmity for his sake, I believe he felt, just as I should have felt, such friendship on such an occasion. (69–70)

Burke paints the scene of remembrance vividly and emotionally. Against the pressure of the public world (and Keppel's trial for fleeing a military engagement), the "fine portraits" provoke thoughts of absence and loss. "[N]ow dead" friends and bygone "better days" stand in for an obsolete world of disinterested, virtuous public conduct. Male friendship is described in terms usually reserved for sexual relationships: "peevishness" and "jealousy" are avoided even through a "final separation."

While the open expression of same-sex affection could be seen to represent a civic ideal of sociability, it also reveals the growing uncertainty of gender categories in a culture of sensibility that disordered (even if ultimately reestablishing in different terms) conventional notions of masculinity. Through a diction of erotic love ("He was much in my heart, and . . . I was in his to the very last beat"), Burke waxes nostalgic for the bonds of heroic masculine affection. The affective link between men gives an "ennobled" version of longing. The sentimental portrait, in Burke's hands, looks two ways at once: it serves male property in its nostalgic investment in the disinterested, homosocial sphere of civic virtue, even as its "anxious affection" and "pious passion" provides a significant harbinger of a new social body, comprised of consumers and held together by shared desires.

The painting of Keppel (figure 17) was a familiar image. Hazlitt would say

FIG. 17. Sir Joshua Reynolds, *Admiral Viscount Keppel*, c.1780. (Copyright Tate, London, 2004)

that it "recall[ed] Lord Keppel's memory oftener than any other circumstance."[60] Burke called it an emblem of "what Englishmen, and what English seamen were, in the days when name of nation, and when eminence and superiority in that profession were one and the same thing."[61] Here the picture is linked with the public spectacle of the "trial at Portsmouth"—Keppel's court-martial for alleged half-heartedness in an engagement with the French off the

Who's in fault? (NOBODY) a view off Uſhant.
The Anatomiſts will have it that it can have no Heart having no Body—but the
Naturaliſts think if it has a Heart, it muſt lay in its Breeches
Pub.d Dec.r 1st 1779 by W.m Humphreys N.o 227 Strand.

FIG. 18. William Humphreys, *Who's in Fault? (Nobody) a view off Ushant*, 1779. (Copyright The Trustees of the British Museum)

Isle of Ushant in 1778. The court-martial inspired an outpouring of nationalistic feeling. Outbursts such as William Hayley's *Epistle to Admiral Keppel* were frequent—"O ye! our Island's Pride! and Nature's boast! / Whose peerless valour guards and gilds our coast." So, too, were portraits of Keppel, five of which Reynolds executed following the trial (and one of which Keppel presented to Burke). Some of these were even reproduced in mezzotint as "an act of congratulation (and circulation) benefiting subject, artist, and engraver alike."[62] Guarding and gilding the British shore, Keppel became a national icon.

But for all the nationalistic feelings he inspired, Keppel was not universally admired, and the gloomy background in Reynolds's portrait reflects the dark cloud that hovered above him after the trial until his death. The mezzotint engravings that Reynolds circulated were subject to parodies whose viciousness must have galled Burke and his circle of friends. The most pointed of these was William Humphreys's *Who's in Fault? (Nobody) a view off Ushant* (figure 18).

FIG. 19. Sir Joshua Reynolds, *Commodore Augustus Keppel*, c.1752–53. (National Maritime Museum, London)

Sending up Reynolds's ennobling portrait, Humphreys's print refers to the lack of accountability, following Keppel's acquittal, for the naval fleet's humiliation at Ushant. The picture challenges Keppel's capacity for affective heroism: lacking a torso, he lacks a heart (or at least a properly located one). As the caption states, "*it* can have no Heart having no Body—but . . . if *it* has a Heart, it must lay in its Breeches." Keppel, pronominally neutered, is presented as deficient in the manly, flesh-and-blood feelings that Burke's idealized word portrait would later insist upon.

Burke's recollection of the Reynolds painting has an urgency, then, as it is designed to contest earlier representations of his friend—and, indeed, of the whole Whig circle that, in opposing the American war, opened Keppel to accusations of military faintheartedness. Writing, in a sense, on behalf of a generation of men, the end of whose lives coincided with the beginnings of Revolution, Burke seems to elevate disinterested friendship over the bonds of family. Since Keppel was the uncle of the Duke of Bedford, Burke's panegyric implies that he was Keppel's "true heir and descendant," to quote Frans de Bruyn, "by spiritual if not physical propinquity."[63] Subordinating inheritance based on blood relationship to a spiritual inheritance based on principles and lasting friendship, Burke tacitly evokes another, even more famous portrait by Reynolds, one painted long before the Duke of Bedford had been "swaddled, rocked, and dandled into a Legislator" (or even born): a dramatic, cliffside full-length portrait of Keppel (figure 19) completed more than four decades earlier. In this painting, Keppel is quite literally *landed*: whereas Burke would later envision Marie Antoinette "just above the horizon, which she hardly seemed to touch," Reynolds plants Keppel firmly in the British landscape. Fuseli thought the image sublime, and in his 1798 memoir of Reynolds, Edmond Malone remarked that it established him as "the greatest painter that England had seen since Vandyck."[64] Its iconic significance is indicated by the fact that, for some time after its execution, Reynolds displayed it in his studio so that "sitters who came with more moderate intentions could see what possibilities of immortality were available" for their own purchase. These "possibilities" were crucially bound up with Keppel's forceful yet elegant pose—the mode of classical sculpture that Reynolds was to promote as his Grand Style over the next several decades.[65]

Classical allusion, however, could also produce gender trouble—the fact that Humphreys's print, with its pointing finger, tacitly gestures to this earlier portrait might indicate as much. The appeal of the *Apollo Belvedere*, often cited as the particular source for Keppel's pose, was its elegant manliness. A famously homoerotic spectacle, the *Apollo* was suited to the representation of masculinity within polite culture, as Chloe Chard has argued, because it was at once sublime and beautiful, naked and classically validated. Travelers' accounts of the sculpture confirm this double meaning. "If I was a Woman, I should be more in love with the *Apollo* than as a man I am with the *Venus* [de Medici]," wrote Lancelot Temple; "I have seen many women whom I should prefer to the *Venus*; but never such a beautiful man as the *Apollo*!"[66] The latent homoerotics of the Keppel pose (especially as it is based on the *Apollo*) plays a critical part in Burke's verbal portrait. When Burke writes: "Lord Keppel was something high. It was a wild stock of pride, on which the tenderest of all hearts had grafted the milder virtues" (73), he admits the investment of his affections. The allusion to *The Winter's Tale*, a play that treats "the art of grafting," helps prepare for a portrait in which the intimate relationship between writer and subject achieves a kind of formal realization, as Burke blends his own identity with that of Keppel. Insisting that "I knew the man that I speak of," Burke makes the picture speak for him—or rather, he speaks for it: "[Keppel] never would have listened to any compromise with the rabble rout of this sans-culotterie of France. His goodness of heart, his reason, his taste, his public duty, his principles, his prejudices, would have repelled him for ever from all connexion with that horrid medley of madness, vice, impiety, and crime" (72). Imbuing his portrait subject with his own peculiar voice—"that horrid medley" is unmistakably his own—Burke finds a rhetorical outlet for interwoven affections. He seemed to have shared a heart with Keppel. Now, through the written portrait, he negates their "final separation."

The missing term here is Reynolds, the unnamed artist whose great skill was self-denial and whose savvy business sense required that he not assert himself. His identity cannot be extricated from this charged complex of emotions, especially as he provides the model for the verbal portraiture. As the boundaries between Burke and Keppel become increasingly uncertain, Reynolds achieves a recessive presence in a pattern of portraiture that culminates with a signature sequence of long and winding rhetorical questions. Six of the final eight paragraphs of the text begin with conditional questions that stress the visual: "Could he with patience bear *to behold* . . . ? Would Keppel have borne *to see* the ruin of the virtuous patricians . . . ? Could Keppel . . . ? Would Keppel . . . ?" (76–78). The result is a verbal portrait whose interrogative framing solicits a reader's consent. Burke's absorption of Keppel's voice was not without detractors. William Miles, in his *Letter on the Extraordinary Pamphlet by Mr. Burke* (1796), writes: "How fortunate it is that the grave conceals the blushes of Lord Keppel! Mr. Burke has introduced a new method of prophesying; he pronounces decidedly what part the gallant admiral would take in the great public questions of the day, as if he were alive."[67] Burke, that is, uses the oblivion of death as a spur to idealization. His portrait of Keppel substitutes for an exact likeness a conveniently refinished conception available to a reader's own idealized self-reading.

The thought of Keppel "blushing" in his grave, however, indicates another consequence of the portrait: the representation of an attenuated masculinity (especially as Burke himself had equated "blushing" with the "affecting" quality of feminine "beauty in distress").[68] This signals Burke's uneasy layering of propertied and consumerist values in his rhetorical portraits, which look nostalgically to the disinterested virtue of the aristocratic past even as they appeal to the private interests of a bourgeois present. Like the genre itself, Burke's portraits at once reinforce dominant social meanings and constitute a performative space where such meanings could be reimagined or reassigned. Though intended to direct his rhetorical address to an audience of propertied men, Burke's Grand Style retains at its core a revolutionary impulse capable of speaking directly to the desires of the middling sort he most wants to exclude. Novalis would indelibly describe the *Reflections* as "ein revolutionäres Buch gegen die Revolution," and in this contradictory quality, Burke's text registers the inheritance of Reynoldsian portraiture, an elite art that nevertheless has, as its governing principle, the upward mobility implicit in the genre.[69]

At a Royal Academy dinner in April 1789—three months before the fall of the Bastille—Burke scribbled some words on a piece of paper and passed it to Reynolds, who in turn handed it to the Prince of Wales to read aloud: "This end of the table, in which, as there are many admirers of the art, there are many friends of yours, wish to drink an English tradesman, who patronizes the art better than the Grand Monarque of France: 'Alderman Boydell, the Commercial Maecenas.' " However overstated, the toast to the print-publisher and entrepreneur extraordinaire John Boydell captures Burke's sense of the enormous transformation his country was undergoing, and it is supremely appropriate that the ever-ambivalent Burke should have championed an undertaking that sought to effect the symbolic accommodation between old property and new money.

If any "English tradesman" could invite comparison with the classical dignity and public virtue of a Roman statesman, it was Boydell. His labors had been instrumental in raising the prestige of British engraving (indeed he was personally responsible for creating an annual print-trade surplus of over £200,000); he made proposals for redesigning the official residence of London's Lord Mayor; and he frequently donated nationalistic paintings for display in public spaces.[70] In the words of the anonymous author of *Observations on the Present State of the Royal Academy*, Boydell could stake "a better claim to the homage of the arts, than the aggregate body of the nobility and gentry of Great Britain."[71] Burke's paean to "the Commercial Maecenas" manifested his sensitivity to the gigantic cultural shift that was actively propelled by the changing relations between art and audience in the late eighteenth century. This shift found its corollary in Boydell's grandest enterprise yet: the Shakespeare Gallery, the eighteenth century's most ambitious artistic undertaking and, before long, its most colossal failure. Turning now to this site of exhibition, where the volatility informing Burke's writings played out in images, we explore some of the difficulties that portraiture presented to those who would try to make it serve a democratic national ideal.

CHAPTER TWO

Everybody's Shakespeare

> What injury (short of the theatres) did not Boydell's "Shakespeare Gallery" do me with Shakespeare! To have Opie's Shakespeare, Northcote's Shakespeare, light-headed Fuseli's Shakespeare, heavy-headed Romney's Shakespeare, wooden-headed West's Shakespeare (though he did the best in "Lear"), deaf-headed Reynolds's Shakespeare, instead of my, and everybody's Shakespeare. To be tied down to an authentic face of Juliet! To have Imogen's portrait!
>
> —Charles Lamb

Charles Lamb's piqued reminiscence of the Shakespeare Gallery (1789–1805) calls attention to the proprietary problems that accompany the illustration of literature.[1] In the case of John Boydell's scheme for commissioning and exhibiting history paintings based on England's representative poet, these problems took on national significance. Conceived as a for-profit experiment in cultural representation, the Shakespeare Gallery—London's premiere exhibition hall in the 1790s—took the aristocratic ideal of the insular family gallery to a wider public. Englishness was now focused on the national poet, and the traditional image of the nation-as-patrimony broadened to include anybody with some money and a taste for Shakespeare.

But inevitably, as Lamb complains, an exclusionary principal prevailed. One person's "Shakespeare" was not another's. Middle-class readers were especially invested in a personalized encounter with the plays, as Deidre Lynch has argued, finding their own "inner regions of selfhood" mirrored back to them by the characters they read about.[2] Yet in making the elite genre of history painting the vehicle for his entrepreneurial nationalism, Boydell rejected portraiture, the genre of characterization. The marriage of art, commerce, and nationalism may have been a stroke of marketing genius, but the marriage of bourgeois and high-aesthetic values was contradictory. Boydell's scheme was an overtly ideological proposition, yet its own politics were strikingly unsettled.

These contradictions are epitomized by the attenuation of generic difference in Boydell's scheme. For all the Shakespeare Gallery's promotion of history painting, the insistent shadow-presence of portraiture in its productions reveals the difficulty in forging a distinctively national culture from the aesthetic values of the ruling class. History paintings, in the schematic language of eighteenth-century art writing, were said to promote civic virtue—but who could afford to buy one, let alone find a large enough space in which to display it? Portraiture, smaller in both size and conception, was the genre for a nation of shopkeepers. Its appeal to a new class of art patrons had to be accommodated if the Gallery was to succeed as a nationalist project and as a commercial venture.

The painters of the Shakespeare Gallery, ironically, are the ones who effected the accommodation between civic virtue and private taste, providing aesthetic solutions to problems that Boydell did not foresee. Entrusted with creating a school of history painting that could rekindle feelings of civic virtue, they instead produced naturalistic scenes of private virtue in mixed modes—"historical portraits," "domestic histories," and "fancy pictures." These not only complicated the schematic divisions between genres, but were better suited to the variousness of the emerging image of the British social body. "The much-envied history painter succeeded as an exponent of civic virtue to the extent that he could expand on the genre of portraiture," argues Louise Lippincott; "the successful history painting 'lived' as closely as possible the market life of a portrait."[3] This miscibility of genres was the main achievement of Boydell's undertaking. The Shakespeare Gallery was a site of aesthetic play, where generic boundaries were actively reconfigured in the effort to produce an art—and a public exhibition space—that could be marketed as genuinely representative.[4]

These dynamics are best studied in historical and textual particulars, rather than in the abstractions that for so long have enabled out-of-hand dismissals of the Shakespeare Gallery—from the romantic-period painter James Northcote, who derided the collection as "such a collection of slip-slop imbecility as it was dreadful to look at," to W. Moelwyn Merchant, who in *Shakespeare and the Artist* (1959) lamented that this "most ambitious attempt to illustrate Shakespeare should give the general impression of a massive irrelevance."[5] Another way of approaching the Gallery's significance seeks to explain what the plays depicted in the Gallery meant to English audiences of the late eighteenth century, and how specific interpretive cruxes within those plays invited artistic treatment.[6] "In what we usually think of as art history," John Barrell writes, "interpretation is often regarded with suspicion; where it is attempted, it is usually with the aim of revealing that a work of art hangs together, has a coherent meaning."[7] Here, however, I am interested in what specific paintings produced for Boydell suggest about the relation between aesthetics and the social body at the end of the eighteenth century.

An especially appealing case for this purpose is *The Winter's Tale*, not the least because it is a genre-mixer, a famous tragicomedy, as well as one of the most widely represented plays in the Gallery. At once about art and artistic reproduction, political authority, and—as adapted in the eighteenth century by Garrick and others—the British middle class, *The Winter's Tale* afforded artists an occasion to reflect on Boydell's political and aesthetic objectives. Shakespeare's treatment of autonomy and collaboration, in particular, stimulated the artists. In order to appreciate the contemporary force of this play, it will be necessary first to understand the origins of the Shakespeare Gallery and its meanings in Georgian Britain. These meanings involved not just a historical sense of Great Britain, but also the way national icons could be adapted to suit the tastes of the respectable middle classes—a modification subtly indicated by Lamb's identification of the Gallery's Shakespearean paintings as "portraits." Against this background, the depictions of *The Winter's Tale* show how these painters' elaboration of a network of dependencies destabilized the Gallery's ideological imperatives. As we shall see, the very painters commissioned to produce "everybody's Shakespeare" proved also to be the most insightful critics (*pace* Lamb) of this nationalist undertaking.

A Revolution in Taste

John Boydell conceived the Shakespeare Gallery as a public space in which to imagine a unified social body. He planned to commission work in painting's most elite genre that would simultaneously be made accessible to middle-class consumers. Whereas Sir Joshua Reynolds, president of the Royal Academy, saw commerce as detrimental to the arts, Boydell embraced commercial processes such as print publishing, which since the success of Benjamin West's *The Death of Wolfe* (1776) had helped to finance high-aesthetic pursuit.[8] History painting's profitable collaboration with engraving assisted the civic imperative of the arts by spreading its vision far and wide. History painting and engraving together were to contribute in elevating "vulgar" tastes so as to bring together multiple social bodies in a common public spirit.

But from the outset, this approach to cultural inclusion was vexed. Describing what she calls "aesthetic democracy," Linda Dowling locates the seeds of this concept in Shaftesbury, who "imagine[s] that his own deep appreciation of [paintings, music, and the Greek and Roman classics] must be, if only latently or potentially, basic to human nature itself."[9] Such a view held that taste was a natural inheritance, as opposed to an acquisition obtained and improved through education and training; its prevalence among the elite was purely coincidental. But the projection of an "aristocratic sensibility outward onto humanity as a whole" was problematic: "the collapse that had threatened aesthetic democracy from the very beginning," Dowling argues, "is the loss or emptying out of meaning that occurs in any context where 'noble' or 'aristocratic' is no longer permitted to function in relation to a set of terms—the ignoble, the vulgar, the base—in opposition to which it had originally assumed its meaning."[10] Boydell's commercialism is a case in point. He wanted no portraits representing a middle-class, commercial, and private society—even though portraiture had been established as one of the nation's aesthetic triumphs, and consumers had underwritten it. Instead, he meant for history painting to *become* middle-class, commercial, and private. Yet if he succeeded, the genre would relinquish the aura of elitism that was the source of its prestige. Even as Boydell fortified existing ideas about rank by making aspiration (toward higher genres; toward elite tastes) the keynote of his project, the vehicle and object of aspiration was emptied of the meanings that imbued it with cultural value in the first place.

To understand how this conflict plays out in the Shakespeare Gallery, it will help to examine the conception, advertisement, execution, and reception of the project. The received view of the Gallery as "a massive irrelevance" belies the sensation it caused in its heyday, when it was an integral part of a thriving exhibition culture and a fashionable place for the nouveau riche to flaunt its status as patrons of the arts. The Gallery originated in a similar site, a dinner party held at the house of Boydell's nephew, Josiah Boydell, on November 4, 1786. There, compliments were offered to the elder Boydell for raising British engraving to the highest ranks while nearly single-handedly creating an annual print-trade surplus of over £200,000. Boydell's response brims with the patriotic sentimentality from which national heroes are made: "The only answer the Alderman made to these compliments was, that he was not yet satisfied with what he had done, and that, old as he was, he should like to wipe away the stigma that all foreign critics threw on this nation—that they had no genius for historical painting." George Nicol (who as a bookseller was hardly an uninterested party) goaded Boydell, noting "that there was one great National subject concerning which there could be no second opinion, and mentioned Shakespeare."[11] With that was born an enterprise dedicated to establishing an English historical school with subjects drawn from the "great National" poet. Before the night was over, a prospectus was taking shape, and within three years "a triumph of the hyperbolic," in Grant Scott's appealing phrase, was a reality.[12]

Hyperbolic as it may have been, Boydell's plan was straightforward and savvy. Two series of oil paintings—one large, one small—were to be commissioned from the principal artists of the day, and a gallery was to be built for their exhibition at 52 Pall Mall. The spectacle of the exhibition hall was something of a decoy; it was primarily intended to promote the commercial heart of the project, an imperial folio edition of 100 engravings taken from the large paintings, and a typographically resplendent edition of Shakespeare's plays embellished with engravings from the smaller paintings. Londoners would circulate through the Gallery en masse, ogling the original compositions of Britain's finest painters, and building on this publicity the engravings would circulate as international commodities on the Boydell-dominated print market that was the financial bloodline for the project.

As an approach to art patronage, this represented a revolution of sorts in its almost entire reliance on middle-class print buyers. On a list of more than six hundred subscribers (as Edmond Malone observed), "there were not above twenty names among them that anybody knew. Such is the wealth of this country."[13] Yet, paradoxically again, one of the prime attractions for potential patrons was the chance to be peer to royalty, since among those subscribers were notables such as George III. Boydell capitalized on this appeal, even designing a medal engraved with the names of subscribers—each asked "to sign his name, with his own hand, on sheets of vellum" supplied by the Gallery. He boldly advertised this cachet:

> The encouragers of this great national undertaking will also have the satisfaction to know, that their names will be handed down to Posterity, as the Patrons of Native Genius, enrolled with their own hands, in the same book, with the best of Sovereigns—the Father of his People—the Encourager of all good Works. They flatter themselves, that, some hundred years hence, the Autographs of all the first Men of Taste, who lived in England at the end of the eighteenth and the beginning of the nineteenth century, with their SOVEREIGN at their head, will be deemed no small curiosity, especially when this circumstance is celebrated by a Medal, struck for that especial purpose.[14]

Boydell promised a kind of immortality to ordinary citizens, elevating them with their king as comrade patrons of the arts. One newspaper declared of the innovative financing: "To *noble* patronage Painting owes little, to *royal* patronage, less.—The spirit of the People, as it accomplished a revolution in Government, so also in Taste."[15] In vivid contrast to the Royal Academy's practice of charging a fee "to prevent the Rooms being filled by improper Persons," Boydell's was a proudly inclusive vision of the arts.[16] The Academy, with its disingenuous disdain for commerce, advertised its exclusivity; the Shakespeare Gallery publicized its inclusiveness.[17]

This was reflected not just in the exhibition hall, but also (and more crucially) in the drawing rooms of countless customers—tradesmen and aristocrats, urban-dwellers and provincials alike. Families who already possessed portable, bound "galleries" of Continental Old Masters could now add British works to their collections. Through a marriage of art and commerce forged in the engraver's workshop, the artist's Shakespeare really might be "everybody's Shakespeare." Ironically but with astounding success, the "highest form of visual art," John Brewer observes, "now came to depend for its success on mechanical reproduction."[18] No painting existed in its own, original splendor, but only and always in tension with its reproductions—107 of the 167 original paintings exist today only in their engraved form.[19] The blurring of distinction between aristocratic and middle-class patrons was thus duplicated on the level of the artwork itself, where reproductions equaled—even superseded—originals.[20] Even the pay scales indicate this shift: the commissions granted for the paintings were only half what engravers, whose work was more labor-intensive, were paid for reproducing them.[21] In this new market, skilled labor set the price. Original genius carried no premium.

This reversal could help explain the complaints in the House of Lords regarding the quality of the engravings. Adam Smith's description of England as a nation of shopkeepers indicates the national character that was to define England's modern potency: nationalism was coming to mean commercial prowess, and vice versa. The Shakespeare Gallery exploited this interdependence by encouraging people to buy into Shakespearean art for the good of the nation. Not surprisingly, these aesthetic "war bonds" encouraged a rhetoric of patriotic sacrifice. To Reynolds's concern that he be compensated for what he could otherwise earn painting portraits, Boydell replied sharply that he "should be sorry to see Sir Joshua the only painter that does not cooperate with him, by giving up part of their profit to the great national object of introducing a taste for historical painting."[22] In a suit brought against defaulting subscribers who had grown impatient with the slow pace of publication (the imperial folio of prints, for instance, was not issued until the Gallery's collapse in 1805), the Boydells complained that they "little saw any of their countrymen and subscribers would desert them in their day of need in so great a National undertaking."[23]

But it was genre, and not desertion, that posed a more vexing dilemma. By seeking to embody nationalism in history paintings drawn from Shakespearean themes, Boydell provoked the question of what kind of art could best represent England. Portraits, on the one hand, were affordable and could fit on the walls of middle-class homes, and they represented the confident individualism of middle-class identity. But their dominance also evoked insecurity. "Foreigners have said, with some severity," Boydell wrote in the preface to his first exhibition catalogue (1790), "that the ability of our best Artists is chiefly employed in painting Portraits of those who, in less than half a century, will be lost in oblivion—While the noblest part of the Art—HISTORICAL PAINTING—is much neglected."[24] The public perception of the Gallery seconded this view. Here is an excerpt from the more than 200 couplets of Edward Jerningham's "The Shakespeare Gallery" (1791):

> Too long, as with the iron power of Fate,
> Hath Custom bolted the Historic Gate;
> Enlighten'd Boydell bursts th' opposing bar,
> On their rude hinge the pond'rous portals jar;
> While the rapt Arts salute, with loud acclaim,
> This rich accession to their rising name.
> . . . .
> Oft have we heard the pure of taste complain
> Of mawkish Portraiture's eternal reign;
> Of exhibitions which the art disgrace,
> And pall the eye with many a vacant face.
> Let Miniature erect her fairy school,
> And 'mid her gewgaws unmolested rule;
> Let her bright dome each pleas'd Narcissus seek,
> To her let Beauty fold her summer cheek!
> Let her delineate, on her iv'ry plane,
> The nuptial simper of the happy swain!
> From these we turn to scenes of higher aim,
> Where Eagle-Genius soars to nobler game;
> Where Fancy, Reason, Taste, in one conjoin'd,
> Unfold the workings of th' impassion'd mind.

Jerningham broadcasts the civic-humanist view, which continued to possess considerable allure among conservatives in the 1790s. Portraits, he argues, are effeminate and domestic, self-pleased and self-pleasing; they mimetically "delineate" their subjects, and epitomize an age of luxury. History painting is altogether "nobler," accessible to the masculine few who can "burst" through its "Gate"; it conveys "the workings of th' impassion'd mind," and is the natural produce of a virtuous and sovereign nation. The "Enlighten'd Boydell," in Jerningham's eyes, was salvaging English dignity against the sneers of a world that would never—and presumably *should* never—take seriously a nation of "mawkish" portraitists.

That it was left to a private entrepreneur to combat Britain's cultural inferiority complex indicates a failure on the part of the Royal Academy to promote, in Barrell's phrase, "a school of history-painting worthy of a great and free nation."[25] Founded in 1768 in response to increasing uncertainty about the public function of the arts, the Academy ironically became a site for the private art of portraiture. Its annual exhibitions were dominated by this genre: throughout the 1780s, Marcia Pointon shows, portraits regularly constituted the largest percentage of Academy exhibits, history paintings the smallest.[26]

The Academy's failure to effectively promote history painting facilitated the emergence of the Shakespeare Gallery, as Boydell sought to involve new segments of the population in a large-scale cultural rejuvenation. For the artists entrusted with carrying out this project, however, this aesthetic version of democracy was problematic. Just as history painting "needed" mechanical reproduction if it was to be a representative art, painters, too, had to face the limits of their autonomy. Production was chained to consumption. Not just the necessity of collaboration with engravers, but also the prevailing taste for visual representations of private virtue, meant that the "fair issue" of their paintings (to adopt the dominant trope of *The Winter's Tale*) rested in the hands of others.[27] Success carried strict conditions. A new kind of "artist" emerged in this marketplace, and its patron was the nation. How did the painters handle this situation?

Portraiture and the Romance of History

"It is Shakespeare's peculiar excellence," Coleridge writes, "that throughout the whole of his splendid picture gallery (the reader will excuse the confest inadequacy of this metaphor), we find individuality every where, mere portrait no where."[28] Though "the confest inadequacy of this metaphor" indicates that Coleridge speaks not of any literal gallery, the metaphor itself nevertheless reveals the power of Boydell's undertaking to shape the perception of the most antitheatrical commentators. This was just as Boydell had boasted: in this gallery "mere portrait" is "no where" to be found. Yet the paintings themselves suggest otherwise. Horace Walpole's description of Reynolds's *Puck* (figure 20) as "an ugly little imp, but with some character," for example, implies what anyone familiar with the composition might suspect: that this is more a portrait than a history painting.[29] In fact, *Puck* was originally modeled on the son of Reynolds's frame maker and appeared as a child portrait at the Royal Academy exhibition of 1789. Boydell, who was "taken with the portrait," followed the canny advice of George Nicol: "Well, Mr. Alderman, it can very easily come into the Shakespeare, if Sir Joshua will kindly place him on a mushroom, and give him fawn's ears, and make a Puck of him." Two pointed ears later, an otherwise standard portrait had become something quite distinct.[30] The painting's transformation offers a strangely comic echo of Reynolds's practice of dressing his subjects in classical garb. Like Boydell, who boldly brought together the venerable genre of history painting and the robust industry of printselling, Rey-

FIG. 20. Luigi Schiavonetti, after Sir Joshua Reynolds, *Midsummer Night's Dream*, 2.2. *The Dramatic Works of Shakspeare*, 1802. (Courtesy of Department of Special Collections, Stanford University Libraries)

nolds—in *Puck* and elsewhere—followed King Polixenes's own unheeded dictum: "We marry / A gentler scion to the wildest stock, / And make conceive a bark of baser kind."[31]

The exhibition of *Puck* at the Royal Academy in spring 1789 would reveal just how touchy a matter the crossing of generic boundaries could be. "This picture has no claim to praise, but is rather disgusting," wrote the reviewer for the *Morning Post* (May 1, 1789); "It is really offensive, and we wonder the taste and feeling of this admirable artist should ever have been employed on such a subject."[32] The admission of "low" subjects into "high" art was nothing less than an affront to establishment taste. Many of the painters working under Boydell nevertheless confronted and capitalized on the likelihood of stylistic compromise. To accommodate historical composition to an age of portraiture, the genre had to be reconfigured—in practice, if not in theory. Not that the established boundaries of history painting were intractable. Even the mere acknowledgment of literature as an appropriate subject for historical painting, as Richard Altick notes, was an eighteenth-century concession to the growing numbers of literate, bourgeois art consumers.[33] But what made adaptation inevitable in the Shakespeare Gallery was the fact that those people who had enabled the undertaking in the first place were the faithful patrons of both the theater and the portrait studio. The audiences who flocked in unprecedented numbers to performances of Shakespeare in the eighteenth century were the same audiences who made portraits a lucrative genre.[34] The Shakespeare Gallery could not have been conceived without them, and it was not likely to flourish unless it met their tastes. Unlike the Royal Academy, with its rent-free quarters, governmental backing, and anticommercial pose, the survival of the Shakespeare Gallery depended on sales. Painters, too, had to concern themselves with a diverse public from which future commissions might be forthcoming. Thus the nationalistic rhetoric of the project had to be adapted to meet the private tastes of a new class of art patrons.

But if the adaptation of history painting was emblematic of a culture in which the authority of consumers was displacing (or imbibing) the authority of property, it also helped to unsettle the foundation of authority within that culture. As Richard Wendorf explains, theatrical portraits—"portraits of actors rehearsing, performing on the stage, sitting in the guise of one of the characters they have portrayed, or . . . gently alluding to their profession"—were not a distinct kind of portrait so much "as paradigmatic of what all successful portraiture embodies."[35] The economic alliance between theater and portraiture was evident in pieces such as Zoffany's *Garrick and Mrs. Pritchard in Macbeth* (1768), or Reynolds's *Mrs. Robinson as Perdita* (1782). But it was a social alliance, as well, as everyday people frequently posed as characters in their favorite plays—or more astrally, as goddesses, angels, or biblical heroines.[36] By adopting the stances of the theater, the British saw and represented themselves in performative terms, rather than in the static postures of the traditional family gallery.

This theatricalization of history painting, however, offered yet one more event of ideological ambivalence. Historical portraits may have appealed to the liberated sensibility of the upwardly mobile citizen, as well as to the painter who could merge the lofty ambition of history painting with the profitability of portraiture; but such subjects, as Reynolds's Puck reminds us, also involved recognizable individuals in the representation of history. This had a two-fold effect. If the adaptation of Shakespeare to history painting was an integral part of rewriting the national past in the teleology of English Protestantism and mercantile virtue, the visual inscription of everyday citizen-consumers as Shakespearean "players" served this agenda. Yet this inscriptive gesture also destabilized the very "history" it sought to uphold. Romance, offering an unfixed story from which to mold a national tale, was a valuable source for the rewriting of history according to present ideological needs. One irony of the Boydell endeavor is that a romance could prove more amenable to providential narrative than an overtly providential and nationalistic play such as *Henry VIII*, whose historicity, Hazlitt observed, was too unwieldy: "The character of Henry VIII is drawn with great truth and spirit. It is like a very disagreeable portrait, sketched by the hand of a master."[37] But the advantages of romance were balanced by the danger that romance could expose the fictions underwriting national ideology. This position of history painting as a brand of high-minded storytelling was always potential in the Shakespeare Gallery, especially given the central position of romances such as *The Tempest* and *The Winter's Tale*. But this potential was activated in historical portraits, which courted the attention of consumers by turning English history into accessible theater. The introduction of poseurs into history painting could be seen to vitiate not just the genre, but the nation it ostensibly represented.

Conservative critics of the Gallery recognized these dangers. Some passed off the accommodation of historical tradition to the new economy of the portrait as lack of skill. The reviewer for *Walker's Hibernian Magazine*, noting that many of the Gallery's paintings are "confounded and overcharged with figures," wrote: "The beauty of many of the heads, considered separately from the figures to which they belong . . . seems intuitively to indicate their proceeding from a school chiefly attentive to portrait painting."[38] Others stated their concerns more bluntly: "There was some reason to fear that our painters would have sought for and gathered their ideas from the theatre, and given us portraits of the well-dressed Ladies and Gentlemen [of the stage]. . . . There was some reason to fear a representation of all that extravaganza of attitude . . . which is tolerated, nay in a degree demanded, at the playhouse."[39] The concern here is aesthetic inclusion. A theater accessible to all classes, and a theatricalized genre that enables posers to play parts, were anathema to proponents of an English historical school. Richard Altick summarizes this resistance: "Literary art should never suggest the tastes of the heterogeneous audiences that filled the great barns of Covent Garden and Drury Lane and, even worse, the 'minor' theaters patronized by the unruly working class."[40] Motivating this view is the fear that "extravaganza of attitude" would deplete Shakespeare's representativeness by underscoring the status of history painting as an extravagant mythologizing practice.

The prestige of history painting rested in its independence from the world of common objects—unlike portraiture, it was not mimetic. And yet, against this expectation, many of the Gallery's historical scenes were, like portraits, posed in studios, while many others were mimetic replications of staged performances. Various leading actors and celebrity personalities were recognizable in several of the paintings. Lady Hamilton was possibly the most represented figure in the Gallery, having sat for Tresham (as Cleopatra) and Romney (as Miranda), among others. Northcote evinces a certain anxiety in explaining away such mixing of genres: "There is not so much difference [between history and portrait] as you imagine. Portrait often runs into history, and history into portrait, without our knowing it."[41] But if painters accepted and even invited genre mixing, Boydell himself was less enthusiastic about such permeability. His project of cultural rejuvenation was based on the encouragement of history painting *proper*: what made the Shakespeare Gallery, in his own words, "so great a National undertaking," was its dissemination of an aristocratic genre as an item of mass consumption, through the democratizing art of engraving. To dilute the integrity of history painting was to defeat the purpose.

In order to safeguard this integrity, Boydell suggested subjects to his painters and even, according to Northcote, hinted at possible treatments.[42] Many of the depictions that appeared in the Gallery, in fact, were completely absent from the period's stage adaptations. The most painted subject from *The Winter's Tale*, for instance, was Leontes in the moments immediately before and after his banishment of the infant Perdita—moments that were removed (along with the rest of Sicilia and the first three acts) from every performance of the play since 1741. But Boydell could control only so much, and despite his best efforts his gallery emerged as a public space where the generic and social contours of history painting were continually redrawn, especially on behalf of historical portraiture—the generic analogue of Shakespearean romance—as a site where national identity proved malleable. In the hands of his artists, Boydell's nationalism proved an ambivalent proposition, caught not just between the social values of history painting and portraiture, but between a democratic historical portraiture and a theatricalized national history. In the end, the artists exploited these undecideables—perhaps nowhere so capably as in their illustrations of Shakespeare's late romance, *The Winter's Tale*, whose mixed generic and political character lent itself to the interrogation of the Gallery's objectives.

"Though the print be little": *The Winter's Tale* as Social Allegory

In 1817, fondly recalling a performance of *The Winter's Tale*, Hazlitt waxed nostalgic over the spirited turns of Siddons, Kemble, and Bannister, before turning his thoughts to the timelessness of theatrical illusion: "We shall never see these parts so acted again; or if we did, it would be in vain. Actors grow old, or no longer surprise us by their novelty. But true poetry, like nature, is always young; and we still read the courtship of Florizel and Perdita, as we welcome the return of spring, with the same feelings as ever." Hazlitt illustrates his point by quoting a lengthy excerpt, crowned with the young prince's profession of a love that desires its object's transformation into living art:

> When you do dance, I wish you
> A wave o' the sea, that you might ever do
> Nothing but that: move still, still so,
> And own no other function.[43]

A poetry sustained in space, and an image moving in time—the terms are those of the "sister arts," and with this meditation Hazlitt analogizes the central preoccupation of *The Winter's Tale* with that of eighteenth-century debate regarding that aesthetic doctrine. It was not a haphazard analogy. As a sophisticated dramatic treatment of aesthetic representation, *The Winter's Tale* was very concordant with the concerns of artists, who made it the second-most represented play in the Shakespeare Gallery, with seven paintings.[44] Its array of cultural meanings in the late eighteenth century suggest its attraction to Boydell's painters, and more broadly point to the main issues at stake in aesthetic democracy.

These effects were not congruent: painters used *The Winter's Tale* as a template to explore and challenge the Boydell endeavor, and this was enabled in no small part by the subject itself. *The Winter's Tale* is Shakespeare's central treatment of "art theory" and "iconic tradition," in Jean Hagstrum's words, the final act in particular "compounded of themes intimately associated with the tradition of *ut pictura poesis* and iconic poetry."[45] But Hermione is transformed into an aesthetic representation long before the celebrated statue scene. Leontes initially complains of Polixenes that he "wears her like her medal, hanging / About his neck"—like a portrait miniature (1.2.309–10)—and when Camillo says of the restored Queen embracing Leontes, "She hangs about his neck" (5.3.112), she resumes this status. The debate between Polixenes and Perdita, inspired by Perdita's rejection of "streaked gillyvors . . . Nature's bastards" (4.4.82–3), foregrounds the manipulation of nature by aesthetic imagination. Finally, Perdita exits the argument by imagining herself as cosmetically "painted"—and by implication, as a portrait:

> I'll not put
> The dibble in earth to set one slip of them,
> No more than, were I painted, I would wish
> This youth should say 'twere well, and only therefore
> Desire to breed by me. (4.4.100–104)

Her words recall her father's desire for a wife as manageable as art—art that sits in space but does not move in time. By imagining her portrait as an insufficient substitute for her identity, Perdita anticipates Florizel's more generous vision of her as a *living* art embodying movement and time all at once. Her words also prepare us for the play's great set piece: the statue scene, in which the idea of portraiture as a living art comes to fruition.

The recurring notion of portraiture in *The Winter's Tale* indicates the significance, for this play, of likeness—the primary criterion for assessing portraits. Unable to guarantee the faithfulness of his wife, the father depends on likeness to ensure the legitimacy of his heirs. Were women "false," raves Leontes,

> As o'er-dyed blacks, as wind, as waters, false
> As dice are to be wished by one that fixes
> No bourn 'twixt his and mine, yet were it true
> To say this boy were like me. (1.2.133–7)

Suited as the mimetic art of portraiture is to the pathological anxieties that fuel this play, what supplies *The Winter's Tale* with its principal metaphor for likeness is the even more mimetic process of printing. Mamillius's nose, Leontes declares, "is a copy out of mine" (1.2.124); upon meeting Florizel, he announces: "Your mother was most true to wedlock, Prince, / For she did print your royal father off, / Conceiving you" (5.1.123–5); and Paulina, urging the agitated king to accept the infant Perdita, announces:

Behold, my lords,
Although the print be little, the whole matter
And copy of the father: eye, nose, lip,
The trick of's frown, his forehead, nay, the valley,
The pretty dimples of his chin and cheek, his smiles,
The very mould and frame of hand, nail, finger. (2.3.98–103)

The recurrent metaphor of printing made *The Winter's Tale* enticing for the painters commissioned by Boydell. What Janet Adelman refers to as the play's treatment of "absolute identity" was pertinent to the collaborative principle of the Gallery: a king whose legitimate authority is wholly subject to the reproductive powers of women neatly allegorizes the situation of a supposedly "sovereign" genre that depends on a process of printing off impure copies. Here, as in Boydell's plan for an English school of history painting, the original to be printed off is always royal, but never fully autonomous. To the extent that, in Coleridge's words, "the passion to be delineated in *The Winter's Tale* was *jealousy*," this is also a play about the intense anxiety regarding autonomy that conditions Leontes' jealousy.[46] "The father, all whose joy is nothing else / But fair posterity" (4.4.395–6), depends for his "fair posterity" on a reproductive process embodied by the mother.[47]

"Childbirth," Carol Thomas Neely argues, "is the literal and symbolic center of the play"; its symbolic function extends to *aesthetic* production, in the printed ballads hawked by Autolycus in the Bohemian countryside.[48] As one Augustan critic observed: "It is impossible for any man to rid his mind of his profession. The authourship of *Shakespeare* has supplied him with a metaphor."[49] Leontes' complaint that Hermione has "sull[ied] the purity and whiteness of my sheets" (1.2.329) evokes the anxieties of an author whose own "fair posterity" depends on a detached manufactory process and on less-than ideal readers like Mopsa and Dorcas. The pregnant female body that "prints [the] royal father off" is at once the sign of a compromised political authority and a metaphoric crux for the mechanical reproduction of works of art. In other words, Hermione's pregnancy (and Perdita's "production"), while serving to mute Leontes' authority, also suggests the collaborative element of the Boydell enterprise, where the art of engraving supersedes the authority of the original painter.

Critics as diverse as Neely and Stanley Cavell have recognized Hermione's pregnant body as a central dramatic image; among other things, her body's metaphoric association with printing emphasizes the proximity between aesthetic and political concerns.[50] It is therefore appropriate that, appealing though *The Winter's Tale* may have been for aestheticians, it was equally appealing for the middle-class beneficiaries of sociopolitical transformation. Here, after all, was a play that embodied the English nostalgia for rural scenes; a plot that celebrated the love between a known Prince and an enigmatic "queen of curds and cream"; and best of all, at a time when George III's mental illness perpetuated an appealing "myth of royal ordinariness," a cast that starred a mad king.[51] Such a production could not help but appeal to Georgian audiences developing a self-image as "Britons" inseparable from their own upward mobility.

Its adaptation on the eighteenth-century stage appealed emphatically to those audiences. Two major versions began appearing about mid-century: Macnamara Morgan's *Florizel and Perdita; or, The Sheep-Shearing* (1754), and Garrick's *Florizel and Perdita* (1756). Accounting almost exclusively for the ninety-eight stagings of *The Winter's Tale* between 1751–1800, both of these confined the action to the springtime world of Bohemia.[52] Such rewritings illuminate the societal values that shaped reception, and in the case of *The Winter's Tale*, as Michael Dobson argues, they strongly endorsed "guardedly egalitarian, and specifically private, contemporary versions of sympathy and domestic virtue."[53] The first three acts, being less than suited to such an endorsement, required drastic revision. Hence Morgan entirely excludes Hermione and Leontes, communicating the Sicilian "prehistory" through narrative reminiscences that contextualize what really mattered to audiences: the against-all-odds love of Florizel and Perdita. This ribald comedy is especially interesting for suggesting a pronounced aristocratic anxiety about continuing class dominance. King Polixenes sanctions the young lovers' sexual liaison, but he will not tolerate their marriage:

> I could have patience with him
> Meant he to sport it with the am'rous wench
> And had he thriv'd, and from the wholesome theft,
> Had bred a mungril hardy as a mule
> I could have kiss'd the sturdy bastard boy
> As he trudg'd barefoot o'er the mountain's brow.

Lines like these gently scorn an aristocratic anxiety concerning its economic dominance: let the lower classes prettify the countryside, Polixenes implies, but don't let them dilute the ruling class. Or, in Morgan's less delicate dialogue: "Had *Florizel* / But thought of bedding without wedding her, / I well cou'd like his liking."[54]

Though considerably more demure than Morgan's adaptation, Garrick's is guided by a similar ethos. Again, Sicilia is omitted in favor of the pastoral world of Bohemia and its youthful lovers.[55] Leontes does appear, but only as a repentant, shipwrecked king haunted by memories of domestic tranquillity. The audience is spared his tyrannical cruelty, which a contemporary critic complained "show[ed] his majesty to be little better than a bedlamite," and is presented "the warmer and more affecting" image of his psychic recovery.[56] This depiction tallies with Linda Colley's observation of "a newly invented royal magic," which encouraged Britons "to see their monarch . . . as ritually splendid and remorselessly prosaic."[57] The refurbished Leontes evokes sympathy as a man of feeling recovering from past emotional excesses; his earlier violence is a mere shadow-presence. In the late 1780s, when George III first felt the indignity of an illness whose details were published daily for all to read, such a royal image was quite familiar. And just like the real king, whose madness the public found endearing, the late eighteenth century saw Leontes as a king with a human face.[58] This sympathetic perspective laid the groundwork for the psychologically and politically complex treatments of *The Winter's Tale* in the Shakespeare Gallery. Painters, for all of their creative agency within the venture, had to balance their role in artistic production with the bottom line of consumption. Their mediating position between the tradesman who founded the Gallery, the poet who was enshrined by it, and the consumers who supported it was critical to the fashioning of "everybody's Shakespeare."

"Mocked with art": Shakespeare for Everybody

The Boydell *Winter's Tale* series included four paintings engraved for the imperial folio edition of large (50 x 63 cm) prints, and three reproduced as small (17 x 27 cm) illustrations for the textual edition. My interest lies in the larger works, which invited the painters' more elevated ambitions, rather than the smaller pieces destined for supplementary status as textual illustrations. These larger pieces included John Opie's portrayal of Leontes commanding Antigonus to expose his infant daughter, Francis Wheatley's image of the shearing festival, Joseph Wright's "Antigonus Chased by a Bear," and William Hamilton's depiction of the statue scene.[59] Throughout these compositions, the challenge to the sovereignty of history painting is embedded in a thematic critique of absolute authority, whether aesthetic, generic, or political. Paint and print, kings and servants, the sublime and the pastoral are all accommodated to one another in these paintings, as power is made to reside in a space of compromised absolutes.

Opie's thematically expansive composition (figure 21), exhibited in 1793, encapsulates these themes. As an image of power that on closer inspection becomes an image of fragility, the painting performs the deficiency of absolutism.

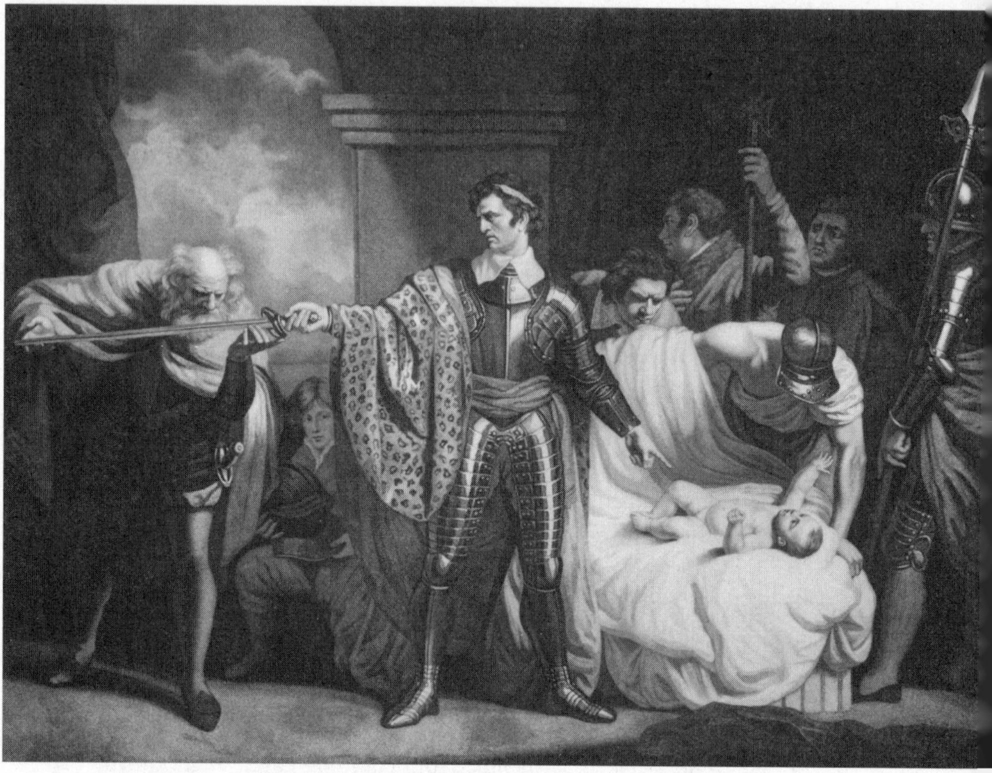

FIG. 21. J. P. Simon, after John Opie, *Winter's Tale*, 2.3. (Rare Books Division. Department of Rare Books and Special Collections. Princeton University Library)

The attenuation of authority emerges, first of all, at the level of genre. While representing (as history paintings conventionally do) a pivotal moment of moral decision—Leontes' command that Antigonus expose the infant Perdita "some place / Where chance may nurse or end it" (2.3.182–3)—Opie also offers a meditation on portraiture. The painting can be seen not only as *suspended* narrative, but also as *expanded* narrative, in what seems to be a multiple representation of Leontes in various life stages: infant, boy-courtier, soldier, king, and old man. Even the faceless soldier on the right, whose helmet completes Leontes' armor, suggests a diminished version of the king, for as an odd antiportrait he attests to the obsolescence of a hierarchy based on likeness. Amid this phantasmically decentered identity, royalty itself is made vulnerable. If, as Janet Adelman has argued, Leontes' "masculine potency and authority" depend on his capacity to "trust in . . . female processes," Opie's image of a king defaulting on this trust undercuts his power—even as it presents him at the height of his absolute command.[60] This is underscored by the textual excerpt that accompanies the image in Boydell's exhibition catalog, which stresses Leontes' insecurity about his legitimate succession by cutting off his speech with the words, "Another's issue."

The subordinate figures in the composition call further attention to this specter of illegitimacy. Antigonus—whose own weapon protrudes emphatically from his left hip—bends to kiss Leontes' sword yet seems rather to squint at it, as if doubting its potency. Opposite him, a courtier glares at the infant, presumably searching for any likeness to his king. Meanwhile, Leontes' Bohemian robe evokes a key visual rhyme with the fabric shared between the infant and the faceless soldier—a rhyme that elicits a comparison between Leontes and this mysterious figure, who, to the king's diminishment, shares something in common with the infant.

The expressive faces of these marginal figures are important because they foreground the importance of facial likeness in the play. Whereas William Hamilton's small picture (figure 22) shows a king tormented by paranoia, Opie—a portrait painter infamous for the perceived similarity of his subjects' features (a phenomenon Coleridge labeled "Opieism")—reclaims Leontes from his foppish stage representations by endowing him with a sense of tragedy.[61] Leontes' solemn expression suggests a psychological complexity far removed from his abrupt outburst. He appears split between a refusal to admit his vulnerability and an inability to deny it—a psychic fissuring that his posture enacts as well. Pointing his arms in opposite directions, he embodies the Janus-face of time. To his right, the elderly Antigonus epitomizes a traditional past, all loyal duty and submission; to his left lies the future, the infant Perdita. The painting's narrative itself is Janus-like: the central action of the infant's banishment anticipates the future, while the concentrated contemplation of her origins dwells on the past. All this attention to the infant is the crowning irony: despite the physical and emotional centrality of Leontes, it is the child bathed in bright light that commands attention. The father is finally subordinate to the "copy of the father."

By balancing the tragic Leontes with the radiant infant, Opie shifts focus from the old guard to the new. Perdita, the royal "print," holds all the hopes of her unwitting father, for only her improbable survival and return will prevent his political extinction. The figure of Perdita, as both infant and adult, appealed to other illustrators as well. Henry Thomson's *The Finding of Perdita* (c. 1790) portrays a magical bundle complete with the belongings that define her existence—scroll, jewels, fabric; while William Hamilton's small depiction of the

FIG. 22. Francesco Bartolozzi, after William Hamilton, *Winter's Tale*, 2.3. *The Dramatic Works of Shakspeare*, 1802. (Courtesy of Department of Special Collections, Stanford University Libraries)

FIG. 23. Joseph Collyer, after William Hamilton, *Winter's Tale*, 4.4. *The Dramatic Works of Shakspeare*, 1802. (Courtesy of Department of Special Collections, Stanford University Libraries)

shearing festival (figure 23) casts her in the urbane image of middle-class aspiration.

All these images recall Paulina's description of Perdita as no longer "prisoner to the womb," but "Free'd and enfranchis'd" (2.2.62–4). For if, as Peter Erickson notes, Perdita "quickly gives up her 'dream' of transcending class hierarchy" in her confrontation with Polixenes, the late eighteenth century viewed her in terms of a liberating social mobility and a royalty inherent in every person.[62] John Guillory argues that Gray's "Elegy" activates "the pastoral topos of the aristocrat-as-peasant" through allusion to Perdita, "a real princess whose 'noble rage' is repressed in her identity as a peasant girl," and indeed, the sentimental culture that Gray helped inaugurate dwelled not on her status as a princess by blood but as royal by theatrical license: "the queen of curds and cream."[63] This mobility is particularly evident in Garrick's adaptation of the play, which represents Bohemia as a site of bourgeois values. A contemporary promptbook in the Harvard Theatre Collection, Michael Dobson observes, emphasizes the leveling aspect of Garrick's play. For example, Leontes' statement to Florizel in Shakespeare—

> Your choice is not so rich in *worth* as beauty,
> That you might well *enjoy* her

—is revised by Garrick as:

> Your choice is not so rich in *wealth* as beauty,
> That you might well *atchieve* her.[64]

By rendering worth as wealth, and enjoyment as achievement, Garrick trumps royalism in favor of social mobility.[65] Perdita's actual bloodlines matter much less than her ability to fashion herself into a woman worthy of a Prince's achievement. If for eighteenth-century audiences Perdita was a "free'd and enfranchis'd" figure liberated from familial ties by her banishment, for *painters* she was something more. She was their particular emblem: the "copy of the father" printed off by a reproductive process embodied in the mother. Perdita is a potent subtext, marking the transition between aristocratic privilege and middle-class social mobility, and—in artistic terms—between royal patronage and public patronage.

This subtext clearly emerges in Francis Wheatley's representation of the shearing festival (figure 24), a painting that seems to bring history painting into its nineteenth-century inheritance as narrative genre, and which organizes itself around Perdita. Here she is shown handing Polixenes some flowers, thus foregrounding the art-nature debate and infusing the scene with all of that debate's implications. This "streaked gillyvor" of a composition enacts the debate by

FIG. 24. James Fittler, after Francis Wheatley, *Winter's Tale*, 4.4. (Rare Books Division. Department of Rare Books and Special Collections. Princeton University Library)

grafting several modes: as with Opie, the expressive faces and polished poses indicate an expertise in portraiture; the festive tableau and lush nook give the air of a pastoral; and in the background, the sea interpolates the sublime. This last element is especially crucial. Looming over the short-lived merriment, the sea accords with the ominousness of the disguised King Polixenes, on the brink of his Leontean outburst.[66]

By symbolizing Polixenes in the sea, Wheatley overlays aesthetic encounter (beautiful meets sublime) with social encounter (commoners meet king). Just as it includes many aesthetic modes, the tableau is socially inclusive as well, running the gamut from king to rustic. The progressive orientation is heightened by the scene's theatrical premise, the shearing festival being, after all, a play within the play, with Polixenes and Camillo in disguise, Florizel's "high self / . . . obscured / With a swain's wearing," and Perdita "no shepherdess but Flora . . .

FIG. 25. Samuel Middiman, after Joseph Wright, *Winter's Tale*, 3.3. (Rare Books Division. Department of Rare Books and Special Collections. Princeton University Library)

most goddess-like prank'd up" (4.4.2–10). As in David Solkin's argument in *Painting for Money* that civic humanism modulates into *civil* humanism, Wheatley conjoins the notion of land as the ground of a virtuous polity—a staple of pastoral representations—with what Shaftesbury calls the "natural affections" that can lead to public good.[67] Such sociability is clearly on display in this composition, which encompasses the intermingling of opposing forces, particularly in the insistent coupling that dominates the backdrop. Although sublimity poses an imperial threat to the festivities, it is forced to submit to a wider collaborative network of social and aesthetic modes.[68]

If for Wheatley the sublime exists in tension with other forces, for Wright of Derby it is unconstrained and indomitable. In "Antigonus Chased by the Bear" (figure 25), Wright depicts a world in which everybody—royal or otherwise—is susceptible to fear. Amid this sublime landscape, the symbolics of power (as embodied by Antigonus, who carries out Leontes' dictum) is overwhelmed by the actual, brute force of the bear. The painting gives a scene of generic transition in *The Winter's Tale*, when "things dying" turn to "things new-born" (3.3.104–5). In the play, Antigonus's demise is at once the brutal denouement of the first three acts' mini-tragedy, and the entrance to a comic world defined by a famously bizarre stage direction ("Exit, pursued by a bear") and Antigonus's equally bizarre response to his impending doom: "Well may I get aboard. This is the chase. / I am gone for ever!" (3.3.56–7). As Charles Frey describes it, the uniqueness of this scene rests on its generic doubleness: " 'I am gone for ever!' cannot help but be funny, drawing attention, as it does, to the actor's last exit in the part. Imagine a circuit or two around the stage circumference—Antigonus rushing, arms outstretched in horror, the bear lumbering after, Perdita in the center oblivious—and one can make real, if also macabre and grotesque, the distance traveled from Leontes' court in Sicilia. The stage has expanded, a new world is freshly circumscribed, the representative of the old world is consumed, and the baby waits at the center of the new."[69] In Wright's vision, however, the comedic aspect is wholly absent. There is no "lumbering" about, no sense of distance from the turbulence of the Sicilian court, and no infant representative of this "new world." Antigonus's awkward pose notwithstanding, the canvas is permeated with the expectation of terrible violence (Antigonus doesn't have much ground to run on, after all). Previous to Wright's painting, Boydell had rejected a subject drawn from this scene by William Hodges, which portrayed "Antigonus *Torn* by a Bear"; it was, Boydell complained, too "hard and raw."[70] Here, by contrast, the scene's vastness is heightened by the suspension of narrative. The Clown's account of what is *about* to happen ("to see how the bear tore out his shoulder-bone" [3.3.97–8]) is postponed beyond the frame. As Sawry Gilpin, who helped Wright with the figure of the bear, wrote: "I think with you, that the pursuit is better than the horrid act of tearing."[71] By privileging the "pursuit" and occluding the inevitable violence, Wright turns his medium's characteristic lack of temporality to his advantage. If we do not get to see the bear devouring Antigonus, we at least know it is coming; such foreknowledge heightens the emotional impact of the composition, creating the impression of an awful moral judgment. This is accentuated by the displacement of the bear's open jaws onto the oval clearing in the middle of the sky: the heavens are hungry. Leontes' paranoid response to his circumscribed authority elicits a sublime wrath that belittles his own solemn judgment on the infant Perdita. The diminutive figures that pock the canvas, such as the storm-tossed boat and the statuesque Antigonus, complete this quasi-apocalyptic image of human inconsequentiality.

While Wright shows us the cosmic retribution for Leontes' domestic tyranny, William Hamilton directs our attention to the redemption of that tyranny. Hamilton's painting of the statue scene (figure 26) imagines the moment when the male desire for absolute identity finally abdicates to collaborative authority. In Hamilton's hands, this abdication is inextricable from the issue of aesthetic reproduction. As a representation of a "statue," the painting prompts questions about the authority of *any* original, questions that ring doubly when the painting is reproduced as a print. In either case the connection between political and aesthetic authority is a charged one, for aesthetic lineage works very much like royal lineage: the print of a painting of a play about a statue of a queen mirrors the tortuous process of succession in any monarchy, and dramatizes the threats to that succession's legitimacy. Perdita's presence in the composition emphasizes this parallel, her half-visible face begging the question of her likeness with either Hermione or Leontes.

The possibility that Hamilton took the stage as his model further complicates the picture's treatment of succession. Theatrical postures aside, the figure of Polixenes strongly resembles the figure of Cymbeline in Hamilton's painting of that play; possibly it is Richard Hurst, who acted both roles in the late 1770s. But whether or not it replicates a stage production, Hamilton's work at the very least addresses the mimetic underpinnings of many of the Boydell paintings, and in this regard it raises trenchant questions about the nature of representation itself. The gaze upon royalty was a charged motif in the revolutionary 1790s, given their intense concern with the status of authority as a representation. As with Opie's painting of Leontes, the representation of a queen *as* a representation reflects the contemporary interest in the role of the monarchy and its legitimate function: is the statue a fraud or is it the real thing?

Such ironies grow out of the statue scene itself, which undoes the oppositions between original and copy, human and statue. Leontes notes this undoing, first asking, "Does not the stone rebuke me, / For being more stone than it?" (5.3.37–8), and then adding: "The fixture of her eye has motion in't, / As we are mocked with art" (5.3.67–8). The boundaries of the visual medium are such that we cannot know what moment Hamilton depicts—whether Paulina has just drawn the curtain (line 21) or is about to re-draw it (line 69), or whether she has already spoken the words that spur Hermione into motion. There is no way to know if Hermione is moving yet: artistic sovereignty is itself "mocked with art." Just as in the play, the "life" of art requires, in Paulina's words, that the public "awake" its "faith" (5.3.94–5). Frederick Burwick has observed Hamilton's "artistic awareness of the respective spatial and temporal preoccupation evident" in the play, but Hamilton goes further yet by putting the temporal inde-

FIG. 26. Robert Thew, after William Hamilton, *Winter's Tale*, 5.3. (Rare Books Division. Department of Rare Books and Special Collections. Princeton University Library)

terminacy of his medium to work for a wider political claim about aesthetic democracy, in which the middle-class public participates in the practice and promotion of the arts.[72] And significantly, he makes the art public visible here, in the form of the crowd assembled for Hermione's unveiling: the actual beholders of his composition are depicted as present at the statue's unveiling, at the same time that the fact of aesthetic representation asserts their distance from the original. This doubleness of representation, the public's access to the original *through the simulacrum*, was critical to the Gallery's vision of aesthetic democracy.

The insistent background presence of onlookers—courtiers, officers, servants—in the Boydell illustrations offers a further manifestation of the painters' critique of absolute authority. Opie's scowling attendant and ambiguous soldiers; Wheatley's tableau of diverse faces surrounding the stern Polix-

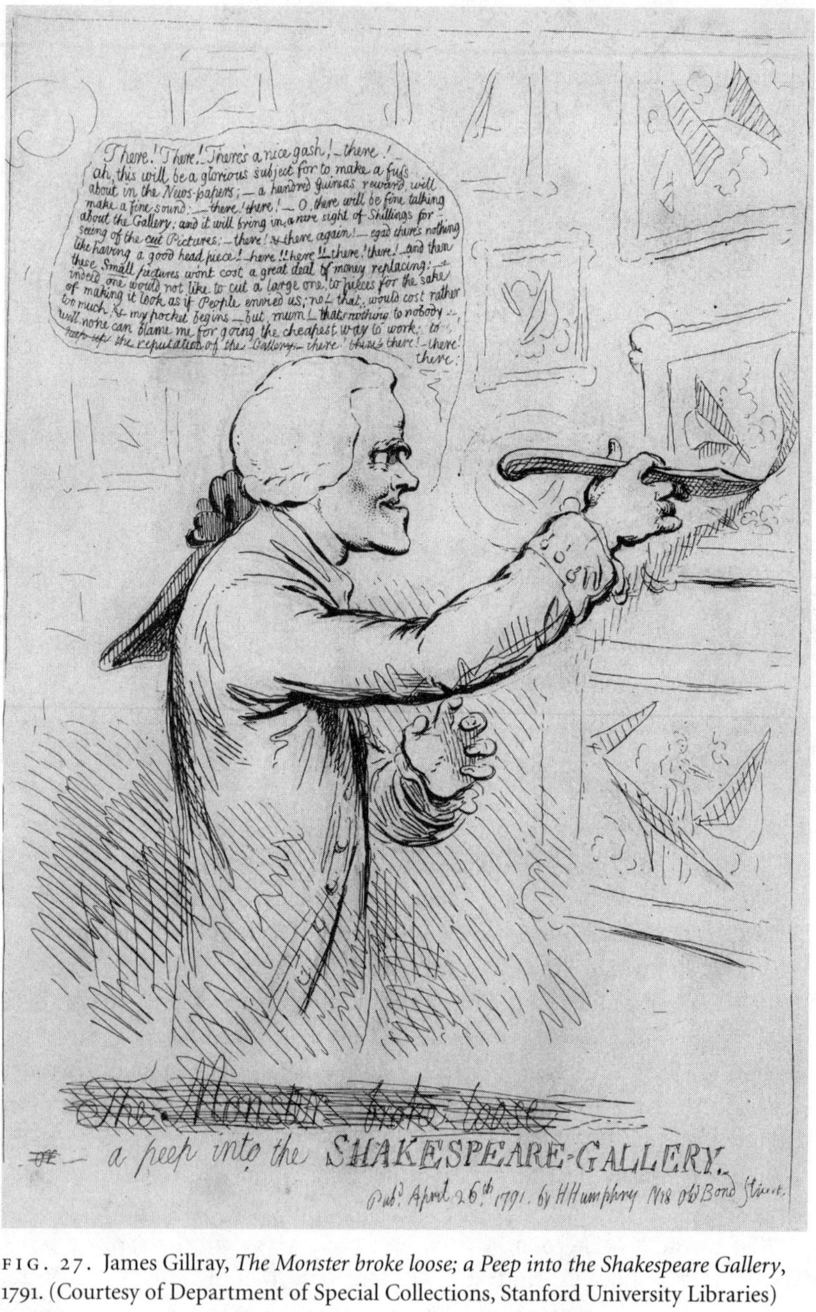

FIG. 27. James Gillray, *The Monster broke loose; a Peep into the Shakespeare Gallery*, 1791. (Courtesy of Department of Special Collections, Stanford University Libraries)

enes; and Hamilton's courtiers, who appear almost bored by Leontes' antics, all remind us that this play's monarchs represent particular instances rather than general attitudes. We might recall Leontes' threat to punish anyone who defends Hermione—"He who shall speak for her is afar-off guilty, / But that he speaks" (2.1.106–7)—a threat that elicits a nearly comical outpouring of verbiage in the Queen's defense. One lord tells Leontes: "For her, my lord, / I dare lay my life down, and will do't, sir, / Please you t'accept it, that the Queen is spotless" (2.1.131–3). Antigonus follows: "Every inch of woman in the world, / Ay, every dram of woman's flesh is false / If she be" (2.1.139–41). And another lord: "More it would content me / To have her honour true than your suspicion, / Be blamed for't how you might" (2.1.161–3). Even at the height of Leontes' irrationality, which should lend some credence to his willingness to carry out a threat, his attendants do not flinch in defending the Queen's virtue, in large part because their own sense of absolute identity is threatened by the prospect of female infidelity. Just like Polixenes, who skips out of Bohemia for nine months without causing a stir in his kingdom, Leontes is made to seem secondary, this time to the symbolic centrality of Hermione. The lords and attendants are not so much worried by the judgment of royal authority as by their psychic investment in the Queen, who functions as a substitute for their own, actual wives or daughters. Representation sustains a kind of value: better a queen in statuary, for these anxious men, than a living, breathing woman.

When several paintings in the Shakespeare Gallery were mysteriously slashed in 1791, James Gillray—who had been rebuffed in his appeal to engrave one of Northcote's paintings—turned his satiric fury against Boydell. In *The Monster broke loose; a Peep into the Shakespeare Gallery*, Gillray shows Boydell himself stealthily cutting paintings: "These *Small* pictures won't cost a great deal of money replacing," the "Monster" Boydell is quoted as saying; "Indeed one would not like to cut a large one to pieces for the sake of making it look as if People envied us" (figure 27). Feeding rumors that the attention-seeking Boydell was the culprit, Gillray underscores the irony of the crime: the ostensible raison d'etre of the gallery, the large-scale paintings that were to help establish an English school, were left untouched. Instead, the vandal gouged at the smaller paintings housed in the basement of the exhibition.

It may not have been the marketing ploy Gillray claims it was, but the slashing of the smaller works did reflect a reality of spectatorship at the time: smaller and less prestigious paintings, generally hung low on the walls where they could be better seen, were the most accessible—and most vulnerable—works of art on display. As Gillray's print reminds us, the success of this grandiose project hinged not on the public spectacle of giant history paintings (which were safe from the vandal's knife) but on the subsequent distribution of the gallery to the private homes of middle-class readers. In images such as Hamilton's portrait of the tearful Leontes, we see the downsizing of the tragic passions, with high-flown sentiment pitched to the more conservative aspects of a middle-class culture of sensibility.

But for all the entrepreneurial savvy that went into its planning, the Shakespeare Gallery would ultimately go down in history as a spectacular bust. The Gallery had long been in dire financial straits, due both to the closing of the European print market and to contradictions in the project's articulation. In January 1805—a month after John Boydell's death—the paintings were auctioned, the anticlimax of a bargain-basement sell-off being the only way for the family to avoid bankruptcy. Cleared of Shakespearean paintings, the rooms at 52 Pall Mall were soon transformed into the British Institution for Promoting the Fine Arts in the United Kingdom, which combined Continental masterpieces lent by country houses with British paintings carrying a frequently militaristic emphasis. Steering history painting away from its classical, biblical, and even English literary sources "and toward," in Morris Eaves's words, "a national mythos," this successor to the Shakespeare Gallery developed the most conservative aspects of a project that had sought problematically to forge a unified social body from the collective pursuit of prestige through high-art consumption.[73]

But its brief existence and various internal contradictions notwithstanding, the Shakespeare Gallery nourished an embryonic and potentially transformative political friction. A highly visible venue in which artists could experiment with the relation between nation and genre, it was an aesthetic harbinger of the complex social transformations that would define nineteenth-century Britain. Here the myth of the original ran smack into the commercial appeal of the copy. Genres on the high end of the hierarchy became subject to the skilled labor of engravers, and authority of all kinds was reimagined in more collective terms. Even John Boydell, visionary entrepreneur, found himself distanced from his brainchild: his vision subject to the painters' variations on national history and romance, his profits contingent on their ability to please potential customers. Oddly enough, it is in this sense that his undertaking was most successful. For by framing nationalism in terms of the division between history painting and portraiture, the Shakespeare Gallery assisted the evolution of these singular genres into hybrid modes, such as narrative genre painting and historical portraiture. Though these genres were unstable, they were also emblematic of the social and political consolidations of the coming century.

CHAPTER THREE

Painting Sorrow

> She was a kind and exemplary wife and her likeness, which is now before the reader, will (if it does not strike his eye as beautiful) prepossess him, perhaps, in her favour, as a mild, plain, and unaffected woman.
>
> —Profile of Charlotte Smith in *Effigies Poeticæ: or Portraits of the British Poets* (1824)

> Ah! then, how dear the Muse's favours cost,
> *If those paint sorrow best—who feel it most!*
>
> —Smith, *Elegiac Sonnets*

At the precise midpoint of her completed, ninety-two-poem sequence of *Elegiac Sonnets* (1797), Charlotte Smith imagines English literary history as a deteriorating country house, and herself as a "musing wanderer" haunting the property's margins.[1] "Written at Penshurst, in autumn of 1788" (sonnet 46) emphasizes the pastness of Penshurst's past. In the sestet, portraits communicate the decay of tradition:

> The spoiling hand of Time may overturn
> These lofty battlements, and quite deface
> The fading canvas whence we love to learn
> Sydney's keen look, and Sacharissa's grace . . .
> (lines 9–12)

Smith revises Ben Jonson's image of Penshurst as a beacon of hospitality, "Where comes no guest but is allowed to eat" ("To Penshurst," line 61). Her Penshurst is gothic, sublime, deserted—as it was throughout the eighteenth century, when it was an abandoned, junglelike pile holding little appeal for the Georgian crowd. As Horace Walpole wrote after visiting in 1752: "This morning we have been to Penshurst—but, oh! how fallen!" Or as Smith's own note to the poem explains: "The house is at present uninhabited, and the windows of the galleries and other rooms, in which there are many invaluable pictures, are never opened but when strangers visit it."[2] Honored guests are now strangers; open windows, signs of a fledgling tourist industry.

The house may seem forbidding, yet it remains curiously accessible. Unlike Smith's ancestral estate of Bignor Park—no longer her own, on account of an arranged marriage gone bad, a profligate husband, and a miswritten will—Penshurst draws in the outsider. Smith walks on the poet Edmund Waller's path, as if self-reflexively noting the poetic "galleries" to which she *can* have access via allusion (lines 6–7). The architectural counterpart to the poetics of sincerity on display in *Elegiac Sonnets*, Penshurst avoids "the closed theatricality that is characteristic" of many country houses, Don Wayne suggests, its "flat facade . . . present[ing] the house openly and directly to the world": "Penshurst *is* the creation of the illusion of 'sincerity,' of an open and direct participation in a community that extends beyond its walls."[3] Likewise Smith's Penshurst is not insular but approachable, its affect a democratic one. Her note to the poem affirms that "Sydney's keen look" refers not to Sir Philip, author of an important precursor sequence (whose keen look hangs in the same gallery), but to Algernon Sidney, a republican martyr executed for his alleged role in the Rye House plot.[4] She develops this subtext by showing how a faithfully observed nature ("timid deer," "matted fern") takes over from "lofty battlements," and also by depicting the decay of the portraits themselves. Time levels all, "quite defac[ing]" the portraits that set history in a spatial order, just as the portraits themselves reveal the symbolic defacement of the national literary inheritance.[5] Together, overgrown nature, overturned "battlements," and decaying paintings describe a juncture when the patrilinear order, figured as the power of history, is under intense strain.

This sense of historical disruption is nowhere so apparent as in lines seven and eight, which contrast the gentle sounds of a (masculine) lyric tradition with the raucous song of (feminine) nature. Here the wanderer walks alongside ferns "which Waller's soothing lyre were wont to hear, / But where now clamours the discordant hern!" The hern is a projection of the sonneteer. Exiled from the heronry that Smith, in a note, observes is located "in the park at Penshurst," the hern "clamours" where once Waller expressed a conventionalized longing for sweetness in songs of unrequited love for Sacharissa. If Waller's desire is sanctioned (and even formulated) by poetic convention, Smith's "discordant" desire for inclusion—in the gentry circles to which she was born; in the "gallery" of English poets—verges on impropriety. This is especially the case given the low status of the form in which she was working: famously ridiculed in Johnson's *Dictionary* as "not very suitable to the English language," the sonnet's "sugred tast," as Rachel Crawford has noted, set it barely above the epigram in a poetic hierarchy described in Thomas Warton's *History of English Poetry* (1774–81).[6] Nevertheless, just as the hern in "Written at Penshurst" unabashedly persists in her complaint and becomes the prevailing voice on the scene, Smith by 1797 had developed into England's preeminent sonnet writer—even, in conjunction with the move from a "georgic-descriptive hierarchy" to a "lyricized hierarchy," helping to elevate the form itself.[7] As indicated by the visual semiotic produced by Smith's enjambment of "overturn" in the line marking the sonnet's turn, portraits and sonnets exist in different relation to the "spoiling hand of time." If time defaces the "fading canvas," it impels the sonnet toward formal fruition. Poetry holds out the promise of access to the ruling pantheon; it is a place where history contains possibilities not available in the culture at large.

Writing against the tradition of the country-house poem, within which "place is identity," Smith posits the value (if not the desirability) of placelessness, alienation, and exile.[8] But whereas Wordsworth, with the support of a powerful paternalist landlord, would later generate poetic capital by making placelessness the special property of the male poet-wanderer, for a woman such as Smith it was a compulsory orientation.[9] Male property owners and the great poets they supported held reserved places in Britain's notional ancestral gallery; women sonneteers in debtors' prison—as Smith was in 1784, when *Elegiac Sonnets* first appeared—most certainly did not. In "Written at Penshurst" and throughout her sequence, as I discuss in this chapter, she conceptualizes this marginalization via the late eighteenth-century culture of art. In sonnets that lament her restricted legal rights as well as her exclusion (as a woman writing sentimental sonnets) from a masculine literary inheritance, Smith evokes painting and its less prestigious cousins, engravings and miniatures, as critical contexts for considering issues of political and cultural belonging.

Sentimentality itself was extraordinarily attuned to the contours of prestige, signaling alternative forms of distinction in a commercial society (a fact that Boydell's goal of disseminating history paintings in the guise of portraits makes clear), but the numerous instances of literal or figurative "painting" in *Elegiac Sonnets* engage this in an even more specific way.[10] Smith deals knowingly with graphic metaphors in ways that suggest her alertness to symbolic capital as well as its material vessels. Against the "fading canvas" of the authoritative portraiture housed at Penshurst, she repeatedly alludes to less prestigious, more informal media (sketching, botanical drawing, and miniature painting), forms of visual art generally kept in portfolios or hung in more private rooms.[11] Writing of her aspiration "to guide the crayon" (sonnet 34, line 4); of her "vain" efforts to sketch flowers with "the mimic pencil" (37.9); of "the scenes" drawn by fancy's "sportive pencil" (47.2); of the botanical drawings that "in happier hours" she "with pencil light . . . drew" (65.4); of her uninspired attempt to "bid the pencil's varied shades arrest / Spring's humid buds, and Summer's musky gems" (91.6–7); and of the miniature of her daughter that she wears on her "bleeding breast" (91.8), Smith activates a cultural context in which the popularity of so-called minor art forms raised serious (and often threatening) questions about the symbolic value of painting. The Royal Academy's exclusion of engravers was only the most prominent of the many reverberations of this dynamic. Andrew Robertson, a rising miniature painter who sought to elevate his work by adopting the rich coloring and varnish of the Old Masters, dismissed traditional miniatures as "but *toys*"—"pretty things, but not pictures. No nature, colouring or force."[12] The oil painter Martin Archer Shee was similarly disparaging: "Blockheads pursu'd through every nobler shape, / In miniature take refuge, and escape."[13] Meanwhile, the establishment of the Society of Painters in Water Colour codified a more elevated style of watercolor practice, its members—"conscious of themselves as members of a profession"—scorning an older, less formal style.[14] Smith, who writes in a form and scale low in the literary hierarchy, mobilizes the meanings of art throughout her sonnets in order to insinuate their importance. Her engagement with a Georgian visual culture increasingly characterized by the fluidity of generic categories reveals *Elegiac Sonnets* as a canny performance extraordinarily alert to the forms of legitimation available to women at the time.

Strange Defeatures

Elegiac Sonnets first appeared in 1784 as a slim quarto of twenty-eight "little poems" that its author hoped could mitigate the financial distress brought on by a spendthrift husband. Over the next sixteen years, however, Smith's elegant collection underwent a dramatic expansion. Through nine editions, the mode was accumulation: sonnets were added to the ends of previous sequences and prefaces amassed at its beginning. In 1800 the remarkable growth industry concluded with the downsizing of the larger quarto into a more affordably reproduced octavo, *Elegiac Sonnets, and Other Poems.*[15] The final, two-volume sequence of ninety-two sonnets was supplemented with a frontispiece portrait, five prefaces, a twelve-page list of subscribers, nine ornamental engravings, twenty-three additional poems, and an advertisement for eleven of Smith's novels.

The material expansion of *Elegiac Sonnets* reflected an effort to personalize the poet's relationship with her public. The prefaces let readers in on the details of Smith's life; the frontispiece portrait let readers see her.[16] At once an authenticating and aesthetically enhancing frame for the sequence, the paratextual apparatus presented an outward face designed to condition a sympathetic reading of the lyrics. It worked: absorbed by her portraits of misfortune, readers sent sonnets of personal advice, offered their help in locating sources for uncited allusions, and gave public testimony of the pleasure they received from her poems. When in 1786 the *Gentleman's Magazine* incorrectly (but with perfect elegiac logic) printed the poet's obituary, it retracted with an apologetic sonnet to "the wife, the mother, and the friend."[17] As indicated by the words of one commentator (quoted in the epigraph), Smith fashioned herself as "a mild, plain, and unaffected woman"—as an eminently believable character, or at least as the kind of character middle-class consumers would wish to believe in.

In the sonnets themselves, Smith plays on the late eighteenth-century public's belief in the veridical nature of the fictional character. The vogue for imagining individuals as portraits (or for seeing through a portrait into individual character) reflected a new mode of literary portraiture: the visual and verbal gallery of *fictional* portraits. The commercial gathering of characters as portraits reflects what Deidre Lynch has described as the emergence of "character" as a desirable commodity. John Hamilton Mortimer's 1775 exhibit at the Society of Artists featuring portraits of Shakespeare's characters, and *Portraits Illustrative of the Novels, Tales, & Romances of the Author of "Waverley"* (1824), are just two examples of imaginary characters finding extratextual life in metaphorical picture galleries. The flourishing of actual literary galleries in the 1790s—Boydell's Shakespeare Gallery, William Bowyers' Historic Gallery, Fuseli's Milton Gallery, Thomas Macklin's Poets' Gallery, to name a few—extended this trend, revealing literary representation to be shaped by visual culture, as visual culture likewise became steeped in literary values.

Smith's own mobilization of the cult of character begins in earnest in 1792, when the ethical basis of her sonnets—nine years in the making—comes into question.[18] In the preface to this sixth edition of her sonnets, Smith complains that she has "unfortunately no reason yet, though nine years have . . . elapsed [since she started publishing "elegiac" sonnets], to *change my tone*." (Nor would she have such a reason before her death in 1806: Smith's predicament, originating in a miswritten will that kept her family property from her children, was a model for the absurd Jarndyce versus Jarndyce legal embroglio in Dickens's *Bleak House*.) The assertion of continuity between poetic grief and painful experience is buttressed by the poem's visual apparatus. Starting with the first edition, the sonnets themselves are introduced by portraiture: a sonnet-sized frontispiece introducing readers to the "real" Smith (figure 28). This portrait presents Smith as a perpetual sufferer whose melancholia continually worsens. Indeed: for the eighth edition of 1797, Smith requested that the portrait be

P. Conde sculp.
Oh! Time has Changed me since you saw me last,
And heavy Hours with Time's deforming Hand,
Have written strange Defeatures in my Face.
Published May 15th 1797. by Cadell and Davies Strand.

FIG. 28. Frontispiece to Volume II, Charlotte Smith, *Elegiac Sonnets*, 1797. (Courtesy of Department of Special Collections, Stanford University Libraries)

physically altered to show this worsening and added this caption, slightly misquoted from Shakespeare's *Comedy of Errors*:

> Oh! Time has Changed me since you saw me last
> And heavy Hours with Time's deforming Hand
> Have written strange Defeatures in my Face![19]

Smith writes and is written on: she authors herself even as she is authored by Time, whose negative prefixes undo the poet's work of forming and featuring. In a repetition that binds and coordinates the sequence, Smith's defeatured face, like the portraits at Penshurst, succumbs to (even as they represent) the "spoiling hand of time." This frontispiece asks readers to understand portraiture as a "faithful art" (to quote Smith's ninety-first sonnet): not as a copy that has been artificially altered—which it is—but as a living art that is shaped and reshaped in accordance with the poet's experience.

The effect of the frontispiece rests on the assumption that one can simultaneously fashion oneself as a deep, inward, believable individual and as a character whose life unfolds as public narrative. This apparent contradiction is embedded in the illustrations to many of the sonnets, which support the frontispiece by giving a visible body to the poet. Sonnet-sized portraits that purport to locate a speaker at the scene of a poem's composition make the sonnets, like little pictures, into physical objects and visual events—printed, decorated, handled, seen—whose diminutiveness contributes to their appearance as two-dimensional images. The illustrations, in their theatricality and conventionality, would seem to undercut the central claim of Smith's initial preface of 1784, which in modestly describing sonnets as "little Poems" that are "no improper vehicle for a single Sentiment," distinguishes an auric melancholy from a tainting circulation. The poems, Smith had claimed, were written to "beguile" some "very melancholy moments," and were only shared with the public when her friends "multiplied the copies" of them "till they found their way into the prints of the day in a mutilated state" (*Poems*, 3). The engravings, themselves copies (and thus not admissible to a prestigious national body such as the Royal Academy), exist in a middle ground between effusion and artifice, or nature and culture.

The illustration for sonnet 4, "To the moon," gives an idealized image of the poet composing (figure 29). "Alone and pensive," hand on her "troubled breast" (lines 2, 6), eyes upturned and arm outstretched: the image "visualizes," as Sarah Zimmerman puts it, "the stylized verbal gestures of Smith's poetry."[20] The mediated quality of verbal expression is matched by visual artifice. Framed in an oval that is encircled by sundry ornaments—owl, foliage, bow and quiver,

Plate. 2.
Sonnet. 4.
Publish'd Jan.y 1.1789. by T. Cadell, Strand.
Queen of the Silver Bow, &c.

FIG. 29. Engraving to illustrate "Sonnet IV. To the Moon," *Elegiac Sonnets*, 1797. (Courtesy of Department of Special Collections, Stanford University Libraries)

book—the engraving calls attention to its preciosity; the oval frame even casts a shadow. The very materiality of the image, its sheer delight in ornate detail, challenges the poet's expressed wish for transcendence, "that I soon may reach thy world serene." As in the opening sonnet's claim that those who "*paint sorrow best*" are also those "*who feel it most*," Smith "conceives of the burden of melancholy as a mark of her learning," in Esther Schor's words, and "of the unlettered classes as exempt from the cultural intercourse of 'sentiments.' "[21] Authentic lyricism, from this perspective (as well as that provided by the plates), derives its effect from reference to an existing tradition.

The framing of the poet's voice by poetic convention is a central problem in *Elegiac Sonnets*, though one that has not been discerned in the sonnets' visual apparatus.[22] Smith's prefaces claim an unproblematic cause and effect for composition ("I wrote mournfully because I was unhappy"), encouraging readers to see through the accoutrements of poetry to an unidealizable, underlying pain; yet her conspicuous use of allusion calls into question the source of that pain, often depleting the personal voice in communicating their dark interiority.[23] Thirty-six of the ninety-two sonnets in the final sequence—including translations of Petrarch, variations on the Italian poet Metastasio, and even poems written for characters in her own novels—are written at a consciously mediated distance from Smith's own personal experience.[24] This self-alienation is nowhere so eye-catching as in sonnet 24, the fourth of five poems in the sequence "Supposed to be written by Werter." Both speaker and auditor are characters out of Goethe:

> The tears shall tremble in my CHARLOTTE'S eyes;
> Dear, precious drops!—they shall embalm the dead!
> Yes—CHARLOTTE o'er the mournful spot shall weep,
> Where her poor WERTER—and his sorrows sleep! (lines 11–14)

Tapping the cult of character, Smith cleverly projects herself into the most popular fiction of the day. While giving voice to Werter, Smith in the guise of "Charlotte" turns herself into an object to be viewed from the outside: an embodied, weeping widow, rather than a melancholic voice.[25] The (repeated) typographical emphasis here theatricalizes the poet's pain, and even functions as a kind of verbal portrait calling attention to the text's artifactual nature. Like Wordsworth's description in *The Prelude* of a street performer on whose chest flames the word invisible (7: 310), this moment obscures the boundary between word and image so as to undermine the romantic priority of the word over the image.

Similarly, in *Elegiac Sonnets* allusion often functions by way of visual sign.

Incorporating major literary figures from Shakespeare, Milton, and Pope, to more minor figures including William Mason and Brook Boothby, the poet does not just substitute quotation for the direct expression of grief, she designates that substitution through punctuation and endnotes. Pinch calls the sonnets "echo chambers, in which reverberate direct quotations, ideas, and tropes from English poetry"; but if echolalia provides an ethereal metaphor, "strange Defeatures" (to use Smith's phrase) provides a more physical one for the way her poems "announce a relationship to poetic language and literary tradition."[26] Since allusion serves as a constant reminder of Smith's "proper" station, it is fitting that her little "written" frontispiece portrait—nicked, worn, and marked—is answered by sonnets that are visibly marked by "strange defeatures" of their own: the ubiquitous quotation marks that turn Smith's character into a defeatured tissue of materiality.

Smith's allusions can even evoke the link between painting and tears—to paint in song being to weep in song—while foregrounding the artifice involved in both. Addressing the profound literariness of Smith's sorrow, the epigraph to the second volume of 1797, taken from Petrarch, ties her theater of allusion to sincerity:

> Non t' appressar ove sia riso e canto
> Canzone mio, nò, ma pianto:
> Non fa per te di star con gente allegra
> Vedova sconsolata, in vesta nigra.[27]

Embodied as a widow dressed in black, Smith's songs are female lyrics that manifest sorrow as a literary masquerade. The external signifiers of grief are separated from its lived experience, as indicated in the epigraph by the wordplay of "pianto," referring to the speaker's "lament" but also to the artifice of that lament. This is a prevalent dichotomy in Petrarch, for as Michael Spiller points out, the Italian words for "to paint" (*pingere*) and "to cry" (*piangere*) share a common origin. Painting in Petrarch provides "the graphic, the permanent form" of tears.[28]

As a self-defacing and defeaturing lyric device, quotation could be read unsympathetically by those seeking serious entrée into the literary canon by way of sentimentality. When Anna Seward blasts Smith's "everlasting lamentables" as "hackneyed scraps of dismality, with which her memory furnished her from our various poets," she picks up Smith's own hint from sonnet 1.[29] The "partial Muse" invoked there can refer to a sympathetic muse partial to the poet, but it can also suggest an *incomplete* or fragmented muse, who inspires poems that seem only partially Smith's own. Yet the voicelessness or lack of poetic authority potentially exposed by allusion can also be seen as a constitutive aspect of the poet's melancholia. Allusion can represent usurpation, but employed to an extreme it can also come to resemble those "sentences that are interrupted, exhausted, come to a standstill," which Julia Kristeva identifies as a symptom of melancholia. Kristeva's account of melancholic speech almost sounds like a negative review of Smith's poems. "A repetitive rhythm, a monotonous melody," she writes, "emerge and dominate the broken logical sequences, changing them into recurring, obsessive litanies."[30] Quotation balances Smith's ongoing and loquacious despondency with the standstill of a search for words that are not her own. Her echo chamber becomes a miniature self-portrait, albeit in an extreme form—an art of defeaturing the poet in the very act of self-presentation.[31]

The visible disfigurement of the text by quotation marks that displace Smith's lyric authority comes into focus within a wider attention to the visual arts in these poems, particularly apparent in the overt materiality of the poem's engraved illustrations. In *Elegiac Sonnets*, portraiture—an art of featuring—is marked by defeatures, a word whose dominant stress is on "defeat" or "ruin" (from the Old French *desfaire*, "to undo") and that in the late eighteenth century came to connote "disfigurement" or "defacement" (*OED*). The engravings ask that readers envision the speaker: she may be looking to the moon in the illustration for sonnet 4, but the reader is always looking at her.[32] The very eighteenth-century spectacle of a poet dressed in modern finery while sitting, as in the illustration for sonnet 12, "on some rude fragment of the rocky shore" (line 1) abets a theatricality that posed a clear enough threat to the poet's ethical project (figure 30). The potential for reading her effusions as rote gestures is registered in a printer's error in the 1797 volume, through which this latter illustration mistakenly appears opposite sonnet 8 (and is even labeled "Sonnet 8," though the caption is from sonnet 12). However errant, the fact of the misprint suggests just how interchangeable Smith's quotations, poetic laments, and dramatic postures can seem. At the end of the day, one wonders how many readers of sonnet 8 have even noticed that the illustration refers elsewhere.

But the risks associated with feminine artifice are recuperated through a play for authority embedded in Smith's theatrical posturing. Sarah Siddons's frequent representation as the tragic muse, as Judith Pascoe proposes, may have provided Smith with an important model.[33] The speaker in sonnet 29 rejects the comic muse, "gay Thalia," in favor of "her fair and pensive sister" (lines 9–10), who hangs constantly over the shoulder of Siddons in Reynolds's *Sarah Siddons as the Tragic Muse* (1784). Functioning much like her literary allusions,

FIG. 30. Engraving to illustrate "Sonnet XII. Written on the Sea Shore.—October, 1784," *Elegiac Sonnets*, 1797. (Courtesy of Department of Special Collections, Stanford University Libraries)

Smith's repetitive and melodramatic self-presentation evokes the flourishing iconography of heroic female "Melancholy" presented in contemporary portraiture.[34] Well-known paintings such as Reynolds's of Siddons and George Romney's *Mary Ann Yates as the Tragic Muse* (1771) yoked Melancholy to the prestige of high drama. Milton's "Il Penseroso," wildly popular at the time, furnished appealing pictorial possibilities with its "Goddes, sage and holy, / . . . divinest Melancholy" (lines 11–12). Portraits such as Thomas Beach's *Sarah Siddons as Melancholy—Il Penseroso* (1782) bore the gravitas of Milton's "pensive Nun" (line 31). Funerary monuments and engravings like those in Bell's British Theater series also made Melpomene a familiar face.[35] Melpomene's "tearful smile" even made an appearance in the above-mentioned twenty-ninth sonnet (line 11).

In sonnet 32 ("To melancholy. Written on the banks of the Arun, October 1785"), word and image combine to produce a strategy that Smith deploys to manage the contradictions of her self-presentation. Although the poet does not explicitly require that a reader envision her—there is no illustration for this sonnet—she nevertheless insinuates a particular image of herself into the verbal texture of the poem. The speaker of this poem, walking through the Arun river valley, fantasizes that "the hollow sighs" (line 2) of the "dim waves" (line 1) might belong to other "night-wanderers" like herself, poets of melancholy "who their woes bewail" (line 8). One figure in particular occupies her imagination: "Here, by his native stream, at such an hour, / Pity's own Otway I methinks could meet, / And hear his deep sighs swell the sadden'd wind!" (lines 9–11). This fantasy of hearing the seventeenth-century tragedian Thomas Otway is made possible by Melancholy's "magic power" (line 12), which supplies a sympathetic audience of similarly afflicted souls, enabling her to hear Otway just as it enables him to hear her.[36] Otway's phantom nighttime presence evokes the dark sensibilities of Smith's male precursors—Shenstone, Collins, Gray, Young, among others whose nightpieces set melancholy genius against Augustan urbanity. Smith imagines, and identifies with, a masculine voice and hence a masculine sadness in the "deep sighs that swell the sadden'd wind." The "hollow sighs" she hears (line 3) may even be seen to originate in Drayton's sonnet, "Love once would daunce within my Mistres[s's] eye," where song becomes a sexualized male desire (line 9).

And yet, working against this image of the poet as a belated entrant in a masculine tradition, Smith ingeniously turns the book's visuality to a different end. Several pages before her imagined encounter with Otway, the magic power of printing had allowed readers to meet with him through Thomas Stothard's

Plate 3.
Sonnet 26.
Stothard del.
Thornthwaite sculp.t
Published Jan.y 1.1789.by T. Cadell Strand.
For with the infant Otway lingering here.

FIG. 31. Engraving to illustrate "Sonnet XXVI. To the River Arun," *Elegiac Sonnets*, 1797. (Courtesy of Department of Special Collections, Stanford University Libraries)

engraving for sonnet 26 ("To the River Arun") of "the infant Otway" (figure 31). This child portrait signifies two things at once. First, and particularly since all the portraits to this point have represented the sonnets' female speaker, it immediately suggests itself as an idealized picture not of the dead male author but of the poet herself as a youth, prior to her "fall" into marriage (which for Smith also became the world of commerce). The association of Smith with Otway is supported by biographical fact—both writers experienced hardship later in life—as well as by the sonnet. "With the infant Otway, lingering here," Smith writes, "Of early woes she bade her votary dream" (lines 5–6), implying both likeness ("*like* the infant Otway . . .") and companionship (whether mental or, given the conventions of the bower, erotic). The potential for seeing Otway as Smith is further contained within a portrait tradition that, in Marcia Pointon's words, "equates femininity and childhood."[37] The instability of child portraiture, where youth partakes of the feminine much as the female portrait often partakes of the infantile (with both children's and women's portraits typically considered a separate genre from portraits of men), informs Smith's self-presentation. In the poem's concluding couplet, she affirms her interchangeability with Otway by projecting her victimization onto him: "kindred spirits, pitying, shall relate / Thy Otway's sorrows, and lament his fate!" (lines 13–14).

The appearance of a child portrait here also activates a recurring motif of *Elegiac Sonnets*, Smith's motherhood. Otway's portrait serves as a crucial visual cue, reminding readers of the poet's own children, who are so frequently cited in the prefaces and in the poems, and of Smith's sufferings on her children's behalf. In this respect the image assists her rhetorical strategy, for Smith performs motherhood throughout her poems in order to offset the risks of publication. For Smith to play, like the nightingale of sonnet 3, the "songstress sad" (especially for profit) is, according to the rules of decorum, a betrayal of domestic duty. She first treats these risks in the idiom of private self-solacing in this sonnet, "To a nightingale," querying "the sounds that swell thy little breast, / When still at dewy eve thou leavest thy nest, / Thus to the listening night to sing thy fate" (lines 6–8). The sonnet concludes, though, on a note of envy: "Ah! songstress sad! that such my lot might be, / To sigh and sing at liberty—like thee!" (lines 13–14). What is striking here is the cost of singing one's fate: to do it, one must leave one's nest. Unlike the "poor melancholy bird" (line 1), who sings at "liberty" from the supposedly paradoxical roles of author and mother, Smith, if she is to profitably sing her fate, has to worry about propriety: she must stay, and play the mother.

Smith's theatricalization of her own social propriety is apparent enough in her prefaces, which imply the details of her suffering and yet cloud its causes in secrecy. "You know the circumstances under which I have now so long been labouring," she tells an imaginary friend in the preface to her sixth edition, at once arousing and frustrating a public desire for knowledge concerning her suffering; "With these, however, as they are some of them of a domestic and painful nature, I will not trouble the Public *now*" (6). When, eight years later in the preface to her sixth edition (1792), she lets the reader in on a dialogue with a "Friend" ("*You know* that when in the Beech Woods of Hampshire, I first struck the chords of the melancholy lyre, its notes were never intended for the public ear!"), Smith's plea of original intent addresses both the poems' unauthorized circulation and her own publication (5). As here, the prefaces publicize privacy in the act of producing it, nicely serving both commercial interests and social propriety that requires genuine emotion to remain private. As Smith concludes this preface: "I am well aware that for a woman—'The Post of Honor is a Private Station'" (6). This effort to signal what cannot be said with honor by a "gentlewoman," however, gives way to a threadbare honesty in her final preface (1797), where Smith directly invokes her children. Depressed following the death of her daughter in 1795 and long unable to write the poems for which subscribers had put up money, Smith assertively defends her honor.[38] Anyone who "could suspect me of a design to accumulate [funds] for a work I never meant to publish," she declares, "must either never have understood, *or must have forgotten*, what I was, what I am, or what I ought to be," namely a woman of honor and financial capability. Her frequent "mention of myself" is not her fault, she claims, but rather that of "the men, who have withheld my family property" (8). Though sadness has delayed publication, to disclose as much would be as inappropriate as silence. She is left hanging onto the barest hint of agency, parenthetically inferring that she alone can judge her fulfillment of the legal contract binding her to her subscribers: "I . . . doubted, whether . . . I should have the power of fulfilling (so as to satisfy myself) the engagement I must feel myself bound by" (7). This binding is principally economic but also textual, for what she "must feel . . . bound by" is, in the end, her own lyric project: the production of a self whose feelings are bound up neatly in a package and circulated as literary merchandise.

Perhaps inevitably, Smith returns in her final preface to a self-presentation as a grieving mother. She justifies her recurrent publications by citing the death of "the loveliest, the most beloved of [her] daughters, the darling of all her family"; the fate of a son who enlisted in the Army where he "was maimed during the first campaign he served in, and is now a lieutenant of invalids"; her other children, all "deprived of every advantage to which they are entitled"; and her own "anxiety," "sorrow," and "anguish" at the "detention of [her children's] property" (7). The body of her work displays the bodies of her children, and the subsequent engraving of "the infant Otway" reminds readers of this fact. Broadcasting her dual status as grieving mother and public poet, Smith shrewdly posits the publication of inward sorrows as a commitment to private affection. In the final section of this chapter, I turn to an actual portrait of one of Smith's children, represented in the sequence's penultimate poem, where she once again displays her affections only to secure their privacy—this time, in an act of withdrawal that makes possible the sequence's movement toward formal closure.

Too Faithful Arts

Given the intensity of her engagement with Georgian visual culture, it is no surprise that Smith's sonnets should deal knowingly with a tradition of literary "painting." In this, Sir Philip Sidney is an important precursor. "Poesy," Sidney writes in his *Defense* (1595), is "a representing, counterfeiting, or figuring forth—to speak metaphorically, a speaking picture."[39] His sonnets evoke such "counterfeiting" as a positive act, in the effort to show "the very face of woe / Painted in my beclouded stormy face" (sonnet 45). The most famous figure of this sort appears in his opening sonnet, where Sidney is overtly rhetorical and seeks out "fit words" with which "to paint the blackest face of woe." Smith's version, as cited in my epigraph, is equivocal: to "paint sorrow," she suggests, to represent it artistically, one must be subject to it—and thence the subject of it. As in her frontispiece, misery is thus the handiwork of "heavy Hours." For Sidney, by contrast, a "face of woe" is witty artifice that anticipates the sonnet's concluding exhortation: "I am not I, pity the tale of me." His speaker is produced by language: we can get inside his head only through his tale. Smith, on the other hand, offers her tale as transparent and sincere.

Yet as we have seen, her portraiture is just as crafty. Scott admired in Smith's novels "the truth and precision of a painter" and J. M. S. Tompkins her "sober, veracious sketches," but Smith's poetry, like the engravings of the sonnets' idealized female speaker, tends to break the bond between truth and portraiture.[40] Smith's opening sonnet figures poetry as a "dear delusive art"—dearly bought, that is, at the expense of the real, as she indicates in sonnet 38, where "cruel Reason" impinges on the poet's fancy: "as the dear delusions leave my brain, / She bids the truth recur—with aggravated pain!" (lines 13–14). Her final two sonnets, however, seem to repudiate this "dear delusive art" in favor of what sonnet 91 describes as the "too faithful art" of grief. They accomplish this by turning to actual art: first by invoking a literal painting, a portrait miniature of the poet's recently deceased daughter, and finally by recalling the politics of exclusion that marks the poet's relation to the picture gallery in sonnet 46.

This shift away from artifice signals the sequence's imminent closure. In her preface to the sixth edition of 1792, Smith addresses a fictional friend who proposes that she attempt "a more cheerful style of composition." The poet demands, "can the *effect* cease, while the *cause* remains?" (5). Her emphasis on personal cause and poetic effect means that melancholy must be her perpetual song. Individual poems might be capable of formal closure, but Smith's sequence of sonnets, like her legal quandary, would go on and on. Not just the strategic incurability of Smith's melancholy (a formal pathology), but also the arrangement of the sequence vexes the process of closure in *Elegiac Sonnets*. Between 1784 and 1800, the sequence takes on a variety of shapes that challenge its formal coherence. The "demand for subsequent editions requiring revision, amendment, and augmentation," Schor writes, "severely strained the unitary conceit of the sonnet cycle."[41] In various ways, Smith's twentieth-century readers see an anticlosural principle at work in the sequence initiated in 1784 and halted, but not concluded, at Smith's death.[42]

Nevertheless, in the final two sonnets, Smith gestures toward formal closure. In sonnet 91, the depiction of a miniature of Smith's deceased daughter Anna Augusta facilitates this closure by making metatextual reference to the sequence as a whole. Like Smith's ninety-two "miniature" poems, the portrait occupies a liminal space between the covert and the displayed. Dangling from the neck, lying upon the poet's "bleeding breast," it is very much of her body (even as the daughter was); yet it is also a display for others, a public declaration of longing for a lost, beloved object. Given the traditional association of flowers with poems, the first half of this sonnet—and especially the opening line—reflects on the form of the sequence as a whole and the manner in which its flowers should be grouped.[43] While it seems to reflect on floral arrangement, and its title purports to reflect on drawings of plants, sonnet 91 reflects most emphatically on the ninety melancholy verbal sketches or miniatures leading up to it:

I can in groups these mimic flowers compose,
  These bells and golden eyes, embathed in dew;
Catch the soft blush that warms the early Rose,
  Or the pale Iris cloud with veins of blue;
Copy the scallop'd leaves, and downy stems,
  And bid the pencil's varied shades arrest
Spring's humid bud, and Summer's musky gems:
  But, save the portrait on my bleeding breast,

I have no semblance of that form adored,
  That form, expressive of a soul divine,
  So early blighted; and while life is mine,
With fond regret, and ceaseless grief deplored—
  That grief, my angel! with too faithful art
  Enshrines thy image in thy Mother's heart.

Speaking after the death of her daughter, the sonnet gives an image of contradiction, as the miniature figures publicity joined to privacy, self-display to inwardness. An extension of the speaker's body, it makes art the essence of her being, especially as it is superseded by the heart that, in the text of the poem, literally underlies it (and contains it linguistically). As always, Smith's world is one where even natural objects are powerless to compensate for the losses they embed: memory ignites, yet it persistently fails to restore joy. At the start of *Elegiac Sonnets* the "dear delusive art" of poetry is the sign of authentic suffering; here authority is situated in the "too faithful art" of grief. The miniature of the daughter is faithful as a *mimesis*: like the repetitive botanical drawings, it is a made thing, a "semblance," its minute stippling as artificial as the pencil swipes of "mimic flowers." But Smith repudiates this picture in favor of a more ineffable image "enshrined" in a "Mother's heart." Her sonnet subsumes material artifice—whether portrait or poem—in interiority, particularly in the final couplet that enshrines the mournful art of sonnet writing in the "mother's heart." The word "enshrine" at once suggests the hidden aura of the daughter's image as well as its exterior casement, making the heart into a corporeal locket containing the daughter's image.

The blurring between art and heart, and between the material and the imaginary, is apparent from the opening lines, where lifeless copies of nature anticipate the copied daughter of the sestet: the "golden eyes," the rose's "soft blush," the iris's "veins of blue" are all answered by the flower-sized portrait with its own eyes, blush, and veins. Earlier in the sonnet sequence, Smith describes drawing as a "light" activity of "happier hours," but one confounded by the weight of grief: "So fail from present care and sorrow past / The light botanic pencil's mimic powers" (sonnet 65, "To Dr. Parry of Bath, with some botanic drawings which had been made some years"). In sonnet 91, these "mimic powers" do not so much fail as surrender to the sorrow aroused by memories of the daughter.

Underscoring the irrepressibility of memory as it overflows the boundaries of artifice, the octave is cut short by one line: the daughter's portrait displaces botanical drawing at line eight, an early turn that splits the sonnet into two septets. The first septet is marked by a numbing repetitiousness: three of its lines exhibit perfect iambic regularity, the other four are unsettled only at their very beginning and thus fall into a metric predictability to go along with the speaker's uninspired drawing. But line eight brings with it a new sense of rhythm, enhancing the effect of interiority so critical to Smith's production of character. The second septet is dominated by third-beat promotions—not caesurae, but rhythmic "falls" that force a line to sink in its middle (e.g., "But save the por[-trait on my] blee-ding breast"; "So ear-ly blight[-ed and while] life is mine"). This absence at the center of the line—a void that repeatedly disappoints the ear—characterizes six of the last seven lines. The distinctiveness of the pattern accentuates the division in the poem, but its more important effect is to reflect the enshrinement of the portrait. The rhythmic surface of each line is punctured, emphasizing what it shields, a sphere of ineffable emotion. The only metrically regular line in the septet—the single line whose rhythm stays afloat, as it were—is line twelve, which describes the unending labor of grief. The poem's rhythm provides the fragile shrine encrypting the speaker's real sorrows.

The extravagant sadness of *Elegiac Sonnets* thus ends with a decisive moment of intense intimacy that is shielded from view. As in D. G. Rossetti's poem, titled "The Portrait," the image is an impenetrable holy site around which unspeakable feelings are scattered. Smith moves inward, from material miniature to ineffable image, from memento to memory. The picture is indispensable to the process of fetishization by which the poet reclaims the aura of melancholy described in the preface of 1784. Yet, despite this emphasis on an enshrinement that preserves the aura of emotion intact, interiority is authenticated through its exterior display. The transparent self-revelation associated with the Georgian miniature (worn on the chest as a window into the heart) is renounced in favor of a rhetoric of opacity, one more suggestive of an Elizabethan culture of "secret self-expression," as the speaker folds her daughter's image within an embodied locket, the heart. If Smith's achievement of authentic interiority is a function of self-display, it is also peculiarly illegible in this denouement. While she publishes the existence of an inner sanctum, the sanctum itself—site of the true self, subject of the faithful art of grief—remains safeguarded by the outer lining of her heart.[44]

The display of the deceased daughter's miniature holds out to public view both ownership and intimacy. Worn on her breast, it allows Smith to show off her property in the portrait itself as well as the more ineffable possession it signifies. But it also reflects the limitations placed upon her by the refusal of the political-legal establishment to grant Smith her rightful inheritance. The miniature is the mobile portrait gallery of a woman estranged from her genteel origins, featuring not a patrilinear inheritance of property but a matrilinear inheritance of sorrow. In its particularized location on her breast, the picture represents an unhoused, embodied display opposed to the extravagant, propertied displays of paternal seats such as Bignor Park.

Miniatures, whether as signs of maternal sorrow or emblems of the poetry of sensibility, provide a private alternative to the ensconced tradition of Penshurst and Bignor Park. As Smith suggests in the finale of *Elegiac Sonnets*, she bears a more positive relation to the former tradition as a poet than to the latter as a woman in a patriarchal society. If Penshurst symbolizes aristocratic decline at the exact midpoint of the sequence, Smith's concluding sonnet, "Written at Bignor Park in Sussex, In August, 1799," signals nostalgia for the personal loss of access to inheritable privileges. The title recalls that of the first edition of her sonnets (*Elegiac Sonnets, and Other Essays by Charlotte Smith of Bignor Park, in Sussex*), which stressed its author's gentry origins that belied her residence in debtor's prison at the time of the book's publication. Here Smith represents one last time that same sense of distance from what she "ought to be":

> Low murmurs creep along the woody vale,
> The tremulous Aspens shudder in the breeze,
> Slow o'er the downs the leaden vapours sail,
> While I, beneath these old paternal trees,
> Mark the dark shadows of the threaten'd storm,
> As gathering clouds o'erveil the morning sun;
> *They* pass!—But oh! ye visions bright and warm
> With which even here my sanguine youth begun,
> Ye are obscured for ever!—And too late
> The poor Slave shakes the unworthy bonds away
> Which crush'd her!—Lo! the radiant star of day
> Lights up this lovely scene anew—My fate
> Nor hope nor joy illumines—Nor for me
> Return those rosy hours which here I used to see!

The lasting image Smith leaves of herself is that of a speaker alienated from her landed origins. Whereas Penshurst, as the symbol of literary inheritance, remains accessible, if only by trespass, Bignor Park enforces an exclusion that is both spatial (she may not enter) and temporal (she may not return in time).

The helplessness and doom associated with Bignor Park's "old paternal trees" starkly contrast the "Mother's heart" of sonnet 91. They carry a far different resonance than do the "old paternal trees" of Smith's male peer in the late eighteenth-century sonnet revival, William Lisle Bowles. Bowles's double-sonnet "On a Landscape by Rubens," for instance, emphasizes a masculine contentedness, a confidence of inclusion, as the speaker "hears / The green leaves of his old paternal trees / Make music, soothing as they stir" (lines 18–20). Whereas Smith's shuddering Aspens and gathering storm make her "old paternal trees" seem foreboding, Bowles's "are to him as companions" (line 23). They also will be companions for

> his infants, who, when he is dead,
> Shall hear the music of the self-same trees
> Waving, till years roll on, and their gray hairs
> Go to the dust in peace. (lines 25–28)

Bowles envisions an uninterrupted succession nurtured by the music of "the self-same trees."[45] In Smith's ninety-first sonnet, by contrast, the indefinite article in the final phrase, "a Mother's heart," indicates not just an identification between the poet and her deceased daughter, but an identification between mothers and daughters generally—a multigenerational song of exclusion. Tracing Smith's unrequited desire for proper possession through to the very end, sonnet 92 posits a melancholy that must extend beyond the close of the printed sequence. The poet is left puzzling over an ambivalent inheritance in her concluding lines, which echo Gray's "Sonnet on the Death of Mr. Richard West." Gray's morning sunlight cruelly contrasts his speaker's sense of never-ending gloom; here it is "the radiant star of day" that "lights up this lovely scene anew," but has no power to cheer the melancholy poet: "Nor for me / Return those rosy hours which here I used to see!" The denial of Smith's property doubles as the impossibility of returning to the "rosy hours" of her childhood. And yet this defeat is expressed through an active usurpation. Allusion need not be merely a sign of self-abnegation. Though cut off from her past and denied her property, Smith freely accesses the treasures of a literary past. Poetry offers an alternative form of belonging; sonnets *can* provide a route into anthologized galleries of poems, if not into the portrait gallery of Bignor Park or, for that matter, the National Portrait Gallery where her male peers will hang.

Coda: Smith in the Gallery

One prominent late-romantic effort to canonize British literature in the form of the textual portrait gallery, *Effigies Poeticæ: Portraits of the British Poets* (1824), illustrates this point. Its two-volume selection ends with Smith—one of only two representatives (with Robert Burns) of what we now call the romantic period. The commentary that is paired with Smith's engraved portrait describes her poetry as a kind of life portrait. Calling Smith a "very amiable woman" and the "pleasing writer . . . of some small poems," it confounds the distinction between her life and her writing: "She was a kind and exemplary wife and her likeness, which is now before the reader, will (if it does not strike his eye as beautiful) prepossess him, perhaps, in her favour, as a mild, plain, and unaffected woman." Smith, it seems, is canonized because of a normative femininity appealing to a male reader. Though "her little poems are very touching," this is only so because "her sad life was employed in harassing her invention for tales and poetry, upon the profits of which her family were in some measure to subsist" (2: 139). Clearly, for a woman writing poems of personal lament in the conventional idiom of sensibility and publishing novels for profit, the path to the literary portrait gallery is vexed—a fact that the paratextual apparatus of *Elegiac Sonnets* makes only too clear. Amiable woman, exemplary wife, plain, unaffected and devoted mother: this is the portrait Smith herself designed to give the public. Here it finds its place alongside other "Portraits of the British Poets."

A related publication of 1826 offers an intriguing bookend to Smith's inclusion in this gallery of poets. Claiming ancestry in the traditional family gallery, Jacob Strutt's *Sylva Britannica: or Portraits of Forest Trees* rested its conservative appeal on the association between trees and ancestral descent. It is positively Burkean (or Bowlesian) in claiming that the trees, "silent witnesses of the successive generations of man," remind Britons "of the illustrious ancestors who may have seen it planted" (vii-viii), especially "The British Oak," said to be "inseparably associated . . . in the minds of Englishmen" with "the ideas of British power, and British independence" (2). But *Sylva Britannica*'s conservatism undermines itself. As a gallery of "portraits," it evokes a commonplace of eighteenth-century family portraiture: the placement of the family at the base of a tree (usually an oak) to symbolize its heritage. The family piece, as Ronald Paulson has argued, often includes formal tensions that forebode far reaching social shifts.[46] Reynolds's *Lady Elizabeth Delmé and her Children* (1777–79), for example, is a classic instance of a portrait that is working hard—*too* hard—to contain the disruptive energy of the young boy to whom the family name and property is entailed.

While the harmony of the domestic scene is made possible in such images by the absent father and the soon-to-be absent son (off on heroic missions or to tend to overseas properties), the boy's outwardly directed energies also suggest a more subversive potential that must be contained. He is thus doubly framed:

FIG. 32. Sir Joshua Reynolds, *Lady Elizabeth Delmé and Her Children*, 1777–79. (Andrew W. Mellon Collection, Copyright 2005 Board of Trustees, National Gallery of Art, Washington)

on one side, the mother wraps an arm around the group and clasps his hand; on the other side, the daughter, looking directly at us, leans into the boy. *Sylva Britannica*, seemingly without irony, follows this subversive potential through to its logical conclusion. These tree portraits dispense with family members: only foliage remains, the bare symbol of an older social order.

This irony is especially sharp in the book's treatment of Penshurst, and "Sir Philip Sidney's Oak" (48–50). The "biographical portrait" of this tree includes quotations, as one might expect, from both Jonson ("That taller tree which of a nut was set / At his great birth where all the Muses met"), and Waller ("yonder tree, which stands the sacred mark / Of noble Sidney's birth"). But history enacts strange reverses, and the profile ends by subordinating these men to Smith, whose sonnet on trespassing at Penshurst tacitly undermines the tradition of the country-house poem. "Sweet sounds often awaken echoes not less sweet," Strutt writes, introducing Smith's "Written at Penshurst"; "so have these lines of Waller, rushing over a poetic mind, . . . brought forth the following interesting picture of the feelings which Penshurst, so long the noble residence of busy and exalted spirits, is calculated to awaken in its present state of comparative desolation and abandonment." Sonnet 46 of *Elegiac Sonnets* follows and concludes the profile (although Smith never explicitly mentions the oak itself). The sonnet, which we have seen meditate on the decay of the great estate and the poet's exclusion from English tradition, offers an apt conclusion for a sequence of tree portraits that, though designed to celebrate national history, contains seeds of its own undoing. Great houses deteriorate and portraits fade, but beauty and old oaks—particularly when captured in engravings that can be reset, endlessly copied, and distributed at low cost—do indeed "defy decay."

CHAPTER FOUR

Monsters, Marbles, and Miniatures

> I turn without shrinking from cloud-borne angels, from prophets, sibyls, and heroic warriors, to an old woman bending over her flower-pot. . . . "Foh!" says my idealistic friend, "what vulgar details! What good is there in taking all these pains to give an exact likeness of old women and clowns? What a low phase of life!—what clumsy, ugly people!"
>
> But, bless us, things may be lovable that are not altogether handsome, I hope? I am not at all sure that the majority of the human race have not been ugly, and even among those "lords of their kind," the British, squat figures, ill-shapen nostrils, and dingy complexions are not startling exceptions. . . . yet to my certain knowledge tender hearts have beaten for them, and their miniatures—flattering, but still not lovely—are kissed in secret by motherly lips.
>
> —George Eliot, *Adam Bede* (1859)

> "How broken they are, a'ant they?"
> "Yes, but how like life."
>
> —Popular anecdote (ca. 1817) about seeing the Elgin Marbles

In 1804, a short-lived periodical, *The Miniature*, described realism as "the style of a MINIATURE": "While the touches are less daring, while less force, and richness of imagination may be found in the following sketches, they may perhaps derive some merit in a humbler scale, from correctness of design, and accuracy of representation." The "humbler scale" of private life is a miniature scale—as echoed by Austen, in her self-belittling description of "the little bit (two Inches wide) of Ivory on which I work with so fine a Brush."[1] It comes as no surprise, then, that George Eliot should cherish realism in the trope of exact portraits, in the excerpt from *Adam Bede* (1859) quoted above as an epigraph. Embracing true-to-life images in all their "squat," "ill-shapen," and "dingy" actuality, Eliot posits realism as an aesthetic of affection and sympathy. The turn away from the idealizing portraiture of the Royal Academy and its first president, Sir Joshua Reynolds, is also a turn toward miniatures "kissed in secret": in private, one's likeness need not be "lovely" to be loved.

But how about in public? Forty years earlier, writing at a moment when realism was taking hold as a dominant aesthetic and when monstrosity held radical connotations, Mary Shelley situated its meanings within a distinctly political context. In *Frankenstein* (1818), Shelley allegorizes the opposition between a populist aesthetic of "exact likeness" and the "cloud-borne angels" of more prestigious modes of portraiture. The various portraits represented in her novel, including full-lengths, miniatures, and most famously the gigantic Creature, mobilize prevalent arguments taking place within the culture of art in order to raise questions about the constitution of the British social body.[2] Embedding class-coded arguments about genre and aesthetic representation, the portraits of *Frankenstein* posit bourgeois identity as a romance that is perilously dependent upon the naturalization of new class hierarchies, which themselves collapse beneath the weight of an all-too-real social instability.[3]

In reading Shelley's aesthetic concerns through the lens provided by Georgian visual culture, I approach *realism*, an admittedly unwieldy term, through debates on art that are as concerned with the image of a social body instantiated by certain kinds of representations as they are with the question of reference itself. My idiosyncratic use of the term hovers somewhere between Raymond Williams's unidealizing and potentially radical aesthetic of "actual existence," and the uncertainty that grounds George Levine's view that monstrosity must always be repressed in a realistic tradition that "belongs, almost provincially, to a 'middling' condition and defines itself against [stylistic and narrative] excesses."[4] Yet Shelley's engagement with visual culture aligns her novel very much with "the extreme, the violent, the ideal," as opposed to "the seductive world of things."[5] Monstrosity, in its uncanny return as actual, unidealized existence, underpins her querying of a politically oriented realism inherited from the culture of art.[6]

The major cultural happening in the post-Napoleonic moment in which *Frankenstein* was produced was the acquisition by the British government of the Elgin Marbles. Arguments over this acquisition had as their tacit subject the sociopolitical implications of realist aesthetics, and later in this chapter I will turn to discussions of the marbles' anatomical precision as a critical context not just for *Frankenstein* but for realism. Embodying an antiestablishment aesthetic of particularity even as they figured forth an ideal of liberty, the marbles appealed to commentators who saw in their internal effects an aesthetic revolution: the return of a material repressed from beneath a surface of culture and artifice. The voluminous writings about the marbles (ca. 1816–1818), contemporaneous with Shelley's novel, inform the nuances of class definition in the portraits of *Frankenstein*, and even undergird Shelley's most famous "portrait": the gigantic Creature, a body overloaded, like the marbles, with "vulgar details." In the Creature, Shelley allegorizes a populist aesthetic, a social body inclusive of the "low" and the "ugly." Not that this reveals a personal politics: Johanna Smith points out the "fluctuation in [Shelley's] views—between fear of the revolutionary working class and sympathy for the laboring poor."[7] But it is perhaps because of her ambivalence that Shelley is so sensitive to the ways in which aesthetic form reflects and propels social reconfiguration. In *Frankenstein*, she observes a mode of class definition that still prevails in Eliot's time: if the British, as "lords of their kind," find sovereignty an accessible (if diminished) ideal, the cachet of high art contributes to this lordly aura and yet is powerless to guard against its potential loss.

Framing Justine: *Frankenstein* and the Art of Emulation

On December 5, 1816, in a letter to her husband, Mary Shelley writes:

> Sweet Elf
>
> I was awakened this morning by my pretty babe and was dressed time enough to take my lesson from Mr West and (Thank God) finished that tedious ugly picture I have been so long about—I have also finished the 4 Chap. of Frankenstein which is a very long one & I think you would like it.[8]

Shelley's drawing lessons from the miniature painter John West coincide with the birth of one of literature's most persevering giants. This "4 chap" includes an "ugly picture" of its own: the verbal portrait of the Creature, with yellow skin, lustrous black hair, pearly white teeth, watery eyes, shrivelled complexion, and straight black lips.[9] Throughout *Frankenstein*, the meanings of scale are elaborated through portraits, which turn class into a function of performance and equipage rather than of birth. Yet paradoxically, even as the portraits disclose social hierarchy as unstable, they also naturalize it. The sociopolitical meanings of artistic scale are first invoked in the novel when Victor, returning home after William's death, enters the family library and views two paintings hanging on the wall: "I gazed on the picture of my mother, which stood over the mantle-piece. It was an historical subject, painted at my father's desire, and represented Caroline Beaufort in an agony of despair, kneeling by the coffin of her dead father. Her garb was rustic, and her cheek pale; but there was an air of dignity and beauty, that hardly permitted the sentiment of pity. Below this was a miniature of William; and my tears flowed when I looked at it" (106). The hanging of these two pictures in the Frankensteins' library brings the late-Georgian exhibition hall into the domestic sphere. The side-by-side display of miniatures and history paintings was customary in exhibition galleries, where the influence of consumerism on art made itself felt in a competition that transformed both genres.[10] The notoriously unmarketable history painting, too large and expensive for most consumers, was physically and thematically downsized into portraits invested with an antique air, which presented family history in classical, literary, or historical guise. By contrast, the tiny, ornamental miniature, in order to compete with the larger paintings, grew from an average diameter of one-and-a-half inches in 1760, to three inches in 1800, to six inches in 1820.[11] In accordance with the miniature's expansion, the site for its display changed as well. Concealable lockets worn on the wrist were replaced, first by oval frames hung from the neck, and then by larger, rectangular miniatures that were hung on the wall. By the 1830s the form was suffering from "elephantiasis," as Graham Reynolds puts it; it was even common to see "works of monster size" produced by suturing together "several separate pieces of ivory."[12]

Shelley records these shifts. The two portraits hanging on the Frankensteins' wall represent evolved forms: one is a diminished history painting, the other an oversized memento. In each case, aesthetic production conforms to consumer desire. The movement is toward a middle ground, as the portraits come to encapsulate both an erasure and a remapping of generic difference. The larger portrait rises to the status of history painting, fostering a contemplative distance in its "air of dignity." The smaller portrait gets associated with the body and with emotions. It requires a physical nearness that eliminates distance, and translates the air of dignity into a flood of tears. Despite the fact that these are generically related—as portraits—they are separated by an arbitrary boundary: one is prestigious, the other is ordinary. The picture of Caroline Beaufort is made to seem more like a history painting than like a miniature. The relation between these portraits gets lost beneath the illusion that the historical one, which is the family's centerpiece, is of a higher order.

In a provocative reading of the portraits in *Frankenstein*, Marie-Hélène Huet finds "the dark desire to reproduce without the other" imaged in the portraits as an effort "to erase the paternal image, to dispel the disquieting presence of a silent father."[13] By contrast, I read these portraits not in terms of the "monstrous births" of the female imagination, but in terms of the theatricality of class. "The fact of increased upward mobility is at once the premise of 'bourgeois ideology'—that anyone can succeed—and its prime source of social anxiety," explains John Guillory; "Hence the continuous appropriation by the bourgeoisie of aristocratic caste traits, precisely in order to reinforce and stabilize a class structure founded upon a necessary degree of instability or fluidity."[14] Likewise in a culture where the consumption of art was increasingly a middle-class province, portraiture helped affirm the naturalness of upward social mobility. The historical style wove a spell of prestige around portraiture, and history painting, made smaller, more private, more sentimental, invited consumers into the genre's air of elitism. This helps explain Victor's programmatic response to the picture of his mother, with its "air of dignity and beauty," as opposed to the strange fit of passion evoked by the miniature of William. As Colin Campbell notes, the aristocratic sensibility is an ethic of restraint that rejects "excess of emotion" as "unseemly and ungentlemanly."[15] Yet this discrimination notwithstanding, the upward mobility promoted by the historical portrait is threatened by the representational reality of the miniature. Mobility can go either way; artistic genres, and the people they represent, can fall just as easily as they can rise. Ironically, the elite "historical subject" denotes such a fall in the form of Caroline's ruined, and now dead, father—"a merchant, who, from a flourishing state, fell, through numerous mischances, into poverty" (63). Caroline's portrait restages a scene of mourning: the pose is heroic and dignified, but the content recalls the tenuousness of her life of privilege. As summarized by this picture, the elevation of the consumer entailed the collapse of an ideal of natural rank, a collapse as threatening to those born into status as to those who have achieved it.

The indeterminate boundary between natural and achieved status, between an aristocratic and a consumerist sensibility, characterizes the narrative dimension of this particular portrait. It depicts a pivotal moment in the Frankenstein family history: Alphonse Frankenstein's abandonment of civic life for private life. The painting's origins are rehearsed by Victor, who begins by describing his father's life of public service: "My father had filled several public situations with honour and reputation. He was respected by all who knew him for his integrity and indefatigable attention to public business. He passed his younger days perpetually occupied by the affairs of his country; and it was not until the decline of life that he thought of marrying, and bestowing on the state sons who might carry his virtues and his name down to posterity" (63). Even family, in this description, is conceived within the parameters of civic virtue, with the pursuit of self-perpetuation figured as a gift to the state.[16] But it is not until Alphonse encounters the mourning daughter of his good friend (the encounter that supplies the impetus for the painting) that he retires into private life:

> Her father died in her arms, leaving her an orphan and a beggar. This last blow overcame her; and she knelt by Beaufort's coffin, weeping bitterly, when my father entered the chamber. He came like a protecting spirit to the poor girl, who committed herself to his care, and after the interment of his friend he conducted her to Geneva,

> and placed her under the protection of a relation. Two years after this event Caroline became his wife.
>
> When my father became a husband and a parent, he found his time so occupied by the duties of his new situation, that he relinquished many of his public employments. (64)

By idealizing the moment that leads to Alphonse's relinquishment of "public employments" for life as "a husband and a parent," the portrait commemorates the retirement to private life of the Frankenstein family. But hanging in the drawing room, the most public of rooms within the private home, this portrayal of his manly altruism also becomes a kind of public performance. Caroline's mourning is staged for the portrait sitting; and the picture itself perpetuates Alphonse's original performance of benevolence, when he "rescues her from the painful fate of working-class womanhood."[17] Caroline is thus preserved as an image of feminine vulnerability, and the viewer becomes a latter-day "protecting spirit." (One suspects that Alphonse is not painted in the background gazing upon his future wife, but rather that the viewer is meant simply to "become" him.) Private virtue emerges as a reproducible performance, enabled by the fact that culture gives patterns for pathos. This is reaffirmed by the repetition of Caroline's pose (kneeling by her dead father "in an agony of despair") by various characters throughout the novel. Its iconic origin may be the scientist hanging over his yet-unliving Creature, but it reappears when Victor discovers the murdered Elizabeth—he "hung over her in the agony of despair" (220)—and yet again at the end of the novel, when Walton encounters the Creature, "hung over the coffin" of the dead Victor" (242). The repetition of this pose narrows the gap between the material portrait (which is hung) and the living individual (who "hangs" over). Private virtue becomes a mere pose that can be emulated by practically anyone. There is nothing natural about its practice, and the social distinction that accrues to it is neither preordained nor permanent.

If historical portraiture lifts the consumer into the elite sphere of history painting while mystifying the influence of consumerism, the story of miniature painting lays that influence bare. To the extent that larger portraits can help to naturalize class position, this naturalization depends on concealing the fact that, in Lynch's words, "Faces made money—the overloaded faces of the popular print market and the minutely detailed portraits that Reynolds relegated to the bottom of the artistic barrel especially so."[18] Miniature painting foregrounded this fact. It was a profit-driven field whose practitioners refused any claim to "original genius." Studio work was rushed; it was not uncommon to paint over ten portraits a day. Neoclassical principles served lucrative ends, as the ideal of "generality" enabled artists to save on labor by letting ivory show through in the face.[19] Generalization increased production, which in turn made miniatures yet more affordable. The oil painter Martin Archer Shee writes in a note to his *Rhymes on Art*: "From the prompt means of subsistence which miniature-painting affords to every manufacturer of a face, it will always be the refuge of imbecility; a receptacle for the poor and disappointed in art, [for] all who want vigour that impels to higher game, or the means to support a larger pursuit. . . . [I]f their fame be more confined, their profit is less precarious."[20] As Shee indicates, miniatures were associated with an erasure of class distinctions, their popularity viewed as a sign of flagging national potency in the arts. His class snobbery is only in part a defensive reaction to the incursion of miniature painting on his own profits; it also responds to the way the practice of miniature painting threatened to unmask all portrait practice as the kind of mercenary service industry Hazlitt would later describe: "The 'numbers without number' who pay thirty, forty, fifty, a hundred guineas for their pictures in large, expect their faces to come out of the Painter's hands smooth, rosy, round, smiling; just as they expect their hair to come out of the barber's curled and powdered. It would be a breach of contract to proceed in any other way. A fashionable Artist and a fashionable hair-dresser have the same common principles of theory and practice; the one fits his customers to appear with *éclat* in a ball-room, the other in the Great Room of the Royal Academy."[21] The portrait painter and the hairdresser, according to Hazlitt, are essentially similar: while both create mass-produced images that mime individuality, they actually fit customers into a culturally scripted formula for prestige. It is this unsettling possibility—that portraits are mere commodities that assist the effort "to appear with *éclat*"—that emerges in the Frankensteins' drawing room. There the juxtaposition of historical portrait and miniature reveals a latent similarity that upsets not just the aristocratic air of historical portraiture, but the natural appearance of middle-class achievement.

This similarity, and the Frankensteins' compulsion to conceal it, gets rehearsed in the saga of Justine Moritz, who is accused of coveting a miniature portrait of Caroline Beaufort. This is the tiny picture that the Creature rips from William's neck. Its discovery in Justine's pocket is the main reason that she is accused of William's murder; at her trial this miniature alone seems to testify against her. "I know . . . how heavily and fatally this one circumstance weighs against me, but I have no power of explaining it," Justine says, "I am only left to conjecture concerning the probabilities by which it might have been placed in my pocket" (111). The miniature achieves its highest value as forensic evidence. Yet it, too, operates within a network of class definition, for while the miniature found in Justine's pocket is evidence of her guilt, it also provides the Frankensteins with evidence of their own social status. Justine, in effect, is accused of coveting not just the portrait, but Caroline's standing. Her personal history is particularly threatening to the bourgeois ideology of upward mobility: Justine was not born to servitude, but rather, after the death of her father, was adopted by the Frankensteins and in time "learned the duties of a servant." In other words, she falls into servitude by learning the role. But the theatricality of her class position hits a telling contradiction in her near-perfect imitation of Caroline Beaufort's "phraseology and manners"—mimicry so skilled that "her mien and expressions continually remind" Elizabeth of her "dear aunt" (94). While learning how to be a servant, Justine also learns how to emulate her mistress. In Shelley's time the emulative, aspiring servant exposed the inherent dangers of social mobility and as a consequence, Campbell explains, commentators "were quick to presume that imitative conduct revealed the presence of emulative motives," biased in part by a "jealous regard for their own privileges, combined with an intense anxiety about the stability of the social order."[22] Justine, who epitomizes the fluidity of status, can therefore be seen to enact its ambiguous mobilities.

A servant's imitation of her employer did not necessarily imply emulative desires. Amanda Vickery notes that maids regularly accepted trinkets and clothes as gifts, but rather than desiring "legitimacy" they were often more attracted by the gifts' resale value: "Clothing was seen as an important part of their *earnings*, rather than merely the coveted equipment of social emulation."[23] If the Frankensteins view Justine as emulative, their suspicion might be seen as a response to the disconcerting fact that class signifiers (Justine's as well as their own) are mobile and not class-bound. They provide a case in point for the paradoxical way that social mobility encourages the reassertion of artificial distinctions and fosters a bias against possible upstarts. When William is discovered, the Frankensteins, quite remarkably, are unable to see beyond the miniature in their search for motives. Alphonse reports that on the evening of William's murder the boy "had teazed [Elizabeth] to let him wear a very valuable miniature that she possessed of [Caroline]," adding: "This picture is gone, and was doubtless the temptation which urged the murderer to the deed" (100). Elizabeth, too, as Kate Ellis notes, "immediately blames herself for having given [William] the miniature to wear" rather than thinking "to find little William's true murderer."[24] The portrait loses its function within a cult of remembrance for the dead mother. It is "teazed away" by William; Elizabeth refers to it as a "bauble" (112); and Justine, wondering how it wound up in her pocket, calls it a "jewel" (111). Value seeps outward, from the picture to the jeweled frame that encases it, until Elizabeth finally dismisses it as "a few jewels" (122). With commodity value (its jeweled case) that supersedes its symbolic value, the miniature is, in Alphonse's eyes, only desirable to a female servant. Social mobility requires the production of a new "other," and Justine becomes that figure. An unattached female "sleeping around" (in the barn), whose sexuality the Creature discerns when he places the miniature "securely in one of the folds of her dress" (170), Justine undermines patriarchal privilege in two registers: as an independent female sexuality who can unsettle patrilinear lines of inheritance, and as a servant capable of "acting" the part of privilege. Having so skilfully imitated her benefactress, Justine effectively stands in for the Creature who declares desire for her, becoming in Alphonse's words a repository of "depravity and ingratitude" (108).

Like the miniature style of portraiture with which she is linked, Justine reveals the unnerving truth about mobility—namely, that it moves in multiple directions. Even the well-intentioned Elizabeth, who comes to believe that Justine is innocent of murder, never quite absolves her of the robbery. Despite her impassioned defense of her "more than sister" (115), to the end Elizabeth assumes that Justine did, indeed, covet the miniature, all the while emphasizing her own solicitude and freedom from such material wants. Elizabeth "would have willingly given [the miniature] to her," she says—if only she'd known the "poor girl" so "earnestly desired" it (112, 108). Just as William's miniature portrait is cordoned off as "common" to foster an artificial distinction, Justine has to be characterized as different, as somebody with a penchant for debased, material objects.

Instead of establishing lineage, the portraits in *Frankenstein* register genealogical ruptures. The historical portrait of Caroline Beaufort figures Alphonse not as a husband, but as a surrogate father. Meanwhile, the purloined miniature bearing Caroline's likeness emphasizes that, for Elizabeth as for Justine, "belonging" is less a matter of resemblance than of possession.[25] Both women are products of benevolent paternalism, and Justine's death seems to magnify Elizabeth's own insecurity. "She had become grave," Victor recalls, "and often conversed of the inconstancy of fortune, and the instability of human life" (121). For all her rhetoric of distinction, Elizabeth is not so far removed from Justine.

Or, as it happens, from the Creature. U. C. Knoepflmacher has argued that "the beautiful and passive Elizabeth and the repulsive, aggressive Monster who will be her murderer" are doubles, a claim that might seem surprising given the contrast between their verbal portraits.[26] The Creature's portrait, as told by Victor, parodies idealized beauty: "His limbs were in proportion, and I had selected his features as beautiful. Beautiful!—Great God! His yellow skin scarcely covered the work of muscles and arteries beneath; his hair was of a lustrous black, and flowing; his teeth of a pearly whiteness; but these luxuriances only formed a more horrid contrast with his watery eyes, that seemed almost of the same colour as the dun white sockets in which they were set, his shrivelled complexion, and straight black lips" (86). Conversely, the angelic portrait of the "uncommonly lovely" Elizabeth that soon follows presents an "open and capacious forehead [that] gave indications of a good understanding, joined to great frankness of disposition. Her eyes were hazel, and expressive of mildness. . . . Her hair was of a rich dark auburn, her complexion fair, and her figure slight and graceful" (108). A commentator for the *London Magazine*, who snidely wrote that "Poetry, and novels and romances, have made a certain combination of auburn hair, blue eyes, Greek noses, and pearl teeth, an indispensable part of the *materièl* of true love," could hardly have wished for a more revealing contrast.[27] Unlike the Creature's portrait, with its numerous but disharmonic parts, the absence of particularity in Elizabeth's portrait makes clear the moral evaluations that attend aesthetic description: loveliness, understanding, and frankness are allied with the supposedly "beautiful" qualities of mildness, slightness, and grace. In the 1831 version, Elizabeth is even said to wear "a crown of distinction" that marks her as naturally elite.[28]

Notwithstanding the stark aesthetic contrast, Elizabeth and the Creature share affinities with the category of the miniature. Stuck in a diminutive domestic sphere, Elizabeth laments her lack of "opportunities of enlarging her experience" (180). Victor reinforces the miniature association by describing her as "gay and playful as a summer insect" (65)—an epithet he also directs, with a difference, at the Creature, whom he calls a "vile insect" (27). As with the portraits on the drawing-room wall, the adjectival distinction is less significant than the common identity: as "insects," Elizabeth and the Creature are both miniatures of a kind. No wonder, then, that the Elizabeth of idealizing portraiture can be reframed by the murderous Creature as a gothic portrait, or that, in the prevailing artistic discourse of 1818 to which I now turn, the Creature would be a "monstrous miniature."[29]

Overloaded Marbles

Victor Frankenstein describes himself as "an artist occupied by his favourite employment" (85), and in constructing the novel's most famous "likeness," he faces the artist's dilemma of how to balance the objective of a beautiful representation with the practical matters of time, labor, and media. Because, in his words, "the minuteness of the parts formed a great hindrance to my speed," he resolves "to make the being of a gigantic stature; that is to say, about eight feet in height, and proportionably large" (82). Gigantism offers a practical solution to the expenditures of labor; it is faster and easier to work with larger parts.[30]

But the ultimate cost is aesthetic, as Hazlitt claims in his *Examiner* article on the Elgin Marbles (June 30, 1816). He contends that large paintings are better than small ones not because of their size alone, but because they provide more room for the artist to furnish details and particulars. Size does not "substitute for grandeur," he says, but rather "assists" it by providing more space for the artist "to finish, fill up, and enrich every part as much as possible"—that is, to load every rift with ore. Hazlitt extends his consideration of the "colossal height" of the marbles to the question of portraiture, vis-à-vis epic art:

> A miniature is inferior to a full-sized picture, not because it does not give the large and general outline, but because it does not give the smaller varieties and finer elements of nature. . . . [T]he copy of a good portrait will always make a highly-finished miniature, but the copy of a good miniature, if enlarged to the size of life, will make but a very vapid portrait. Some of our own Artists, who are fond of painting large figures, either misunderstand or misapply this principle. They make the whole figure gigantic, not that they may have room for nature, but for the motion of their brush, regarding the quantity of canvas they have to cover as an excuse for the slovenly and hasty manner in which they cover it; and thus in fact leave their pictures nothing at last but monstrous miniatures.[31]

The irony is that the gigantic Creature shares the qualities of Hazlitt's "monstrous miniatures." Notwithstanding Victor's effort to "select . . . his features as beautiful," the Creature is at once made on a grand scale, but also lacks "the smaller varieties and finer elements of nature." James Whale's Frankenstein films of the 1930s, which depict the monster with smooth, powder-white skin set off against distinct sutures, had the visual aesthetics right after all. His surface mass is largely blank, void of details, which enables the hideous "work of muscles and arteries beneath" the skin to obtrude upon the sight. This is different from the effect of Swift's Brobdignagian women, who horrify because of their magnified particularity: "so coarse and uneven, so variously coloured when I saw them near, with a Mole here and there as broad as a Trencher, and Hairs hanging from it thicker than Pack-threads."[32] The viscera of Shelley's Creature stand out because there is nothing to distract from them: the aesthetic surface (the "yellow skin" that "scarcely covered" him) is too thin. He is autonomously deconstructing. In Swift, details are disgusting; in Shelley, the inadequacy of details allows more disgusting ones to emerge.

As Hazlitt indicates, the Elgin Marbles organized arguments about particularity and generality, serving in Jacob Rothenberg's words "as a focal point around which the most significant aesthetic and critical issues of the day were fought out."[33] I now turn briefly to contemporaneous discussions of the marbles as a major expression of the late-romantic reform aesthetic on display in *Frankenstein*.[34] Like Shelley's Creature, the marbles embodied an incipient "realism" that was said to be rude and unmannered, or in the words of a popular anecdote (quoted as an epigraph), "Broken" and "like life." Byron parodied their aesthetics, calling them "Phidian freaks, / Misshapen monuments and maim'd antiques," and Sir George Beaumont wished them restored to Greece, not because of cultural politics but because "they excite rather disgust than pleasure in the minds of people in general, to see parts of limbs, & bodys, stumps of arms, &c.—"[35] Their advocates, however, praised them for these very reasons. As witnesses testifying to their value before the Select Committee of the House of Commons, the portrait painter Thomas Lawrence cited their "great truth and imitation of nature," and the Italian sculptor Canova referred to their "perfect flesh," adding: "Every thing here breathes life."[36] Those who championed the marbles saw them as combining mimetic naturalness with a stylistic grandeur that incorporated details, rather than leaving them out.

As such, the collection was an affront to the prevailing Reynoldsian aesthetic. The Elgin Marbles, Hazlitt writes, "repudiate [the] doctrine" according to which "grandeur of style consists in giving only the *masses*, and leaving out the details." Such disapprobation was implicitly political. As Paul Magnuson observes, to call Reynolds's ideal into question was "to challenge the Royal Academy that had supported it and the system of patronage that in turn supported the Royal Academy." Hazlitt's complaint about how Reynolds's "principle of conformity" at once excludes a "principle of contrast, of discrimination and identity" and the corporeal intensity of these "living men turned to stone" registers a preference that is also a protest against academic authority.[37]

The protest is sharpened by its appeal to natural philosophy. Arguing that each statue, "instead of being a block of marble," has an "internal machinery of nerves and muscles," Hazlitt emphasizes a fluidity between marble and nerves, man and stone. The anatomist's encounter with "the coats of the stomach laid bare" or "the transverse section of the brain" furnishes a model for artistic creation. "Art is the microscope of the mind," Hazlitt writes, situating Percy Shelley's claims for the power of poetry in a scientific context; it "may be said to draw aside the veil from nature."[38] If Reynoldsian portraiture removed an individual's deformities, this alternative aesthetic brought them into the open. Art is said to comprise a surgical penetration through layers of idealization and custom—Burke's decent drapery, or Reynolds's general air—to an elemental nature that exists prior to such superadded strata. To such connoisseurs as Richard Payne Knight, testifying before the select parliamentary committee (and not inclined to endorse the greatest treasure of a bourgeois exhibition culture), the value of the marbles is uncertain because "their surface is gone mostly."[39] But this is precisely the appeal for such advocates as Hazlitt. To him, the marbles are beautiful because their veins and muscles, bones, bowels, and intestines, are visible to the eye. They turn the body inside out, demystifying depth by making it visible. By reading in the marbles the underlying equality of human bodies, Hazlitt defines a progressive aesthetic that promotes the exposure and synthesis of anatomical details (their active "enlightenment"), rather than the naked authority of the central form.[40]

Yet even this is figured as a distinctively masculine impression of power. The machismo underpinning Hazlitt's rhetoric is evident in his dismissal of the *Apollo Belvedere* as "a modern fine gentleman" and "a theatrical coxcomb." Preferring instead the marbles' "negligent grandeur and manly strength," Hazlitt expresses a preference for the particular, not so much as a brand of realism but as an effect of imaginative force. His meticulous descriptions that laud the marbles' scientific exactness, their "loose folds in the skin [and] veins under the belly," reveal a paradox. The turn toward mimetic precision is inclusive of aesthetic details, and yet it is exclusive in its representation not just *of* men, but also *for* men: "Let any one, for instance, look at the leg of the Ilissus or River-God, which is bent under him—let him observe the swell and undulation of the calf, the inter-texture of the muscles, the distinction and union of all the parts, and the effect of action every where impressed on the external form, as if the very marble were a flexible substance, and contained the various springs of life and motion within itself, and he will own that art and nature are here the same thing."[41] Hazlitt corroborates Magnuson's argument that to "both liberals and conservatives, [the marbles] embodied all forms of liberty, including sensuality."[42] But even the sensuality that the marbles seem to license signifies a very limited ideal of liberty, one that can be seen to reaffirm the status quo. By fixating on a "principle of fusion, of motion, so that the marble flows like a wave [with] all the flexibility, all the malleableness of flesh," Hazlitt delineates a gendered anatomical aesthetic, a male gaze enamored of male particulars.[43]

Hazlitt's dismissive attitude toward the *Apollo Belvedere* epitomizes a romantic prejudice against neoclassicism and suggests a gendered preference for genius over fashion. Above all, however, it reveals the influence of Hogarth, who bequeaths to Hazlitt not just an aesthetic program but also a tacit, counter-establishment politics. It is from Hogarth that Hazlitt inherits his preference for particularity, roughness, even crudeness; and the insistent masculinity of his spectatorship can be seen as an outright rejection of Burkean "beauty" along with the reliance of establishment aesthetics on a conception of the art object as feminine.[44] Hazlitt's masculine erotics of viewing suggests an effort aligned with a Hogarthian countertradition, in its move toward a rougher conception of the aesthetic.

This turn could take on an explicitly populist dimension in postwar Britain, a fact that is even more pronounced in some of the marbles' other advocates. Take Benjamin Haydon, whose first sight of the marbles provoked an impassioned response—first, to the representation of female figures: "The first thing I fixed my eyes on was the wrist of a figure . . . in which were visible, though in a feminine form, the radius and the ulna. I was astonished, for I had never seen them hinted at in any female wrist in the antique. I darted my eye to the elbow, and saw the outer condyle visibly affecting the shape as in nature. I saw that the arm was in repose and the soft parts in relaxation. That combination of nature and idea which I had felt was so much wanting for high art was here displayed to midday conviction. My heart beat!" Haydon's response is conditioned by his trade: he reads the statues with an artist's eye. Yet his tone shifts palpably in the face of masculine figures:

> If I had seen nothing else I had beheld sufficient to keep me to nature for the rest of my life. But when I turned to the Theseus and saw that every form was altered by action or repose,—when I saw that the two sides of his back varied, one side stretched from the shoulder-blade being pulled forward, and the other side compressed from the shoulder-blade being pushed close to the spine as he rested on his elbow, with the belly flat because the bowels fell into the pelvis as he sat,—and when, turning to the Ilissus, I saw the belly protruded, from the figure lying on its side,—and again, when in the figure of the fighting metope I saw the muscle shown under the one arm-pit in that instantaneous action of darting out, and left out in the other arm-pits because not wanted—when I saw, in fact, the most heroic style of art combined with all the essential detail of actual life, the thing was done at once and for ever.
>
> Here were principles which the common sense of the English people would understand.[45]

British "common sense," which prefers a realism whose "actual life" is represented in "the most heroic style of art," is activated in a trained male gaze on male anatomy.[46] Though the female forms are "sufficient" for Haydon, he sees more—and more detail—in the male. The marbles focus an aesthetic of particularity that brings depth to the surface—an "aesthetics," to quote Paulson on Hogarth, "of seeing under or into," which emphasizes an underlying human "nature" that is good, innocent, and replete with rights.[47] Haydon hints at the practical extension of such an aesthetic: "The Elgin Marbles will as completely overthrow the old antique, as ever one system of philosophy overthrew another more enlightened."[48] The marbles' "realism" serves national self-definition; it is, in Haydon's estimation, peculiarly *English*.

For all his passion, though, Haydon's preference for details also suggests another destination for anatomical extravagance, one that verges on monstrosity. Of the Farnese *Hercules*, Hazlitt complains that its "ostentatious and over-laboured display of anatomy . . . is so overloaded with sinews, that . . . if life could be put into it, it would be able to move."[49] If such criticism barely conceals his enthusiasm for an art that extols details over an idealized central form, it also reveals misgivings. Whereas Haydon recalls how, when studying the Elgin Marbles at night, "a transcendant limb, here and there a shattered head . . . instinct with life, have trembled into light, and seemed ready to move, so evident was their life and circulation"; and the poet William Haygarth extols the way "the metopés / Start into ambient air, and breathe with life," Hazlitt shrinks at the thought that representation might take on an uncontrollable life of its own.[50] He seems disturbed not just by the visibility of all this effort—which seems to reveal the achievability of "high art" to the detriment of a romantic ideal of the natural genius—but also by the ease with which an aesthetic that accents the bodily detail can slip into caricature. In contrast to Hazlitt's romantic emphasis on the synthesis of details, caricature magnifies the part at the expense of the whole. Its truth claim, Lynch relates, depends on the rejection of synthesis in favor of representational surplus.[51] As the grotesquerie of the surface, caricature brings to light a significant repression within the glorification of classical statuary, namely, that even the internality and depth it posits is an external effect. The "ostentatious," "over-laboured," and "overloaded" *Hercules* reveals an unstable boundary between the high-art "realism" of sculpture and the low-art likenesses of caricature.

Yet this instability was an integral, if often unspoken, aspect of the anti-establishment aesthetic embodied by the marbles. For although the controversy that surrounded the marbles focused on British cultural imperialism, there was also the sense that latent in their aesthetics were the seeds of a populist aesthetic—if not exactly radical, then certainly volatile, nonetheless. The writings that champion the marbles register the same, affected nationalism of Allan Cunningham's Reform-era memoir of Hogarth, in which he calls that artist "the spontaneous offspring of the graphic spirit of his country, as native to the heart of England as independence is."[52] Keats's sonnet "Addressed to Haydon" lauds their purchase as, in John Kandl's words, "a national plebeian victory," praising Haydon as a "stout unbending champion" for whom "unnumbered souls breathe out a still applause" (lines 11, 13). Haydon is said to exalt the "high-mindedness" of "people of no name, / In noisome alley, and in pathless wood" (lines 3–4). The marbles, Keats implies, are not "freaks" (as Byron would have it), whose mutilated bodies can only bear value in their original Athenian context; they are, rather, "relics of former grandeur bearing the aura of ancient Greek liberty."[53] Barry Cornwall's poem, "On the Statue of THESEUS in the Elgin Collection of Marbles," ironically figures the statue of the famously tyrannical Athenian king first as a revolutionary (against a Roman god), and then as a victim of monarchical discipline:

> —Aye, this is he—
>   A proud and mighty spirit:—how fine his form
> Gigantic!—moulded like the race that strove
> To take Jove's heaven by storm, and drive him from
> Olympus. . . .
> . . . .
> His mighty Sire, in anger when he saw
> How dark his course and impious, must have stay'd
> (So carv'd to nature is that Phidian stone)
> The flow of life, and with his trident-touch
> Have *struck him into marble.* (lines 1–5; 16–20)

While developing the motif of the marbles' naturalism by staying the flow of life, Cornwall's antiestablishment figurations emphasize that the marbles' visual realism generates political meanings. Haydon similarly argues that embedded within their sublimity is a "fire" and "rashness of violence" that Phidias manages to contain, but that poor imitators might carry "to a vicious excess."[54] After Waterloo, when popular attention returned with a fury to the shortcomings of the home government, such terms as "violence" and "excess" were fraught with insurgent connotations. The expansive and inclusive frame of the novel, the vogue for grand-scale theatrical spectacle, and a trend toward oversized group portraits—all cultural versions of the activism for parliamentary reform—exemplify how excess functions as a trope for a public culture deemed potentially violent in the post-Napoleonic moment. It is this same charged vocabulary that Shelley brings to life in her 1818 novel, by allegorizing what I call a reform aesthetic in the body of her most famous character.[55]

Monstrous Realism

Through the trope of portraiture, Shelley develops the anatomical aesthetic associated with the marbles into a theory of the novel. Reviewing Godwin's *Cloudesly* in 1829, she turns portraiture and anatomy into twin metaphors for novel writing. Godwin's "portraiture is endowed with the very essence and spirit of our nature," she writes; "he conceives, in its entireness, the living picture of an event with all its adjuncts; he sets it down in its vivid reality: no part is dim, no part is tame."[56] Like the Elgin Marbles, whose anatomical realism brings them to the brink of life—and like Shelley's own Creature, himself a "living picture"—Godwin's "portraiture" represents the "machinery of nerves" beneath the skin of his subject. Reading him, Shelley writes, "we felt . . . that we wandered among giants' rocks, 'the naked bones of the world waiting to be clothed' " (713).

Shelley, however, does not promote "realism" as a passive form of mimesis, but instead praises what she calls Godwin's "master art" for following "rules of grouping or colouring." Though lauding Sir Walter Scott's "individual portraiture," she adds that his "wholes want keeping"—thus echoing Walton in *Frankenstein*, whose "extended and magnificent dreams" are said to "want (as the painters call it) *keeping*."[57] Godwin, on the other hand, "sketches in his own mind, with a comprehensive and bold imagination, the plan of his work; he digs at the foundations . . . examines his materials, and sees exactly to what purpose each is best fitted." Unlike Victor, who carelessly speeds to the larger, more general parts, Godwin is meticulously detailed: "He transfuses himself into the very souls of his personages; he dives into their secret hearts, and lays bare, even to their anatomy, their workings; not a pulsation escapes him,—while yet all is blended into one whole, which forms the pervading impulse of the individual he brings before us" (712). Again, portraiture—bringing an "individual . . . before us"—is presented as the novelist's filthy task. The overhasty Victor, for his part, lacks the requisite imaginative sensitivity; he fails to blend his materials "into one whole," to "transfuse himself into the very soul" of his Creature. Shelley's discussion of *Cloudesly* promotes the going out of the self as the basis for a radical realism that entails an aesthetic of sympathy and affection rather than of power.[58] Godwin is said to evoke an inclusive ideal through a broad scope of imaginatively realized detail. Unlike Reynoldsian portraiture, which works to conceal distasteful particulars in the service of promoting an elite vision of the body politic, Godwin's "living picture" brings the diverse elements of society to life as a unified whole.

Characterizing the novelist as both portraitist and resurrectionist, Shelley resuscitates a key context for *Frankenstein* that bears directly on her reform aesthetic: the phenomenon of bodysnatching, which as Tim Marshall has established, contributes to that novel's representation of anatomical science. A notorious problem in Shelley's time, bodysnatching was encouraged by medical schools and the emerging discipline of anatomy. Its prominence led to heated parliamentary debates and, ultimately, the Anatomy Act of 1832, which provided for the legal sale of state-institutionalized bodies to British medical schools.[59] "The distribution of political power in the reformed electorate," Ruth Richardson argues, "closely resembled the redistribution of risk decreed by the Anatomy Act"; for if Reform married the upper gentry with the aristocracy in order to guard the rights of property against the claims of the working class, the Anatomy Act, by "demarcating and isolating the propertyless as its victims," effectively "bought off the allegiance of the propertied classes with legal apparatus to protect their defunct remains."[60] Despite the fact that, prior to the Anatomy Act, all social classes were potential victims of graverobbers, the poor were by far the most vulnerable. This was due to the development of sturdy coffins that allowed those with means to purchase a sense of funerary security. Such inventions were all the rage; in the year of *Frankenstein*'s initial publication, for instance, Edward Bridgman's "Patent Coffin" made a sensational debut, and broadsheet poems celebrated Bridgman as a "prince of coffin makers" for an intricate, wrought-iron design with "concealed spring catches on the inner side of the lid" to "prevent levering," and which were "joined in such a way as to thwart any attempt to force the sides of the coffin apart."[61] But since such inventions were beyond the means of the working classes, when Victor "dabbled among" the "damps of the grave," he came away primarily with a particular class of corpse. Contrary to Lee Sterrenburg's claim that Shelley's novel "serves to depoliticize the monster tradition," the Creature animates the "realism" of the Elgin Marbles in/as a political body.[62] Transforming physiological aesthetics into a "reform aesthetic," the novel engages debates over the right of the working class to vote that had raged since the 1790s.

The several cartoons that labeled the Reform Bill a "Political Frankenstein," then, while rightly sensing the rise of the politically repressed, can also be understood to be inexact.[63] The framers of the Bill were careful to exclude the bodies with which Frankenstein made his Creature. These base materials are only "landed" in the material sense, having been exhumed from the property that defines their absence from the body politic. Despite Victor's effort to reintegrate them so as to keep distasteful, defective, or deformed particularities out of sight, the Creature's thin, translucent skin opens up to view an inner space of muscles, organs, and veins that recedes toward the microscopic. This anatomical realism, verging on sublimity, usurps the neoclassical order. Like Lord Elgin's "Phidian freaks," the Creature brings to light the particularities that Reynolds's drapery had sought to conceal. Portraiture summons the specter of the missing original even as it eradicates that original. But the Creature does not embody the absence of any one person; rather he evokes a plurality of absences. He literalizes the dictum that portraiture invokes the absence of its subject by the fact that the subject in this case is already an absence, politically speaking. Sutured together with negative presences, this heteroglossic body discloses the pleasing illusions of an idealizing portraiture. Even though he is outwardly denied class identity, the Creature, as an assemblage of exposed viscera, figures the "ugly" potential for working-class political visibility. His vivified body gives life to an aesthetic of particularity, thus presenting the ultimate threat to middle-class stability.[64]

Read alongside this culture of bodysnatching, Shelley's reanimation of portraiture as a charged and flexible metaphor in her review of *Cloudesly* suggests how "realism" as a novelistic mode could, at its best, facilitate a democratic aesthetics based on sympathy. More than a decade before, she had anticipated this vision in *Frankenstein* by affirming and even amplifying the liberal attack on Reynoldsian portraiture as an establishment aesthetic. The appearance of Shelley's Creature is characterized neither by the idealized generality of neoclassicism nor by the synthesized particularity of Hazlitt's naturalism, but rather by a radical accessibility that resists containment and synthesis, as it invites overflow and spillage. Whereas Burke had mystified the British polity as "a permanent body composed of transitory parts" (*Reflections*, 33), Shelley responds by anatomizing that body politic, laying it bare in all its ugly and uncontrollable detail. Realism is a "consensually oriented" discourse, as Katherine Kearns puts it, that assumes a "congeniality among addressor and addressee."[65] Seen in this light, the Creature, as he faces the commonplace gaze of spectators, is all too real. His is a monstrous realism that, if it would ultimately assist the literary reproduction of a status quo (as many today argue), is shown here to carry an equally explosive potential to unveil a minutely detailed body politic that, once pieced together from the fragments of humanness the novel has to offer, would be difficult to suppress.

Shelley activates this metaphor for the radical inclusiveness that Bakhtin would come to associate with the novel almost in spite of her own ambivalence regarding parliamentary reform. Her later delight at the passage of "a Reform Bill which excluded the working classes from the vote," Johanna Smith argues, "demonstrates both her reformist enthusiasm for an extended franchise and her conservative relief that the more revolutionary bill was defeated."[66] Such ambivalence might be understood as an effect of Shelley's own economic uncertainty and dependence on the middle-class gift-book market. But if her personal situation left her exposed to the fluctuations of social mobility, it also made her a sensitive observer of middle-class anxiety, finely attuned to the radical possibilities of realistic representation. This sensitivity is perhaps best summarized by the encounter between the Creature and the miniature portrait of Caroline Beaufort. Unlike the rest of the Frankensteins, who refer to this miniature as a material quantity, the Creature is transfixed by its aesthetic quality: "As I fixed my eyes on the child, I saw something glittering on his breast. I took it; it was a portrait of a most lovely woman. In spite of my malignity, it softened and attracted me. For a few moments I gazed with delight on her dark eyes, fringed by deep lashes, and her lovely lips" (170). Like the Creature, Caroline's portrait is rhetorically transparent. She is a collection of visible parts: "dark eyes," "deep lashes," and "lovely lips." But the mirroring of the lovely miniature and the monstrous miniature is only momentary, for the picture soon becomes a revelatory portrait, its beauty giving way to the Creature's recognition of his own ugliness: "In regarding me," he realizes, she would "have changed that air of divine benignity to one expressive of disgust and affright" (170). The scene allegorizes the Creature's situation as the *disjecta membra* of society.[67] Comprehended only as the negative reflection of another's portrait, his visceral actuality forces itself on the sight of a social order effectively constituted by his exclusion. Seeing beauty for what it is, he simultaneously sees his own aesthetic—or counteraesthetic—power, which necessitates his alienation. For the Creature, the miniature holds out a pleasing illusion of social acceptance, a romance of "fitting" into a consensual economy of realism. But this illusion quickly fades, succumbing to the reality of a class- and genre-system that guards against the disruptive potentiality represented in extremis by his own body, the frighteningly mobile product of Frankenstein's unhallowed arts.

CHAPTER FIVE

The Look of a Poet: Wordsworth

> It is not enough for an artist to draw a cold map of the human countenance, and because he has placed the nose right, and the eyes not wrong, and opened a mouth where a mouth should be, to think he has done enough and wipe his brushes and desist. No, the genius of art must do more; we demand for Wordsworth, not a look equal to the management of the stamp revenue for Westmoreland alone, but something of that dignity of intellect which dictated his truly noble poems; we want a little inspiration; we desire such expression as will induce the spectator to say, "that is the look of a poet."
>
> —*The Athenæum*, on the portrait of Wordsworth (ca. 1832) painted for St. John's College, Cambridge, by Henry William Pickersgill

As a child, William Wordsworth entered his grandfather's drawing room and struck a whip through an ancestral portrait.[1] It would seem to have been a propitious episode, a precursor to his later call for poets to break with their "common inheritance."[2] But, recalling this encounter with portraiture more than seven decades later, Wordsworth—by this time England's Poet Laureate—repudiates the youthful act of rebellion, concluding his recollection of it on a caustic, dismissive note: "No doubt, though I have forgotten it, I was properly punished."[3] Endorsing a punishment that he cannot even remember, Wordsworth in his old age pointedly refuses to sanction a childhood uprising symbolized by violence against a family portrait.

It is a refusal in keeping with both the conservative spirit of Wordsworth's later career and the enormous influence of portraiture in defining that career for Victorian audiences. From 1830 on, Wordsworth turned more and more frequently to portrait painting as a topic for poetry, writing some dozen poems, mainly but not exclusively sonnets, based on painted portraits.[4] These poetic interests coincided with the proliferation of Wordsworth's own portrait. For even as he urged a decommercialization of poetry so that quality could prevail over sales, he sat for scores of portraits that promoted "Wordsworth" as literary merchandise. Read in tandem, these poems and paintings shed light on how he managed the intersection of poetic form and self-presentation to shape his later and eventually posthumous reputation.[5] They also elucidate a crucial moment in the career of the "romantic poet," when, iconized in "Wordsworth," its image was marketed to Victorian readers and prepared for future generations. Poems and portraits alike perpetuate a marketable self-presentation that could accommodate Wordsworth's status as an icon of domesticity and desire to be perceived as a culturally powerful man of genius. Together they merge what Felicia Hemans called "the true Poet at Home" with the poet of imagination, nourishing a celebrity that would culminate in his 1843 appointment as Poet Laureate.[6]

But this is not just a story about Wordsworth. It is also a story about anxieties pervasive within literary culture after 1832, with Wordsworth at the nucleus of a wider debate about the author's role as figurehead in an age of cultural democratization and (ongoing) political disenfranchisement. Especially at a time when arguments about the reform of copyright placed "original genius" in opposition to literary democratization—the solitary poet made the antithesis of an expanding reading public—Wordsworth's management of his public image, as well as the use of that image by others, summarizes a cultural nexus between romantic authorship and the circulation of goods. Following on the heels of the First Reform Bill, the debate over copyright adds an ironic dimension to Wordsworthian self-presentation: even as his authority as a "man of genius" was undone by illicit copies of his poems, he himself sanctioned the mass production of countless counterfeit "Wordsworths" designed to promote his work. At such cross-purposes, Wordsworth would make the poet a potent and autonomous public figure, even while recognizing his dependence on a series of commercial forces beyond his control. In what follows, I explore how Wordsworth dealt with this paradox—how the prototypical "Romantic" successfully negotiated a Victorian literary culture that would anoint him as England's national poet.

Fashioning "Wordsworth"

Wordsworth famously resented his lack of public stature, yet by the 1830s he was becoming a national icon. The public could view him by traveling to the Lake District—and many did—but more often, access to the poet was obtained by textual encounter: poems printed in newspapers and literary annuals. More and more, these poems were graced by portraits, as the "second self" constituted by his body of work was joined by the growing number of "Wordsworths" created by portrait painters.[7] Though not featured, like Dickens, in the poster portraits used in omnibuses to promote authors, small engravings that marketed the private man as a public icon made Wordsworth, by the end of his life, a familiar face.[8]

The best-known image of Wordsworth in his lifetime was Henry William Pickersgill's 1832 oil portrait, painted at the request of St. John's College, Cambridge.[9] Through its widespread dissemination as an engraving, the "St. John's Pickersgill" (as it is now called) became the dominant nineteenth-century image of Wordsworth (figure 33). It adorned his 1836 collection of *Poems* as a frontispiece engraved by W. H. Watt (the first time Wordsworth had authorized such a use of his engraving), and was subsequently reprinted in six more editions of his poems throughout the 1840s. The engraved portrait also turned up in gift-book "profiles," as the frontispiece for the first American edition of *Harper's Magazine* in 1850, and on the cover of the liberal philanthropic periodical *Social Notes* in 1879. The flocks of tourists at Rydal notwithstanding, the St. John's Pickersgill provided the primary means by which nineteenth-century readers saw Wordsworth.

Although its request by St. John's seemed to confirm Wordsworth's status as a national icon, his developing response to the portrait indicates concern regarding his increasing popularity. Unlike his poems, whose materiality he could mystify in a language of genius, portraits gave a "Wordsworth" of the surface, courting publicity even while subjecting his image to misappropriation. Wordsworth's handling of the promotional opportunity afforded by this portrait summarizes his ambivalence about a literary marketplace that rewards an author's willingness to undertake theatrical self-promotion.

A cosmospolitan painter of political and military worthies, Pickersgill had brought with him to Rydal, after a delay of over a year, both glamor and excitement. As Wordsworth's daughter Dora tells it, "The 10 days Mr Pickersgill was with us [were] the happiest and most memorable I had well nigh said, of my life." The preliminary chalk drawing that "Pick" (as Dora called him) completed was beloved by all the household: "All that I need say," she writes, "is none of the females of this house could gaze upon it for 5 minutes with eyes undimmed by tears—and as for mine I often wonder they were not washed out of their sockets quite."[10] Wordsworth gave a more stoic endorsement: "We all like it exceedingly," he wrote to the bookseller Edward Moxon, adding this awkward request: "In all probability it will be engraved, but not unless we could secure beforehand 150 Purchasers. I do not say *Subscribers* for it would not be asked as a favor. To further the intent may I beg of you to receive the names of such persons as it *might* suit, to write them down in your Shop? . . . [I]t is not wished to have a *Board* or Advertisement of this intention in your Shop, but merely that you should receive such Names as might offer" (*Later Years*, 2: 554–5). Wordsworth

FIG. 33. Henry William Pickersgill, *William Wordsworth*, 1833. (Courtesy of St. John's College, Cambridge)

envisions the portrait as more than a simple family piece. Engraved portraits were, to use his own word, "business" (3: 115). Yet here he betrays discomfort with the appearance of being marketed—or worse yet, *self*-marketing. On the one hand, he seeks a kind of independence in the marketplace, asking not for the "favor" of subscriptions but for actual purchasers. On the other hand, he seeks these phantom purchasers in the most discrete manner possible—to be advertised on "a *Board*" in a printing shop would be particularly disagreeable—as if Moxon could field unsolicited offers for a product that nobody knows exists. Wordsworth is well aware of the paradox: he wants his "head," as painted by the most fashionable portrait painter of the day, to be engraved and circulated as a public sign and vehicle of his greatness, yet this very circulation entails turning his image into a commodity that broadcasts his self-promotion.

As it happened, the picture was not engraved until 1836 (figure 34), by which time Wordsworth, as was his wont, had lost any affection he had had for it. Henry Crabb Robinson protested that the portrait made Wordsworth's eyes look sickly ("The picture wants an oculist," he wrote); the reviewer for the *Athenæum*, quoted in the epigraph, worried that it was too much the "stamp collector," not enough "the poet"; and when Wordsworth himself viewed the painting at St. John's in March 1835, he lamented its location—not in the prestigious Dining Hall but rather in an adjacent room for which it was "of too large a size." By 1840, Wordsworth was imagining opportunities to "revise" it: "If I go to London in the Spring, and my eyes should be in as good order as they are at present, the picture shall meet me there and I will get P. to retouch it." He wanted, as it were, to correct the proofs.[11]

But even as the family circle soured on the picture, the reading public came more and more to know it *as* Wordsworth, largely through engravings that ornamented the gift books' popular "profiles," and which were placed at the front of seven different authorized collections of his poems (1836, 1840, 1841, 1842, 1843, 1846, 1849). Put simply, Pickersgill's was the public face of "Wordsworth," in spite of the poet's ambivalence about this sign and vehicle of his fame. W. H. Watt's engraving, placed at the front of the 1836 *Poems*, exacerbated the problem by circulating what Wordsworth deemed an emasculated version of an original. The engraving has, he writes, "an air of feebleness" and "a weakness of expression about the upper lip." Reduced to a mere head, the poet appears as an image of "decrepitude"—the consequence, he claims, "of the whole Person not being given" (*Later Years*, 3: 304). In a letter to Moxon, he laments the "reclining attitude" (3: 307); months later, writing to his nephew Christopher, he repeats his dissatisfaction with its "air of decrepitude, and the maudlin expression about the upper lip" (3: 343–44). Not only did the engraving diminish—to the point of deleting—the poet's body, it also unnaturally magnified and fetishized a mere part of that body, the lip. There was something compromising about being represented as less than entire, as if a vigorous, laboring body (scaling Helvellyn or walking to and fro) were essential to the portrayal of the poet-at-work. At a time when British society was, to Wordsworth's mind, in need of guidance from "men of real power," he saw his image circulated publicly in a form that signified weakness.[12] Yet, remarkably, Wordsworth authorized the en-

FIG. 34. W. H. Watt, engraving after Henry William Pickersgill, 1835. Frontispiece to Volume I of *The Poetical Works of William Wordsworth*, 1843. (Courtesy of Department of Special Collections, Stanford University Libraries)

graving for six further editions of his works throughout the 1840s—this despite telling Christopher that "an engraving from [Frances] Chantrey's Bust shall replace it" should he "live to see another Ed[ition]" (*Later Years*, 3: 344). Chantrey's bust, which portrayed Wordsworth as a manly Roman senator, would in fact replace the Pickersgill on some editions, but not until 1845; in the meantime the poet had "lived to see" four new editions, each adorned with the fashionable St. John's Pickersgill. Like a gift-book "beauty," Wordsworth's reclining head was repeatedly displayed to catch the eyes of would-be readers.

But Wordsworth also aggressively sought to manage both the public and private dimensions of this image, an effort nowhere more apparent than in his sonnet "To the Author's Portrait," paired with the engraving at the front of his 1836 *Poetical Works*. While conceding his status as icon of the domestic sphere, this sonnet also joins that status to a more active political voice. The sonnet was originally composed in 1832, and in 1836 it became a vehicle through which Wordsworth attempted to accomplish several disparate, even contradictory tasks: first, transforming the Watt engraving's aura of sentimental weakness; second, codifying a Wordsworthian affect that transcends the mimesis of portraiture; and third, voicing a political position through a prototypically Wordsworthian finessing of historical chronology.

The dedicatory poem to *Poetical Works*, "To the Author's Portrait" appears overleaf from the sonnet-sized frontispiece, on the right-hand page.[13] The turn of the page marks a turn into poetry, as the portrait is covered over and left behind. But if the turn of the page *overlays* the portrait, the sonnet *overwrites* it:

> Go, faithful Portrait! and where long hath knelt
> Margaret, the saintly Foundress, take thy place;
> And, if Time spare the colours for the grace
> Which to the work surpassing skill hath dealt,
> Thou, on thy rock reclined, though kingdoms melt
> And states be torn up by the roots, wilt seem
> To breathe in rural peace, to hear the stream,
> And think and feel as once the Poet felt.
> Whate'er thy fate, those features have not grown
> Unrecognized through many a household tear
> More prompt, more glad to fall than drops of dew
> By morning shed around a flower half-blown;
> Tears of delight, that testified how true
> To life thou art, and, in thy truth, how dear![14]

It is important to note the multiple contexts for the sonnet. Written in response to Pickersgill's original chalk drawing in 1832, the poem as published in the dedication to the *Poetical Works* tacitly refers to the engraving with which it is paired. A closer look, however, reveals a lingering nostalgia for the original that it initially celebrated—for example, in the phrases "take thy place" (referring to the original to be hung at St. John's) and "spare the colours" (referring not to the colorless engraving but to a missing original).

The poem's political reference, too, is contemporaneous with the original painting. The apocalyptic vision of lines five through seven, with its "states . . . torn up by the roots," gestures toward the 1832 Reform Bill.[15] In a letter to Thomas Arnold (September 19, 1832) containing the sonnet, Wordsworth moves freely between the Pickersgill portrait and Arnold's support for Reform:

> We have had Mr Pickersgill with us who has done all that was needful on the spot and in my presence, towards completing a Portrait of me, for St John's Coll. The Likeness is said to be admirable, and every one is pleased w[it]h [it]. It will be engraved, if as we presume the College has no objection. Since your departure I have carefully read your Letters printed in the Sheffield paper. With a great portion of their Contents I can clearly agree, but there are points seeming to me material, on which you are for pushing change farther than I am prepared to go—I hope it will not be disagreeable to you and Mrs Arnold if I fill the remainder of this Sheet with a Sonnet called forth by the Pickersgill Picture.— [The sonnet follows, in full.][16]

What I find striking is the fact that, consciously or not, Wordsworth joins politics and portraiture: an argument about Reform participates in a sonnet about his own, soon to be circulated image. This conjunction spills into the sonnet, with its attempt to unite the public voice of lines five through seven with a self-portrait as a domestic icon. Though "kingdoms melt" and "states be torn up by the roots," Wordsworth finds salvation in the portrait, the pictorial version of stable subjecthood. Yet this static identity soon attenuates to a less certain "those features" (line 9), suggesting that this "second self" is secondary indeed: if the portrait is first addressed as the person in the portrait, reclining on a rock, it soon becomes mere features that can be copied and arranged.

This shift emphasizes that the preservation of "Wordsworth" depends on the affective power of likeness. In this regard the sonnet resembles the final movement of "Tintern Abbey," a poem in which Wordsworth famously turns to his sister as a vessel to sustain him, not only through the preceding dark "five years" (extending back to the start of the war with France), but through an uncertain future as well. The displacement of the political, as well as the salvation from it, depends on Wordsworth finding sustenance in a domestic sphere figured in pictorial terms: "Just as he had framed a 'picture of the mind' for his own memory," Susan Wolfson writes, "so now he frames and bequeaths this picture to the mansion of his sister's mind."[17]

Similarly, in the 1836 sonnet, the sustainer of the poet's "features" is the "household tear": "Tears of delight" that "testified how true / To life thou art, and in thy truth, how dear!" (lines 10, 13–14). Likeness elicits tears: the portrait and the Wordsworth women become his mutual preservers. Ironically, the portrait cannot *mean* much to a reader unable to compare its "likeness" to the original. It is only a familiarity with the original that gives the portrait its value. Yet these are not just the tears of Dorothy, Dora, and Mary; when the sonnet is made to refer to the engraving at the front of the book, it imagines these tears as belonging to *readers*. Wordsworth as domestic merchandise belongs to everyone. The volume becomes a vessel for the poet's fame, and also a dear domestic object, reproduced like Wedgwood china for display in the home. Figuring the nation as a private space, Wordsworth at once projects his unreproducible "originality" and codifies his status as national domestic object.

The conjunction of sentiment and nation was hardly unique to this moment in the history of Wordsworthian iconography; indeed, it continued to inform the nineteenth-century illustration of Wordsworth well beyond 1850 (and, some would argue, even through the present day). The countless unauthorized, illustrated editions published after the poet's death, reports Stephen Gill, show Wordsworth "as the celebrant of an idealized British rural life, of domestic virtues, of children and old age, and of benignity."[18] This is woman's poetic territory, and as Peter Manning argues, Wordsworth was "more than susceptible" to being read in a manner that violated his "repeated emphasis on his 'manly' style and ethical gravity."[19] In 1879, when *Social Notes* used as its cover design a copy (by W. Ballingall) of Watt's Pickersgill, surrounded by a Lake District scene complete with a humble cottage and a girl feeding her pet lamb (February 8, 1879), this sentimentalizing tendency reached a pinnacle. In the 1830s, however, debates over copyright reform gave Wordsworth an out. Arguing about a literary and political issue that shares a common vocabulary with the discourse of portraiture, Wordsworth discovered a site where he could project a different image: that of a poet whose prestige and cultural importance are said to derive from his powers of solitary absorption and originality. In copyright, Wordsworth engaged issues of democratization and originality to similar ends, as part of a self-presentation that merged Victorian domesticity with an older ideal of the civic-minded poet.

The "Poet at Home" and the Pose of Absorption

When the St. John's Pickersgill appeared in the 1834 Royal Academy show, *The Athenæum*—as quoted in my epigraph—remarked on the missing sense of solitary sublimity so often associated with Wordsworth. The picture failed to capture the "essence" of "Wordsworth": the "look of a poet," according to the reviewer, should exude the noncommercial aura of "truly noble poems," as opposed to a coldly mimetic portraiture that has affinities with revenue-producing stamps. Around this same time, Wordsworth himself was making a similar argument for copyright reform: authors such as himself, he wrote in a petition to Parliament, "have engaged and persevered in literary labour, less with the expectation of producing immediate or speedy effect, than with a view to interest and benefit society, though remotely, yet permanently." This long-term public benefit depended on a literature of high quality that "would be circulated in the shape which the last hand of their respective Authors gave them."[20] Cheap, unauthorized copies of a poem—like the copy of the poet's face—lacked the aura, the "little inspiration," of the original.

That Wordsworth had genuine reason to be concerned about copyright is not in doubt—he did, after all, have a family to support. But the debate about copyright also provided Wordsworth an additional forum for self-presentation. He knew a good marketing opportunity when he saw it, and was pleased to recognize that the controversy had helped to "widen the circulation of my works" (*Later Years*, 3: 314). Wordsworth used the occasion to promote himself as a poet whose cultural centrality and prestige derived from "original genius"—an argument that unfolds both in rhetorical portraits *of* Wordsworth that are used throughout the debate, and in a series of poems *about* portraits, in which Wordsworth activates the shared vocabulary of copyright and portraiture.

To Wordsworth, who wrote over fifty letters lobbying for copyright reform, longer terms of copyright were required in order to preserve the integrity of works of genius from corruption by cheap, unauthorized reproductions. Whereas proponents of the status quo held that extended terms would raise the price of books and halt the democratizing spread of literacy, Wordsworth countered that an expanded reading public was not, by itself, a civic good. "[F]or the great body of the people *dirt-cheap* literature, excuse the term, is rather a disadvantage than a benefit," he argues. "They are as carelessly treated and as recklessly destroyed, as they were unthinkingly bought" (3: 576). Having to pay dearly for a book would, in theory, intensify the attention one pays to that book. Though Wordsworth would elsewhere contradict himself by arguing that author's rights would lower the cost of books, his key point stands: quality of literature trumps quantity of books. And "quality," it turns out, depends on a diluted form of authenticity: "It is the very Books which we are attached to, in the very shape in which we have often read them, that do us the most good," Wordsworth writes, "that sink into our hearts, fix our opinions, direct our views, and rectify our [judgment]" (3: 599). The conceptions of men of genius—men such as Wordsworth—had to sustain their aura to promote the public good.[21]

Sergeant Thomas Noon Talfourd, the chief parliamentary advocate for reform, tapped this appeal to Wordsworthian genius in his speech for the Copyright Bill on April 25, 1838. Like Michel Beaupuy pointing to a hunger-bitten girl as a sanctioning image for the French Revolution, Talfourd adduced verbal portraits of wronged authors, citing Wordsworth as his central case. In an autonomous and excerptible description pieced together from Wordsworth's poetics, he pictures "an author, of true original genius" who has disclaimed "the inane phraseology" of lesser poets "unskilled in the moving accidents of fortune." Wordsworth's work is said to supply an "antidote to the freezing effects of the scientific spirit of the age"; he "has cast a glory around the lowliest conditions of humanity, and traced out the subtle links by which they are connected with the highest"; he has sought to "create the taste by which he shall be appreciated." And yet, Talfourd laments, when finally Wordsworth's "copyright becomes valuable, it is gone!"[22] Not surprisingly, Wordsworth was pleased by Talfourd's verbal portrait. He expressed a desire to "have it printed separately" since, he felt, "its circulation would do good." He even hoped to "bind it up" as "a sort of heir-loom in my family"—a private documentation of public importance (3: 563).

But despite Talfourd's promotion of Wordsworth as a poet "of true original genius," the persuasive power of his speech depended on Wordsworth's status as exemplar of the domestic sphere. For it was as a private man, who Felicia Hemans called "the true Poet at Home," that he was known to the reading public. Wordsworth and Rydal Mount were practically interchangeable. Maria Jane Jewsbury's poem "A Poet's Home" (1826) metonymized him as his domestic circle through a poetic gallery of portraits: Coleridge, with "locks of partial grey" and a "bright and beaming eye," and Dorothy, "Sportive, tender, graceful, wild, / Scarcely woman, more than child." Christopher Wordsworth's *Memoirs* open with a long description not of the poet, but of his home, while remarking that Rydal Mount "has been made familiar to many eyes by engravings" that at times have even stood in as frontispieces to his poems. Wordsworth's public image as so private a man gave special, if unspoken, force to the argument for reform. The present law was an affront to what that poet essentially *was*: the champion of domestic virtue and the exemplar, in Hemans's words, of the "home affections."[23]

Yet it was the very cachet contained in Wordsworth's name and his power as a household icon that paradoxically constituted the dispossession of which Talfourd complains. "Because their thoughts become our thoughts, and their phrases unconsciously enrich our daily language," Talfourd claims of such men as Wordsworth, "we cannot fancy them apart from ourselves, or admit that they have any property except in our praise."[24] To be influential is to become common property. Wordsworth anticipated the point in 1808, when the term was fourteen years, by claiming that under present law "men of real power, who go before their age, are deprived of all hope of their families being benefited by their exertions."[25] This gendered rhetoric (which among other things admits men alone to the sphere of genius) suggests a split between "men of real power" who serve the public, and lesser men who meet domestic obligations. But as Wordsworth indicates in a letter he sent anonymously to the *Kendal Mercury*, even the poet-prophet needs to profit from poetry to support a family: "A conscientious author, who had a family to maintain, and a prospect of descendants, would regard the additional labour bestowed upon any considerable work he might have in hand, in the light of an insurance of money upon his own life for the benefit of his issue; and he would be animated in his efforts accordingly, and would cheerfully undergo present privations for such future recompense."[26] Against the standard complaint that domesticity is antithetical to independent, "manly" power, Wordsworth here links the private interest of middle-class authors with the public benefit that can potentially issue from literary works, by viewing copyright protection as a kind of insurance policy. Denied the opportunities enjoyed by "men who rise to eminence in other professions"—to form "family establishments in business" and thereby "to provide at once for their descendants"—the self-possessed man of genius becomes a figure of wronged virtue and, potentially, a father prevented from leaving a legacy.[27] Thus, no matter how vigorously advocates for reform invoked Wordsworth's importance as a man of genius, their arguments invariably came to rest on Wordsworth the family man, whose situation revealed the law as a violation of domestic affection.

Wordsworth, for his part, tried to finesse this distinction. In "A Poet to His Grandchild" (1838), for example, he expands the ideal of "family" to include the British public:

> 'Son of my buried Son, while thus thy hand
> Is clasping mine, it saddens me to think
> How Want may press thee down, and with thee sink
> Thy Children left unfit, through vain demand
> Of culture, even to feel or understand
> My simplest Lay that to their memory
> May cling;—hard fate! which haply need not be
> Did Justice mould the Statutes of the Land.
> A Book time-cherished and an honoured name
> Are high rewards; but bound they nature's claim
> Or Reason's? No—hopes spun in timid line
> From out the bosom of a modest home
> Extend through unambitious years to come,
> My careless Little-one, for thee and thine!'

Just as natural affection, in Wordsworth's neo-Burkean view, undergirds national potency, so, too, the present law damages not just the author as father of *children*, but the author as father of *culture*.[28] Idiot boys become the author's inheritance: his own grandchild, even, proves an "unfit" audience, unable "to feel or understand" his "simplest lay." Not just private, material gains, then, but cultural and intellectual profit is at stake. Ultimately, the argument goes, Wordsworth's victimization as a private man is a matter of public concern. Not only is his immediate family deprived of his literary earnings, but the nation as a whole is disinherited of his intellectual wealth.

That wealth was increasingly seen to belong to the aura of solitary genius. Wordsworth's "works have found their way to the heart of the nation," George Gilfillan writes in 1849, because "his spirit has preserved its severe seclusion."[29] In this reading (as in Wordsworth's argument for copyright reform), the cultural value of poetry resides in its originality. Absorption, paradoxically, signifies civic engagement. Whereas Thomas Wakley, MP for Finsbury and an avid opponent of monopolies, complained "that the mere rhetorical combination of words should be claimed as an absolute property" of the author, Wordsworth embodied the idea that poetry was the offspring of a unique genius.[30] Poems, Wakley held, were mere aggregations of words that could not be said to belong to any one person; lyric was a product of random, arbitrary, and transferable labor. For Wordsworth, conversely, poetry was not about arrangement but expression—a point he would emphasize through portraiture, in a series of ekphrastic poems that deny their natural affinity with visual arrangement in favor of an aesthetic of expressive encounter.

Michael Fried has described "a tradition of absorptive painting" in which "engrossment, reflection, reverie, obliviousness, and related states are represented" as if such poses were caught from life; they "treated the beholder as if he were not there."[31] Wordsworth's portrait poems enact a similar dynamic by situating the poet as an absorbed beholder. In these poems, Wordsworth models "the look of a poet" as one that merges private affection and inward power. If the copyright debates show Wordsworth wavering (or being tossed) between two different roles, his poems about portraits attempt a reconciliation. The self-portraiture contained in these poems assists him in working through concerns about self-possession that are intrinsic to having one's portrait taken. By shifting the traditional emphasis of portraiture away from imitation and onto the expressive encounter with a portrait, Wordsworth's portrait poems show the poet in two very different yet equally "public" roles: as an absorbed man of genius, and as a model of domestic piety. They discriminate the physical (painted) likeness from the ethereal (remembered, imagined, sentimentalized) conception; they are invested with a "perfect fidelity" to the "precise features of the pictures within" (so Walter Pater described Wordsworth's poetic power).[32]

Yet, as poems about the most domestic genre of painting, they extend this interior mode of picturing to the private sympathies.

The Paterian "picture within" descends from Wordsworth's own pictorial vocabulary. The "picture of the mind" in "Tintern Abbey" and a manuscript version of the meditation on Snowden in which "the perfect image of a mighty Mind" is said to be "embodied in material portraiture" offer two prominent sites where the "the bodily eye, . . . the most despotic of all our senses" meets a mental gallery of pictures.[33] Such pictures as fixed forms of Wordsworth's genius always refer to mental pictures whose best medium of communication is language. Hence the greater value of memory over pictorial realism in Wordsworth's sonnet "To a Painter," on Margaret Gillies's 1839 portrait of Mary Wordsworth:

> Couldst thou go back into far-distant years,
> Or share with me, fond thought! that inward eye,
> Then, and then only, Painter! could thy Art
> The visual powers of Nature satisfy. (lines 9–12)

With a self-reference to the "flash upon the inward eye" of "I wandered lonely as a Cloud," Wordsworth imagines the painter as a discrete "viewer" of his idealized mental picture. But the interjection—"fond thought!"—emphatically withdraws that possibility, uniting interiority with uniquely personal experience in the defining act of "picturing" within these portrait poems.

Wordsworth's unique encounter with a painting takes precedence over not only Gillies's portrait, but even his own ekphrasis. What begins as an exercise in mere verbal replication often becomes, through the formings of ekphrasis, a completely new portrait, an original viewing. Even in these poems based on the most mimetic form of painting, imitative arrangement is subordinated to expressive interpretation. This is especially true of the sonnets, the structure of which demarcates a clear hierarchy: a visually descriptive octave on the portrait is superseded by a sestet on subjective response. One of Wordsworth's first forays into the portrait poem genre, "Recollection of the Portrait of King Henry Eighth, Trinity Lodge, Cambridge" (publ. 1827), shows this hierarchy:

> The imperial Stature, the colossal stride,
> Are yet before me; yet do I behold
> The broad full visage, chest of amplest mould,
> The vestments 'broidered with barbaric pride:
> And lo! A poniard, at the Monarch's side,
> Hangs ready to be grasped in sympathy
> With the keen threatenings of that fulgent eye,
> Below the white-rimmed bonnet, far-descried.

Who trembles now at thy capricious mood?
'Mid those surrounding Worthies, haughty King,
We rather think, with grateful mind sedate,
How Providence educeth, from the spring
Of lawless will, unlooked-for streams of good,
Which neither force shall check nor time abate!

The title describes this as recollection rather than description, but starting with line two the painting is replicated as if on a mental screen. The octave becomes an icon, a vessel filled with visual details: "colossal stride," "full visage," "chest of amplest mould," "vestments 'broidered," hanging "poniard," "fulgent eye," and "white-rimmed bonnet." The turn from octave to sestet coincides with a turn from visible likeness to subjective response—from what viewers see to what they "think." Invoking the royal "We" to meet the royal subject, Wordsworth sees and speaks for all: his is a public voice. In the face of the King's haughty ferocity, the sonnet argues, viewers maintain "a grateful mind sedate" by reducing his image to a miniature in a national gallery of "surrounding worthies." By eclipsing the visual object in the sestet, Wordsworth makes his encounter with this portrait more important than its physical presence.[34]

Though the portrait of Henry VIII is public, not domestic, its chief force is to produce a personal encounter, of a piece with the drama that recurs in Wordsworth's poems about private portraits of family and friends. Sonnets on his wife's portrait (both titled "To a Painter"), and a group of poems on pictures of Isabella Fenwick are types of what John Hollander calls "notional ekphrases": verbal descriptions of paintings for which the reader has no objective referent. The value of these private portraits is entirely private; their "meaning" is the drama of the poet's look. Similarly, in "Lines Suggested by a Portrait from the Pencil of F. Stone" (1834), Wordsworth "reads" the portrait to us to involve us in his response:

Look at her, whoe'er
Thou be that, kindling with a poet's soul,
Hast loved the painter's true Promethean craft
Intensely—from Imagination take
The treasure,—what mine eyes behold see thou,
Even though the Atlantic ocean roll between. (lines 22–27)

It takes "a poet's soul" to understand such verbal "painting." The speaker offers himself as an originary seer who provides select readers the "treasure" of encounter; the syntactic chiasmus of line 26 ("what mine eyes behold see thou") underscores the duplication of the poet's look. Since the focus of the poem is on the viewing poet, the identity of the sitter is practically irrelevant.[35] It hardly seems to matter that he is confronted with the opacity of an unfamiliar face when, perplexed, he questions the portrait: "Offspring of soul-bewitching Art, make me / Thy confidant! Say, whence derived that air / Of calm abstraction?" (lines 41–43). To all appearances, the portrait is abstract and unknowable. The speaker is left to create a narrative that emphasizes that it is his encounter, and not the portrait itself, that is the meaningful dynamic:

> Can the ruling thought
> Be with some lover far away, or one
> Crossed by misfortune, or of doubted faith?
> Inapt conjecture! . . .
> . . . The floweret, held
> In scarcely conscious fingers, was, she knows,
> (Her father told her so) in youth's gay dawn
> Her Mother's favourite; and the orphan Girl,
> In her own dawn—a dawn less gay and bright,
> Loves it, while there in solitary peace
> She sits, for that departed Mother's sake.
> (lines 43–52; 63–69)

The speaker answers his own question about the origin of her "calm abstraction" by producing a narrative to go along with the portrait, thus remaking it as his own creation. The "mirror" of portraiture becomes the "lamp" of lyric. The trope here is prosopopeia, which Paul de Man describes as "the fiction of an apostrophe to an absent, deceased or voiceless entity, which posits the possibility of the latter's reply and confers upon it the power of speech." De Man elaborates his definition in terms of portrait making: "Voice assumes mouth, eye and finally face, a chain that is manifest in the etymology of the trope's name, *prosopon poien*, to confer a mask or a face (*prosopon*)."[36] Yet what makes Wordsworth's poem so dramatic is the way it simultaneously senses the possibility of prosopopeia and doubts its force:

> —Not from a source less sacred is derived
> (Surely I do not err) that pensive air
> Of calm abstraction through the face diffused
> And the whole person. (lines 70–73)

The parenthetical pause "(Surely I do not err)" calls attention to a margin of error while putting the weight on the poet's reading. With it, Wordsworth indicates his investment of the portrait with meaning and hence his own creative displacement of it. Meditating on the imaginative deficiencies of portraiture taken on its own terms, he turns lyric into a self-meditation on the ekphrastic poet, absorbed in a creative act of beholding.

Yet there is another pressure. Because portrait poems present doubly still images—verbal likenesses of visual likenesses—they are charged with the potential for what W. J. T. Mitchell has called "ekphrastic fear," the anxiety that "the difference between the verbal and visual representation might collapse, and the figurative, imaginary desire of ekphrasis might be realized literally and actually."[37] On the one hand, this double stillness enables Wordsworth to emphasize the timelessness of "lyric" in opposition to the temporality of narrative. But it also results, paradoxically, in an uncanny sense of motion that further underlines the creative encounter with art as the main dynamic. For example, in "More may not be by human Art exprest" (1839–40), Isabella Fenwick's portrait seems to "share / A seeming intercourse with vital air. / Such faint sweet sign of life as Nature shows / A sleeping infant or the breathing rose" (lines 7–10). A more emphatic quickening characterizes the opening of "Lines Suggested by a Portrait from the Pencil of F. Stone":

> There she sits
> With emblematic purity attired
> In a white vest, white as her marble neck
> Is, and the pillar of the throat would be
> But for the shadow by the drooping chin
> Cast into that recess—the tender shade,
> The shade and light, both there and everywhere,
> And through the very atmosphere she breathes,
> Broad, clear, and toned harmoniously . . .
> (lines 11–19)

The statue-like woman in the portrait, with her "marble neck" and "pillar" of a throat, at first seems a throwback to neoclassical imitation. But when the speaker, "[b]eguiled into forgetfulness" and framed by a window (lines 1, 5), transforms from passive register into active recreator, the woman breaks out of her marmoreal restraint. Ekphrastic fear is conquered by a freshly asserted gaze that animates the still and silent woman. The sitter's unframing is the poet's as well; the central "portrait" here is Wordsworth's.

In these poems we see Wordsworth using ekphrasis to define his prestige as a product of absorption and its concomitant, "true original genius." He achieves the most extreme transvaluation of the domestic icon into the absorbed man of genius through what I call "counterekphrasis": the verbal description of a *refusal* to represent a mental image. As a version of Mitchell's "ekphrastic indifference" (a preliminary and ephemeral acceptance that verbal language cannot replicate a visual image), Wordsworthian counterekphrasis is a more overt rejection of language itself as too material to adequately represent an idealized mental image.[38] Hence in a paean to Margaret Gillies's portrait of Mary

Wordsworth, the visual image does not accord with the poet's pristine "picture of the mind," which is expressed only in negative terms:

> All praise the Likeness by thy skill portrayed;
> But 'tis a fruitless task to paint for me,
> Who, yielding not to changes Time has made,
> By the habitual light of memory see
> Eyes unbedimmed, see bloom that cannot fade,
> And smiles that from their birthplace ne'er shall flee
> Into the land where ghosts and phantoms be;
> And, seeing this, own nothing in its stead.
> ("To a Painter," lines 1–8)

The sonnet presents Wordsworthian experience as timeless and ego-based. The portrait is trapped in the moment of its making, whereas the mental image discloses "eyes unbedimmed" and "bloom that cannot fade." The sonnet presents memory as an extreme form of personal property that is qualitatively unrepresentable except as poetry. This accent on ownership is expressed in line eight ("And, seeing this, own nothing in its stead"), which indicates the inalienability of the poet's "picture within." It is heightened in a draft version of this line in which the speaker's possession by the mental image is contrasted with the absence that distinguishes its physical portrayal: "See this, *own this*, but nothing in its stead."[39] To use the phrase made current by the copyright debate, this image is the "absolute property" of the poet. Hence the poem's enactment of a key tenet of Wordsworthian counterekphrasis: an insistence on ineffability that values poetry not as an arrangement of words but as an art of absorption pointing beyond words.

While providing occasions to present the self in solitary absorption, Wordsworth's portrait poems also make "absolute property" a performative quality, by staging domesticity as a public affair. We see this in this sonnet's pendant, also titled "To a Painter." Though couched as a retraction to the painter, it reads like an apology to Mary Wordsworth for the previous poem's tacit insult:

> Though I beheld at first with blank surprise
> This Work, I now have gazed on it so long
> I see its truth with unreluctant eyes;
> O, my Belovèd! I have done thee wrong,
> Conscious of blessedness, but, whence it sprung,
> Ever too heedless, as I now perceive:
> Morn into noon did pass, noon into eve,
> And the old day was welcome as the young,
> As welcome, and as beautiful—in sooth
> More beautiful, as being a thing more holy:

Thanks to thy virtues, to the eternal youth
Of all thy goodness, never melancholy;
To thy large heart and humble mind, that cast
Into one vision, future, present, past.

As line four makes clear (and his title notwithstanding), Wordsworth's offense is less against Gillies than against his wife. Praising "the old day" over "the young"—"More beautiful, as being a thing more holy"—Wordsworth expresses his awkward awareness of having replaced the portrait of his "Belovèd" with his own remembered image of her. "Your mother tells me she shrinks from Copies being spread of those Sonnets," Wordsworth explains to Dora, "her modesty and humble-mindedness were so much shocked that I doubt if she had more pleasure than pain from these compositions, though I never poured anything more truly from the heart" (*Later Years*, 4: 59). Attributing Mary's reaction to female modesty (as opposed to embarrassment at her husband's grudging acceptance of her), Wordsworth again takes up ekphrastic contest as a form of self-portraiture, asserting the nonreproducible "truth" generated by his "inward eye."

In their rebuke and retraction, the sonnets illustrate a tension between two poetic stances: one private, the other public. Wordsworth's embodiment of "home affections" (as Hemans put it) is felt to conflict with the civic virtues of "the true, original genius." Wordsworth manages the contradiction by using his ekphrastic portrait poems to model domestic affection publicly, advertising his exemplary status as an icon of moral benevolence in these dramas of encounter with the image of absence—and, in particular cases, the images of aging or deceased friends. Wordsworth's poems were public documents, whether they adopted the publicly oriented voice of the later Christian lyrics or the private voice that, in some cases, would remain private until the inevitable posthumous publication. By offering opinions on everything from capital punishment to railway construction, all while comfortably ensconced at Rydal with family and friends, mountains and lakes, he merged his domestic self-portrait into a persona of public concern. Both "Wordsworths"—the tender "Poet at Home" and the civic-minded man of genius—circulated in his steady flow of writings, sometimes in contradictory currents. Domesticity *was* public: the poet's response to art, be it sympathy or absorption, was, as framed by Wordsworth, a civic act.

Ekphrastic Sociability

The absorptive pose of Wordsworth's portrait poems finds a visual counterpart in Benjamin Robert Haydon's *Wordsworth on Helvellyn* (1842; figure 35). A monument to the mind-in-creation, the portrait is one of romanticism's iconic

FIG. 35. Benjamin Robert Haydon, *Wordsworth on Helvellyn*, 1842. (National Portrait Gallery, London)

images. It gives concrete form to William Hazlitt's description of a Wordsworth who "lives in the busy solitude of his own heart; in the deep silence of thought," transforming the effete poet reclining on a rock into a brooding figure of "heroic proportions."[40] For many, the picture seems to resist the category of "portraiture" altogether. "It shows the influence of history painting," Frances Blanshard writes, "indeed it *is* a history painting of Wordsworth on a mountain top, inspired to create." For A. C. Sewter, it was not just the best portrait of Wordsworth, but "the finest portrait of the nineteenth century." And Stephen Gill says that it is "what an image of Wordsworth should be." Such comments extend the initial adoration within the Wordsworth circle. On her deathbed in 1847, the poet's daughter Dora said of the portrait: "It is perfection."[41]

Widespread esteem for this painting within romantic circles reflects the longstanding valorization of romantic solitude: what better icon than that of the poet in heroic isolation, absorbed in deep thought atop a blustery mountain? Yet, against expectation, *Wordsworth on Helvellyn* belongs to a complicated network of cross-references that qualifies its appeal to romantic solitude and asks us to rethink the nature of Wordsworthian inwardness. A closer look at the origins and early reception of this emblematic painting reveals, beneath its overt featuring of the solitary mind-in-creation, what Gillian Russell and Clara Tuite call romanticism's "sociable other."[42] *Wordsworth on Helvellyn* embeds its own peculiar history of sociability, discernible through noncanonical forms of cultural production ranging from painted portraits to letters. This "quintessential image of Romantic genius" offers a valuable point of departure for rethinking the collaborative, interactive, and theatrical aspects of the romantic enterprise.[43]

Wordsworth on Helvellyn originates in an exchange of letters and artistic gifts. Having received from Haydon an etching of a grandly heroic, nine-by-eleven-foot portrait of the Duke of Wellington, Wordsworth returned to him, on September 2, 1840, a thank-you sonnet "actually composed while I was climbing Helvellyn last Monday":

By Art's bold privilege Warrior and War-horse stand
On ground yet strewn with their last battle's wreck;
Let the Steed glory while his Master's hand
Lies fixed for ages on his conscious neck;
But by the Chieftain's look, though at his side
Hangs that day's treasured sword, how firm a check
Is given to triumph and all human pride!
Yon trophied Mound shrinks to a shadowy speck
In his calm presence. Since the mighty deed
Him years have brought far nearer the grave's rest,
As shows that face time-worn. But genuine seed
Has sowed—that bears, we trust, the fruit of fame
In Heaven; hence no one blushes for thy name,
Conqueror, 'mid some sad thoughts, divinely blest!

Composed while ascending Helvellyn Monday Aug 31st 1840
Wm Wordsworth (*Later Years*, 4: 100–1)

This miniature response to a gigantic portrait proves to be the inspiration for *Wordsworth on Helvellyn*: a portrait of Wordsworth composing a sonnet about *another* portrait by Haydon. The unlikely antecedent of the quintessentially "Wordsworthian" image, it offers a glimpse of Wordsworth at ekphrasis, attempting to contest the priority of Haydon's portrait through strategic rearrangements aimed at establishing the sonnet as its own point of origin.

Ekphrasis, understood specifically as the verbal representation of a visual representation, is frequently read as a topos of interartistic rivalry: the ekphrastic poet "ensures the permanence of its own composition at the expense of the art work," argues Grant F. Scott, and "at times even delights in the ephemerality of the painted or sculpted image."[44] In this particular instance, though, something more personal is being contested. Wordsworth's revisions, which aim to generate a kind of poetic self-portraiture, emerge from a set of exchanges that reflects the social nature of portraiture itself. Engaging Haydon's painting in a dynamic series of private letters, Wordsworth might be said to exemplify what I will call "ekphrastic sociability." Put another way, if ekphrasis (from the Greek *ek phrassein*, "to speak out" [*OED*]) literally means "to tell in full," Wordsworth's sonnet gives voice to a rivalry among friends who alternately admire and mirror one another's strengths and ambitions.[45] What the sonnet does *not* tell in full—what it keeps in reserve—is the epistolary exchange that is its imaginative basis.

Wordsworth made numerous revisions over the three weeks following the initial draft, as described in a frenetic series of letters (to Haydon, Isabella Fenwick, Crabb Robinson, and Henry Reed) that shows the poet, in his own words, "considering and reconsidering, changing and rechanging" the sonnet's final quatrain (4: 107). The revisionary effort was ostensibly designed to deepen the poem's faithfulness to the painting, but Wordsworth's stated aim of producing a sonnet in which "the presence of the Portrait is . . . carried thro' " conceals a contrary struggle to exalt the poem over Haydon's portrait (4: 108). The goal of this struggle is a sonnet that concentrates Haydon's heroic grandeur into a self-authored, self-portrait in miniature: an ekphrasis in which Wellington is a double or stand-in for Wordsworth.

The various epistolary exchanges in which the revisions unfold expose the radically social underpinnings of poetic creation. Revision commenced just two days after Wordsworth first sent the poem to Haydon, with a curt request that the painter

> Correct thus the lines toward the close of the Sonnet:
>
> As shows that time-worn face. But he such seed
> Hath sown, as yields, we trust, the fruit of fame
> In Heaven etc— (4: 105)

Three days later, another letter to Haydon intensified this drama of indecision:

> I am quite ashamed to trouble you again, but after considering and reconsidering, changing and rechanging, it has been resolved that the troublesome passage shall stand thus:
>
> In his calm presence. Him the mighty deed
> Elates not brought far nearer the grave's rest
> As shows that time-worn face. but [sic] he such seed
> Hath sown as yields, we trust, etc.

On September 10, Wordsworth repeats this third version, "as last sent, and in which state I still consider it finished" (4: 108). Yet by the very next day (September 11), his certainty has dissolved:

> I know not what to do with the passage, if it be not well corrected as follows
>
> Him the mighty deed
> Elates not: neither doth a cloud find rest
> Upon that time-worn face; for He such seed
> Hath sown etc. (4: 110)

Later that day, Wordsworth sends yet another letter "beg[ging]" Haydon "to read it thus":

> His life is brought far nearer the grave's rest,
> As shews that time-worn face. But he, such seed
> Hath sown, as yields etc—. (4: 111)

Finally, on September 14, Wordsworth confesses in a letter to Fenwick: "I know not how [the sonnet] will come out at last" (4: 115). Yet that very same day, writing to Henry Reed, Wordsworth distills the poem's swelling history of revision by introducing it, simply, as "a Sonnet composed the other day while I was climbing our Mountain—Helvellyn" (4: 116). Only such an air of authority could validate Wordsworth's later complaint that the poem had "been published in several Newspapers but with such gross blunders that I have ventured to send you a corrected Copy" (4: 117–18). He may have felt that "gross blunders" had violated the sanctity of a stable, finished text object, yet in truth there does not appear to have been such any such text object to suffer violation at that period. Even a partial list of the various titles he gave the sonnet over these few weeks summarizes the instability of the poem's textual authority: "On the Ground of Waterloo Painted by Hayden [*sic*]" (MS. 146); "Upon Hayden's Portrait of The Duke of Wellington, Supposed to be on the field of Waterloo 20 years after the Battle" (letter to Henry Reed); "a Sonnet Suggested by Haydon's Picture of the Duke and Copenhagen on the Field at Waterloo 20 years after the

Battle (Berg MS. 5); "Suggested by Haydon's Picture of the Duke of Wellington and his Horse, Copenhagen, on the Field of Waterloo, Twenty Years after the Battle. Painted for St. George's Hall, Liverpool, and now engraving by Lupton" (*Literary Gazette*); "Sonnet composed by Mr. Wordsworth on accomplishing the ascent to Helvellyn August 1840, Suggested by Hayden's picture of the Duke of Wellington and his War Horse" (Monkhouse Album); "On a Portrait of the Duke of Wellington, upon the field of Waterloo by Haydon" (Haydon MS. 151.2); and, most appropriately, it was twice given no title at all (MS. 89, Rydal Mount MS.).[46] Far from honing in on his central idea, Wordsworth's revisions to this point bear witness to an extraordinary inability to decide how to shape his sonnet.

Such indecision, unremarkable in itself, is expressed and worked through in a distinctly social manner. These letters reveal the basis of the sonnet's revision in friendship and friendly rivalry. The visual-verbal conflict that informs the Wellington sonnet from the outset also registers a more personal conflict. Wordsworthian ekphrasis proves not just a competition between arts, but a social game of one-upmanship between colleagues. Just as portraiture—an art so critical to establishing the romantic myth (think of famous images such as Joseph Severn's Keats, Thomas Phillips's Blake, or Amelia Curran's Shelley)—is itself an art of collaboration between painter and sitter, so too Wordsworth's poetic *self*-portraiture unfolds in dialogue.

When he first sent it to Haydon, Wordsworth included the "earnest request that it may not be put into circulation for some little time, as it is warm from the brain, and may require, in consequence, some little retouching" (4: 100)—as if the poem were a portrait. The very same day, however, in a letter to Crabb Robinson, Wordsworth pointedly subordinated Haydon's vast portrait to his own miniature ekphrasis: "Haydon has just sent me a spirited Etching of his Portrait of the Duke of Wellington taken 20 years after the Battle of Waterloo, from the Life. He is represented upon the field; but no more of the Picture—take my Sonnet which it suggested the other day. The lines were composed while I was climbing Helvellyn. . . . I was seven hours on my feet without being at all tired; so that if we are to see Italy again together in tolerable time I am still capable of some exertion."[47] The portrait is ousted by the sonnet, just as Wellington "upon the field" gives way to Wordsworth "climbing Helvellyn." Likewise, Wordsworth counters Haydon's gigantism with a principle of miniaturization: Waterloo "*shrinks* to a shadowy speck" (line 8) as history's long view swallows it whole. Whereas Haydon boldly claims of his portrait, "Inspired by History I fear not making my grandest thing," Wordsworth is more elegiac. If time shrinks even the most magnificent of historical canvasses, as Bishop Hunt has argued, Wordsworth's sonnet abets, eclipsing an enormous painting.[48] Even in his eclipse, Haydon proves a vital point of departure.

Wordsworth's revisions build upon the central fiction of Haydon's portrait: its temporal disjuncture, an aging Wellington revisiting and reveling in his past glory (yet still enjoying the fruits of that seed). Haydon's conventional depiction of a hero represented long after his defining triumph at the site of that triumph provides a visual analogue to what Carlos Baker has called Wordsworth's "double-exposure technique." As in "Tintern Abbey," where the speaker revisits a former haunt and meditates on the difference between past and present selves, the effect, Baker argues, is something like "a double exposure on photographic film": "The same person appears in the same setting, except that ten years have elapsed between exposures."[49] Here, developing the temporal discrepancy intrinsic to Haydon's painting, Wordsworth makes Wellington a figure in his signature trope.

For the viewer of Haydon's picture, the double exposure is immediately apparent. The reader, however, confronts ambiguity encouraged by Wordsworth's revisions—particularly his alternation of lines 9 and 10, "Since the mighty deed / Him years have brought far nearer the grave's rest," to, "Him the mighty deed / Elates not brought far nearer the grave's rest." Wordsworth explains: "As the passage first stood, 'Since the mighty deed'—there was a transfer of the thought from the picture to the living Man, which divided the Sonnet into two parts—the presence of the Portrait is now carried thro', till the last line where the Man is taken up." The explanation insinuates a faithful submission to the painting ("the Portrait is now carried thro' "). But by delaying the "transfer of the thought from the picture to the living Man," Wordsworth also delays the revelation of the second exposure, what Baker calls "the picture of things as they are in the historical 'now.' "[50] In the poem the two exposures appear as one; the distinction between "living Man" and history disappears. Through the deletion of the phrase "Since the mighty deed"—a phrase that signals the pastness of the past—Wordsworth's revision hides Wellington's age. "It was necessary to advert to the Duke being much older," he writes, "which is yet done in the words time-worn face—but not so strongly as before" (4: 110–11). While noting the Duke's age, Wordsworth nevertheless maintains a productive ambiguity—the "time-worn face" could just as easily refer to the conqueror of 1815, reflecting perhaps a war-weary encounter with death. The double exposure in Haydon's portrait becomes a sign of emotional complexity in Wordsworth's sonnet, which in turn becomes a more nuanced and psychologically "true" type of the portrait.

Yet this effort to achieve an *original* portrait of Wellington is also an effort to develop *self*-portraiture out of an interactive foundation. The poet gazing on the portrait gives a mirror image of Wellington gazing on the field of Waterloo. Hunt calls Wellington "yet another version of the Wordsworthian Solitary, the isolated, somber figure, often set in the midst of a desolate landscape, which so haunted the poet's imagination," and it is important to recall the way Wordsworth's border-figures so often call attention to the figure of the poet beholding.[51] Even as we (yet again) watch Wordsworth watching, ekphrasis becomes a nostalgia for past glory, identification with Wellington an expression of faith in abandoned powers. (Not coincidentally, this was the theme of the "Intimations Ode," whose reissue was the chief poetic event of 1815—the year of Wellington's victory at Waterloo.)

Previously, Wordsworth had entered into a similar identification in a sonnet written on another of Haydon's oversized pictures. "To B. R. Haydon, On Seeing His Picture of Napoleon Buonaparte on the Island of St Helena" (1831) refers to one of more than two dozen Napoleons that Haydon produced in a lifelong act of homage qua identification.[52] "My skull is like Napoleon's," Haydon once wrote, yet here Wordsworth claims the identification for himself.[53] Having seen this painting exhibited in 1831, he was struck by Haydon's explanatory description of "such a genius in captivity," and the "mysterious associations of the sky, the sea, the rock and the solitude with which he was enveloped."[54] If Napoleon's confined genius struck Haydon as an almost painful reflection of his own, it was the theme of "genius in captivity," for which the sonnet itself is a sign, that appealed to Wordsworth:

> Haydon! let worthier judges praise the skill
> Here by thy pencil shown in truth of lines
> And charm of colours; *I* applaud those signs
> Of thought, that give the true poetic thrill;
> That unencumbered whole of blank and still,
> Sky without cloud—ocean without a wave;
> And the one Man that laboured to enslave
> The World, sole-standing high on the bare hill—
> Back turned, arms folded, the unapparent face
> Tinged, we may fancy, in this dreary place
> With light reflected from the invisible sun
> Set, like his fortunes; but not set for aye
> Like them. The unguilty Power pursues his way,
> And before *him* doth dawn perpetual run.

Wordsworth finds room enough in his scanty plot of ground for an "unencumbered whole of blank and still, / Sky without cloud—ocean without a wave" (lines 5–6). Enjambment heightens even as it condenses the "poetic thrill": with the turn of a line, "signs / Of thought" (lines 3–4) shifts the reader from the visual and determinate to the mental and indeterminate, while "laboured to enslave / The World" (lines 7–8) figures the magnitude of Napoleon's ambition as the natural expanse that envelops him. The italicized final line concludes matters on a note typical of the later Wordsworth, by exalting the private virtue of humility. Though ostensibly aimed at both Napoleon and Haydon, this closing admonishment also indicates that Wordsworth, too, recalls the allure of the apocalyptic imagination.

The Napoleon sonnet, like the Wellington, pays homage to a painter who was (like Wordsworth for much of his life) unappreciated. But these poems also miniaturize Haydon's appetite for glory by squeezing upwards of a hundred square feet of paint into the two-inch space of a sonnet. The special quality of language is to be unaffected by physical diminution: "A reduction in dimensions," Susan Stewart writes, "does not produce a corresponding reduction in significance."[55] Characterized by their capacity to fit so much into so little, these sonnet-pictures based on Haydon's grand historical representations show Wordsworth translating the spectacle of the heroic portrait into the intimacy of a private miniature. Usurping the figure of the military conqueror for his own self-portraiture, Wordsworth anticipates George Gilfillan's hypermasculine depiction of 1849 of the sublime and solitary poet as "the sole king of Rocky Cumberland, the lord of Rydal Mount, the sultan of Skiddaw, the warlock of Windermere, William Wordsworth."[56]

The degree to which Wordsworth's ekphrastic self-portraiture is a performance modeled on other men's poses is striking.[57] But Wordsworth's identification with Wellington was particularly ironic. Among the most caricatured men of the age, Wellington's unauthorized image multiplied and circulated in ways Wordsworth could hardly imagine. Wellington was also a frequent spectator at the print-shop windows where his image was displayed (a famous caricature by Charles Heath makes fun of this habit).[58] Therefore, notwithstanding the attempt to generate a sublime image of the poet, the sonnet remains haunted by the possibility that one's image could be misappropriated or multiplied beyond one's control, as a commodity within that explicitly social world of shopping.

This possibility was present to Wordsworth at the time he composed the sonnet, for September 1840 was marked not only by poetic revision but also by the return to Rydal of the portrait painter Henry William Pickersgill, to paint a portrait commissioned by Sir Robert Peel. So it is that in Wordsworth's letters about the sonnet, the poet's thoughts sometimes turn to the earlier portrait painted by Pickersgill. At one point Wordsworth recalls his dismay with that picture: as the sonnet is in need of "some little retouching," so, too, the look of a poet. It was apparently no accident when Wordsworth responded to Haydon sending him the sonnet as it appeared in the *Literary Gazette* ("I wrote 'On ground *yet* strewn,' and so read and repeat it, not 'On ground *still* strewn,' as it stands. The twists are to my ear intolerable.") by extending an invitation to his friend and rival: "I and mine would be most happy to see you here next Summer, for the purpose" of "painting me on my own ground poetically" (4: 132, 111). This proposition would result in *Wordsworth on Helvellyn*, a realization of the self-portrait "actually composed on Helvellyn" as a monument to the poet's enduring power. That the quintessential portrait of Wordsworth imagined him in the act of poetic *self*-portraiture is no surprise. More surprising is that this portrait of introspection-in-solitude—the product of a series of epistolary exchanges—would soon figure in the Victorian perception of a social Wordsworth.

Introspective Sociability

When Matthew Arnold in 1879 transformed the popular image of "Wordsworth" as a poet of rural life and domestic piety, he chose for the frontispiece the relatively obscure portrait by Haydon, whose lone previous book publication was in Gilfillan's 1849 memoir of Wordsworth.[59] By championing the now-familiar poet of the "golden prime" of 1797–1807, Arnold replaced (to quote Stephen Gill) "the gigantic monolith that was Wordsworth" with "a new one of more manageable size."[60] The downsizing of Wordsworth's corpus also entailed rearranging its parts. As Arnold put it, "He will come out better, and more effective in my arrangement, I think, than he has ever come out before."[61] This "improved" Wordsworth was said to be most justly understood by dismissing his "formal philosophy" as an "illusion" and by accepting, in its place, the "extraordinary power with which [he] feels the joy offered to us in nature, the joy offered to us in the simple primary affections and duties." The various Victorian faces of Wordsworth—the tender domestic poet, the prophet and sage, the somber poet-philosopher—were concentrated by Arnold into a humanist figure who could teach his readers "how to live."[62]

For Arnold, this figure was embodied by *Wordsworth on Helvellyn*, a painting that was definitively not in vogue at the time. By joining a Wordsworth "who lives in the busy solitude of his own heart" with a poet who sets an example of joy in the common life, Arnold staged "Wordsworthianness" as simultaneously absorptive and civic. As in the "tradition of absorptive painting" described by Fried, for Wordsworth absorption denotes an obliviousness to the fact of being beheld: "No Man sees his own face when he is absorbed in meditation, with his head downwards," he wrote to Abraham Cooper in 1844; "The position of the head [in *Wordsworth on Helvellyn*] in my own opinion merely cannot be favorable to *likeness*" (*Later Years*, 4: 555). Yet Arnold's is a social Wordsworth, a poet who teaches readers "how to live": "Wordsworth's poetry is great because of the extraordinary power with which Wordsworth feels the joy offered to us in nature, the joy offered to us in the simple primary affections and duties; and because of the extraordinary power with which, in case after case, he shows us this joy, and renders it so as to make us share it" (9: 51). Such is the intensity of Wordsworthian experience that, even in its inwardness, it is outward: his personal feeling is a common one "offered to *us*"; his expression compels us to partake. Like John Stuart Mill, who four decades earlier had found in Wordsworth a "medicine" that "could be shared in by all human beings," Arnold saw this sense of a "power" so "extraordinary" that we are compelled to share it as the mark of the poet's greatness.[63]

In a selection of poems that aims to share, enlighten, and teach, therefore, the rhetoric of the *Wordsworth on Helvellyn* frontispiece is paradoxical (though it continues to define Wordsworthian scholarship today): solitude is social, not solitary; the poet is most deeply involved with his readers in his brooding isolation atop Helvellyn. Of course, on the face of it, this understanding of Haydon's portrait seems contradictory. The image clearly displaces the physical exertion of climbing into the mental exertion of composing; contemplative repose masks an intensity of creation, rendering literary labor as a product of upward ascent and inward thought. What could seem more counterintuitive than to signify civic engagement by depicting the poet of genius absorbed in meditation in a landscape of the symbolic sublime?[64] Yet in this Arnold echoes Wordsworth's own claim, made while lobbying for copyright reform in the 1830s, that solitary mental exertion serves public ends. The intellectual labor of men of genius, according this argument, is necessarily solitary and isolated. The poet is most "civic" when most absorbed—that is, when most *himself.* As Gilfillan was later to put it, Wordsworth's national significance requires his spiritual seclusion.[65]

The paradox is demonstrated by the Victorian reception of *Wordsworth on Helvellyn.* The most famous poetic tribute to the portrait, Elizabeth Barrett's sonnet "On a Portrait of Wordsworth by B. R. Haydon" (1842), echoes the claim that the distillation of Wordsworthian inwardness reveals an essentially social power. Barrett, who had the picture in her possession when writing the sonnet, reads Wordsworth's portrait as "historical" in the same way she reads poems as "historical": both capture a sense of daily life at odds with conventional portraiture.[66] To this end, Barrett's sonnet quibbles with its own title by declaring that this is not a portrait (at least not an "academic" one):

Wordsworth upon Helvellyn! Let the cloud
Ebb audibly along the mountain-wind,
Then break against the rock, and show behind
The lowland valleys floating up to crowd
The sense with beauty. He with forehead bowed
And humble-lidded eyes, as one inclined
Before the sovran thought of his own mind,
And very meek with inspirations proud,
Takes here his rightful place as poet-priest
By the high altar, singing prayer and prayer
To the higher Heavens. A noble vision free
Our Haydon's hand has flung out from the mist:
No portrait this, with Academic air!
This is the poet and his poetry.[67]

Barrett's initial apostrophe is both to Wordsworth and to the painted figure in her room, "Wordsworth upon Helvellyn." Just below this, she playfully inserts her own initials, "Ebb," thus equating Wordsworth's figure with the "figures" of her name.[68] And through this opening, Barrett actually participates in the portrait, asking readers in lines 3 and 4 to reimagine the scenery behind Wordsworth: Barrett turns the portrait into a moving picture that requires spectators for its activation.

For Barrett, Wordsworth's greatness stems from his ability to overcome the opposition between lived and poetical selves, and thereby to bring history—not epic history but daily history—into poetry (as in her epic of daily life, *Aurora Leigh*). "What is most remarkable in this great writer," she writes, "is his poetical consistency. There is a wonderful unity in these multiform poems of one man: they are 'bound each to each in natural piety,' even as his days are: and why? because they *are* his days—all his days, work days and Sabbath days—his life, in fact, and not the unconnected works of his life, as vulgar men do opine of poetry and do rightly opine of vulgar poems, but the sign, seal, and representation of his life—nay, the actual audible breathing of his inward life's spirit."[69] What is striking is the extent to which Barrett feels she *knows* Wordsworth. This correspondence between the poet's life and work would dominate Victorian interpretations, as in the first authorized life of the poet, Christopher Wordsworth's *Memoirs* (1851): "He wrote as he lived, and he lived as he wrote."[70] Barrett, for her part, takes the correspondence into an interior province of meditation and thought, honing down Wordsworth's "days" to his "life" and finally to "his inward life's spirit"—the same trajectory traced by her sonnet. For Barrett as for Arnold, Wordsworthian power abides in his union of solitary meditation with a poetry that speaks of "life."

For both of these viewers of Haydon's portrait, Wordsworth's potency as a poet is realized in his ability to engage others. Thus in the first two lines of Barrett's sonnet, "Wordsworth" becomes a vehicle for the insertion—and assertion—of "Ebb." And if Wordsworth's "life's spirit" finds expression in the outward "sign, seal, and representation" of his lyrics, and if his identity becomes an "actual audible breathing" captured in this image of absorption, it is also true that he is indebted for the image to "Haydon's hand" (line 12). Even at the height of his powers, atop Helvellyn in solitary meditation, Wordsworth gets recognized by Barrett as a figure dependent upon others for his completion.

This perception of a reciprocal Wordsworth is reinforced by the implicit narrative situation of *Wordsworth on Helvellyn*, which, after all, shows the poet composing *another* ekphrastic portrait poem—the sonnet on Haydon's portrait of the Duke of Wellington. Returning to the scene of that poem's composition, *Wordsworth on Helvellyn* participates in the myth of poetic inspiration. Ironically, though, the painting is an image of romantic sociability: as a picture of Wordsworth-at-ekphrasis, it mediates Haydon's earlier portrait of Wellington in giving a portrait of Wordsworth. Barrett's correspondence with Haydon made her well aware of the image's triangulated network of inspirations. Hers is therefore a sonnet on a portrait that captures the composition of *another* sonnet about a portrait. While explicitly arguing for the inalienability of the poet's labor, Barrett tacitly figures inspiration and composition as an ever-circulating dynamic, an ongoing engagement with others. In her very faith in Wordsworthian representation, Barrett recognizes and brilliantly captures the sociability that informs his absorptive self-presentation.

It took less than a year after Wordsworth's death in 1850 for Henry William Pickersgill to complete a new large, full-length picture of him, based partly on the portrait for St. John's. The painting "aimed at something like the effect of *Wordsworth on Helvellyn*," Stephen Gill writes, yet failed entirely: "This elegantly clad and shod, white-haired gentleman, sitting with pencil in hand, looks like an elderly clergyman with a taste for improving verses." Sara Coleridge, who saw the portrait exhibited at the Royal Academy in 1851, wrote to Isabella Fenwick that the image "of our dear departed poet is *insufferable*," lamenting in particular its "sombre sentimentalism of countenance." The portrait was not, in fact, authorized by the family. Instead, it was shrewd business on the part of a painter who, in Crabb Robinson's words, considered it as "his own property" and "look[ed] forward to [it] as of great value to his family in the next generation."[71] Pickersgill's wish to turn a profit on Wordsworth's likeness was fulfilled in 1860, when the picture became the first of the poet to be purchased by the newly established National Portrait Gallery. Just as he had lamented during the debates over copyright reform, the author was shown to be exploitable for others' gain. Painted posthumously, without permission, and for profit: *this* was the "look of the poet" that for six decades would be, quite literally, Wordsworth's "national" portrait.

When Wordsworth visited Liverpool in 1831 and neglected to visit a friend, he apologized by writing: "I could not profit by that nor any good thing, for they were all driven out of my Mind, by the Reform Bill, inflammations in my eyes and the stupid occupation of sitting to four several Artists.—I can assure you that from these and other causes I was in anything but a comfortable state of feeling" (*Later Years*, 2: 506). That he would associate the First Reform Bill with sitting for his portrait is appropriate, since the circulation of Wordsworth's image was enabled by the expansion of literacy and the widespread availability of words and images. As we have seen, it was left to Wordsworth himself (and, after his death, the efforts of family, friends, and admirers) to contest the less desirable fictions of identity with competing fictions of the poet; to balance his self-presentation as a marketable domestic icon by championing the poet as an original genius, whose cultural centrality derives from the labor of solitary absorption. In sitting for his portrait he reluctantly gave himself over to the requirements of the market, which made his self-advocacy as a national poet dependent upon a kind of low-grade entrepreneurial flair. Like Burke and Boydell in the previous generation, Wordsworth associated portraiture with a British body politic whose face was changing for the worse. Like them, he also had much to gain much from it.

Epilogue

> No line is drawn—no standard of eligibility established, but it is considered indispensable to cover the walls from top to bottom—array them *en cap-à-pié*—if possible with good paintings, if not, with such as are to be had. Nothing like margin is allowed; for, it should seem, an exhibition is expected to be a dense crowd of frames and canvasses, wedged together as their forms and dimensions will best permit, without any regard to arrangement, except that certain places are provided for the privileged and for some of the stars; whilst the rest are looked upon as so many ciphers, valueless in themselves, yet adding importance to the significant figures—a very fallacious kind of arithmetic. . . . Rather does the majority of inferior works tend to "swamp" the entire assemblage.
>
> —*Fraser's Magazine*, "Our Royal-Academical Lounge" (1832)

Writing just a month after the passage of the first Reform Bill, the reviewer for *Fraser's Magazine* barely masks his high-Tory outrage while lamenting the hubbub of the 1832 Academy show.[1] It is easy to dismiss the attitude as mere partisanship, especially since the review goes on to make explicit the subtext of democratization: "Now-a-days every thing must be for 'the people'—the million" (711). For this writer, art exhibition was a disturbing microcosm of the nation, an echo in the cultural sphere of the diverse imagined community brought into political existence by Reform. Yet the apparent democracy of art, like Reform itself, can be understood less as a bustling and inclusive diversity of social bodies than as a phantasmatic multeity-in-unity: an abstract, exclusive, and idealized national self-image.

In concluding this book, I want to approach this problematic through a consideration of Sir George Hayter's gigantic group portrait, *The House of Commons, 1833* (1833–43; figure 36). Purchased by the government in 1858 and almost immediately presented to the newly established National Portrait Gallery, Hayter's "history by portraiture," as he described it, celebrated Reform as a sublime national aesthetic.[2] The painting's size made a powerful claim on viewers' attention: the title page of its accompanying *Descriptive Catalogue* proudly an-

FIG. 36. Sir George Hayter, *The House of Commons, 1833*, 1833–43. (National Portrait Gallery, London)

nounced that it was "Painted on one hundred and seventy square feet of canvass." Hayter himself observed its rareness as portraiture: "Few such complicated compositions have been presented to the eye in any age; the history of painting may describe pictures containing a greater number of heads, but no author alludes to any picture containing nearly four hundred portraits, where every person sat to the artist, who faithfully represented them" (vi). A portrait of Britain's leading representative body, *The House of Commons, 1833* carves out a space of representation in which the entirety of the nation is said to be present. In its sheer scale it makes the staggering claim to be a national portrait; through the extended metonymies of democracy its nearly 400 figures purport to an almost unimaginable comprehensiveness. Hayter's emphasis on the fact that these are not mere "heads" but individually painted portraits is significant. Ridding his composition of the whiff of mass production, he defines it instead as a portrait gallery in its own right, an assemblage of several hundred *detailed works of art*, each one necessitating a degree of labor, attention, and absorption equivalent—so he seems to suggest—to the attention a representative gives to his constituents.

But as an attempt to recuperate a form of representative presence, this claim for the originality of each portrait registers the tremendous strain under which mass imagery places this ideal. Jeffrey Schnapp, describing crowd images in the 1930s, articulates the problem. "Crowds presented themselves as so enormously variegated that individual identity no longer appeared fully legible," he writes, yet "this extreme diversity combined with large scale produced the impression that they had merged into abstract homogeneous masses. Extreme heterogeneity seemed to equal extreme homogeneity."[3] As in Pre-Raphaelite paintings, where a superabundance of detail leads, paradoxically, to a sense of aesthetic unnaturalness and abstraction, particularity verging on excess returns the viewer, against expectation, to the Reynoldsian general air.[4] It is at this point of abstraction and extreme derealization that an individual viewer's response comes into play—and where that response proves most malleable. A radically decentralized form overflowing with detail can encourage viewers to project their own desires onto an image. Such is the paradox of portraiture as it enters an age of realism and expanded political representation—also an age, as Poovey has shown, when "technologies of representation" brought a newly imagined social body, mapped and plotted in overwhelming detail, into view as a single, coherent abstraction.[5]

Hayter's painting illustrates this aesthetic and political dilemma. Like many others that populate the post-Reform national imaginary, *The House of Commons, 1833* seems insufficient to describe the profound empowerment for some and the ongoing disenfranchisement for most that characterizes the British polity after 1832. It is the painting of a myth, the imagining of an ideal—like the event it celebrates. F. R. Ankersmit's recent account of the affinity between government and art describes the work such an image performs: "Each (civil) society needs an image of itself in order to function properly; without such a mirror image of itself it will stumble around erratically and aimlessly like a blind man."[6] Reform was just such an image, providing an aesthetic national representation. The nation had gone through several ordeals of reaction en route to Reform, and for many the 1832 bill was a concession by the elite to stave off revolution (with the evolution of Reform from within taking another thirty-odd years). After the bill's passage, a stark discrepancy continued to exist between the implied cultural presence of the people and their actual political representation. Although Reform made Britain "considerably more democratic," Linda Colley observes, it still left four out of every five adult males, and all women, without the vote. Lacking a provision for a secret ballot, it also allowed landowners and employers to exert considerable pressure on those who did vote.[7] Even in the reformed Commons, where a property qualification for MPs continued in effect until 1858, the percentage of merchants, manufacturers, and bankers was actually lower than a year before.[8] As a contributor to *The Poor Man's Guardian* wrote in October 1832: "The promoters of the Reform Bill projected it, not with a view to subvert, or even remodel our aristocratic institutions, but to consolidate them by a reinforcement of sub-aristocracy from the middle-classes."[9] It is telling that Hayter, having completed a portrait sketch of each MP, offered it to his sitters for a price of ten guineas—more than the £10 qualification that 80 percent of the country was unable to meet.[10]

Against this set of political realities, *The House of Commons, 1833* staked its symbolic claim not simply as a group portrait but as Britain incarnate. The unique qualities of the painting become apparent in a brief comparison with an earlier image of the Commons by Thomas Rowlandson, published in Rudolph Ackermann's *Microcosm of London* in 1808 (figure 37). Hayter, aiming for grandeur, apologizes for the plainness of his sitters' dress: "The colour of European costume cannot be considered favourable to an artist," he says, "the colours worn are nearly the same, and, from the material of which they are composed, are less calculated to reflect light than silks and satins" (vii); Rowlandson, seemingly artless, conveys the unadorned simplicity of the Commons. Hayter's painting, with dimensions of seventeen-by-ten feet, is designed for a blockbuster show—it can accommodate countless viewers at a time (if only it can find a wall on which it will fit); Rowlandson's drawing fits in a book—it sits on a table and addresses one person at a time. Hayter's Commons is full to

FIG. 37. Thomas Rowlandson, *The House of Commons*, from R. Ackermann, *The Microcosm of London*, 1808. (Art and Architecture Library, Stanford University)

overflowing; Rowlandson's is half-empty. Hayter's MPs are serious, involved, purposive; Rowlandson's (those who are present at least) are distracted, some even dozing.

In part, these differences reflect the artists' respective backgrounds. Celebrated by Hazlitt for his "resplendent miniatures," Hayter was known to charge the highest prices in London, thus assuring himself an exclusive clientele.[11] He was also a longtime recipient of royal patronage: at twenty-four he was named Portrait Painter to Princess Charlotte, and in 1837 Queen Victoria appointed him Royal Painter of Portraits and History. He made a fortune on these royal connections, his *Coronation of Queen Victoria* alone netting him 2000 guineas. Conversely, Rowlandson, the son of a tradesman, worked in a sensuous, energetic style that was at odds with his academic training. His art, which purchased its comedy at the expense of privilege, was naturally attuned to what W. Charles

Townsend in 1844 recalled as the "paltry dimensions, confined space, and want of accommodation" of the Commons; it "could only be adequately described in the vernacular of Cobbett, who possessed the peculiar faculty of disenchanting his readers from all charms of poetry, of vulgarizing the noble, and debasing the sublime." Townsend underscores just how out of touch Hayter's grand aims were with the affect of the Commons. "Who that has sat in the gallery of the old House of Commons," he asks, "can fail to recollect his first feeling of disappointment, as he gazed with a sense of wounded pride around the dark and narrow room, and looked in astonishment at honourable members grouped in various attitudes of carelessness and indifference!"[12] It is precisely this plain and disappointing realism, suited to a humbler scale of representation, that Rowlandson captures and for which the Commons, as a national representative space, is celebrated.

It may be, however, that so gentle a demystification of the system of representation was not possible after 1832, when the Commons became a focus for the most extreme of political fears and desires. Tory opponents felt they were witnessing a virtual apocalypse. Robert Peel called Reform "a fatal precedent" and warned that "the monarchy would last for no more than five years." The Duke of Wellington felt he was "witnessing a revolution"; three weeks after its passage, he wrote to the Duke of Buckingham, "The Government of England is destroyed."[13] Against such fatalism, others embraced Reform with an equally fervent optimism. Cobbett declared that it "would take its place alongside . . . the Protestant Reformation and the revolution of 1688," and the *Westminster Review* described it as "our taking of the Bastille . . . the first act of our great political change."[14] Spectacular jubilees, appealing even to those still excluded from the franchise, were held throughout the nation, as "reform" became an idea whose symbolic value overshadowed its complex realities.[15]

It did have its concrete consequences, however. In addition to extending parliament's working year well beyond the leisurely five months of the eighteenth century, it provided a Whig majority for other legislation, such as that which effected the abolition of the slave trade.[16] The slave-trade legislation, in fact, being the most significant accomplishment of 1833, casts an enormous shadow here. A viewer unaware that the moment represented is ceremonial—"the moving the Address to the Crown on opening the first reformed parliament"—could easily assume that the Commons was engaged in serious discussion about the slave trade. This potential confusion of ceremony and political debate lies behind the painting's ideological effect. Hayter tells us that he was careful to choose a moment in which the House would be full and would be acting as a unified body: "The occasion represented is one on which the members of parliament have usually been unanimous, as opposition to an Address to the Crown rarely occurs, and it was one which would surely fill the House, as all the greatest men of the country were called on by their rank, their power, and intellect, to be present" (7). This helps to account for the difference between this image and Rowlandson's: the moment is a special one, which attracts all of the MPs and even some members of the Upper House (represented on each side, at the front of the painting). There is, moreover, very little in the way of disagreement or disruption. The emotional impact of so vast a representative body seeming to act as one is impressive, and one that Hayter claims is best conveyed by the visual artist: "Painting can represent the scene to posterity better than poetry or prose," he writes, for it presents "details, which must belong to the features, dress, or habits, of our present day, and which do not come within the province of an author" (5–6).

Why this should matter is not entirely clear, except for the fact that the painting strikes the viewer at one blow, with the overwhelming impact of a multiplicity that—for all its many particulars—can only be absorbed as a unified, abstract idea. Hayter's attention to an unusual moment of unanimity is telling. Democracy requires that the idea of unanimity be subsumed within the reality of a plurality. "A political association represents the achievement of the unanimous will of its members," argues Emmanuel Sieyès; but "in a society of several million individuals, ... plurality becomes legitimately a substitute."[17] Such an understanding of democracy "transsubstantiates *majority* into *unanimity*," writes Bernard Manin; "Majority *must* be considered as equivalent to unanimity."[18] The emotional impact of this painting requires that Hayter avoid revealing this transsubstantiation: to give visual form to Reform as an idea, majority must not simply be considered a substitute for unanimity—the two must be one and the same.

This is reflected in the painting's central formal tension, between the many particular portraits that comprise the picture and the unified body it presents. Aesthetically, this tension is resolved by a focus on the space of representation itself. The image is drawn from a perspective inaccessible to any spectator. It is an artificial perspective, omniscient and all-encompassing, that together with the framing of the figures by the room (not to mention the physical breadth of the 170-square-foot canvas) helps forge a compromise between the neoclassical "central form" and a decentered mass.[19] These effects relocate emphasis away from the many, individually painted portraits and onto the massive space in which they are made present, making this a portrait of a representative body *in which the space that contains that body is primary*. If, in the Hobbesian formulation, the unity of the state rests in the fact that all citizens share the same representative (the king), whose body gives form to the abstraction known as "the People," Hayter resolves a social body understood as so many "particular people in particular places" into an abstract universality: one unified representative body acting as one, in one particular place and time.

In 1776, John Adams described the American government as an appealing, if impossible, mimesis: it "should be in miniature, an exact portrait of the people at large."[20] As we saw in chapter four, attempts to manipulate scale—to make large portraits of small ones, and small portraits of large ones—are dogged by the specter of exclusion: details get expelled, absences magnified. Both sides of this dynamic are activated here. As the canvas widens to include ever more figures, each individual, himself representative of many others, shrinks to a miniature whose presence fades into abstraction. Like all portraits, it is haunted by the ghost of its referent.

Insofar as the painting incarnates the distinctly aesthetic quality of Reform, it also reproduces Reform's occlusions. It translates the detail into the universal but fails to acknowledge either the collapsing humanist faith in the concept of representativeness or the looming threat of atomism.[21] In its grandeur it also subsumes the related problematic of selection and exclusion that haunts realist representations—what Barthes in "The Reality Effect" describes as the arbitrary imposition of a frame: "Nothing could indicate why we should halt the details of the description here and not there."[22] Against these potential threats, Hayter posits a vigorous national unity that reflects Reform as well as its countless cultural extensions—the jubilees, knick-knacks, engravings, and sundry other commodities it spawned, which together united the nation under the banner of a patriotism woven out of shared desires.[23] Fostering an illusion of national totality, the gigantic portrait becomes little more than an emblem or abstract design, like a flag, standing in for a more general social relation.[24] At once a spectacular, large-scale national group portrait and a gallery of portraits in its own right, *The House of Commons, 1833* reproduces the philosophical, aesthetic, and political tensions that define the romantic legacy to the Victorian period, tensions that are keenly concentrated in the discourse of portraiture.

The localness and familiarity of portraiture, as we have seen, exist in a constant tension with—indeed are constituted by—what is most abstract, generalizable, anonymous. Encounters with portraits often invest the experience of mass-cultural sociality with an appealing illusion of personal intimacy. As in John Pinkerton's *Iconographia Scotia; or Portraits of Illustrious Persons of Scotland* (1797), where portraiture "renders us personally acquainted, so to speak, with former ages"; or *Portraits of the British Poets* (1824), with its offer to introduce readers "*personally* as it were" to figures in literary history, portraits promise to make intimate those relations that seem alien or imposing.[25] Perhaps for this reason, Elizabeth Bennet, in the passage with which I began this book, remains flatly unimpressed with Darcy's ancestral portraits: "In the gallery there were many family portraits, but they could have little to fix the attention of a stranger." Elizabeth, though new to Pemberley, is no stranger to Darcy. She may be precisely the kind of person upon whom these symbolic images of power are meant to work, but knowing Darcy personally entails a kind of affective immunity: the cold impersonality of power proves less impressive than the warm memory of what is familiar.

In a room dedicated to the display of carefully arranged objects, Susan Stewart writes, "each sign is placed in relation to a chain of signifers whose ultimate referent is not the interior of the room—in itself an empty essence—but the interior of the self."[26] This explains the refraction of Elizabeth's attention from the outward portrait to the remembered one, as well as Austen's own claim, upon visiting the gallery at Spring Gardens in May, 1813, to have found "a small portrait of Mrs Bingley, excessively like her. I went in hopes of finding one of her Sister, but there was no Mrs Darcy;—perhaps, however, I may find her in the Great Exhibition which we shall go to, if we have time;—I have no chance of finding her in the collection of Sir Joshua Reynolds Paintings which is now shewing in Pall Mall & which we are also to visit.—Mrs Bingley's is exactly herself, size, shaped face, features and sweetness; there never was a greater likeness."[27] Locating Jane Bennet's picture in a public gallery, a portrait that "is exactly herself, size, shaped face, features and sweetness," Austen indicates how the mass appeal of the portrait actually depends, oddly enough, upon the genre's simultaneous inscription of the abstract and the particular, the alien and intimate. The very fact that one tends to think of portraits by the artist's name rather than the sitter's indicates the strangeness of most public portraits.[28] Here "the collection of Sir Joshua Reynolds Paintings" would presumably feature individuals too well-known to provide Austen with the spitting image of a Mrs. Darcy. A familiar face may be like; but only an imaginary one can be *excessively* like.

This paradox, whereby a particular identity at once embodies an intractable otherness and implies a similarity that exists on a mass scale, sheds light on the effectiveness of portraits in helping to convey a sometimes genuine, sometimes hallucinatory sense of community.[29] A recent and rather direct example is provided by "Portraits of Grief," the *New York Times*' Pulitzer prize-winning response to the events of September 11, 2001. This serial gallery of portraits provided a virtual space where Americans could congregate and reimagine a collective body constituted by an accumulation of local details. Ultimately collected in a book titled *Portraits: 9/11/01*, these thousands of verbal and visual snapshots, intended to give a face to the tragedy, quickly became an occasion for imagining "America."[30] It was, to use the *Times*' own words, a "democratic" gallery that sought to erase distinctions of class, race, and gender, in which "executive vice presidents and battalion chiefs appeared alongside food handlers and janitors" in equal descriptions of two hundred words apiece.[31] Like the mournful snapshots covering the walls around Ground Zero (its street-level complement), "Portraits of Grief" was both moving and communalizing. Weaving together the personal and the conventional, it exemplified what Tricia Lootens refers to as the Möbius strip of national sentimentality, whereby textual effects that are deeply and genuinely affecting simultaneously carry subtle, potentially insidious, cues.[32] Local and nationalistic affects are here indistinguishable; even the web address for the permanent archive suggests as much: "nytimes.com/pages/national/portraits."

The incredible impact of this textual portrait gallery is accounted for by this transformation of an anonymous mass into a set of distinct and recognizable individuals, local details that are then aligned with the nation itself. The author Paul Auster wrote that the experience of reading the portraits was like having "real lives . . . jumping out at you. . . . We weren't mourning an anonymous mass of people, we were mourning thousands of individuals."[33] Yet the steadiness with which the profiles poured forth had an opposite effect as well: how, after all, *can* one mourn thousands of individuals *except* as a kind of abstraction? (It is a telling irony that "Portraits of Grief" evolved from a series originally titled "Among the Missing"—a fact that literalizes the inscription of absence in any portrait.) In *The American Scholar*, Thomas Mallon has observed the weirdly homogenizing effect of the series' emphasis on a fantasy of unproblematic domesticity.[34] But it is not so much that "Portraits of Grief" churned out multiple versions of the same desirable story as that its serial form and massive scale meant that even the most genuine of local details were bound to be swallowed up in the relentless multiplication of detail.[35] Put another way, it is not that "Portraits" mass-produced grief, but that it made grief an object of mass consumption. In the words used to advertise *Portraits: 9/11/01*: "There's more than one Ground Zero—there are thousands of Ground Zeros. *Portraits: 9/11/01*, a collection of the over 1,800 profiles published in the *Times*, helps us visit them all."[36]

To call such grief touristic, a form of mental traveling, is to recognize the gallery of portraits as an ever-widening vista of imagined social relations. Like the spectacle, the gallery is, in Guy Debord's words invoked at the start of this book, "not a collection of images, but *a social relation, mediated by images*." But what, precisely, is this sociality that it incarnates? Even as "Portraits of Grief" multiplied, decentered, and localized the tragedies of September 11, its proliferation of faces and personal details, in a gallery read daily by countless other Americans, helped to generate a social body that could only exist, could only *survive*, as an abstraction. Such effects can be unifying or terrifying. Witness Thomas De Quincey's hallucinatory vision, in which the ocean becomes a massive space of representation: "The sea appeared paved with innumerable faces, upturned to the heavens: faces, imploring, wrathful, despairing, surged upwards by thousands, by myriads, by generations, by centuries." De Quincey, attributing the vision to living in London, a place he says is ruled by "the tyranny of the human face," again shows the particular body lost amidst mass culture's sea of faces.[37] His nightmare vision of urban alienation augurs modern images of social inclusiveness, such as Mirko Ardemagni's *The New Masses* (1935), a photograph of a crowd with no shape except that conferred arbitrarily by the picture's edge. Startlingly undifferentiated and homogeneous, such imagery illustrates the diffusion of actual bodies into aesthetic abstraction.[38] That readers might have an interest in their own abstraction—or analogously, in an aestheticization that promises inclusion in a phantom social body—is at once a curious outcome of the discourse of portraiture and a perplexing symptom of modernity.

Notes

Introduction

1. Jane Austen, *Pride and Prejudice* (1813), ed. Robert Irvine (Peterborough, ON: Broadview Press, 2002), 88. The epigraphs are from Franco Moretti, *Atlas of the European Novel 1800–1900* (London and New York: Verso, 1998), 17; and Guy Debord, *La Société du Spectacle* (1967; Paris: Gallimard, 1992), 4. ("Le spectacle n'est pas un ensemble d'images, mais un rapport social entre des personnes, médiatisé par des images.")

2. Darcy's annual income of £10,000 makes his family among the richest few hundred in all of England, but lacking a seat in the House of Lords, he is by law a commoner, not an aristocrat. He does, however, have aristocratic ancestry, his maternal grandfather having been a member of the peerage. On money and class in Austen's time and in this novel in particular, see Lawrence Stone and Jeanne C. Fawtier Stone, *An Open Elite? England 1540–1880* (Oxford: Clarendon Press, 1984), and James Heldman, "How Wealthy is Mr Darcy—*Really*? Pounds and Dollars in the World of *Pride and Prejudice*," *Persuasions: Journal of the Jane Austen Society of North America* 12 (1990), 38–49.

3. Edmund Burke, *Reflections on the Revolution in France* (1790), ed. L. G. Mitchell (Oxford: Oxford University Press, 1993), 33. On the country-house gallery, see Shearer West, "Framing Hegemony: Economics, Luxury and Family Continuity in the Country House Portrait," in Paul Duro, ed., *The Rhetoric of the Frame: Essays on the Boundaries of the Artwork* (Cambridge: Cambridge University Press, 1996), 63–78 (esp. 76–77).

4. Richard Steele, *The Spectator* no. 109 (5 July 1711); in *The Spectator*, ed. Donald F. Bond, 5 vols. (Oxford: Clarendon Press, 1965), 1: 449–50.

5. The phrase "representative space" is adapted from Oliver Arnold's work on the ideology of Commons in the seventeenth century: "a virtual space in which the whole realm was, according to Commons' rhetoric, present"; "Absorption and Representation: Mapping England in the Early Modern House of Commons," in *Literature, Mapping, and the Politics of Space in Early Modern Britain*, eds. Andrew Gordon and Bernhard Klein (Cambridge: Cambridge University Press, 2001), 17.

6. Linda Colley, *Britons: Forging the Nation, 1707–1837* (New Haven, CT: Yale University Press, 1993), 177.

7. *The Sociology of Georg Simmel*, ed. and trans. Kurt Wolff (Glencoe, IL: The Free Press, 1950), 46, 48.

8. Bruce Robbins, "Introduction: The Public as Phantom," *The Phantom Public Sphere*, ed. Robbins (Minneapolis and London: University of Minnesota Press, 1993), xix-xx.

9. *The Literary Career of Sir Joshua Reynolds*, ed. Frederick W. Hilles (Cambridge: Cambridge University Press, 1976), 38.

10. On the Signboards (or Sign Painters') Exhibition, see Brandon Taylor, *Art for the Nation: Exhibitions and the London Public* (New Brunswick, NJ: Rutgers University Press, 1999), 14–19; and Ronald Paulson, *Popular and Polite Art in the Age of Hogarth and Fielding* (Notre Dame, IN, and London: University of Notre Dame Press, 1979), 31–48.

11. Newspaper clipping dated 1789, in *Press Cuttings from English Newspapers on Matters of Artistic Interest, 1686–1835*, 6 vols. (London, Victoria and Albert Museum), 2: 509; quoted in Richard D. Altick, *Paintings From Books: Art and Literature in Britain, 1760–1900* (Columbus: Ohio State University Press, 1985), 44.

12. Colley, *Britons*, 176.

13. On the role of museums in nurturing fictions of the social body, see Vera Zolberg, "'An Elite Experience for Everyone': Art Museums, the Public, and Cultural Literacy," in *Museum Culture: Histories, Discourses, Spectacles*, eds. Daniel J. Sherman and Irit Rogoff (Minneapolis: University of Minnesota Press, 1994), 49–65; and Carol Duncan, "Art Museums and the Ritual of Citizenship," in *Exhibiting Cultures: The Poetics and Politics of Museum Display*, eds. Ivan Karp and Stephen D. Lavine (Washington, DC: Smithsonian, 1991), 88–103.

14. *Annals of the Fine Arts* 1 (1817), 52.

15. Jonathan Richardson, *An Essay on the Theory of Painting* (London: John Churchill, 1715), 41.

16. Quoted in Marcia Pointon, *Hanging the Head: Portraiture and Social Formation in Eighteenth-Century England* (New Haven, CT and London: Yale University Press, 1993), 2. Pointon documents the price scales as well, on pages 2–3, 38.

17. Marcia Pointon, "Portrait! Portrait! Portrait!!!" in *Art on the Line: The Royal Academy Exhibitions at Somerset House, 1780–1836*, ed. David H. Solkin (New Haven, CT: Yale University Press, 2001), 95–96.

18. David Cannadine, *Aspects of Aristocracy: Grandeur and Decline in Modern Britain* (New Haven, CT and London: Yale University Press, 1994), 10.

19. Pointon, *Hanging the Head*, 38; Cannadine, *Aspects of Aristocracy*, 19.

20. John Cannon, *Aristocratic Century: The Peerage of Eighteenth-Century England* (Cambridge and New York: Cambridge University Press, 1984), 114.

21. Cannadine, *Aspects of Aristocracy*, 20; *The Opinions of William Cobbett*, eds. G. D. H. and Margaret Cole (London: Cobbett Publishing Co., [1944]), 281.

22. Cannadine, *Aspects of Aristocracy*, 19.

23. Charles Rosen and Henri Zerner, *Romanticism and Realism; The Mythology of Nineteenth-Century Art* (New York: Viking, 1984), 38.

24. Wordsworth, *The Prelude* (1805), 7: 686, 692, in *The Prelude: 1799, 1805, 1850*, ed. Jonathan Wordsworth, M. H. Abrams, and Stephen Gill (New York and London: W. W. Norton, 1979).

25. Robert L. Vales, *Peter Pindar* (New York: Twayne, 1973), 36.

26. Mark Girouard, *The English Town: A History of Urban Life* (London and New Haven, CT: Yale University Press, 1990), 119.

27. Cannadine, *Aspects of Aristocracy*, 34; Michael McCahill, *Order and Equipoise: The Peerage and the House of Lords, 1783–1806* (London: Royal Historical Society, 1978), 148. "Peerage mania" was a phenomenon that saw more than 200 peerages created between 1776 and 1830; see also Cannadine, *Aspects of Aristocracy*, 29–32.

28. Jacob George Strutt, *Sylva Britannica; or, Portraits of Forest Trees*, (London: Longman, Rees, Orme, Brown, and Green, 1826).

29. For three powerful accounts of formalism and historicist criticism, see Seth Lerer, "Medieval English Literature and the Idea of the Anthology," *PMLA* 118 (2003), 1251–67; Alan Liu, "The Power of Formalism: The New Historicism," *ELH* 56 (1989), 721–71; and Susan J. Wolfson, *Formal Charges: The Shaping of Poetry in British Romanticism* (Stanford, CA: Stanford University Press, 1997), esp. 1–30.

30. Henry James, "Preface" to *The Tragic Muse*, in *Henry James: The Critical Muse: Selected Literary Criticism*, ed. Roger Gard (Harmondsworth: Penguin, 1987), 514–16.

31. This shift was spearheaded by John Barrell, *The Political Theory of Painting from Reynolds to Hazlitt: "The Body of the Public"* (New Haven, CT: Yale University Press, 1986), and ed., *Painting and the Politics of Culture: New Essays on British Art 1700–1850* (Oxford and New York: Oxford University Press, 1992); Morris Eaves, *The Counter-Arts Conspiracy: Art and Industry in the Age of Blake* (Ithaca, NY: Cornell University Press, 1992); W. J. T. Mitchell, *Iconology: Image, Text, Ideology* (Chicago: University of Chicago Press, 1986); and David Solkin, *Painting for Money: The Visual Arts and the Public Sphere in Eighteenth-Century England* (New Haven, CT and London: Yale University Press, 1992). Others whose work on romantic visual culture has propelled this turn include: William Galperin, *The Return of the Visible in British Romanticism* (Baltimore, MD: The Johns Hopkins University Press, 1994); Eric Gidal, *Poetic Exhibitions: Romantic Aesthetics and the Pleasures of the British Museum* (Lewisburg: Bucknell University Press, 2001); Bruce Haley, *Living Forms: Romantics and the Monumental Figure* (Albany: State University of New York Press, 2003); Andrea Henderson, "Passion and Fashion in Joanna Baillie's 'Introductory Discourse'," *PMLA* 112 (March 1997), 198–213; Judith Pascoe, *Romantic Theatricality: Gender, Poetry, and Spectatorship* (Ithaca, NY: Cornell University Press, 1997); Grant F. Scott, *The Sculpted Word : Keats, Ekphrasis, and the Visual Arts* (Hanover, NH: University Press of New England, 1994); Richard C. Sha, *The Visual and Verbal Sketch in British Romanticism* (Philadelphia: University of Pennsylvania Press, 1998); Jonah Siegel, *Desire and Excess: The Nineteenth-Century Culture of Art* (Princeton, NJ: Princeton University Press, 2000); and Gillen D'Arcy Wood, *The Shock of the Real: Romanticism and Visual Culture, 1760–1860* (New York: Palgrave, 2002). This list is not exhaustive, of course, as reflected by the insightful and influential work cited throughout these notes.

32. Samuel Taylor Coleridge, "On Poesy or Art," in *Biographia Literaria, with his Aesthetical Essays*, ed. J[ohn] Shawcross, 2 vols. (Oxford: Oxford University Press, 1907; repr. 1979), 2: 259. There has been a recent surge of interest in the ways that portraiture helps to market literature and fashion identity—one that makes the recognition of the politics underlying the discourse of portraiture all the more urgent. On portraiture and authorial self-presentation, see Simon Bainbridge, "From Nelson to Childe Harold: The Transformations of the Byronic Image," *Byron Journal* 27 (1999), 13–25; Christine Kenyon

Jones, "Fantasy and Transfiguration: Byron and his Portraits," in *Byromania: Portraits of the Artist in Nineteenth- and Twentieth-Century Culture*, ed. Frances Wilson (New York: St. Martin's Press, 1999), 109–36; Morton D. Paley, *Portraits of Coleridge* (Oxford: Clarendon Press, 1999); Pascoe, *Romantic Theatricality*; Linda H. Peterson, "Female Autobiography, Narrative Duplicity," *Studies in the Literary Imagination* 23 (1990), 165–76; Eleanor Ty, "Engendering a Female Subject: Mary Robinson's (Re)Presentations of the Self," *English Studies in Canada* 21 (1995), 407–31; and Sarah M. Zimmerman, "Charlotte Smith's Letters and the Practice of Self-Presentation," *Princeton University Library Chronicle* 53 (1991–2), 50–77, and *Romanticism, Lyricism, and History* (Albany: State University of New York Press, 1999).

33. Foundational considerations of visual-verbal romanticism include James A. W. Heffernan, *Museum of Words: The Poetics of Ekphrasis from Homer to Ashbery* (Chicago: University of Chicago Press, 1993), and *The Re-Creation of Landscape: A Study of Wordsworth, Coleridge, Constable, and Turner* (Hanover, NH and London: University Press of New England, 1984); Christopher Hussey, *The Picturesque: Studies in a Point of View* (London: Putnam, 1927); Karl Kroeber, *British Romantic Art* (Berkeley: University of California Press, 1986); Stephen Larrabee, *English Bards and Grecian Marbles* (New York: Columbia University Press, 1943); Ronald Paulson, *Representations of Revolution (1789–1820)* (New Haven, CT and London: Yale University Press, 1983); and J. R. Watson, *Picturesque Landscape and English Romantic Poetry* (London: Hutchinson, 1970). Then there is Blake studies, a visual-verbal industry unto itself. Blake observed the bourgeois ideology of portraiture, as in his incisive annotations to Reynolds's *Discourses*. For exemplary treatments of his theory of words and images, see Barrell, "A Blake Dictionary," in *The Political Theory of Painting*, ch. 5; Eaves, *The Counter-Arts Conspiracy*; and W. J. T. Mitchell, *Blake's Composite Art: A Study of the Illuminated Poetry* (Princeton, NJ: Princeton University Press, 1978).

34. Until recently, a member needed simply to have declared: "Mr. Speaker, I spy strangers." The Stranger's Gallery has not been cleared since 1958, though motions for its clearance have been posited, and denied, on several occasions since then. See Norman W. Wilding and Philip Laundy, *An Encyclopaedia of Parliament* (New York: Praeger, 1968), and L. A. Abraham and S. C. Hawtrey, *A Parliamentary Dictionary* (London: Butterworth, 1956).

35. In the seventeenth century the word began to refer to the "persons who occupy the gallery portion of a theatre, . . . Hence fig. the less refined or instructed portion of the public" (*OED* 4.a)—a usage that was soon to become common.

36. Barrell, *The Political Theory of Painting*, 1–2.

37. The new model of society, Barrell claims, was economic: its "health and progress" were no longer a function of competing political interests, but rather depended "on the exercise of 'private' virtues, by the merchant, the trader, the manufacturer, the artisan, and the husbandman"; *The Birth of Pandora and the Divison of Knowledge* (Basingstoke and London: Macmillan, 1992), 10.

38. Ian Watt, *The Rise of the Novel: Studies in Defoe, Richardson and Fielding* (London: Chatto & Windus, 1957), 31. For a penetrating treatment of the figure of the "national body," see Marc Redfield, *The Politics of Aesthetics: Nationalism, Gender, Romanticism* (Stanford, CA: Stanford University Press, 2003), 45–92. Redfield gives a concise and very helpful discussion of the frequently employed trope of the body on pages 74–81.

39. Pierre Manent, *Intellectual History of Liberalism*, trans. Rebecca Balinski (Princeton, NJ: Princeton University Press, 1994), 49.

40. William Makepeace Thackeray, *Vanity Fair: A Novel Without a Hero* (1848; London: Everyman Modern Library, 1991), 604.

41. On this humanizing trend (and this particular print), see Colley, *Britons*, ch. 5. Theresa Kelley's argument that allegory survives into modernity by "shuttling . . . awkwardly between human attributes and abstract ideas," making "border raids" on the real (including the human and pathetic), suggests a helpful gloss on this bourgeoisification of the image of the royal body; Kelley, *Reinventing Allegory* (Cambridge: Cambridge University Press, 1997), 2, 9.

42. Mary Poovey, *Making a Social Body: British Cultural Formation, 1830–1864* (Chicago: University of Chicago Press, 1995), 7–8.

43. Peter Stallybrass and Allon White, *The Politics and Poetics of Transgression* (Ithaca, NY: Cornell University Press, 1986), 93.

44. On Britannia as feminine allegory for the nation, see Anne K. Mellor, *Mothers of the Nation: Women's Political Writing in England, 1780–1830* (Bloomington and Indianapolis: Indiana University Press, 2000), 139–46. On "John Bull" as a metaphor for public opinion, see Miles Taylor, "John Bull and the Iconography of Public Opinion in England c. 1712–1929," *Past and Present* 134 (1992), 93–128; and Dror Wahrman, "Public Opinion, Violence, and the Limits of Constitutional Politics," in *Re-reading the Constitution: New Narratives in the Political History of England's Long Nineteenth Century*, ed. James Vernon (Cambridge: Cambridge University Press, 1996), 83–122.

45. Gordon Teskey, *Allegory and Violence* (Ithaca, NY and London: Cornell University Press, 1996), 126. On the neoclassical unease with allegory, see Kelley, *Reinventing Allegory*, esp. 6–9, 70–92.

46. William Blake, "Annotations to Sir Joshua Reynolds's Discourses," in *The Complete Poetry and Prose of William Blake*, ed. David Erdman (Berkeley: University of California Press, 1982), 641.

47. Bernard Mandeville, *The Fable of the Bees: or, Private Vices, Publick Benefits*, Part II (1729), ed. F. B. Kaye, 2 vols. (Oxford: Clarendon Press, 1924), 2: 32–34.

48. On Hogarth's anti-academic position and influence on later artists, see several works by Ronald Paulson, including *Emblem and Expression: Meaning in English Art of the Eighteenth Century* (Cambridge: Harvard University Press, 1975); *The Beautiful, Novel, and Strange: Aesthetics and Heterodoxy* (Baltimore and London: Johns Hopkins University Press, 1996); *Popular and Polite Art*; and "English Painting: One School or Two?" *Eighteenth-Century Life* 17 (1993), 104–19. For an especially thorough and wide-ranging treatment of the enduring Hogarthian countertradition, see Robert Patten, *George Cruikshank's Life, Times, and Art*, 2 vols. (New Brunswick, NJ: Rutgers University Press, 1992–96). For a view oriented to the influence of civic humanism, see Solkin, *Painting for Money*, 78–105.

49. See Paulson, *Beautiful, Novel, and Strange*, 83–84.

50. William Hogarth, *Analysis of Beauty*, ed. Joseph Burke (Oxford: Oxford University Press, 1955), 123–24; quoted in Paulson, *Beautiful, Novel, and Strange*, 94.

51. Rouquet, quoted in Paulson *Beautiful, Novel, and Strange*, 258; Barry, *The Works of James Barry*, 2 vol. (London: Cadell and Davies, 1809), 2: 224, 306, 385.

52. Paulson, *Beautiful, Novel, and Strange*, xv.

53. Amal Asfour and Paul Williamson, *Gainsborough's Vision* (Liverpool: Liverpool University Press, 1999), 3.

54. Paulson, *Emblem and Expression*, 210, 211.

55. Blake, "Annotations to Sir Joshua Reynolds's Discourses," 641; *The Complete Works of William Hazlitt*, ed. P. P. Howe, 21 vols. (London: J. M. Dent, 1934), 6: 132.

56. Barrell, *Birth of Pandora*, 48. The British cultural-materialist school of art history, Paulson argues, has neglected Hogarth's influence in describing an art world dominated by an ethos of civic humanism. Hazlitt, for one, was powerfully affected by Hogarth (as I discuss in chapter four), and it is telling that Barrell, whose book *The Political Theory of Painting* (1986) has had a profound impact on recent art-historical writing (and, indeed, on the present study), takes issue with Hazlitt's disjoining of aesthetics and history, or taste and politics. Andrew Hemingway, who offers penetrating commentary on Barrell's argument, presents a spirited defense of Hazlitt, noting that "by 1816, the defeat of Napoleon, the break-up of the radical movement with which he had grown up, and the extremely repressive political climate of Regency Britain had reduced Hazlitt to a condition of political despair. . . . With the public forms of culture so irremediably compromised in his eyes, it is not surprising that he came to believe that true discernment was only possible for a few"; "The Political Theory of Painting Without the Politics," *Art History* 10 (1987), 381–95 (392).

57. Colley, *Britons*, 210.

58. J. P. Hemm, *Portraits of the Royal Family in Penmanship* (Nottingham : Hemm, Oliver & Co., 1831). Elizabeth Fay introduces the phrase "book-form portrait gallery" as a descriptive for the genre in her essay "Portrait Galleries, Representative History, and Hazlitt's Spirit of the Age," *Nineteenth-Century Contexts* 24 (2002), 151–75.

59. In considering this use of the medium, I am indebted to Jeffrey Schnapp's discussion of Xanti Schawinski's poster *1934-XII*, a Leviathan-like image of the Italian masses gathered in the torso of Mussolini. In representing Mussolini's face, Schawinski preserved the dots that are a natural result of industrial lithography. Choosing not to use a higher resolution image, he generated a visual echo (between the members of the crowd and the dots in Mussolini's face), emphasizing a similarity between the people and their medium of representation. The image thus suggests the use of technology to subsume the will of the people into one man's will. Schnapp, *Staging Fascism: 18BL and the Theater of Masses for Masses* (Stanford, CA: Stanford University Press, 1996), 108.

60. Teskey, *Allegory and Violence*, 136.

61. John Horne Tooke, *Two Pair of Portraits presented to all the unbiassed electors of Great-Britain and especially to the electors of Westminster* (London, 1788), 26.

62. Vales, *Peter Pindar*, 36.

63. *Literary Gazette* 2 (1818), 299.

64. On "Terramania," see Cannadine, *Aspects of Aristocracy*, 12.

65. Barry, *Works*, 2: 309.

66. John Boydell, *Collection of Prints, from Pictures Painted for the Purpose of Illustrating the Dramatic Works of Shakspeare, by the Artists of Great Britain*, 2 vols. (London: John and Josiah Boydell, 1803), [vi].

67. See Pierre Bourdieu, *Distinction: A Social Critique of the Judgement of Taste*, trans. Richard Nice (Cambridge, MA: Harvard University Press, 1984).

68. Paulson, *Beautiful, Novel, and Strange*, 76.

69. Barry, *Works*, 2: 309, 342.

70. Robert Jephson, *Roman Portraits: A Poem in Heroick Verse* (London: G. G. and J. Robinson, 1794); William Hazlitt, *The Spirit of the Age; or, Contemporary Portraits* (London: H. Colburn, 1825); Hazlitt, *Works*, 4: 305; Thomas Carlyle, "Sir Walter Scott," in *The Works of Thomas Carlyle*, ed. H. D. Traill, 30 vol. (London: Chapman and Hall, 1896–99), 29: 77–78.

71. [Mrs. A. Maddocks], *Scripture Female Portraits* (London: E. Wallis, 1820), 10.

72. *A Mother's Portrait, Sketched soon after her Decease* (London: Knight and Lacey, 1823), 1, 3, 4. Edgeworth writes: "We cannot judge either of the feelings or of the characters of men with perfect accuracy from their actions or their appearance in public; it is from their careless conversations, their half finished sentences, that we may hope with the greatest probability of success to discover their real characters"; *Castle Rackrent* (London: J. Johnston 1800), iv.

73. There were small, inexpensive "galleries" such as *The Eccentric Magazine; or, Lives and Portraits of Remarkable Characters* (1812), and *Portraits of Curious Characters in London* (1814), and larger, more expensive ones, such as R. S. Kirby's *Wonderful and Scientific Museum: or, Magazine of Remarkable Characters* (1803–1809), and John Thomas Smith's *Vagabondiana* (1817), which sought to underscore the distinctiveness and variety of English life for a higher-class audience. On this trend, see Deidre Shauna Lynch, *The Economy of Character: Novels, Market Culture, and the Business of Inner Meaning* (Chicago: University of Chicago Press, 2000), 260–61, and Pointon, *Hanging the Head*, 91–94.

74. James Caulfield, *Portraits, Memoirs, and Characters, of Remarkable Persons, from the Revolution in 1688 to the End of the Reign of George II*, 4 vols. (London: H. R. Young and T. H. Whitely, 1819–20), 1:iii.

75. Barrell, *Birth of Pandora*, 1.

76. Not that such galleries were unproblematic in their performances of social inclusion. Though Pointon says that Caulfield generated "a subversive effect" by using portraiture "to remind readers . . . of the antithesis of polite society," it is important to note that in his preface he stresses the *exceptionality* of his subjects: their very singularity is not "representative" but non-normative and deviant. Caulfield also boasts that the images are "taken from originals of the greatest scarcity and value. . . . [N]ot a life or character is recorded, but is accompanied by a portrait of unquestioned authenticity"—the emphasis falling not on breadth but on the scarcity and authenticity of the prints. These may be "low" characters, but within an economy of rare goods they are precious commodities. Pointon, *Hanging the Head*, 92, 94; Caulfield, *Portraits*, 1: ix. For alternative readings of the element of "play" in eighteenth-century art, see Paulson, *Emblem and Expression*, and Solkin, *Painting for Money*, 89–93.

77. John Thomas Smith, *Vagabondiana; or, Anecdotes of Mendicant Wanderers Through the Streets of London* (London: [John Thomas Smith], 1817), iv, 44.

78. Hazlitt, *Works*, 12: 285–86; Sir Joshua Reynolds, *Discourses on Art* (1769–90), ed. Robert R. Wark, 3rd ed. (New Haven, CT and London: Yale University Press, 1997), 140.

79. This complexity is nicely summarized by W. J. T. Mitchell, who describes the recent suspicion into which the referential realism of the photograph has fallen: "It is getting increasingly hard to find anyone who will defend the view (variously labeled 'positivist,' 'naturalistic,' or 'superstitious and naïve') that photographs have a special causal

and structural relationship with the reality that they represent"; *Picture Theory: Essays on Verbal and Visual Representation* (Chicago: University of Chicago Press, 1994), 282. "The romantic visible" is Galperin's phrase: a "more legitimate opposition to romanticism" than what Carol T. Christ, describing the dominant mode of Victorian cultural production, calls "the aesthetic of particularity"; *The Return of the Visible*, 288. Christ's study is important for the understanding of Victorian representation; *The Finer Optic: The Aesthetic of Particularity in Victorian Poetry* (New Haven, CT and London: Yale University Press, 1975).

80. Letter to *Le Messager*, 19 Nov 1851, quoted in T. J. Clark, *Image of the People: Gustave Courbet and the Second French Republic 1848–1851* (Greenwich, CT: New York Graphic Society, 1973), 23. ("Non seulement socialiste, mais bien encore démocrate et républicain, en un mot, partisan de toute la Révolution et par dessus tout, réaliste, c'est-à-dire, ami sincère de la vraie vérité.") John Tagg uses the phrase "democratization of the image" to introduce what he reads as the duplicitous nature of photography in *The Burden of Representation: Histories and Photographies* (Amherst: University of Massachusetts Press, 1988), 34.

As the reference to Tagg suggests, the question of photographic representation haunts the margins of this study. The formal relation between photography and an aesthetics of particularity, as well as the political effects of photography, is an exceedingly complex matter about which much has been written. Many in the nineteenth century intuited a genuine democratization. According to Nancy Armstrong, over 300 million *cartes des visites* were sold in England between 1861 and 1867 alone, an explosion in the sphere of representation that led Lachan Maclachlan to view the photograph as a development binding "every grade of society, from the Queen on the throne to the peasant in his humble cottage," and, on the other side of the Atlantic, Ralph Waldo Emerson to call it "the true Republican style of painting." Armstrong, *Fiction in an Age of Photography* (Cambridge, MA: Harvard University Press, 1999), 17; Maclachlan, "A National Photographic Portrait Gallery," *British Journal of Photography* (15 August 1863): 333; Emerson quoted in Mary Warner Marien, *Photography and Its Critics: A Cultural History, 1839–1900* (New York: Cambridge University Press, 1997), 4. Tagg's is the most powerful account of the shadow-side of democratization. As he observes, the proliferation of photographic portraits meant that portraiture not only "furnished the cosier spaces of the bourgeois home" but "also found a place in files—in police stations, hospitals, school rooms and prisons. . . . It was no longer a privilege to be pictured but the burden of a new class of the surveilled"; *The Burden of Representation*, 58–59.

81. "New Design," *Punch* 13 (1847), 20.

82. Henry Bromley, *A Catalogue of Engraved British Portraits, from Egbert the Great to the Present Time* (London, 1793), vi.

83. I quote Desenfans's title, *A Plan . . . to preserve among us, and to transmit to posterity, The Portraits of the most distinguished characters of England, Scotland and Ireland, since his Majesty's accession to the Throne* (London, 1799).

84. John Hayes, "Introduction," *National Portrait Gallery in Colour*, ed. Richard Ormond (New York: St. Martin's Press, 1979), 3.

85. John Burke, *The Portrait Gallery of Distinguished Females, including Beauties of the Courts of George IV and William IV* (London: E. Bull, 1833). For a reading of this book-form gallery, see Fay, "Portrait Galleries, Representative History, and Hazlitt's Spirit of the Age," 155–61.

86. For a fascinating account of some of the ways that the new British elite "enfolded themselves in all the romantic extravagance of a spurious antiquity," see Cannadine, *Aspects of Aristocracy*, 34.

87. William Jerdan, *National Portrait Gallery of Illustrious and Eminent Personages of the Nineteenth Century*, 4 vols. (London: Fisher, Son, and Jackson, 1830–34). I quote from the anonymous review: *Gentleman's Magazine* 101: 1 (1831), 49. The close relation between books such as this one and the (actual) National Portrait Gallery is indicated by an early review of the exhibition, which claimed that it "ought to become an illustrated English history of all classes"; *The Athenaeum*, no. 1580 (1858): 181.

88. Dickens, *Bleak House*, ed. Stephen Gill (Oxford and New York: Oxford University Press, 1996), 305–6. Dickens indicates how female portraits in general, and book-galleries of female portraits in particular, codified femininity as a site for defining the tasteful disinterestedness that helped to ground nationalist discourse. See Kathy Alexis Psomiades, *Beauty's Body: Femininity and Representation in British Aestheticism* (Stanford, CA: Stanford University Press, 1997), 1–23; and Redfield, *Politics of Aesthetics*, 34–40.

89. *Portraits of the Spruggins Family, arranged by Richard Sucklethumkin Spruggins, Esq.* [pseud.], written and illustrated by Walter Sneyd; arranged for publication by Frances, Countess of Morley ([London], 1829). For another example of a satirical gallery of portraits—albeit one with a different set of investments—see Sir Frederick Fopping [pseud.], *Portraits of Fops; or Illustrations of the Foppish Character in all its Curious Variety* (London: J. Johnston, 1811).

90. Benedict Anderson, *Imagined Communities: Reflections on the Origin and Spread of Nationalism*, 2nd ed. (New York: Verso, 1991 [1983]), 77. In this revised edition Anderson includes a chapter on "Census, Map, Museum," which indicates the role these cultural institutions played in shaping how "the colonial state imagined its dominion." He writes that "museums, and the museumizing imagination, are both profoundly political" (178). The picture gallery is one kind of museum—if not, like the British Museum, a collection of artifacts testifying to Britain's imperial reach. For particularly strong treatments of nationalism and the aesthetic, see Gidal, *Poetic Exhibitions*, and Redfield, *The Politics of Aesthetics*.

91. Wordsworth, *Lyrical Ballads*, ed. R. L. Brett and A. R. Jones, 2nd ed. (New York and London: Routledge, 1991), 311; Samuel Taylor Coleridge, *The Friend*, ed. Barbara E. Rooke, 2 vols. (Princeton, NJ: Princeton University Press; London: Routledge and Kegan Paul, 1969), 1: 457; Hazlitt, *Works*, 12: 280; Moretti, *Atlas of the European Novel*, 17.

92. *The Adventures of Count Ferdinand Fathom*, ed. Jerry C. Beasley (Athens: University of Georgia Press, 1989), 4.

93. Reynolds, "Preface to the Ironical Discourse," *Portraits*, ed. Frederick W. Hilles (New York: McGraw-Hill, 1952), 145.

94. Recently F. R. Ankersmit has defended the aestheticization of politics by arguing that the gap between signified and signifier, representative and constituent, is the source for "the unparalleled political creativity of representative democracy": "What makes art interesting, what made the evolution of art possible, is precisely this indeterminacy in the relationship between art and reality. And if this is true about aesthetic representation, it is no less true of political and historical representation"; *Historical Representation* (Stanford, CA: Stanford University Press, 2001), 276. As Redfield has argued, however, Ankersmit's *apologia* for top-down political models reflects a thoroughly romantic ideal, wherein an entire *lack* of correspondence is precisely the *unity* of representation. (It is

indeed difficult—particularly in times like the present—to defend a view of political representation as *interesting*); *Politics of Aesthetics*, 204–5.

95. Alex Woloch, *The One Versus the Many: Minor Characters and the Space of the Protagonist* (Princeton, NJ: Princeton University Press, 2003), 31.

96. This image is discussed (for its documentary value as well as for its interest as a text in its own right) by several commentators in the remarkable collection of essays (cited previously) published by the Courtauld Institute to accompany its 1990 show: *Art on the Line: The Royal Academy Exhibitions at Somerset House, 1780–1836*. Among the contributors to this volume who treat the print are: John Murdoch, "Architecture and Experience: The Visitor and the Spaces of Somerset House, 1780–1796," 17; John Sunderland and David H. Solkin, "Staging the Spectacle," 24, 25; C. S. Matheson, " 'A Shilling Well Laid Out': The Royal Academy's Early Public," 47–48; Marcia Pointon, "Portrait! Portrait! Portrait!!!" 96; Greg Smith, "Watercolourists and Watercolours at the Royal Academy, 1780–1836," 193, 196.

97. On the symbolic importance of women at the Academy shows, see K. Dian Kriz, " 'Stare Cases': Engendering the Public's Two Bodies at the Royal Academy of Arts," in *Art on the Line*, ed. Solkin, 55–63. Kriz argues that the visibility of feminine politeness and sociability was as essential to the Academy's authority as was the aura of liberal masculinity. These particular women, as objects of the connoisseur's gaze, could be understood as embodying the precariousness (as Kriz describes it) of this feminine ideal. On the disruptive effect of having "two competing orders of attention," with smaller paintings subordinated and yet "nearest to the audience's eye," see Sunderland and David H. Solkin, "Staging the Spectacle," in *Art on the Line*, 24.

98. *Shelley's Poetry and Prose*, eds. Donald H. Reiman and Sharon B. Powers (New York and London: W. W. Norton, 1977), 242.

99. Kelley reads *The Cenci* in this light in *Reinventing Allegory*, 154ff. The reactions of Dickens and Mark Twain show how easily the personal response to such non-narrative images could slip into subjectivism. For Dickens, Beatrice Cenci's portrait is "almost impossible to be forgotten": "There is an expression in her eyes—although they are very tender and gentle—as if the wildness of a momentary terror, or distraction, had been struggled with and overcome, that instant; and nothing but a celestial hope, and a beautiful sorrow, and a desolate earthly helplessness remained." Twain is more skeptical of the expressive capacity of a portrait: "In Rome," he writes, "people with fine sympathetic natures stand up and weep in front of the celebrated 'Beatrice Cenci the Day Before Her Execution.' . . . It shows what a label can do. If they did not know the picture, they would inspect it unmoved, and say, 'Young Girl with Hay Fever; Young Girl with Her Head in a Bag.' " A portrait without a narrative or a label, Twain suggests, *means* only insofar as a particular viewer *responds*. Dickens, *American Notes and Pictures from Italy* (London: Oxford University Press, 1957); Twain, *Life on the Mississippi*, ed. John Seelye (London: Oxford University Press, 1990), 291.

100. Kelley, *Reinventing Allegory*, 155.

101. Christ, *The Finer Optic*, 11.

102. *Shelley's Poetry and Prose*, 473–74.

103. Coleridge, "On Poesy or Art," 259–60. On the internalization of mimesis in Coleridge, see Frederick Burwick, *Mimesis and its Romantic Reflections* (University Park: Pennsylvania State University Press, 2001), ch. 3. On Coleridge and portraiture, see

Denise Degrois, "Making the Absent Present: Self-Portraits and Portraits of the Artist in Coleridge's Work," *Wordsworth Circle* 22 (1991), 30–35; and Paley, *Portraits of Coleridge.*

104. Coleridge, *Biographia Literaria, or Biographical Sketches of My Literary Life and Opinions* (1817), ed. and intro. George Watson (London and Melbourne: J. M. Dent, 1975; repr. 1987), 57.

105. "On the Diversity of Opinions with regard to Likenesses in Portraits," *London Magazine*, 6 (1822), 34: 321–22.

106. Lavater's *Essays on Physiognomy*, one of the period's most extensive interpretations of portraiture, celebrates expressive portraits as "speaking portraits." Van Dyck's painting of Anthony Triest, for example, he calls "One of the most speaking portraits I am acquainted with"; John Casper Lavater, *Essays on Physiognomy, Designed to Promote the Knowledge and the Love of Mankind*, trans. Henry Hunter (London, John Murray, 1792), 226.

107. "Ekphrasis" can be read broadly as any verbal description of the three-dimensional world, but even in my more local concern with what Heffernan calls "the verbal representation of visual representation," disagreements exist. For Wendy Steiner, ekphrasis is "a pregnant moment" reproduced in words, "the concentration of action in a single moment of energy," whereas for Heffernan it is a "narrative response to pictorial stasis"; Heffernan, *Museum of Words*, 3, 5; Wendy Steiner, *The Colors of Rhetoric* (Chicago: University of Chicago Press, 1982), 41. Murray Krieger and Jean Hagstrum, in two of the classic treatments, hint at the priority of the image within an otherwise comfortable alliance of "sister arts"; Murray Krieger, "Ekphrasis and the Still Movement of Poetry; or, *Laokoon* Revisited," in *The Poet as Critic*, ed. Frederick McDowell (Evanston, IL: Northwestern University Press, 1967), 5; Jean Hagstrum, *The Sister Arts: The Tradition of Literary Pictorialism and English Poetry from Dryden to Gray* (Chicago: University of Chicago Press, 1958), 18. Heffernan and Grant F. Scott, on the other hand, view ekphrasis as a topos of struggle and interartistic rivalry.

108. Heffernan, *Museum of Words*, 93.

109. "On a Portrait" (lines 15–20). *The Poems of Anna Letitia [Aikin] Barbauld*, ed. William McCarthy and Elizabeth Kraft (Athens: University of Georgia Press, 1994), 139.

110. Samuel Johnson, *Idler* no. 45 (24 February 1759); in *The Idler and The Adventurer*, eds. W. J. Bate, J. M. Bullitt, and L. F. Powell (New Haven, CT: Yale University Press, 1963), 140.

111. *Letters of John Keats*, ed. Hyder E. Rollins, 2 vols. (Cambridge: Harvard University Press, 1958), 1: 369.

112. *Magazine of the Fine Arts* 1 (1821): 9–10.

113. "Stanzas to Painting," lines 33, 55, *The Poetical Works of Thomas Campbell* (Boston: Little, Brown and Co., 1864), 207–9.

114. Lines 1–2, 11–14, 33–40. *Andrew Marvell: Selected Poems*, eds. Frank Kermode and Keith Walker (Oxford and New York: Oxford University Press, 1990), 37–38. For a helpful discussion of this poem in the context of portraiture, see Michael Cohen, *Engaging English Art: Entering the Work in Two Centuries of English Painting and Poetry* (Tuscaloosa and London: The University of Alabama Press, 1987), 99–101.

115. Hazlitt, *Works*, 6: 149; 10: 112.

116. Lines 1–5. *The Poetical Works of Robert Southey*, 10 vols. (Boston, 1880), 2: 225–26.

117. Lines 1–6. *Selected Poems, Letters, Reception Materials*, ed Susan J. Wolfson (Princeton, NJ and Oxford: Princeton University Press, 2000), 467–69.

118. Henry F. Chorley, *Memorials of Mrs. Hemans* (London, 1836), 2: 150.

119. Lines 168–71. *The Poetical Works of Robert Browning*, eds. Ian Jack and Robert Inglesfield, 9 vols. (Oxford: Clarendon Press, 1995), 5: 31–53.

120. It is this specifically political orientation that distinguishes this study from Nancy Armstrong's similar, important effort to unfold such a prehistory; see "The Prehistory of Realism," the first chapter in her book *Fiction in an Age of Photography*. For a significant study of pre-photographic visual culture that seeks "to illuminate the largely unwritten pre-history of our millenial visual age," see Gillen D'Arcy Wood, *Shock of the Real*, 15.

121. Elizabeth Basye Gilmore Holt, *The Triumph of Art for the Public* (Garden City, NY: Anchor, 1979); Linda Dowling, *The Vulgarization of Art: The Victorians and Aesthetic Democracy* (Charlottesville: University Press of Virginia, 1996); George Orwell (on Dickens's "vivid pictures"), *The Collected Essays, Journalism and Letters*, eds. Sonia Orwell and Ian Angus, 4 vols. (New York: Harcourt, Brace & World, 1968), 1: 443, 455.

122. After the Bill's passage, the *Poor Man's Guardian* acknowledged the power of illusion. Hinting that Reform was an idealist aesthetic program, popular radicalism a realist-representationalist one, the writer continued: "The only difference between the Whigs and the Tories is this—the Whigs would give the shadow to preserve the substance; the Tories would not give the shadow, because stupid as they are, the millions will not stop at shadows but proceed onwards to realities" (25 Oct 1832); quoted in E. P. Thompson, *The Making of the English Working Class*, (New York: Vintage, 1966 [1963]), 812.

Chapter One: The Many Bodies of Edmund Burke

1. The epigraph is drawn from *The Correspondence of Edmund Burke*, ed. Thomas W. Copeland, 10 vols. (Cambridge/Chicago: Cambridge University Press & The University of Chicago Press, 1958–1978), 7: 75.

2. Reynolds, *Portraits*, 158.

3. This is the image given by Richard Wendorf in his excellent, critical biography, to which I am much indebted: *Sir Joshua Reynolds: The Painter in Society* (Cambridge, MA: Harvard University Press, 1996).

4. James Northcote, *The Life of Sir Joshua Reynolds*, 2 vols. (London, 1819), 2: 249–50.

5. Several years ago, Robert W. Uphaus detailed the affinities between the two men's politics, particularly their mutual view of genius and discovery as threatening "the massive disruption of the past"; "The Ideology of Reynolds's Discourses on Art," *Eighteenth-Century Studies* 12.1 (Autumn 1978), 59–73 (67). Burke's influence on Reynolds has been much remarked upon. Dr. Johnson once lamented that Reynolds was, as he put it, under "the *Irish constellation*," and after Johnson's death, Reynolds grew increasingly reliant on Burke for conversation and friendship. The painter was among those from whom Burke sought feedback on his *Reflections on the Revolution in France*, and in the years 1789–90—when Burke was writing the *Reflections* and Reynolds was conceiving his final discourse (as well as its ironic inverse)—the two were continually together. In addition to Uphaus, see Wendorf, *Sir Joshua Reynolds*, 196–98.

6. Burke, *Correspondence*, 7: 75.

7. Edmond Malone, ed., *The Works of Sir Joshua Reynolds, Knight . . . [and] An Account of the Life and Writings of the Author*, 2nd ed., 3 vols. (London: T. Cadell, 1798), 1: ci–ciii.

8. E. H. Gombrich, *Norm and Form* (London and New York: Phaidon, 1966; repr. 1971), 133.

9. Barrell, *Political Theory of Painting*, 70–71. On Reynolds's and Burke's interiorization of the discourse of custom, see Thomas Pfau, *Wordsworth's Profession: Form, Class, and the Logic of Early Romantic Cultural Production* (Stanford, CA: Stanford University Press, 1997), 272–88.

10. Barrell describes these ambiguities in *Political Theory of Painting*; see especially 98–99 and 140–1.

11. In Reynolds's female portraiture, Gill Perry argues, the "increasing instability of the portrait genre" finds expression in conventions that reveal the "constantly renegotiated status" of femininity; "Women in Disguise: Likeness, the Grand Style and the Conventions of Feminine Portraiture in the Work of Sir Joshua Reynolds," in *Femininity and Masculinity in Eighteenth-Century Art and Culture*, eds. Gill Perry and Michael Rossington (Manchester: Manchester University Press, 1994), 18, 32.

12. *General Evening Post*, February 25–28, 1792; quoted in Martin Postle, *Sir Joshua Reynolds: The Subject Pictures* (Cambridge: Cambridge University Press, 1995), 256.

13. Isaac Kramnick, *The Rage of Edmund Burke: Portrait of an Ambivalent Conservative* (New York: Basic Books, 1977), 10.

14. C. B. Macpherson, *Burke* (New York: Hill and Wang, 1980), 7.

15. *The Works of the Rt. Hon. Edmund Burke*, ed. Henry Rogers, 2 vols. (London: Holdsworth, 1842), 2: 500.

16. Stephen H. Browne, *Edmund Burke and the Discourse of Virtue* (Tuscaloosa: University of Alabama Press, 1993), 28. Browne, who emphasizes the emergence of "virtue" from "the active exchange between author and reader," here discusses what he calls Burke's "rhetorical portraiture" in the 1770s. Stephen Blakemore reveals the benefits of a tightly focused intertextual analysis of the *Reflections* in *Intertextual War: Edmund Burke and the French Revolution in the Writings of Mary Wollstonecraft, Thomas Paine, and James Mackintosh* (Madison, NJ: Fairleigh Dickinson University Press, 1997).

17. Hazlitt, *Works*, 12: 112.

18. Edmund Burke, *A Philosophical Enquiry into the Origin of Our Ideas of the Sublime and Beautiful* (1757), ed. James T. Boulton (London: Routledge and Kegan Paul, 1958), 42, 150. On the potentially debilitating effects of beauty in Burke's aesthetic account, see Frances Ferguson, "Sublime of Edmund Burke, Or the Bathos of Experience," *Glyph, Johns Hopkins Textual Studies* 8 (1981), 62-78; and Tom Furniss, *Edmund Burke's Aesthetic Ideology: Language, Gender, and Political Economy in Revolution* (Cambridge: Cambridge University Press, 1993). On the relationship between the aestheticized body and a gendered viewer, see the essays in *Femininity and Masculinity in Eighteenth-Century Art and Culture*, eds. Perry and Rossington, especially those by Perry ("Women in Disguise," 18-40) and Chloe Chard ("Effeminacy, Pleasure and the Classical Body," 142–61).

19. Wollstonecraft, *A Vindication of the Rights of Men* (1790; repr. with *A Vindication of the Rights of Woman* and *Hints*), eds. D. L. Macdonald and Kathleen Scherf (Peterborough, ON: Broadview Press, 1997), 37; Kramnick, *Rage of Edmund Burke*, 8, 138.

20. It has even led Seamus Deane to read it as travel literature—and as such, as a foundational text of Irish cultural studies; *Strange Country: Modernity and Nationhood in Irish Writing since 1790* (Oxford: Clarendon Press, 1997). See also Nicholas K. Robinson, *Edmund Burke: A Life in Caricature* (New Haven, CT: Yale University Press, 1996).

21. Thomas Paine, *Rights of Man* (1791–92), ed. Eric Foner (New York: Penguin, 1985), 50; Joel Barlow, *The Conspiracy* (1793), quoted in *Edmund Burke*, ed. Isaac Kramnick (Englewood Cliffs, NJ: Prentice-Hall, 1974), 126; Wollstonecraft, *Vindication of the Rights of Men*, 58.

22. Walter Benjamin uses the term "death's head" in describing allegory as *facies hippocratica*: "In allegory the observer is confronted with the *facies hippocratica* of history as a petrified, primordial landscape. Everything about history that, from the very beginning, has been untimely, sorrowful, unsuccessful, is expressed in a face—or rather in a death's head"; *The Origins of German Tragic Drama*, trans. John Osborne (London: NLB, 1977), 166.

23. Frans de Bruyn, *The Literary Genres of Edmund Burke: The Political Uses of Literary Form* (Oxford: Oxford University Press, 1996), 7. Relevant here, as well, is James Vernon's work on images of political leaders in nineteenth-century Britain, in support of the notion that "Politics, then as now, was about people"; *Politics and the People: A Study in English Political Culture, c. 1815–1867* (Cambridge: Cambridge University Press, 1993), 251–91 (290). Also see Vernon's claim elsewhere that "the mode of communication in which political discourse was articulated was critical to its meaning and reception"; "Notes Towards an Introduction," in *Re-reading the Constitution*, ed. Vernon, 20.

24. *Gallery of Portraits of the National Assembly, supposed to be written by Count de Mirabeau*, 2 vols. (London: G. G. J. and J. Robinson, 1790). See Pointon on how "the development of party-political machinery [was] served by the discourse of portraiture" in her account of "the phantom portrait gallery"; *Hanging the Head*, 97.

25. *Sketches from Nature, in High Preservation* (London: G. Kearsly, 1779), i.

26. I quote Pointon from *Hanging the Head*, 101. Gillray's print appears in *The Antijacobin Review and Magazine* 1 (December 1798) and is reprinted in *The Works of James Gillray* (London: Henry G. Bohn, 1847).

27. *Jane Austen's Letters*, ed. Deirdre Le Faye, 3rd ed. (London and New York: Oxford University Press, 1995), 323.

28. Frances Burney, *The Diary and Letters of Madame D'Arblay*, ed. Charlotte Francis Barrett, 7 vols. (London: Henry Colburn, 1842), 2: 62, 160.

29. Tony Tanner, *Jane Austen* (Cambridge, MA: Harvard University Press, 1986), 117. Students of the novel are familiar with the form's emphasis on the individual, an emphasis that modern readers in particular have institutionalized. Dorrit Cohn writes of the twentieth century's "predilection for novels with thoughtful characters and scenes of self-communion," and Elizabeth Kraft too has observed the veneration of "the individualistic, the internal, as though that were the nature of identity"; Cohn, *Transparent Minds: Narrative Modes for Presenting Consciousness in Fiction* (Princeton: Princeton University Press, 1978), v; Kraft, *Character and Consciousness in Eighteenth-Century Comic Fiction* (Athens: University of Georgia Press, 1992), 5.

30. Peter Brooks, *The Novel of Wordliness* (Princeton, NJ: Princeton University Press, 1969), 15.

31. Browne describes the *Speech of Taxation* as "a gallery of character portraits"; *Edmund Burke and the Discourse of Virtue*, 27.

32. *The Writings and Speeches of Edmund Burke: Volume 1, The Early Writings*, eds. T. O. McLoughlin and James T. Boulton (Oxford: Clarendon Press, 1997), 59–61. Background for this sketch is provided by James Prior, *Memoir of the Life and Character of the Right Hon. Edmund Burke* (1854), 2 vols. (New York: Burt Franklin, 1968), 1: 92.

33. J. G. A. Pocock, *Politics, Language, and Time: Essays on Political Thought and History* (New York: Atheneum, 1971), 212.

34. For Burke, the terms of the 1688 Declaration of Rights form a Constitution that is binding for all time. Paine, however, notes Burke's reluctance to go "into a comparison of the English and French constitutions, because he could not but perceive, when he sat down to the task, that no such thing as a constitution existed on his side of the question"; and he later cites Burke's desire to hide "some radical defect in what is called the English constitution"; *Rights of Man*, 72, 93. James Vernon, describing the "always unstable and endlessly contested" meanings of this "unwritten" text, writes that "the very word constitution itself conveys . . . fluidity and lack of fixity"; "Notes Towards an Introduction," *Re-reading the Constitution*, ed. Vernon, 2.

35. Hazlitt, *Works*, 10: 7.

36. Lynch, *The Economy of Character*, 58, 60.

37. Reynolds, *Discourses on Art*, 72. On caricature, see Diana Donald, *The Age of Caricature: Satirical Prints in the Reign of George III* (New Haven, CT: Yale University Press, 1996); Lynch, *The Economy of Character*, esp. chapter 1; and Pointon, *Hanging the Head*, 79–102.

38. Richard Brinsley Sheridan, *The School for Scandal* (1777), ed. F. W. Bateson (New York: W. W. Norton, 1979), 79.

39. On Burke's gendering of international commerce and mobile capital, see Deidre Lynch, "Domesticating Fictions and Nationalizing Women: Edmund Burke, Property, and the Reproduction of Englishness," in *Romanticism, Race, and Imperial Culture, 1780–1834*, eds. Alan Richardson and Sonia Hofkosh (Bloomington: Indiana University Press, 1996), 40–71; and Linda M. G. Zerilli, "Text/Woman as Spectacle: Edmund Burke's 'French Revolution'," *The Eighteenth Century: Theory and Interpretation* 33.1 (1992), 47–72.

40. I allude to Benjamin's essay on the reproducibility of the artwork; he writes: "[T]hat which withers in the age of mechanical reproduction is the aura of the work of art. This is a symptomatic process whose significance points beyond the realm of art. One might generalize by saying: the technique of reproduction detaches the reproduced object from the domain of tradition. By making many reproductions it substitutes a plurality of copies for a unique existence. And in permitting the reproduction to meet the beholder or listener in his own particular situation, it reactivates the object reproduced. These two processes lead to a tremendous shattering of tradition . . ."; Walter Benjamin, "The Work of Art in the Age of Mechanical Reproduction," trans. Harry Zohn, in *Illuminations*, ed. Hannah Arendt (New York: Schocken Books, 1968), 221. The fact that Benjamin uses "aura" to describe the experience of an autonomous, private, and leisured subjectivity—as opposed to the representation of royalty to a subject people—indicates the extent to which bourgeois subjectivity would take as its model the aristocratic sensibility it supposedly displaced. On the vital connection between writing and money, see Peter De Bolla: "The transferability of debt signified in the signature and authenticated by it places enormous power in the authority of the pen and the act of writing or inscribing: it states, at its margin, that one may *write* money"; De Bolla, *The Discourse of*

the Sublime: Readings in History, Aesthetics and the Subject (New York: Basil Blackwell, 1989), 110.

41. On symbolic castration in revolutionary iconography, see Neil Hertz, *The End of the Line: Essays on Psychoanalysis and the Sublime* (New York: Columbia University Press, 1985), 161–93.

42. Joseph Addison, *The Spectator*, no. 411 (21 June 1712); in Daniel McDonald, ed., *Selected Essays from "The Tatler," "The Spectator," and "The Guardian,"* (Indianapolis and New York: Bobbs-Merrill, 1973), 462.

43. Christopher Reid, who positions Marie Antoinette's feminine distress alongside the theatrical performances and public reputation of Sarah Siddons, is one of the few commentators to attend to the material culture in which Burke's imagery is enmeshed; "Burke's Tragic Muse: Sarah Siddons and the 'Feminization' of the *Reflections*," *Burke and the French Revolution: Bicentennial Essays*, ed. Steven Blakemore (Athens: University of Georgia Press, 1992), 1–27. Reid's focus on theater history and theatrical conventions—on, for instance, the appeal of the sentimental tableau as a focused instant of emotional stress—runs parallel to my emphasis on the influence of painting, and suggests that Siddonian portraiture (particularly Reynolds's own portrait of the actress, but also, perhaps, theater portraits of her) might also provide a fruitful way of approaching Burke's depiction of the French queen.

44. Kramnick, *The Rage of Edmund Burke*, xii.

45. Northcote, *Life of Reynolds*, 2: 58. On Reynolds's use of mirrors, see Wendorf, *Sir Joshua Reynolds*, 115–16.

46. Pulteney quoted in Wendorf, *Sir Joshua Reynolds*, 115; "On the Diversity of Opinions with regard to Likenesses in Portraits," *London Magazine*, 6 (1822), 34: 321; Hazlitt, *Works*, 12: 108.

47. Barrell, *The Political Theory of Painting*, 94.

48. Jacques Revel, "Marie-Antoinette in Her Fictions: The Staging of Hatred," trans. Terri J. Nelson and Bernadette Fort, in *Fictions of the French Revolution*, ed. Bernadette Fort (Evanston, IL: Northwestern University Press, 1991), 114.

49. On the "always-proliferating literature of derision preoccupied with [Marie Antoinette's] sexual body," see Lynn Hunt, "The Many Bodies of Marie Antoinette: Political Pornography and the Problem of the Feminine in the French Revolution," in *Eroticism and the Body Politic*, ed. Lynn Hunt (Baltimore, MD: Johns Hopkins University Press, 1991) 108–30 (116).

50. *Letters of Sir Joshua Reynolds*, ed. Frederick W. Hilles (Cambridge: Cambridge University Press, 1929), 84–85.

51. Furniss, *Edmund Burke's Aesthetic Ideology*, 154.

52. *The Works of the Rt. Hon. Edmund Burke*, 2: 500.

53. Robert W. Jones, *Gender and the Formation of Taste in Eighteenth-Century Britain: The Analysis of Beauty* (Cambridge: Cambridge University Press, 1998), 121. Barrell, however, provides a more nuanced account of the relationship between eroticism and civic discourse, arguing that what appears to be disruptive to the civic discourse is ultimately contained within it: "The sexuality which is constituted in [the civic] discourse and repressed at the public level of content, of narrative, returns at the private level of aesthetic form and of aesthetic response," Barrell writes; "a public display of renunciation, which by granting legitimacy to an interest in the aesthetic, gives a license to exactly what it appears to have renounced"; *Birth of Pandora*, 86–87.

54. *Livy*, trans. B. O. Foster, vol. 1 in the Loeb Classical Library (Cambridge, MA: Harvard University Press, 1957), 201. J. G. A. Pocock points out the allusion to Lucretia in his edition of the *Reflections* (Indianapolis, IN: Hackett, 1987; 223). Furniss argues that by summoning the specter of Lucretia here, Burke is implicated in the queen's suffering: "The language's very decorum (rape is 'the last disgrace') plays upon the possibility of the queen's rape in the moment it pays court to her. . . . After all, it is Burke's text, rather than the revolutionary 'mob,' which exposes the queen to 'the last disgrace' in order to activate its rhetorical resonance"; Furniss, *Edmund Burke's Aesthetic Ideology*, 155.

55. Payne's comment is cited in Christopher Reid, "Burke's Tragic Muse," 11.

56. Dio Cocceianus Cassius, *The Roman History: The Reign of Augustus*, trans. Ian Scott-Kilvert (Harmondsworth: Penguin, 1987),18; *Livy*, trans. Foster, 205.

57. Elinor S. Shaffer, "Illusion and Imagination: Derrida's *Parergon* and Coleridge's *Aids to Reflection*. Revisionary Readings of Kantian Formalist Aesthetics," in *Aesthetic Illusion: Theoretical and Historical Approaches*, eds. Frederick Burwick and Walter Pape (Berlin/New York: Walter de Gruyter, 1990), 143. The narrative sources alone were enough to ensure that—no matter how faddish the vogue for allegorical portraits—few if any women in the late eighteenth century would have posed in the guise of Lucretia. The care that such a portrayal required is made apparent by the sixteenth-century painter Lorenzo Lotto, whose *A Lady as Lucretia* (c.1534) depicted a Venetian woman, fully clothed, holding a picture of a nude Lucretia. Lotto's portrait thus analogized the women's purity of character while carefully distinguishing their actual circumstances; see Donaldson, *The Rapes of Lucretia*, 15–16. On the effects of Cranach's supplemental use of jewelry, see Jacques Derrida, *The Truth in Painting*, trans. Geoff Bennington and Ian McLeod (Chicago: University of Chicago Press, 1987), 73–74.

58. Ian Donaldson, *The Rapes of Lucretia: A Myth and its Transformations* (Oxford: Clarendon Press, 1982), 139; Claudia L. Johnson, *Equivocal Beings: Politics, Gender, and Sentimentality in the 1790s* (Chicago: University of Chicago Press, 1995), 81. It is also worth noting that portraits of Sarah Siddons as Volumnia in Shakespeare's *Coriolanus*—which, as adapted by John Philip Kemble in 1789, was subtitled *The Roman Matron*—may have provided a model for Burke as well. See Reid, "Burke's Tragic Muse," 11.

59. *A Letter from the Right Honourable Edmund Burke to a Noble Lord, on the attacks made upon him and his pension, in the House of Lords, by the Duke of Bedford, and the Earl of Lauderdale, early in the present sessions of Parliament* (London: J. Owen and F. and C. Rivington, 1796), 28–29.

60. Hazlitt, *Works*, 12: 115.

61. *The Correspondence of Edmund Burke*, 4: 169.

62. [William Hayley], *Epistle to Admiral Keppel* (London: Fielding and Walker, 1779), 19; Wendorf, *Sir Joshua Reynolds*, 160.

63. De Bruyn, *The Literary Genres of Edmund Burke*, 55.

64. Malone, ed., *The Works of Sir Joshua Reynolds*, 1: xxii-xxiii.

65. Ellis K. Waterhouse, *Reynolds* (London: Phaidon, 1973), 19. It is an art-historical commonplace to attribute the pose to the *Apollo Belvedere*, though recently there has been much debate over the extent to which Reynolds directly "quoted" classical sources. For a dissenting opinion, see David H. Solkin, "Great Pictures or Great Men? Reynolds, Male Portraiture, and the Power of Art," *Oxford Art Journal* 9 (1986), 42–49.

66. Quoted in Chard, "Effeminacy, Pleasure and the Classical Body," 151. Chard treats the appeal of the *Apollo Belvedere* for eighteenth-century spectators.

67. William Miles, *A Letter to Henry Duncombe, Esq. on the Subject of the very Extraordinary Pamphlet lately addressed by Mr. Burke, to a Noble Lord* (London, 1796), 66.

68. Burke, *Philosophical Enquiry*, 110.

69. Novalis quoted in Paulson, *Representations of Revolution*, 9.

70. Winifred H. Friedman, *Boydell's Shakespeare Gallery* (New York: Garland, 1976), 42.

71. Quoted in Eaves, *The Counter-Arts Conspiracy*, 22.

Chapter Two: Everybody's Shakespeare

1. *The Letters of Charles Lamb*, ed. E. V. Lucas., 3 vols. (London: J. M. Dent, 1935), 1: 394.

2. Lynch, *The Economy of Character*, 137.

3. Louise Lippincott, "Expanding on Portraiture: The Market, the Public, and the Hierarchy of Genres in Eighteenth-century Britain," in *The Consumption of Culture: World, Image and Object in the Seventeenth and Eighteenth Centuries*, eds. Ann Bermingham and John Brewer (New York: Routledge, 1995), 76.

4. On the importance of Shakespearean illustration in helping to define a national art, including discussion on the Shakespeare Gallery, see Ronald Paulson, *Book and Painting: Shakespeare, Milton, and The Bible: Literary Texts and the Emergence of English Painting* (Knoxville: University of Tennessee Press, 1982), 25ff.

5. *Conversations of James Northcote, R.A. with James Ward on Art and Artists*, ed. Ernest Fletcher (London, 1901), 114–15; W. Moelwyn Merchant, *Shakespeare and the Artist* (London: Oxford University Press, 1959), 66.

6. Recent examples of such an approach to the Shakespeare Gallery include Marcia Pointon, "Representing *The Tempest* in Boydell's Shakespeare Gallery," and Grant Scott, "To Play the King: Illustrations from *The Tempest* in the Boydell Shakespeare Gallery"—both included in *The Boydell Shakespeare Gallery*, eds. Walter Pape and Frederick Burwick (Bottrop, Germany: Peter Pomp, 1996), which also contains indispensable reproductions and annotations. My argument accords with Scott's observation of the "tension that emerges between the brave public rhetoric used to advertise, announce, and introduce the gallery . . . and the more private, skeptical rhetoric exhibited in a number of the paintings themselves" (114).

7. Barrell (intro.), *Painting and the Politics of Culture*, 2.

8. Boydell published and made a killing on William Woolett's print of West's painting. See Friedman, *Boydell's Shakespeare Gallery*, 39, and Eaves, who writes: "That coalition of patriotic subject, history painter, printmaker, and publisher held the potential for commercial success that Boydell . . . later tried to organize and magnify with his Shakespeare Gallery project"; *The Counter-Arts Conspiracy*, 33–34.

9. Dowling, *The Vulgarization of Art*, xiv.

10. Ibid., 15, xii.

11. Quoted in Friedman, *Boydell's Shakespeare Gallery*, 4–5.

12. Scott, "To Play the King," 114.

13. Quoted in Friedman, *Boydell's Shakespeare Gallery*, 69. On the Gallery as a form of "revolution," see Eaves, who claims that "The Boydell experiment in England and the revolutionary experiment in France are . . . parallel events that trade in the same public"; *The Counter-Arts Conspiracy*, 94.

14. Boydell, *Collection of Prints,* [iii].

15. Newspaper clipping dated 1789, in *Press Cuttings from English Newspapers on Matters of Artistic Interest, 1686-1835*; quoted in Altick, *Paintings From Books*, 44. For the wider context of this "revolution . . . in Taste," see the discussion above (especially page 5).

16. *The Literary Career of Sir Joshua Reynolds*, 38.

17. The Gallery's inclusiveness had its own disingenuous element. Even as Boydell's marriage of high art and commerce fostered an unprecedented access to the arts, it also disarmed the art criticism that taught consumers how to look at pictures. Boydell effectively silenced criticism by characterizing it in advance as anti-English. As the reviewer for *Walker's Hibernian Magazine* recognized, "The preface to the catalogue of the Shakespeare Gallery has warily endeavoured to preclude the strictures of criticism by affixing the opprobrium of malignity to all animadversions which should not be favourable to the performances there exhibited, yet the very author himself could hardly suppose that such premature stigma would be found able to stifle the voice of truth"; *Shakespeare: The Critical Heritage*, ed. Brian Vickers, 6 vols. (London, 1981), 6: 509–10. Since reviews were a significant factor in the middle-class participation in the arts, it is striking that the Shakespeare Gallery indirectly regulated them, thus compromising its ability to perform its civic function legitimately.

18. John Brewer, *The Pleasures of the Imagination: English Culture in the Eighteenth Century* (London: Harper Collins, 1997), 457.

19. Friedman, *Boydell's Shakespeare Gallery*, 220–45.

20. Additionally, the various methods of reproduction yielded disparate results. Line engraving and mezzotint were the highest quality modes of reproduction for history painting and portraiture, respectively. But since mezzotint plates wore quickly, they could not accommodate the large quantity of engravings that the Boydell project required. Line engraving (atop the hierarchy of printmaking) was a problem, since it was very time consuming and required a level of talent that the Gallery could not afford. Most of the Boydell prints were thus done in stipple (a process that came into favor in the 1770s), which was perfect for small, textual illustrations, but did not reproduce high-quality large prints—a fact to which the demise of the Gallery has often been attributed. For the particularities of the engraving in and around the Boydell venture, see David Alexander, "Print Makers and Print Sellers in England, 1770–1830," in *The Painted Word: British History Painting, 1750–1830*, ed. Peter Cannon-Brookes (Rochester, NY: Boydell Press, 1991), 23–29; John Gage, "Boydell's Shakespeare and the Redemption of British Engraving," in *The Boydell Shakespeare Gallery*, eds. Pape and Burwick, 26–31; and Christopher Lennox-Boyd, "The Prints Themselves: Production, Marketing, and their Survival," in *The Boydell Shakespeare Gallery*, eds. Pape and Burwick, 45–53.

21. Gage, "Boydell's Shakespeare and the Redemption of British Engraving," 27–28.

22. Recorded in a letter from Mary Palmer to John Boydell, December 1791, published in Reynolds, *Portraits*, 183.

23. Quoted in Friedman, *Boydell's Shakespeare Gallery*, 91. In fact, "only 700 of the original 1300 subscribers remained faithful and purchased all their numbers" (92).

24. Boydell, *Collection of Prints*, [vi].

25. Barrell, *The Political Theory of Painting*, 64.

26. Pointon, *Hanging the Head*, 38.

27. 2.1.152. All citations to Shakespeare are from *The Norton Shakespeare*, ed. Stephen Greenblatt et al. (New York: W. W. Norton, 1997).

28. Coleridge, *The Friend*, 1: 457.

29. Algernon Graves and William Vine Cronin, *A History of the Works of Sir Joshua Reynolds, P.R.A.*, 3 vols. (London, 1889), 3: 1189–90.

30. The story is related in Charles Robert Leslie and Tom Taylor, *The Life and Times of Sir Joshua Reynolds*, 2 vols. (London, 1865), 2: 504; Nicol is quoted in a note on page 536. For background on this painting, see Postle, *Sir Joshua Reynolds: The Subject Pictures*, 255–58.

31. *The Winter's Tale*, 4.4.92–4.

32. Quoted in Postle, *Sir Joshua Reynolds: The Subject Pictures*, 258.

33. Altick, *Paintings from Books*, 19–20.

34. Although Shakespeare was performed fairly continuously (in various forms) throughout the seventeenth and eighteenth centuries, it was not until the Enlightenment that we see "Bardolatry's rise to orthodoxy as a *national* religion," to quote Michael Dobson in *The Making of the National Poet: Shakespeare, Adaptation and Authorship, 1660–1769* (Oxford: Clarendon Press, 1992), 6. This rise peaked in 1769 with the Shakespeare Jubilee in Stratford. Bardolatry's emphasis on "character," Paulson adds, deepened the theater-portraiture alliance by "stimulat[ing] artists to yoke Shakespeare with the English portrait tradition"; *Book and Painting*, 32. Between 1750 and 1800, one out of every six plays performed in London was by Shakespeare. On Shakespeare in eighteenth-century theater and culture, see also Charles Beecher Hogan, *Shakespeare in the Theater 1701–1800*, 2 vols. (Oxford: Clarendon Press, 1957); Dennis Bartholomeusz, *The Winter's Tale in Performance in England and America 1611–1976* (Cambridge: Cambridge University Press, 1982); Jonathan Bate, *Shakespearean Constitutions: Politics, Theatre, Criticism, 1730–1830* (Oxford: Clarendon Press, 1989); Gary Taylor, *Reinventing Shakespeare: A Cultural History, from the Restoration to the Present* (New York: Oxford University Press, 1989), 100–62; and Margreta De Grazia, *Shakespeare Verbatim: The Reproduction of Authenticity and the 1790 Apparatus* (Oxford: Clarendon Press, 1991).

35. Wendorf, *Sir Joshua Reynolds*, 153, 245.

36. See Altick, *Paintings from Books*, 23–28 on the emergence of literature as a basis for "impersonation" portraits. On the increasing emphasis after 1830 on the character being impersonated, see Tricia Lootens, *Lost Saints: Silence, Gender, and Victorian Literary Canonization* (Charlottesville and London: University Press of Virginia, 1996), 84–85.

37. Hazlitt, *Works*, 4: 316.

38. Vickers, ed., *Shakespeare: The Critical Heritage*, 6: 510–12.

39. *Public Advertiser*, 6 May 1789; quoted in Friedman, *Boydell's Shakespeare Gallery*, 75.

40. Altick, *Paintings from Books*, 219.

41. *Conversations of James Northcote, Esq., R.A.*, in Hazlitt, *Works*, 11: 193.

42. Ibid., 11: 289.

43. Hazlitt, *Works*, 4: 326–27.

44. Only *Merry Wives of Windsor* had more representations (eight).

45. Hagstrum, *The Sister Arts*, 86.

46. *Coleridge's Shakespearean Criticism*, ed. Thomas Middleton Raysor, 2 vols. (London: Constable, 1930), 2: 276.

47. This key point occupies a vexed position in the play's recent commentary. In

Broken Nuptials in Shakespeare's Plays (New Haven: Yale University Press, 1985), Carol Thomas Neely inaugurated the feminist approach to maternal nurturance by arguing that birth—"the play's central miracle" (191)—aids the transition from "a static, masculine world that appears self-sufficient and self-sustaining" (192) to the play's concluding acknowledgment of women's centrality. According to Neely, Leontes changes from "want[ing] to possess a Hermione who was . . . a statue" to wanting a "reunion with the woman Hermione" (206). Peter Erickson counters her account of the male embrace of "the living woman" (207) in *Patriarchal Structures in Shakespeare's Drama* (Berkeley: University of California Press, 1985). While "Hermione changes from art object to particularized human being" in the statue scene, he claims, she nevertheless "remains an icon" (163). Erickson finds in the play's final reconcilations "a loss since the women suffer a contraction of power" (162). Though acknowledging that "Hermione's pregnancy is very visible and in and of itself acts as a provocation to male insecurity" (148), he finds that ultimately, rather than empowering women, *The Winter's Tale* offers "a version of procreation that includes the woman only as the vehicle by which the father's mirror image is produced and that implies male control of reproduction" (167). These two extreme positions have since been mediated by Gail Kern Paster, *The Body Embarrassed: Drama and the Disciplines of Shame in Early Modern Europe* (Ithaca, NY: Cornell University Press, 1993), and Janet Adelman, *Suffocating Mothers: Fantasies of Maternal Origin in Shakespeare's Plays, Hamlet to The Tempest* (New York: Routledge, 1992), both of whom recognize (to varying degrees) the male dependence on women while finding in Neely an excess of optimism concerning the play's acceptance of women. For Paster, "Leontes' hyperactive disciplinary regime" (279) results from structural, not idiosyncratic causes—specifically a male competition for the maternal body coupled with a recognition of "the limits of patriarchal control over the female body" (271). Paster takes issue with Neely by arguing: "To suggest that [Hermione's transformation from statue to woman] return[s] her to sexual being and demand[s] acceptance by her husband of the meaning of female sexuality and reproductivity is to miss the key point that this Hermione is visibly altered and diminished by her experience of patriarchal discipline, as may be suggested by the silence in which she embraces Leontes" (279). Finally, Adelman—to whose reading I am most indebted here—preserves and develops the notion that Hermione's maternity severely damages Leontes' sense of autonomy. She finds an impossible fantasy of "pure male identity" embedded in the two kings' nostalgia for twinship and homosociality: "The alternative to the masculine identity conferred through this mirror is the masculine identity originating in the female and everywhere marked by vulnerability to her: the conflicted identity for which Hermione's pregnant body comes to stand" (223). Although "the trauma of tragic masculinity" is its dependence on separation from the female, Adelman argues that "in the end, [Leontes] can find himself as husband and father only by giving himself into [Paulina's] hands, rediscovering his masculine potency and authority through trust in her and in the female processes she speaks for" (219).

48. Neely, *Broken Nuptials in Shakespeare's Plays*, 191.

49. Vickers, ed., *Shakespeare: The Critical Heritage*, 5: 108.

50. Neely, *Broken Nuptials in Shakespeare's Plays*, 191–92; Stanley Cavell, *Disowning Knowledge in Six Plays of Shakespeare* (Cambridge: Cambridge University Press, 1987), 208–13.

51. Colley, *Britons*, 233.

52. See Hogan, *Shakespeare in the Theater 1701–1800*, 2: 718. Of the ninety-eight performances Hogan lists between 1751–1800, ninety-three are the versions by Morgan or Garrick, the remaining five being adaptations by Hull (1771–72) and George Colman the Younger (1772–83).

53. Dobson, *The Making of the National Poet*, 190.

54. *Florizel and Perdita; or, The Sheep-Shearing*, in *A Collection of the Most Esteemed Farces and Entertainments, Performed on the British Stage*, 6 vols. (Edinburgh, 1787), 1: 88, 95.

55. However, as Stephen Orgel points out in his fabulously detailed introduction, individual productions varied stylistically. Thus Elizabeth Farren's Hermione (*c.* 1780), as captured in Zoffany's theater portrait, "returns the play to the classical world" through its iconography; while around the same time, "Elizabeth Hartley . . . is strictly contemporary, wearing an elaborate coiffure and an informal evening gown," and "posed in a neoclassical niche that suggests Marie Antoinette"; *The Winter's Tale*, ed. Stephen Orgel (Oxford and New York: Oxford University Press, 1996), 67.

56. Vickers, ed., *Shakespeare: The Critical Heritage*, 6: 97.

57. Colley, *Britons*, 232.

58. Colley argues that George's much-publicized mental troubles softened his image: "The horrifying illness he suffered in the winter of 1788 made the king appear deeply vulnerable, and the surge of public pity that ensued cancelled out many of the earlier fears of his arbitrary and corrupt intentions"; *Britons*, 212.

59. Hamilton painted all three small pieces as well. There were other paintings—such as Henry Thomson's *The Finding of Perdita*, and William Hodges' *Antigonus Torn by a Bear*—which Boydell commissioned but subsequently dropped from the Gallery.

60. Adelman, *Suffocating Mothers*, 219. Bate sees this as a generic phenomenon as well, with the image unwittingly foregrounding its own unstable status as history painting. Arguing that the gesture of finger-pointing, so frequent in the Boydell compositions, thematizes the attempt to raise lower forms of art into higher ones, Bate concludes: "All limbs have to manifest the heroic energy of the 'Historical' style; exaggerated gesticulation seems to be the only method of making them do so"; *Shakespearean Constitutions*, 57.

61. Morton Paley tells me of Coleridge's coinage, which appears in the second volume of his notebooks.

62. Erickson, *Patriarchal Structures*, 160.

63. John Guillory, *Cultural Capital: The Problem of Literary Canon Formation* (Chicago: University of Chicago Press, 1993), 112. In G. Wilson Knight's foundational argument, Perdita's "royalty" extends beyond her "actual descent" to both "her natural excellence and that more inclusive category from which both descend, or to which both aspire, in the eternity-dimension." She denotes a "concept of spiritual royalty corresponding to Wordsworth's (in his *Immortality Ode*); with further political implications concerning the expansion of sovereignty among a people"; Knight, *The Crown of Life* (New York: Oxford University Press, 1947), 108.

64. Quoted in Dobson, *The Making of the National Poet*, 194; emphasis added.

65. Whether *The Winter's Tale* endorses royalism is a matter of perennial debate. Northrop Frye's observation that Shakespearean romances "set up a hierarchy of behavior" suggests how it can undermine standard notions of political hierarchy. In Frye's es-

timation, *The Winter's Tale* gives us "clowns and rustics who become gentlemen, and very decent ones at that," while only the king reaches a "lower depth of evil"; *A Natural Perspective: The Development of Shakespearean Comedy and Romance* (New York: Columbia University Press, 1965), 109, 110. I would agree with Charles Frey that the play "mocks . . . absolutists"; but even if its treatment of royal authority is not *overtly* subversive, it at least provokes questions about such authority—a contention that the gendered readings of the play all support to varying degrees; Frey, *Shakespeare's Vast Romance: A Study of The Winter's Tale* (Columbia: University of Missouri Press, 1980), 197.

66. Perdita's gift of medicinal flowers, as B. J. Sokol suggests, acknowledges the lurking turbulence: they are "floral gestures toward abating the passions of dignified middle-aged guests before these passions explode"; Sokol, *Art and Illusion in "The Winter's Tale"* (New York: Manchester University Press, 1994), 135. Needless to say, as gestures they are futile, as the festival soon ends in violent threats and slanderous accusations.

67. Anthony Ashley Cooper, 3rd Earl of Shaftesbury, *Characteristics of Men, Manners, Opinions, Times, Etc.*, ed. John M. Robertson, 2 vols. (London, 1900), 1: 286.

68. This sense of variety might also be understood through Wheatley's practice as a watercolorist, as well as his role in helping to invest watercolor painting with the authority of oil painting and historical composition. See Barrell, *Birth of Pandora*, 20.

69. Frey, *Shakespeare's Vast Romance*, 150.

70. Isabel Combs Stuebe, *The Life and Works of William Hodges* (New York: Garland, 1979), 344.

71. Quoted in William Bemrose, *The Life and Works of Joseph Wright, A.R.A., commonly called "Wright of Derby"* (London, 1885), 98.

72. Frederick Burwick, "Introduction" to *The Boydell Shakespeare Gallery*, eds. Pape and Burwick, 15.

73. On the British Institution and other responses to the failure of the Shakespeare Gallery, see Eaves, *The Counter-Arts Conspiracy*, 75–78; I quote from page 84.

Chapter Three: Painting Sorrow

1. The epigraphs are drawn from *Effigies Poeticæ: or, Portraits of the British Poets*, 2 vols. (London, 1824), 2: 139; and from the first sonnet of Charlotte Smith's *Elegiac Sonnets* (1784–1800), in *The Poems of Charlotte Smith*, ed. Stuart Curran (Oxford: Oxford University Press, 1993), 3. All subsequent references to Smith's poems are based on this edition and, where appropriate, are cited by sonnet and line number.

2. Walpole quoted in Randolph S. Churchill, *Fifteen Famous English Homes* (London: Derek Verschoyle, 1954), 53; *The Poems of Charlotte Smith*, 43. The complete passage of Walpole's complaint summarizes the decay of patriarchal order as imaged at Penshurst: "This morning we have been to Penshurst—but, oh! how fallen! The park seems to have never answered its character: at present it is forlorn: and instead of Sacharissa's cypher carved on the beeches, I should sooner have expected to have found the milkwoman's score. . . . There are loads of portraits; but most of them seem christened by chance, like children at a foundling hospital."

3. Don E. Wayne, *Penshurst: The Semiotics of Place and the Poetics of History* (Madison: University of Wisconsin Press, 1984), 51, 99.

4. Smith's reference to Algernon Sidney's portrait carries revolutionary connotations since, as William Senior notes, he leans on a volume entitled "Libertas," and "in the

background of the picture, added, as was the custom, after his death, the frowning front of the Tower of London and the headsman's axe sum up the reward of the patriot's devotion"; "Penshurst Place," *Historic Houses of the United Kingdom: Descriptive, Historical, Pictorial* (London: Cassell, 1892), 129.

5. Churchill, *Fifteen Famous English Homes*, 53. Smith's emphasis on the aura of history at Penshurst hints at a similarly ideological aspect of its physical being, for in its various and plainly visible architectural additions the house contains "legible records of social history" that are reinforced by the "custom of the Sidney family in using chiselled inscriptions and heraldic designs to indicate any new structural operations"; Peter Mandler, *The Fall and Rise of the Stately Home* (New Haven, CT and London: Yale University Press, 1997), 51; Ralph Dutton and Baron Angus Holden, *English Country Houses Open to the Public* (London: George Allen and Unwin, 1934), 72.

6. See Rachel Crawford, *Poetry, Enclosure, and the Vernacular Landscape, 1700–1830* (Cambridge: Cambridge University Press, 2002), 171–78. Thomas Warton, *The History of English Poetry, from the Close of the Eleventh to the Commencement of the Eighteenth Century*, 4 vols. (London: J. Dodsley, 1774–81), 4: 88.

7. The phrases are Clifford Siskin's in *The Historicity of Romantic Discourse* (New York: Oxford University Press, 1988), 12.

8. James Turner, *The Politics of Landscape* (Cambridge, MA: Harvard University Press, 1979), 5–6.

9. For Wordsworth's (not uncritical) relationship with Lord Lowther, see Timothy Fulford, *Landscape, Liberty, and Authority: Poetry, Criticism, and Politics from Thomson to Wordsworth* (Cambridge: Cambridge University Press, 1996), 192–95.

10. Though the cultural historian G. J. Barker-Benfield has argued for the radical effects of sensibility, claiming that its literature did nothing less than enable feminism as a collective movement, literary scholars have expressed skepticism on the politics of sentiment. Adela Pinch suggests that the expressive force of sentimental literature is attenuated by its location at the boundary of the personal and the conventional; Claudia L. Johnson describes sentimentality as a masculine dispensation that updates gender boundaries only to reenact old power structures; and Robert Markley argues that "the theatrics of sentimental virtue preclude any action" that would remove the object of its self-aggrandizing benevolence. Sentimental *poetry* has seemed particularly culpable, by giving voice to what Patricia Meyer Spacks calls an exclusionary community whose "acts of self-differentiation imply superiority and consequent power." "The authors of sentimental texts did not themselves understand sentimentality as a sociocultural negotiation," Julie Ellison summarizes, "The ideological function of sentiment [is] that it represses the consciousness or expresses the unconsciousness of power relations." G. J. Barker-Benfield, *The Culture of Sensibility: Sex and Society in Eighteenth-Century Britain* (Chicago and London: University of Chicago Press, 1992), xviii-xix; Adela Pinch, *Strange Fits of Passion: Epistemologies of Emotion, Hume to Austen* (Stanford, CA: Stanford University Press, 1996), 69; Johnson, *Equivocal Beings*, 12; Robert Markley, "Sentimentality as Performance: Shaftesbury, Sterne, and the Theatrics of Virtue," in *The New Eighteenth Century: Theory, Politics, English Literature*, eds. Felicity Nussbaum and Laura Brown (New York and London: Methuen, 1987), 227; Patricia Meyer Spacks, "The Poetry of Sensibility," in *The Cambridge Companion to Eighteenth-Century Poetry*, ed. John Sitter

(Cambridge: Cambridge University Press, 2001), 249–69; Julie Ellison, *Cato's Tears and the Making of Anglo-American Emotion* (Chicago and London: University of Chicago Press, 1999), 7. Ellison summarizes the prevailing view in order to register her departure from it, and my own reading accords with her view "that much of the literature of sensibility exposes a complicated awareness of the human costs of national and imperial economies, as well as the knowledge that sensibility itself is a privilege" (7). On the literary culture of sentimentality, also see R. F. Brissenden, *Virtue in Distress: Studies in the Novel of Sentiment from Richardson to Sade* (London: Macmillan, 1974); Northrop Frye, "Towards Defining an Age of Sensibility" (1963), in *Poets of Sensibility and the Sublime*, ed. Harold Bloom (New York: Chelsea House, 1986), 11–18; Chris Jones, *Radical Sensibility: Lectures and Ideas in the 1790s* (London and New York: Routledge, 1993); Jerome J. McGann, *The Poetics of Sensibility: A Revolution in Literary Style* (Oxford: Clarendon Press, 1996); John Mullan, *Sentiment and Sociability: The Language of Feeling in the Eighteenth Century* (Oxford: Clarendon Press, 1988); and Janet Todd, *Sensibility: An Introduction* (London and New York: Methuen, 1986).

11. Barrell, *Birth of Pandora*, 14–15. On the rise of amateurism and especially the increasing distinction attached to female sketching, see Ann Bermingham, *Learning to Draw: Studies in the Cultural History of a Polite and Useful Art* (New Haven, CT: Yale University Press, 2000).

12. Quoted in Graham Reynolds, *English Portrait Miniatures* (New York: Cambridge University Press, 1988), 163.

13. Martin Archer Shee, *Rhymes on Art; or, The Remonstrance of a Painter*, 2nd ed. (London, 1805), 33–34.

14. Barrell, *Birth of Pandora*, 20.

15. Though the 1800 publication marked the end of its material expansion, *Elegiac Sonnets* was reissued several more times before and after Smith's death.

16. In her excellent essay "'Out in Left Field': Charlotte Smith's Prefaces, Bourdieu's Categories, and the Public Sphere," *Modern Language Quarterly* 58: 4 (1997), 457–73, Elizabeth W. Harries offers a variation on this argument, drawing on the work of Pierre Bourdieu to argue that "Smith deploys autobiographical elements . . . to disarm her readers and critics and to clear a space for herself in the cultural field"; 663.

17. *Gentleman's Magazine* 56 (1786), 620.

18. Situating Smith's sonnets within the late eighteenth-century culture of elegy, Esther H. Schor describes the seemingly paradoxical requirement that the poet speak sincerely about her experience even while communicating her authority through allusion to the literary tradition; *Bearing the Dead: The British Culture of Mourning from the Enlightenment to Victoria* (Princeton, NJ: Princeton University Press, 1994), 61–66.

19. On this frontispiece and the details behind Smith's request to have the portrait altered, see Sarah Zimmerman, "Charlotte Smith's Letters and the Practice of Self-Presentation," *Princeton University Library Chronicle* 53 (1991), 50–53. Zimmerman's essay, one of the first serious treatments of Smith's work in a decade that saw a blossoming of interest, is grounded in archival work to which I am much indebted here. The original lines read: "Oh! grief hath changed me since you saw me last, / And careful hours with time's deformèd hand, / Have written strange defeatures in my face" (5.1.298–300). The reappearance of this same verbally elaborated frontispiece as the first page of a bio-

graphical notice in the *European Magazine and London Review* of November 1806 (50: 338) shows it to be widely recognized as Smith's public face.

20. Sarah Zimmerman, *Romanticism, Lyricism, and History* (Albany: State University of New York Press, 1999), 44.

21. Schor, *Bearing the Dead*, 63.

22. For the definitive accounts of this problem, see Schor, *Bearing the Dead*, 61–66, and Pinch, *Strange Fits of Passion*, 51–71. See also Rachel Crawford, "Troping the Subject: Behn, Smith, Hemans and the Poetics of the Bower," *Studies in Romanticism* 38 (1999), 249–79.

23. *The Poems of Charlotte Smith*, 5. On the ambiguous heritage of literary feelings, see Pinch, *Strange Fits of Passion*.

24. Stuart Curran tallies this in his introduction to *The Poems of Charlotte Smith*, xxvi.

25. On the complication of Petrarchan gender roles in *Elegiac Sonnets*, see Curran, "Introduction," xxv, and Pinch, *Strange Fits of Passion*, 62. Crawford later rehearses the same theme to argue that the gender trouble here "provokes questions about the figuration of invention"; "Troping the Subject," 265–66.

26. Pinch, *Strange Fits of Passion*, 60, 61.

27. James Wyatt Cook translates: "Where song and laughter are, do not approach, / My song—no, my lament; / To dwell with joyous people will not do, / Widow disconsolate, in weeds of black"; *Petrarch's Songbook* (Binghamton, NY: Medieval & Renaissance Texts & Studies, 1995), 313.

28. Michael R. G. Spiller, *The Development of the Sonnet* (London and New York: Routledge, 1992), 60.

29. *Letters of Anna Seward*, 6 vols. (Edinburgh: Constable, 1811), 2: 287.

30. Julia Kristeva, *Black Sun: Depression and Melancholia*, trans. Leon Roudiez (New York: Columbia University Press, 1989), 33.

31. On the varied effects of quotation, see Marjorie Garber, "Quotation and Cultural Authority," *Quotation Marks* (New York and London: Routledge, 2003), 1–32.

32. Zimmerman reads this image in relation to Michael Fried's work on absorption, arguing that "the poet's apparent obliviousness to an audience . . . proves captivating" to a reader who "must feel forgotten in order to forget himself or herself and make the necessary leap of identification"; *Romanticism, Lyricism, and History*, 47–48.

33. Pascoe discusses Siddons's perceived sexual ambiguity, particularly in performing Lady Macbeth—a role she played, oddly enough, while six months pregnant (and thus very feminine indeed)—and calls this "an enabling reality" for women writers of the time; *Romantic Theatricality*, 20–21.

34. On the association of melancholy with male genius in the Renaissance as well as a wide-ranging cultural history of melancholy in the West, see Jennifer Radden, ed., *The Nature of Melancholy: From Aristotle to Kristeva* (New York: Oxford University Press, 2000).

35. On Bell's series as an influence on Reynolds's later painting of Siddons, see Robyn Asleson, " 'She Was Tragedy Personified': Crafting the Siddons Legend in Art and Life," in *Sarah Siddons and Her Portraitists*, ed. Robyn Asleson (Los Angeles: The J. Paul Getty Museum, 1999), 41–96; on the iconography of "Melancholy," see 69–73. Asleson also notes the irony that Siddons's performance in Thomas Southerne's *Isabella* was con-

fused with Beach's painting, resulting in Thomas Stothard's print, *Sarah Siddons as Isabella—Il Penseroso.*

36. Compare Pinch, who asserts that "Melancholy has the magic power to make one imagine other poets' misery in the landscape, and hence allows an imagined relation to other poets"; *Strange Fits of Passion*, 66.

37. Pointon, *Hanging the Head*, 184.

38. Only a handful of subscribers, in fact, required explanation, for as Judith Stanton observes in her meticulous accounting of Smith's literary business, "only one-third of the subscribers on her list" had paid up after three years; "Charlotte Smith's 'Literary Business': Income, Patronage, and Indigence," *The Age of Johnson* 1 (1987), 375–401 (387–88).

39. I quote from page 217 of Sidney's *Defense*, in *The Oxford Authors: Sir Philip Sidney*, ed. Katherine Duncan-Jones (Oxford: Oxford University Press, 1989). Hagstrum discusses the interartistic aspect of Sidney's formal definition of poetry in *The Sister Arts*, 64. Fumerton, who also treats Sidney, observes that "the sonneteers of the 1590s literally speak the language of limning," repeatedly using "the technical term of the miniaturist—'limn'—instead of the more general 'paint' to describe their verbal portraits of their loves." Examples she cites include Daniel: "Then take this picture which I heere present thee, / Limned with a Pensill not all unworthy"; the *Zepheria* (1594) poet: "never shall that face so fayre depayneted / Within the love-limn'd tablet of mine hart / Emblemisht be, deface or unsaynted"; and Drayton: "My Hart's the Boord, where limnde you may her see; / My Teares the Oyle, my Blood the Colours bee"; " 'Secret' Arts: Elizabethan Miniatures and Sonnets," *Representations* 15 (1986), 87–88.

40. *The Miscellaneous Prose Works of Sir Walter Scott*, 28 vols. (Edinburgh, 1834–36), 2: 64; J. M. S. Tompkins, *The Popular Novel in England, 1770–1800* (London: Constable, 1932), 355.

41. Schor, *Bearing the Dead*, 61.

42. Several have noted the "shape" of *Elegiac Sonnets* in passing: Pascoe emphasizes the sense of process that informs "Smith's additive, evolving opus" (*Romantic Theatricality*, 16); Judith Hawley suggests that, because Smith's poems enact a process of mourning which "is for her partly a legal process of recovering an inheritance in the courts," the formal completion of her sequence depends on events that occur outside of her poems ("Charlotte Smith's Elegiac Sonnets, Losses and Gains," in *Women's Poetry in the Enlightenment: The Making of a Canon, 1730–1820*, eds. Isobel Armstrong and Virginia Blain [New York: St. Martin's Press, 1999], 195); and Curran considers the sequence (in its final form only) as a "finished" whole, a "collection" achieved only with Smith's death ("Romantic Poetry: The I Altered," in *Romanticism and Feminism*, ed. Anne K. Mellor [Bloomington: Indiana University Press, 1988], 200).

43. The tradition Smith activates here is that of the poet as gardener—an association reflected in the fact that the word "anthology" originates in the Greek for "a collection of flowers."

44. I here evoke Patricia Fumerton's description of Elizabethan miniatures; " 'Secret Arts,'" 70.

45. *The Poetical Works of William Lisle Bowles*, ed. George Gilfillan, 2 vols. (Edinburgh: J. Nichol, 1855).

46. Paulson, *Emblem and Expression*, 154.

Chapter 4: Monsters, Marbles, and Miniatures

1. "Solomon Grildig" (pseud.), *The Miniature: A Periodical Paper*, ed. Thomas Rennell, H. C. Knight, G. Canning, and others (London, 1804), 3–4; *Jane Austen's Letters*, 323. The first epigraph is from George Eliot, *Adam Bede* (1859), ed. Carol A. Martin (Oxford: Clarendon Press, 2001), 166–67; the anecdote about the Elgin Marbles is quoted in Grant Scott, *The Sculpted Word*, 190.

2. On the portraits of *Frankenstein* as an extension of a prominent gothic motif, see Jerrold Hogle, " 'Frankenstein' as Neo-Gothic: From the Ghost of the Counterfeit to the Monster of Abjection," in *Romanticism, History, and the Possibilities of Genre: Re-forming Literature 1789–1837*, eds. Tilottama Rajan and Julia M. Wright (Cambridge: Cambridge University Press, 1998), 176–210. As I do below, so too Hogle describes the Monster as a portrait: "A larger-than-life stitching together of dead body-parts torn from the 'natural' former owners" that "haunts his guilty maker . . . by being an artificial 'portrait' of dead life set in motion, the phantasm of an act of counterfeiting" (180).

3. This is not to argue that *Frankenstein* is a "realist" novel. Like George Levine and Katherine Kearns, I describe Shelley's novel as engaged with the *idea* of realism rather than as realistic in itself. See Levine's conclusion, for instance, that Shelley's novel is "the myth of realism," or Kearns's claim that it offers a "space in which to examine realism's necessary complicity with and resistance to" canonical male language; Levine, "The Ambiguous Heritage of *Frankenstein*," in *The Endurance of Frankenstein: Essays on Mary Shelley's Novel*, eds. George Levine and U. C. Knoepflmacher (Berkeley: University of California Press, 1979), 30; Kearns, *Nineteenth-Century Literary Realism: Through the Looking Glass* (Cambridge: Cambridge University Press, 1996), 122–23.

4. Raymond Williams, *Keywords: A Vocabulary of Culture and Society*, 2nd ed. (New York: Oxford University Press, 1983), 259; George Levine, *The Realistic Imagination: English Fiction from Frankenstein to Lady Chatterley* (Chicago: University of Chicago Press, 1981), 5. My understanding of this problematic term is also indebted to Catherine Belsey, *Critical Practice* (London: Routledge, 1980), 67–84; Elizabeth Deeds Ermarth, *Realism and Consensus in the English Novel* (Princeton, NJ: Princeton University Press, 1983); and to the readings in Michael McKeon's anthology *Theory of the Novel: A Historical Approach* (Baltimore and London: Johns Hopkins University Press, 2000).

5. Levine, *Realistic Imagination*, 167.

6. Theresa Kelley, writing on Turner and Napoleonic caricature, argues that Turner uses "extremes of scale to push away from realist norms and interpretation"; *Reinventing Allegory*, 176. Whether tending toward the miniature or the gigantic (or, as I discuss below, caught compellingly between), however, I understand such scalar extremes not as realistic per se, but as performative in that they ask that readers imagine a heightened perception of "reality" that is potential in larger scales and that disappears in smaller ones.

7. Johanna Smith, *Mary Shelley* (New York: Twayne, 1996), 17. Less tentative readings include Betty T. Bennett, whose comparison of Elizabeth Lavenza with Elizabeth Raby (the heroine of *Falkner*) is premised on a confident claim about "the author's remarkably consistent reformist sociopolitical ethos" (" 'Not this time, Victor!': Mary Shelley's Reversioning of Elizabeth, from *Frankenstein* to *Falkner*," in *Mary Shelley in Her Times*, eds. Bennett and Stuart Curran [London: Johns Hopkins University Press, 2000], 1); Lee Sterrenburg, who just as confidently observes Shelley's "gravitation toward conser-

vatism" ("Mary Shelley's Monster: Politics and Psyche in *Frankenstein*," in *The Endurance of Frankenstein* [eds. Levine and Knoepflmacher], 143); and the Marxian allegories of Paul O'Flinn ("Production and Reproduction: The Case of Frankenstein," *Literature and History* 9 [1983]: 194–213) and Warren Montag ("'The Workshop of Filthy Creation': A Marxist Reading of *Frankenstein*," in *Frankenstein*, ed. Johanna Smith [New York and Boston: Bedford-St. Martin's Press, 1995], 384–95), who view the Creature as a figure for an emergent working class; and Tim Marshall, who reads *Frankenstein* as "a proleptic allegory of the 1832 political marriage between the aristocracy and the upper ranks of the middle class" (*Murdering to Dissect: Grave-robbing, Frankenstein and the Anatomy Literature* [Manchester: Manchester University Press, 1995], 15). Shelley herself, without necessarily contradicting any of these readings, hints that she is not ready to accept an inclusiveness like that embodied in her Creature. In 1832 she writes to her friend Fanny Wright that "The people *will* be redressed," yet a day earlier she had lamented that "*Progressiveness*" can only be achieved by the "*sick destructiveness*" of radical activism; *The Letters of Mary Wollstonecraft Shelley*, ed. Betty T. Bennett, 3 vols. (Baltimore: Johns Hopkins University Press, 1980), 2: 122, 124. Sterrenburg, despite declaring Shelley's "growing detachment from radicalism," begins to get at her ambivalence by arguing that *Frankenstein* "goes beyond both the radical and conservative traditions it appropriates"—that it "internalizes political debates" by drawing on "revolutionary symbolism . . . in a postrevolutionary era when collective political movements no longer appear viable." Refreshing though this complicated reading is, however, Sterrenburg's certainty that Shelley's monster metaphor contains no "reference to collective movements" seems odd given the political volatility of the years following Waterloo; "Mary Shelley's Monster," 143, 144, 145, 157.

8. *The Letters of Mary Wollstonecraft Shelley*, 1: 22.

9. Mary Shelley, *Frankenstein; or, The Modern Prometheus* (1818), eds. D. L. Macdonald and Kathleen Scherf (Peterborough, ON: Broadview Press, 1994), 86. Except where noted, this provides the source for all subsequent page references.

10. The following account of Georgian miniatures owes much to Daphne Foskett, *Miniatures Dictionary and Guide* (Woodbridge, UK: Antique Collectors' Club, 1987); Patrick J. Noon, "Miniatures on the Market," in *The English Miniature*, eds. John Murdoch, Jim Murrell, Patrick J. Noon, and Roy Strong (New Haven, CT: Yale University Press, 1981), 163–209; and Graham Reynolds, *English Portrait Miniatures*, 133–76.

11. See Noon, "Miniatures on the Market," 177–80; and Reynolds, *English Portrait Miniatures*, 133–42.

12. Reynolds, *English Portrait Miniatures*, 172.

13. Marie-Hélène Huet, *Monstrous Imagination* (Cambridge, MA: Harvard University Press, 1993), 126.

14. John Guillory, *Cultural Capital*, 95.

15. Colin Campbell, "Understanding Traditional and Modern Patterns of Consumption in Eighteenth-Century England: A Character-Action Approach," in *Consumption and the World of Goods*, eds. John Brewer and Roy Porter (London: Routledge, 1993), 50.

16. Pointing to this scene, Kate Ellis notes: "Alphonse Frankenstein retired from public life entirely in order to pursue this self-perpetuation"; "Monsters in the Garden: Mary Shelley and the Bourgeois Family," in *The Endurance of Frankenstein*, eds. Levine and Knoepflmacher, 128–29.

17. Ellis, "Monsters in the Garden," 129.

18. Lynch, *The Economy of Character*, 61.

19. Noon, "Miniatures on the Market," 173.

20. Martin Archer Shee, *Rhymes on Art*, 33–34.

21. Hazlitt, *Works*, 18: 107–8.

22. Campbell, "Understanding Traditional and Modern Patterns of Consumption in Eighteenth-Century England," 41. See also Henderson, "Passion and Fashion in Joanna Baillie's 'Introductory Discourse,'" 201.

23. Amanda Vickery, "Women and the World of Goods," in *Consumption and the World of Goods*, eds. Brewer and Porter, 284.

24. Ellis, "Monsters in the Garden," 133. Ellis also observes the strange rush to judgment displayed by the Frankensteins, and she finds incredible the unquestioning response to the servants who discover the picture in Justine's pocket: "This act on the part of two servants is certainly one that might reasonably arouse suspicion on the part of their employers, but the Frankensteins appear to view their inability to suspect anyone as one of their greatest virtues."

25. Or "being a possession": in the 1818 edition, as Betty T. Bennett argues, Elizabeth Lavenza is like a commodity "in a business negotiation" between Alphonse and his brother (Elizabeth's father), her adoption into the Frankenstein family finalized by "a guarantee that the child will retain her mother's fortune." And in the 1831 edition, "Caroline Frankenstein . . . gives the four-year-old Lavenza to the five-year-old Victor Frankenstein 'as a pretty present'"; Bennett, "'Not this time, Victor!'" 3.

26. U. C. Knoepflmacher, "Thoughts on the Aggression of Daughters," in *The Endurance of Frankenstein*, eds. Levine and Knoepflmacher, 109.

27. "On the Diversity of Opinions with regard to Likenesses in Portraits," *London Magazine*, 6 (1822), 34: 324.

28. This quote appears on page 323 of the Macdonald and Scherf edition, which includes the 1831 revisions in an appendix.

29. A tacit reference to Fuseli's *The Nightmare* has been observed by Gerhard Joseph, "The Child is Father of the Monster," *Hartford Studies in Literature* 7 (1975), 109; and Anne K. Mellor, "Possessing Nature: The Female in *Frankenstein*," in *Romanticism and Feminism*, ed. Mellor, 225.

30. The unpleasant results of Victor's production process suggest a source for Henry James's "fear of too ample a canvas"—a fear that extremity of scale can result not in "a deep-breathing economy" and "a mighty pictorial fusion," but in "such large loose baggy monsters" as had become common, in James's view, in the tradition of the novel; James, "Preface" to *The Tragic Muse*, 514–16.

31. *The Examiner*, no. 444 (30 June 1816), 411.

32. Jonathan Swift, *Gulliver's Travels* (1726), ed. Robert A. Greenberg (New York: W. W. Norton, 1970), 95.

33. Jacob Rothenberg, "*Descensus ad terram*": *The Acquisition and Reception of the Elgin Marbles* (New York: Garland, 1977), 5.

34. Brought to Britain by Lord Elgin in 1803–4, the marbles immediately became a focus for stylistic debate. And when, in 1816, the government debated whether, and for how much, to purchase them from Elgin, their aesthetics became a matter of public interest. The House of Commons executed a lengthy investigation into their value. Wit-

nesses—the leading artists and connoisseurs of the day—were called, and their testimony was published. These grandest of portraits were finally purchased for £35,000 (about half of Elgin's outlay) and displayed in the British Museum, where they were to aid in a seemingly interminable task: "to improve our national taste for the Fine Arts"; *Report from the Select Committee on the Earl of Elgin's Collection of Sculptured Marbles &c.* (London, 1816), 6. The significance of the marbles in national culture is compellingly described by Eric Gidal, who, in revealing the British Museum as a location where "private experiences of beauty and recollection" are joined "to the identification of a national body," cites the marbles "as exemplary objects of national aesthetic desire"; Gidal, *Poetic Exhibitions*, 114.

35. Byron, *English Bards and Scotch Reviewers*, lines 1029–30; Beaumont quoted in *The Diary of Joseph Farington*, eds. Kenneth Garlick and Angus Macintyre, 16 vols. (New Haven, CT: Yale University Press, 1978–1998), 9: 3290. Byron critiques the British removal of the marbles in *The Curse of Minerva* and, more famously, *Childe Harold's Pilgrimage*, where he bemoans that the British have "snatch'd [Greece's] shrinking Gods to northern climes abhorr'd" (2: 135)—the scalar adjective suggesting not just their fragmentation (and hence physical diminishment) but also their depleted value outside of their original context.

36. *Report from the Select Committee*, 38, 68.

37. Hazlitt, *Works*, 16: 354, 8: 137, 18: 81; Paul Magnuson, *Reading Public Romanticism* (Princeton, NJ: Princeton University Press, 1998), 184.

38. Hazlitt, *Works*, 16: 353, 4: 74.

39. *Report from the Select Committee*, 93.

40. Heringman observes, however, that in a practical (not aesthetic) register, the cost of purchasing the marbles was often compared with the "rude wasting" of a hungry underclass—though even this rhetorical seizure of a superior morality was contested by the opposing sides of the debate over their value; "Stones so wonderous Cheap." *Studies in Romanticism* 37 (1998), 43–62.

41. Hazlitt, *Works*, 10: 28, 10: 222, 12: 329, 18: 81, 18: 145–46.

42. Magnuson, *Reading Public Romanticism*, 182.

43. Hazlitt, *Works*, 16: 353.

44. On gender and the aesthetic, see Terry Eagleton, *The Ideology of the Aesthetic* (Oxford: Blackwell, 1990); Psomiades, *Beauty's Body*, 1–23 (and see 18–22 on the play of gender in Eagleton); and Redfield, *The Politics of Aesthetics*, 34–40, 80–81. Barrell, who concludes his influential book with a consideration of Hazlitt's attempt to divorce taste from politics, laments that by making "power" an effect of individual genius Hazlitt effectively denies "those who are unable to exhibit individuality of character . . . the right to regard themselves as full members of human society"; *Political Theory of Painting*, 338. Paulson, conversely, defends Hazlitt (whom he views as Hogarth's chief inheritor) through a schematic contrast with Reynolds: "The difference between Reynolds and Hazlitt is that Reynolds wrote for a small ruling elite, while Hazlitt supported the ideals of the French Revolution"; *Beautiful, Novel, and Strange*, 96. Hemingway offers a more helpful explanation for Hazlitt's position, arguing that recent history had by 1816 "reduced Hazlitt to a condition of political despair from which he never really emerged. With the public forms of culture so irremediably compromised in his eyes, it is not surprising that he came to believe that true discernment was only possible for a few. The

writers of his generation whom he had most admired, Wordsworth and Coleridge, had become out-and-out reactionaries, and it is therefore hardly surprising that he could find little connection between taste and the political principles he believed in"; "Political Theory of Painting Without the Politics," 392.

45. *Autobiography and Memoirs of Benjamin Robert Haydon* (1853), ed. Tom Taylor, intro. Aldous Huxley, 2 vols. (London: P. Davies, 1926), 1: 66–7. Haydon was among the first and most avid supporters of the marbles. He had read Charles Bell's *Anatomy and Philosophy of Expression as connected with the Fine Arts* (1806) and attended Bell's London lectures, and when he bought John Bell's *The Anatomy of the Bones, Muscles & Joints* (1793) in 1805, he "took the book home, hugging it" (1: 18). Late in life, he analogized his attitude to the marbles to Reynolds's toward Michelangelo: "Reynolds said, the last words he should wish to pronounce in the Academy, were, Michael Angelo! Michael Angelo! the last words I should wish to utter in this world, till art gave way to more awful reflections, while my voice was articulate, and a fibre of my vitality quivered,—are, Elgin Marbles! Elgin Marbles!"; *Lectures on Painting and Design*, 2 vols. (London, 1846), 1: 105.

46. The "Englishness" of the marbles, Heringman argues, extended to a national "economy depleted by the Napoleonic Wars, presenting an appearance of ruin that links the physical state of the Marbles suggestively with the state of the nation"; "Stones so wonderous Cheap," 59. Andrew Hemingway has observed in Haydon's writings a "crucial nationalistic dimension" heightened by a wartime impulse to compete with the cultural achievements of the Continent; "Political Theory of Painting Without the Politics," 391.

47. Ronald Paulson, "Introduction" to William Hogarth, *The Analysis of Beauty* (1753) (New Haven, CT: Yale University Press, 1997), xliii.

48. Haydon, *Autobiography*, 1: 235. Haydon's responses to the marbles were conditioned in part by the circumstances of his viewings. He wandered among them and experienced them physically: they were, he recalls, "within sight and reach," and once, a "Marble fell down and cut my leg" (Autobiography, 1: 66, 70). His close proximity to the gigantic statues may have forced an attention to parts rather than wholes; in Susan Stewart's words, "we know the miniature as a spatial whole or as temporal parts, [but] we know the gigantic only partially"; *On Longing: Narratives of the Miniature, the Gigantic, the Souvenir, and the Collection* (Durham, NC: Duke University Press, 1984), 71. Poor lighting (Haydon often stole by night into Burlington House to view them by candlelight: *Autobiography* 1: 108) may also have contributed. The flickering light suggests an explanation for the marbles' apparent lifelikeness; the literally giant shadows they cast are perhaps registered by Keats (who undoubtedly had heard a great deal about the marbles from Haydon before he saw them in March 1817) in the last line of "On Seeing the Elgin Marbles."

49. Hazlitt, *Works*, 18: 115.

50. Haydon, *Lectures on Painting and Design*, 2: 219–20; Haygarth quoted in Larrabee, *English Bards and Grecian Marbles*, 273.

51. Lynch, *The Economy of Character*, 58. Lynch observes a related concern about the "overlaboured display" of low-art forms: "High art set about defining itself in contradistinction to popular and amateur art by identifying itself with an ideal of 'pictorial abstemiousness' and identifying others with excess" (59).

52. Allan Cunningham, *Lives of the Most Eminent British Painters*, quoted in Paulson, *Beautiful, Novel, and Strange*, 96.

53. This and the previous quotation are drawn from John Kandl, "The Politics of

Keats's Early Poetry," in *The Cambridge Companion to Keats*, ed. Susan J. Wolfson (Cambridge and New York: Cambridge University Press, 2001), 14.

54. Cornwall's poem appears in the *Gentleman's Magazine* 88 (1818), 157. For brief commentaries, see Larrabee, *English Bards and Grecian Marbles*, 274–75, 279; and Scott, *The Sculpted Word*, 61–64. Haydon is quoted from his *Autobiography*, 1: 231–32.

55. As affordable commodities read by the masses, novels were often considered agents of literary democratization. By animating the Elgin Marble aesthetic, however, Shelley explores the democratic potential not of *novel reading* but of *novelistic representation*. I use "reform aesthetic" to designate an aesthetics that embodies developing ideas about political reform.

56. Mary Shelley, "Review of *Cloudesly; A Tale*," in *Blackwood's Edinburgh Magazine* 27 (May 1830), 711–16 (711). Compare Croker's association of a "low" realism with Dutch painting in his review of *Waverley* (*Quarterly Review* 11 [1814]: 355). Shelley's review provides a stepping-stone between Croker and Eliot.

57. Shelley, *Frankenstein*, 53. *Keeping* denotes the "maintenance of the proper relation between the representations of nearer and more distant objects in a picture" (*OED*).

58. See Percy Shelley's *Defence of Poetry* ("The great secret of morals is Love; or a going out of our own nature . . ." [*Shelley's Poetry and Prose*, 487] and "On Love" [whose 1829 publication in *The Keepsake* Mary Shelley oversees]). In the latter essay, the elucidation of sympathy involves a miniature, whose aesthetic of particularity splits the difference between the material and the ideal: "We dimly see within our intellectual nature a miniature as it were of our entire self, yet deprived of all that we condemn or despise, the ideal prototype of every thing excellent or lovely. . . . Not only the portrait of our external being, but an assemblage of the minutest particulars of which our nature is composed: a mirror whose surface reflects only the forms of purity and brightness. . . ."; *Shelley's Poetry and Prose*, 473–74.

59. Since anatomical study was the province of artists as well as surgeons—a fact that became widely recognized during the Elgin Marble affair—both groups benefited from bodysnatching. On bodysnatching and the Anatomy Act of 1832, see Ruth Richardson, *Death, Dissection and the Destitute*, 2nd ed. (Chicago and London: University of Chicago Press, 1987; repr. 2000). Richardson, who remarks that her research began when Shelley's novel prompted her to further explore bodysnatching (xiii), can be credited with inspiring at least three readings of *Frankenstein*: Marshall's full-length work; along with essays by Clara Tuite, "Frankenstein's Monster and Malthus' 'Jaundiced Eye': Population, Body Politics, and the Monstrous Sublime," *Eighteenth-Century Life* 22.1 (1998), 141–55; and Emma Liggins, "The Medical Gaze and the Female Corpse: Looking at Bodies in Mary Shelley's *Frankenstein*," *Studies in the Novel* 32 (2000), 129–46.

60. Richardson, *Death, Dissection and the Destitute*, 262–63.

61. Ibid., 81.

62. Sterrenburg, "Mary Shelley's Monster: Politics and Psyche in *Frankenstein*," 157.

63. William St. Clair notes "at least three cartoons titled 'The Political Frankenstein' were printed in 1832"; "The Impact of *Frankenstein*," in *Mary Shelley in her Times*, eds. Bennett and Curran, 61. Sterrenburg reproduces and briefly discusses one of these, a cartoon by the portrait painter and engraver James Parry entitled "Reform BILL's First Step Amongst His Political Frankensteins"; "Mary Shelley's Monster: Politics and Psyche in *Frankenstein*," 167.

64. My argument here registers Franco Moretti's claim that "Whoever dares to fight

the monster automatically becomes the representative of the species, of the whole of society"; "Dialectic of Fear," trans. David Forgacs, in *Signs Taken for Wonders: Essays in the Sociology of Literary Forms* (New York: Verso, 1988), 84. An analogy is provided by the reaction of Parisians to Manet's exhibition of his portrait of the courtesan, *Olympia*. As suggested by Louis de Laincel's review of the painting, in which he asked why "the Realists choose unclean women as their models and, having done so, reproduce even the filth which clings to their contours," Manet's painting threatened to make "the real" all too apparent, seemingly doing away with art in the process. Georges Bataille, discussing the same image, says that "in her provoking exactitude, she is *nothing*; . . . what she is, is the 'sacred horror' of her own presence—of a presence as simple as absence. Her hard realism, which for the Salon visitors was the ugliness of a 'gorilla,' consists for us in the painter's determination to reduce *what he saw* to the mute simplicity, the open-mouthed simplicity, of *what he saw*"; *Manet: Etude biographique et critique*, 66–67, quoted (as is de Laince) in T. J. Clark's fascinating discussion of this painting: 96, 146.

65. Kearns, *Nineteenth-Century Literary Realism*, 116.

66. Johanna Smith, *Mary Shelley*, 47.

67. Denise Gigante reads this exclusion in aesthetic terms: in his ugliness, she argues, the Creature "symbolizes nothing but the unsymbolized: the repressed ugliness at the heart of an elaborate symbolic network that is threatened the moment he bursts on the scene, exposing to view his radically uninscribed existence"; "Facing the Ugly: The Case of *Frankenstein*," *ELH* 67 (2000), 567.

Chapter Five: The Look of a Poet: Wordsworth

1. The epigraph appears in *The Athenæum* no. 342 (17 May 1834), 379.

2. Wordsworth discusses "the common inheritance of poets" in his "Preface" to *Lyrical Ballads, The Prose Works of William Wordsworth*, eds. W. J. B. Owen and Jane Worthington Smyser, 3 vols. (Oxford: Clarendon Press, 1974), 1: 132.

3. The anecdote is given in Christopher Wordsworth, *Memoirs of William Wordsworth*, 2 vols. (London, 1851), 1: 9.

4. Eleven, to be exact, after 1830. A twelfth was published in 1827 ("Recollection of the Portrait of King Henry Eighth, Trinity Lodge, Cambridge"); and a thirteenth, published in the 1829 issue of *The Keepsake* as "The Country Girl" (but subsequently retitled "The Gleaner"), is said by Wordsworth to be based "on the Picture of a beautiful Peasant Girl bearing a Sheaf of Corn"; *The Letters of William and Dorothy Wordsworth: The Later Years, 1821–1853*, ed. de Selincourt, 2d. ed. rev. and arranged Alan G. Hill, 4 parts (Oxford: Oxford University Press, 1978–88), 1: 590.

5. On Wordsworth's iconic poems as latter-day "spots of time," see Matthew C. Brennan, "Wordsworth's 'Lines Suggested by a Portrait from the Pencil of F. Stone': 'Visible Quest of Immortality'?" *English Language Notes* 35.2 (December 1997), 33–43. On Wordsworth's "theatrical" mode of posing for portraits as an actualization of his poetry's paradoxical "performance" of sincerity, see Pascoe, *Romantic Theatricality*, 184–228.

6. Hemans, *Selected Poems, Letters, Reception Materials*, 492. I am grateful to an anonymous reader for helping me formulate the following paragraph.

7. Frances Blanshard counts eighty-seven portraits of Wordsworth, most painted in the last twenty years of his life; *Portraits of Wordsworth* (Ithaca, NY: Cornell University Press, 1959), 67, 139. Wordsworth uses the phrase "second self" in "Michael" to refer to his

literary heirs, but he also "seems to have thought of his literary corpus as a second self," argues Susan Eilenberg; *Strange Power of Speech: Wordsworth, Coleridge, and Literary Possession* (New York: Oxford University Press, 1992), 207. On the anthologizing of Wordsworth and the relation between promotion and piracy, see Stephen Gill, *Wordsworth and the Victorians* (Oxford: Clarendon Press, 1998), ch. 3. I am grateful to an anonymous reader for helping me formulate the preceding paragraph.

8. On the spectacle of authorial promotion, including such poster portraits, see Gerard Curtis, *Visual Words: Art and the Material Book in Victorian England* (Aldershot, England; Brookfield, VT: Ashgate, 2002).

9. Blanshard concisely summarizes the production, circulation, and reputation of this portrait—a summary to which my own account and understanding of sources is much indebted; *Portraits of Wordsworth*, 74–78.

10. Quoted in Blanshard, *Portraits of Wordsworth*, 76.

11. Robinson quoted in Blanshard, *Portraits of Wordsworth*, 78; *Athenæum* no. 342 (17 May 1834), 379; Wordsworth, *Later Years*, 3: 35, 4: 120. Dora, in describing Pickersgill's manner in painting portraits, suggests the problem in part: "Mr P. liked to have people with him to keep the Poet from thinking of where he was and what he was doing" (Wordsworth, *Later Years*, 2: 554). As a sitter, Wordsworth was thus emptied of precisely what made him "Wordsworth": a sense of reflective identity situated in a specific location.

12. *The Letters of William and Dorothy Wordsworth: The Middle Years, 1806–1820*, ed. de Selincourt; *Part 1, 1806–1811*, 2d ed. rev. Mary Moorman (Oxford: Clarendon Press, 1969), 266. The fact that Wordsworth has no problem with being represented as a sculpture bust—which similarly removed the body but did so in a prestigious and idealizing form associated with senatorial ideals of public virtue—underscores his concern with appearing as a man of "real power," a public poet.

13. The sonnet first appears in 1835's *Yarrow Revisited*, and next as the dedicatory sonnet for the 1836 *Poetical Works*. It later disappears from that prominent position, however, and in fact is replaced by a different sonnet in 1846—"If thou indeed derive thy light from Heaven," which similarly answers the portrait with an emphasis on the poet's God-like immateriality.

14. Unless otherwise noted, all references to Wordsworth's poetry are to the *Poetical Works*, eds. Ernest de Selincourt and Helen Darbishire, 5 vols. (Oxford: Clarendon Press, 1940–49; rev. ed. 1952–59).

15. The lines had previously read: ". . . though Kingdoms melt / Before the breath of Change, unchanged, wilt seem / Green hills in sight, and listening to the stream . . ."; *Last Poems, 1821–1850*, ed. Jared Curtis (Ithaca, NY: Cornell University Press, 1999), 229.

16. This letter receives its first substantial printing in Cecil Y. Lang's edition, *An Arnold Family Album*, special issue of *The Arnoldian* 15.3 (1990): 5–6.

17. *The Questioning Presence: Wordsworth, Keats, and the Interrogative Mode in Romantic Poetry* (Ithaca, NY: Cornell University Press, 1986), 69.

18. Gill, *Wordsworth and the Victorians*, 98.

19. "Wordsworth in *The Keepsake*, 1829," in *Literature in the Marketplace: Nineteenth-century British Publishing and Reading Practices*, eds. John O. Jordan and Robert L. Patten (Cambridge: Cambridge University Press, 1995), 66.

20. "Petition of Wm. Wordsworth, Esq.," in T. N. Talfourd, *Three Speeches Delivered*

in the House of Commons in Favour of a Measure for an Extension of Copyright (London, 1840), 112; Wordsworth, *Later Years,* 3: 597.

21. On Wordsworth's linking an author's unambiguous ownership in his poems with their civic function of producing "more actively and securely virtuous" readers, see Richard G. Swartz, "Wordsworth, Copyright, and the Commodities of Genius," *Modern Philology* 89 (1992), 482–509, esp. 503.

22. Talfourd, *Three Speeches,* 24–25.

23. C. Wordsworth, *Memoirs,* 1: 26; Hemans, *Selected Poems, Letters, Reception Materials,* 492.

24. Talfourd, *Three Speeches,* 20.

25. Wordsworth, *Middle Years,* 266.

26. Wordsworth, *Prose Works,* 3: 312.

27. Wordsworth, "Petition," 112–13.

28. On Wordsworth's complicated intellectual relationship with Burke, see James K. Chandler, *Wordsworth's Second Nature: A Study of the Poetry and Politics* (Chicago and London: University of Chicago Press, 1984).

29. Gilfillan, "William Wordsworth," in *The Eclectic Magazine of Foreign Literature, Science, and Art* 17 (1849), 569.

30. Quoted in Swartz, "Wordsworth, Copyright, and the Commodities of Genius," 500–501.

31. Michael Fried, *Absorption and Theatricality: Painting and Beholder in the Age of Diderot* (Chicago and London: University of Chicago Press, 1980), 5, 43–45.

32. Walter Pater, *Appreciations* (New York: Macmillan, 1910 [1889]), 51. Pater argues that Wordsworth transforms a poetics of temporality into a poetics of being by privileging an aesthetic rather than empirical epistemology: the Paterian "picture within" is more "real" than "rocks, and stones, and things." The phrase "pictures within" itself echoes the "picture of the mind" of "Tintern Abbey" in describing a visionary subjectivity that filters out visibility, an "inward eye of solitude" that displaces (or "re-realizes") the real with the mental, the perceived with the half created. On Pater's reading of Wordsworth in relation to the interpretations of peers like Arnold, Ruskin, and Stephen, see David J. DeLaura, "The 'Wordsworth' of Pater and Arnold: 'The Supreme Artistic View of Life'," *Studies in English Literature* 6 (1966), 651–67; Paul de Man, *The Rhetoric of Romanticism* (New York: Columbia University Press, 1984), 83–92; William Galperin, *Revision and Authority in Wordsworth: The Interpretation of a Career,* (Philadelphia: University of Pennsylvania Press, 1989), 15–27; Gill, *Wordsworth and the Victorians,* ch. 7; and Elizabeth Helsinger, "Ruskin on Wordsworth: The Victorian Critic in Romantic Country," *Studies in Romanticism* 17 (1978), 267–91.

33. Wordsworth's account of the despotism of "the bodily eye" is in *Prelude* 12: 128–29. His involvement of portraiture in the Snowden passage occurs in DC MS. 52; *The Thirteen-Book Prelude,* ed. Mark Reed, 2 vols. (Ithaca, NY: Cornell University Press, 1991), 2: 967. For an extensive catalogue of Wordsworth's pictorial metaphors, see Swingle.

34. My reading of Wordsworth's ekphrastic portraits engages William Galperin's treatment of the "authority" of Wordsworth's later poetry. Galperin uncovers a self-critical impulse, "a Wordsworth answerable to Wordsworth"; Galperin, *Revision and Authority in Wordsworth,* 5. The later Wordsworth, according to Galperin, forgoes intentionality and thus, unwittingly, relinquishes the authority that is the primary

characteristic of the earlier work. Galperin's argument paves the way for my concern with ekphrasis in Wordsworth's later work. Ekphrasis, however, invariably stages struggles *for* authority—not only between poet and painter, but also between poet and reader. The encounter between poet and painting affirms the ekphrastic poet's authority because, put plainly, he controls the reader's access to art—much as Wordsworth attempts to control his own self-presentation in these later years. Thus in the "Sonnet to a Picture by Lucca Giordano in the Museo Borbonico at Naples" (publ. 1847), Wordsworth provides a verbal translation of the portrait to readers who may not be able to access the original—the titular emphasis on the portrait's location is belied by the transportability of poetic language. "Ekphrasis is about physical as much as verbal translation," writes Grant F. Scott, "about moving the visual object from its original residence into the house of words and then restoring and revivifying it"; *The Sculpted Word*, 19. Wordsworth's late ekphrases, then, far from diminishing the importance of his individual authority, emphasize that authority by celebrating a unique encounter between poet and artwork.

35. Though the subject of the portrait is often said to be Jemima Katharine Quillinan, Edward's daughter, Brennan notes that the picture's provenance has not been established, and the poem itself seems deliberately ambiguous on this score; Brennan, "Wordsworth's 'Lines Suggested by a Portrait from the Pencil of F. Stone': 'Visible Quest of Immortality'?" 43.

36. De Man, *The Rhetoric of Romanticism* (New York: Columbia University Press, 1984), 78.

37. Mitchell, "Ekphrasis and the Other," *South Atlantic Quarterly* 91 (1992), 697.

38. Ibid., 696.

39. Wordsworth, *Last Poems*, 334; Wordsworth's emphasis.

40. Hazlitt, *Works*, 19: 11; Haydon, *Autobiography*, 2: 730–31.

41. Blanshard, *Portraits of Wordsworth*, 109; A. C. Sewter, "A Revaluation of Haydon," *Art Quarterly* 5 (1942), 324; Gill, *Wordsworth and the Victorians*, 38; Dora Wordsworth quoted in Blanshard, *Portraits of Wordsworth*, 167.

42. Gillian Russell and Clara Tuite, eds., *Romantic Sociability: Social Networks and Literary Culture in Britain 1770–1840* (Cambridge: Cambridge University Press, 2002), 4.

43. David Blayney Brown, Stephen Hebron, and Robert Woof, *Benjamin Robert Haydon: Painter, Writer, Friend of Wordsworth and Keats* (Grasmere: Wordsworth Trust, 1996), 18.

44. Grant F. Scott, "Ekphrasis as Ideology," *Yearbook of Interdisciplinary Studies in the Fine Arts* 2 (1990), 95.

45. Hagstrum, *The Sister Arts*, 18.

46. Wordsworth, *Last Poems, 1821–1850*, ed. Jared Curtis (Ithaca, NY: Cornell University Press, 1999), 351n.

47. Wordsworth, *Later Years*, 4: 106–7. The editors of the letters assume this etching to be an engraving by Thomas Lupton (1791–1873), as does Bishop C. Hunt Jr. in his survey of the letters in Princeton's Taylor Collection: "Wordsworth, Haydon, and the 'Wellington' Sonnet," *Princeton University Library Chronicle* 36 (1975), 111–32. I agree with the editors of the Cornell Wordsworth that there is no reason to believe anything other than that this is Haydon's etching of his own painting, Lupton's engraving having been in production, according to Wordsworth's admittedly unreliable account.

48. Haydon, *Diary*, ed. Willard Bissell Pope, 5 vols. (Cambridge, MA: Harvard University Press, 1960), 4: 534; Hunt, "Wordsworth, Haydon, and the 'Wellington' Sonnet," 130.

49. Carlos Baker, "Sensation and Vision in Wordsworth," in *English Romantic Poets: Modern Essays in Criticism*, ed. M. H. Abrams (New York: Oxford University Press, 1960), 106. Bishop Hunt argues for the relevance of this paradigm in Wordsworth's sonnet; "Wordsworth, Haydon, and the 'Wellington' Sonnet," 131. A "very clear manifestation," Baker adds, is "Elegiac Stanzas Suggested by a Picture of Peele Castle," where a remembered, tranquil picture is juxtaposed with Beaumont's stormy painting. "Between these two moralized landscapes," he argues, "stretches the poem" (108). In much the same way, Wordsworth's sonnet produces a portrait of its own out of the gap that separates Haydon's two exposures.

50. Baker, "Sensation and Vision in Wordsworth," 107.

51. Hunt, "Wordsworth, Haydon, and the 'Wellington' Sonnet," 131. Hunt additionally argues that Wordsworth, by identifying with Wellington, revived his stance on copyright reform. Indignation at the present political system that seemed not to understand or appreciate "greatness" was expressed in his adulation of Wellington, a former Prime Minister whose leadership at Waterloo had helped to shape the course of European history.

52. The painting of which Wordsworth writes is *Napoleon musing on St Helena*, a pendant to the Wellington.

53. Haydon, *Diary*, 3: 499.

54. Haydon, *Autobiography*, 2: 506.

55. Stewart, *On Longing*, 43.

56. Gilfillan, "William Wordsworth," 569.

57. On Wordsworth's performances of inwardness, see Pascoe, *Romantic Theatricality*, 184–228.

58. Richard D. Altick, *The Shows of London* (Cambridge, MA: Harvard University Press, 1979), 222–25.

59. The *Eclectic Magazine* for August 1849, which contains the memoir by Gilfillan (author of *The Literary Gallery of Portraits*), has for its frontispiece an engraving of the painting by H. S. Sadd. On arguments about "Wordsworth" in the 1870s and '80s, see Gill, *Wordsworth and the Victorians*, 211–14.

60. Gill, *Wordsworth and the Victorians*, 108.

61. *The Complete Prose Works of Matthew Arnold*, ed. R. H. Super, 11 vols. (Ann Arbor: University of Michigan Press, 1960-), 9: 42.

62. Arnold, *Prose Works*, 45, 51, 338. Arnold exercised broad control over the design of his Wordsworth. He dictated such matters as typeface and page layout. The portrait was engraved for Arnold by Charles Henry Jeems, whose work he considered "a treat": "It is better than I had even ventured to expect: for there is something not quite *right* about the picture, fine as it is"; Arnold to Macmillan, 30 June 1879, quoted in William E. Buckler, ed. *Matthew Arnold's Books: Toward a Publishing Diary* (Geneva: Librairie E. Droz, 1958), 141. On the making of Arnold's edition, see the annotations to the introductory essay in Arnold, *Prose Works*, ed. R. H. Super, 9: 336–40; Jared Curtis, "Matthew Arnold's Wordsworth: The Tinker Tinkered," in *The Mind in Creation: Essays on English Romantic Literature in Honour of Ross G. Woodman*, ed. J. Douglas Kneale ([Montreal:] McGill-Queen's University Press, 1992), 49–50; and Buckler, *Matthew Arnold's Books*, 132–45.

63. John Stuart Mill, *Autobiography, and Other Writings*, ed. J. Stillinger (Boston: Houghton Mifflin, 1969), 89.

64. The portrait, as Pascoe notes, was actually posed over the course of several days in a London studio; *Romantic Theatricality*, 217.

65. Gilfillan, "William Wordsworth," 569.

66. Haydon, *Autobiography*, 2: 818.

67. *The Complete Poetical Works of Elizabeth Barrett Browning*, ed. Harriet Waters Preston (New York: Houghton Mifflin, 1900), 98.

68. "Ebb" would have been even more apt after Barrett's marriage to Robert Browning in 1844. Here "Eb." can be read as short for her surname, the final "b" for her last.

69. *The Complete Works of Elizabeth Barrett Browning*, eds. Charlotte Porter and Helen A. Clarke, 6 vols. (New York: AMS, 1973), 6: 303.

70. C. Wordsworth, *Memoirs*, 1: 3.

71. Gill, *Wordsworth and the Victorians*, 38; Sara Coleridge quoted in Blanshard, *Portraits of Wordsworth*, 102; Henry Crabb Robinson, *Books and Their Writers*, ed. Edith J. Morley, 3 vols. (London: J. M. Dent, 1938), 2: 715.

Epilogue

1. "Our Royal-Academical Lounge," *Fraser's Magazine* 5 (1832), 710–11.

2. *A Descriptive Catalogue of the Historical Pictures of the Meeting of the First Reformed House of Commons, in 1833* (London: [Wright and Co.], 1843), vi.

3. Schnapp, *Staging Fascism*, 101.

4. Framing the issue in terms of Pre-Raphaelite aesthetics, Carol Christ similarly describes the abstracting effect of "extreme heterogeneity": while "even the smallest [of] objects" becomes "a possible focus of contemplation," its ontological status comes into question, "poised precariously and deliberately on the brink between being aesthetic objects and being natural objects." On account of "the unnaturalness of painting each object, no matter how near or far, how central or insignificant, with the same microscopic clarity," Christ argues, the Pre-Raphaelites, against expectation, "most often strike us with their lack of realism"; Christ, *Finer Optic*, 53.

5. Poovey, *Making a Social Body*, 4.

6. F. R. Ankersmit, *Aesthetic Politics: Political Philosophy Beyond Fact and Value* (Stanford, CA: Stanford University Press, 1996), 191.

7. Colley, *Britons*, 349.

8. Valerie Cromwell, "The Victorian Commons, 1832–1884," in *The House of Commons: Seven Hundred Years of British Tradition*, eds. Robert Smith and John S. Moore (London: Smith's Peerage, 1996), 121. On the different restrictions for voters and for MPs, see J. V. Beckett, *The Aristocracy in England, 1660–1914* (Oxford and New York: Blackwell, 1986), 455.

9. Quoted in Thompson, *Making of the English Working Classes*, 812.

10. Thompson describes the startling precision with which the government calculated the qualification so as to keep the working classes out of government. He quotes from a letter from Edward Baines, who had undertaken to find out how many and how respectable were the £10 householders in Leeds, to Lord John Russell: "The £10 qualification did not admit to the exercise of the elective franchise a single person who might not safely and wisely be enfranchised," Baines concluded; indeed, "they were surprised to find how comparatively few would be allowed to vote." In Leeds's working-class neighborhoods, "not one householder in fifty would have a vote. . . . In the township of Holbeck, containing 11,000 inhabitants, chiefly of the working classes, but containing

several mills, dye-houses, public-houses, and respectable dwellings, there are only 150 voters. . . . Out of 140 householders, heads of families, working in the mill of Messrs. Marshall and Co, there are only two who will have votes. . . . Out of 160 or 170 householders in the mill of Messrs. O. Willan and Sons, Hobeck, there is not one vote. Out of about 100 householders in the employment of Messrs. Taylor and Wordsworth, machine-makers,—the highest class of mechanics,—only one has a vote. It appeared that of the working classes not more than one in fifty would be enfranchised by the Bill." Thompson adds that "even this estimate would appear to have been excessive. Returns made to the Government in May 1832 showed that in Leeds (poulation, 124,000) 355 'workmen' would be admitted to the franchise, of whom 143 'are clerks, warehousemen, overlookers, &c.' The remaining 212 were in a privileged status, earning between 30s. and 40s. a week"; *Making of the English Working Class*, 818. On the other hand, as Colley describes, "the new British electorate of 656,000 was very large indeed, bearing in mind that Austria, Denmark, Russia, and Greece still had no popularly elected national legislative assemblies at all. A much bigger proportion of men could now vote in Britain than in France, Spain, Belgium or the Netherlands"; *Britons*, 349.

11. Hazlitt, *Works*, 10: 126.

12. W. Charles Townsend, *Memoirs of the House of Commons, from the Convention Parliament of 1688–9 to the Passing of the Reform Bill, in 1832*, 2 vols. (London: Henry Colburn, 1844), 2: 463–64.

13. Beckett, *The Aristocracy in England*, 451; Eric J. Evans, *Parliamentary Reform in Britain, c. 1770–1918* (Harlow, UK, and New York: Longman, 2000), 30.

14. Cobbett, quoted in Colley, *Britons*, 348; *Westminster Review* 25 (4 April 1836), 271, 276.

15. Colley, *Britons*, 349.

16. Evans, *Parliamentary Reform in Britain*, 35.

17. Emmanuel Sieyès, quoted in Bernard Manin, "On Legitimacy and Political Deliberation," in *New French Thought: Political Philosophy*, ed. Mark Lilla (Princeton, NJ: Princeton University Press, 1994), 187.

18. Ibid., 188.

19. I am grateful to Morton Paley for pointing out to me the artificiality of this perspective.

20. John Adams, "Thoughts on Government" (April 1776), in *Papers of John Adams*, volumes 3 and 4 (May 1775 - August 1776), eds. Robert J. Taylor, Gregg. L. Lint, and Celeste Walker (Cambridge, MA: Belknap Press, 1979), 4: 87.

21. On Victorian skepticism regarding representationalism, universality, and liberal-humanist subjectivity, see Christ, *The Finer Optic*; Kelley, *Reinventing Allegory*; and Levine, *The Realistic Imagination*. Kelley succinctly summarizes: "As Victorian writers became more skeptical of the positivist faith that fueled liberal humanist hopes for the things of this world, realism's presentation of particulars and individuals began to look less convinced about its representational status"; *Reinventing Allegory*, 218.

22. Roland Barthes, "The Reality Effect" (1968), in *The Rustle of Language*, trans. Richard Howard (Berkeley and Los Angeles: University of California Press, 1986), 145.

23. Colley, *Britons*, 349.

24. Redfield and Kelley lucidly describe the Hegelian distinction between sign and symbol (Redfield in terms of national imagery); *Politics of Aesthetics*, 50 and n.; Kelley, *Reinventing Allegory*, 136.

25. John Pinkerton, *Iconographia Scotia or Portraits of Illustrious Persons of Scotland, Engraved from the most Authentic Paintings &c With short Biographical Notices* (London: F. Herbert, 1797), iv. *Effigies Poeticæ*, 1: 1.

26. Stewart, *On Longing*, 158.

27. *Jane Austen's Letters*, 212.

28. See Haley, *Living Forms*, 13.

29. For this reason, Benedict Anderson cites as "the hallmark of modern nations" what he calls the "remarkable confidence of *community in anonymity*"; *Imagined Communities*, 36.

30. And not, I stress, anyplace else—as indicated by the fact that Global Exchange, an international human rights organization, has since published its own gallery, titled "Afghan Portraits of Grief," to commemorate the thousands killed in bombing by the US military in the months after 9/11. Indeed, Michael Massing titles his pointed critique of the American media's failure to attend to the grief of Afghan people and the victims of the war there "Grief Without Portraits"—suggesting the essential role of the portrait in producing, or at least in signifying, sympathy. Michael Massing, "Grief Without Portraits," *The Nation* 274 (4 February 2002), 6–8.

31. Janny Scott, "Closing a Scrapbook Full of Life and Sorrow," *New York Times* (31 December 2001; http://www.nytimes.com/2001/12/31/national /portraits/31PORT.html).

32. Lootens graciously shared this idea with me, which she discusses in her book-in-progress, titled *Privatizing the Poetess*.

33. Quoted in Scott, "Closing a Scrapbook Full of Life and Sorrow."

34. "To read the Portraits one would believe that work counted for next to nothing, that every hard charging bond trader and daredevil fireman preferred—and managed—to spend more time with his family than at the office," Mallon writes. "If Mayor Rudolph Giuliani had perished in the attacks, as he nearly did, he would be remembered in the Portraits as a rabid Yankee fan who sometimes liked to put on lipstick"; "The Mourning Paper," *The American Scholar* 71.2 (Spring 2002), 7.

35. The story, as David Simpson argues, is very much at the heart of a phantasmatic national self-image, of "happy people, fulfilled in their jobs, fountains of love and charity, pillars of their families and communities"; "The Mourning Paper," *London Review of Books* 26.10 (20 May 2004): 3.

36. This statement helps to advertise the book on the Amazon website.

37. Thomas De Quincey, *Confessions of an English Opium-Eater* (1822), ed. Grevel Lindop (Oxford and New York: Oxford University Press, 1985), 72.

38. *Staging Fascism*, 101. Given the tendency to abstract away particulars in the imagining of a social whole, Teskey urges that we keep in mind the plural existence of actual bodies that undergird the image of the corporate nation; *Allegory and Violence*, 123. Redfield provides penetrating analysis of these cultural-political investments: "Culture names the subject's identification with anonymity as 'disinterestedness,'" he argues, "with anonymity as the formal, abstract identity of the nation and the human"; *Politics of Aesthetics*, 56.

Index

Absorption, 72, 158, 162, 166–68, 185; and civic engagement, in Wordsworth, 177–78, 180–81. *See also* Genius

Abstraction, 41, 42, 189–93; and allegory, 38–39; and body of the state, 3, 183; and Coleridge, 39; and idealized portraiture, 8, 24, 29, 38–40, 183, 185; opposed to intimacy, 165, 190; overabundance of detail as, 185, 189–90; and "Portraits of Grief," 192–93; and social imaginary, 189–90, 192–93. *See also* Detail(s)

Ackermann, Rudolph, 186

Adams, John, 190

Addison, Joseph, 59

Adelman, Janet, 89, 92, 215

Aesthetics: academic, 4, 13–16, 29, 43, 44, 57, 61, 63, 65, 77, 98, 130–31, 136, 141–44, 148, 185; of particularity, 4, 13–16, 19, 29, 43, 44, 130–31, 141–44, 148, 202; politics of, 4, 7, 13–16, 19, 29, 43–44, 53, 57, 60–61, 77, 89, 98, 130–31, 135, 139, 142–45, 148, 185–86, 189, 200, 203, 225. *See also* Beauty; Civic humanism; Deformity; Monstrosity; Politics, of art; Realism; Sublime, the

Aikin, Anna, 40

Allegory: Benjamin on, 208; and body politic, 11–13, 16–22, 34, 146–48, 199–200; *The Winter's Tale* as social, 87–91. *See also under* Abstraction; Nation; Portraits; Social body

Allusion, 16, 23, 71–72, 106, 109, 113–15, 211, 219. *See also* Portraits, allegorical; *and under* Gender; Melancholy; Property

Altick, Richard D., 84, 86, 214

Amateurism, 219, 226

Anatomy, 131, 141–47, 227; and novel-writing, 145–48

Anatomy Act (1832), 146–47, 227

Anderson, Benedict, 3, 32, 203, 235

Ankersmit, F. R., 186, 203

Anonymity, 190, 192, 235

Apollo Belvedere, 71–72, 142, 211

Apostrophe, 165, 179

Ardemagni, Mirko: *The New Masses*, 193

Armstrong, Nancy, 202, 206

Arnold, Matthew: and Wordsworth, 177–78, 180, 232

Arnold, Oliver, 195

Arnold, Thomas, 157

Asleson, Robyn, 220–21

Assignats, 58–59. *See also* Money

Austen, Jane: and miniatures, 54, 130; at Spring Garden, 191; *Emma*, 54; *Pride and Prejudice*, 1–4, 191, 195

Auster, Paul, 192

Author portraits, 8, 42; and Smith, 108, 109–11; and Wordsworth, 150, 151, 152–58, 177–80

Authority: academic, 141–42; of beauty, 59–61; economic, of consumers, 84; emotional, 123; of history, 3; of history painting, 23, 50; dispersal of, 11, 13, 58; and femininity, 89, 92, 103, 115, 215; legislative, 13, 16; Locke on, 11; lyric, 115; and money, 58–59; of originals, 89, 100; patriarchal, 43, 44, 57, 125, 138, 217; royal, 11, 77, 89, 101, 103; treatment of, in Shakespeare Gallery, 91–103; treatment of, in *The Winter's Tale*, 87–91, 215. *See also* Authorship; Canon; Property; *and under* Ekphrasis; Engraving; Smith
Authorship, 89, 111, 151, 158–62, 167. *See also* Copyright
Autonomy: critique of, in Shakespeare Gallery 77, 82, 89, 214–15

Baker, Carlos, 174, 232
Barker-Benfield, G. J., 218
Barlow, Joel, 52
Barrell, John, 11, 16, 26–27, 48, 61, 76, 81, 197–98, 200, 210, 225
Barrett, Elizabeth, 178–80; "On a Portrait of Wordsworth by B. R. Haydon," 178–80
Barry, James: on Hogarth, 15; Irish radical sympathies of, 15; on portraiture, 23, 24; *Commerce, or the Triumph of the Thames*, 24; *The Distribution of the Premiums in the Society of Arts*, 24; *Portraits of Barry and Burke in the Characters of Ulysses and a Companion*, 24
Barthes, Roland, 190
Bataille, Georges, 228
Bate, Jonathan, 216
Beach, Thomas: *Sarah Siddons as Melancholy—Il Penseroso*, 117
Beaumont, George (Sir), 141, 232
Beauty, 85, 96, 97, 134; Burke on, 48, 50, 55, 59–63, 143; and civic membership, 50; in distress, 48, 52, 59, 73; gift-book "beauties," 31–32, 156; Hogarth on, 15; and nation(alism), 31–32, 45, 48, 52, 56–57, 59–60, 62; of Reform, 45; and social order, 143, 149; vs. ugliness, 138–40, 143, 149. *See also* Aesthetics; Eroticism; Politics, as art; *and under* Authority
Bedford, Duke of, 57, 66–67, 71
Benjamin, Walter, 15, 58, 77, 143, 168, 208–9
Bermingham, Ann, 219
Bible, 85, 104
Biography, 24–26, 61, 129, 144, 177. *See also under* History; Portraiture; Smith
Blake, William, 198; on Reynolds, 13, 16; portrait of, 173
Blanshard, Frances, 169, 228–29
Blind Granny, 26–28
Body, bodies, 121, 142, 159, 163; abstraction, of actual, 16–19, 193, 235; central form of, 61–62; fable of the belly, 19; and the heart, 71; allegory of body politic, 11–13, 16–22, 34, 146–48, 181, 190, 199–200; and beauty, 48; king's, 11–13, 19–20, 22, 59, 190; as mobile gallery, 125; naked, 61–65; of the poet, 111, 113–14, 122–24, 154; pregnant, 89–90, 96; queen's, 59–65, 89–90; of the state, 1, 3, 29, 34, 48, 55–57, 59–63, 148, 183; working-class, 26–30, 44, 147, 159. *See also* Allegory; Beauty; Bodysnatching; Deformity; Detail(s); Femininity; Monstrosity; Pregnancy; Social body
Bodysnatching, 146–48, 227
Boothby, Brook, 114
Bourdieu, Pierre, 219
Bowles, William Lisle: "On a Landscape by Rubens," 126, 127
Boydell, John, 23–24, 31, 43–44, 73–104, 107, 181, 216; accused of slashing paintings, 103–4; and "aesthetic democracy," 75–76, 77–78, 82, 212; appeal to middle class, 78, 79, 104, 212; artists' critique of, 76–77, 87, 89, 91–103; and British trade surplus, 73, 78; Burke on, 73–74; and printmaking, 73, 77–78, 82, 104, 212; nationalism of, 77, 82, 87, 104;

nationalist rhetoric of, 80; praised as national hero, 73–74, 78, 81; revolutionizes art patronage, 78–80, 82, 104; subordinates portraiture to history painting, 23–24, 78, 80–81, 82, 86; suggests subjects to painters, 86. *See also* Shakespeare Gallery
Boydell, Josiah, 78
Brennan, Matthew C., 228, 231
Brewer, John, 80
Bridgman, Edward, 147
British Institution for Promoting the Fine Arts, 5, 31, 104
Bromley, Henry, 31
Brooks, Peter, 55
Browne, Stephen, 50, 207–8
Browning, Robert, 43, 45
Burke, Edmund, 1, 24, 43, 47–74, 127, 141, 143, 148, 161, 181, 206, 209; adapts civic humanism, 49, 55, 63, 65; on beauty and politics, 48, 50, 55, 59–63; on Bedford, Duke of, 56, 66–67, 71; on body of the state, 1, 48, 55–56, 59–63, 148; on Boydell, 73–74; as caricaturist, 66; compared to Cicero and Longinus, 52–53; on the Constitution, 209; on deformity, 56, 61, 143; and eroticism, 50, 57, 59–65; and history, 49, 56, 62–63; and homosociality, 67, 71–73; ideological ambivalence of, 43, 49, 55, 66, 73; on inheritance, 55–56, 58, 127; Irish background of, 53; and Keppel, 67–73; on Marie Antoinette, 43, 48, 59–65, 71; and money, 57–58; and nakedness, 60–61, 63–65; Paine on, 52, 209; perversity of, 50–51; as portraitist, 43, 50, 52, 55, 59–65, 66–67, 71–72, 207; and print culture, 52–53; representations of, 24, 50–51, 52–53; and Reynolds, 43, 47–50, 59–63, 67, 71, 72, 206; and sentimentality, 49, 63, 65; on state as a family, 48, 55; Wollstonecraft on, 50, 52; "Character of —— [Jane Burke]," 55–56; *A Letter to a Noble Lord*, 57, 65, 66–73; *Philosophical Enquiry into the Origins of Our Ideas of the Sublime and Beautiful*, 50; *Reflections on the Revolution in France*, 43, 47–52, 56–65, 66, 71, 73, 148, 206; *Speech on Taxation*, 55. *See also under* Barry; Beauty; Canon; Character(s); Clothing; Keppel; Masculinity; Narrative; Nostalgia; Novalis
Burney, Charles, 24
Burney, Frances, 54–55
Burns, Robert, 126
Burwick, Frederick, 100, 212
Byron, George Gordon, Lord, 8; on Elgin Marbles, 141, 145, 225

Campbell, Colin, 134, 137
Campbell, Thomas, 41
Cannadine, David, 6, 7, 8, 203
Cannon, John, 6–7
Canon, 114, 125–27; Burke's "canonized forefathers," 57, 59; gallery of portraits as, 57, 59, 105–7, 125–27; and Reynolds, 47, 48–49; and Smith, 126–27, 129. *See also* Allusion; Inheritance
Caricature, 50–51, 54, 57–59, 61, 66, 144. *See also under* Character(s); Wellington
Carlyle, Thomas, 24–25
Caulfield, James, 26–29, 31, 201
Cavell, Stanley, 89
Chantrey, Frances, 155
Character(s), 4, 7, 145; in Austen, 2, 3, 54; bardolatry and, 214; in Burke, 50, 52–53, 55, 62–63; Burney and, 54–55; in the novel, 10, 33–34, 55, 208; and caricature, 53; "character-system," 33–34; curious, 26–29, 201; galleries of, 109, 201; and history, 24, 84–86; and inwardness, 2, 3, 25, 63, 109–13, 124, 208; and middle class, 75, 84–85, 109; and narrative, 62–63; and *portrait moral*, 55; portraits of, 82–85, 109, 201; sketches of, 4, 25, 32, 43, 53–55, 67; Charlotte Smith as, 109–14, 124; and theater, 84–85, 214; typographical, 25, 55
Chard, Chloe, 72

Christ, Carol D., 38, 202, 233
Chubb, John, 7, 9
Civic humanism, 15–16, 48–50, 59, 63–66, 67, 76, 77, 81, 98, 134, 158, 159, 162, 168, 177, 200, 210. *See also* Aesthetics, academic, politics of; *and under* Absorption; Beauty; Burke; Masculinity
Clark, T. J., 228
Clothing (drapery), 216; in Burke, 48, 49, 59–65; and emulation, 137; vs. nakedness, 60–61, 63–65; in portraiture, 7, 26, 48, 49, 186; and social body, 59–61. *See also* Eroticism; Theatricality, of class
Cobbett, William, 7, 188
Cohn, Dorrit, 208
Coleridge, Samuel Taylor, 89, 93, 160; on portraiture, 8, 39; on Shakespeare's "picture gallery," 32, 82
Coleridge, Sara, 180
Colley, Linda, 4, 19, 91, 186, 216, 234
Constitution, English, 209
Consumerism, 213; and art, 5, 134; and democratization, 11, 22, 38, 48, 77, 84, 86, 104; and desire, 11, 62, 133; and distinction, 24, 84, 104, 134–35; as middle-class ethos, 59, 73; and portraiture, 49, 78, 84, 85, 86, 104, 133–35; and production, 82, 91, 133; and social body, 5, 48, 67; *See also* Marketplace; Taste
Copying, 5, 47–48, 88–89, 96, 100–101, 104, 111, 123, 140, 151, 159, 168. *See also* Copyright; Engraving; Mimesis
Copyright, 151, 158–62, 167, 178, 181. *See also* Authorship; Property; *and under* Wordsworth
Cornwall, Barry, 145; *Effigies Poeticæ: Portraits of the British Poets*, 105, 126–27, 190
Country house(s), 1–4, 5, 32, 104–7, 111, 125, 129, 191
Country-house poem, 107, 129
Courbet, Gustav, 31
Cranach, Lucas, the Elder: paintings of Lucretia, 64, 65, 211
Crawford, Rachel, 106, 220
Cunningham, Allan, 144
Curran, Stuart, 220–21

De Bolla, Peter, 209
De Bruyn, Frans, 52, 71
De Man, Paul, 165
De Quincey, Thomas, 193
Deane, Seamus, 208
Debord, Guy, 1, 192
Deformity, 56, 60–61, 141, 143. *See also* Monstrosity
Democratization, 4–5, 6, 31, 34–38, 44, 79, 106, 127–29, 147–48, 151, 158, 183, 186, 192, 202, 227. *See also* Reform Bill; Representation, political; Social body; *and under* Authority; Boydell; Consumerism; Politics
Desenfans, Noel, 3, 31
Desire, 2, 3, 11, 61–63, 65, 67, 100, 106, 117, 120, 126, 133, 166. *See also* Eroticism; *and under* Consumerism; Narrative
Detail(s), 16–19, 29, 33–34, 45, 60, 113, 130, 132, 140–44, 146, 148, 185, 189–93. *See also* Aesthetics, of particularity; Caricature; *and under* Abstraction
Dickens, Charles, 32, 45, 109, 151, 204; and authorship, 151; on Beatrice Cenci's portrait, 204; and "Galaxy Gallery of British Beauty," 32; Orwell on, 45; realism of, 32, 45; *American Notes and Pictures from Italy*, 204; *Bleak House*, 32, 109, 203
Distinction, 5, 10, 43, 57–58, 96, 103, 107, 111, 154; class, 7, 23–24, 26, 34–38, 49, 66, 73, 77–79, 85, 90–91, 93, 95, 125, 131–39, 148–49, 192; generic, 7, 23–26, 29, 34–38, 44, 49, 75–77, 84, 86, 92, 96, 104, 106–8, 132, 163, 216, 226; social and aesthetic, analogies between, 23–24, 49, 73, 78, 132–34. *See also* Genre, hierarchy of; Middle class; Social mobility; *and under* Consumerism; History painting; Portraiture
Dobson, Michael, 90, 96, 214
Domesticity, 139, 164, 166, 192; and art, 76, 81, 133; and national imaginary, 13, 56,

158; and virtue, 90–91, 119–20; and Smith, 119–20; theatricality of, 167; Wordsworth as icon of, 152, 156–58, 160–62, 168, 177, 181
Donaldson, Ian, 65
Dowling, Linda, 45, 77–78, 87, 101

Eaves, Morris, 104, 197, 212
Edgeworth, Maria, 25, 201
Eilenberg, Susan, 229
Ekphrasis, 8, 39–40, 44, 162–63, 165–66, 168, 171, 173, 175–76, 180; and authority, 231; counterekphrasis, 166–67; and fear, 166; notional, 164; and rivalry, 171; and sociability, 171. *See also* Sister arts
Elgin Marbles, 44, 130–32, 140–47; and aesthetic debate, 141, 224–25; and anatomy, 141–42; and antiacademic aesthetics, 141; Byron on, 141, 147, 225; Canova on, 141; Englishness of, 143–44, 226; and equality, 141–45; Haydon on, 143, 226; Hazlitt on, 140–44, 148, 225; Keats on, 226; Lawrence on, 141; purchase of, 224–25; realism of, 131–2, 140–46
Eliot, George: and realism, 130–32, 227
Ellis, Kate, 137, 223–24
Ellison, Julie, 218–19
Emulation, 132, 135–38
Englishness, 11, 13, 14, 32, 68, 75, 80, 90, 143–44, 228. *See also* History, and national identity; Nation; *and under* Elgin Marbles; Masculinity; Middle class
Engraving, engravers, 22, 24, 25, 32, 73, 77–80, 107, 108, 111, 113, 115, 117, 119, 121, 190, 213; and art production, 69, 77, 80, 82, 103; and author portraits, 42, 108–11, 127, 151–58; and authority, 58, 86, 89, 103, 154, 156; and circulation, 58, 61, 69, 79, 152, 154, 160; and history painting, 77, 80, 82; methods for, 213; Royal Academy's exclusion of, 5, 108, 111; and textual portrait galleries, 24–27, 31, 45, 127, 129. *See also* Copying; Printing
Erickson, Peter, 96, 214–15
Eroticism, 50, 57, 59–65, 119, 142–43, 210–11. *See also* Beauty; Clothing; Desire; *and under* Sentimentality

Fay, Elizabeth, 200
Femininity, 13, 59, 73, 106, 115, 119, 135, 143, 203–4, 220. *See also* Gender; Motherhood; *and under* Authority
Fenwick, Isabella, 164, 166, 171–72, 180
Frey, Charles, 99, 217
Fried, Michael, 162, 177–78, 220
Frontispiece(s), 26, 53; to Hobbes's *Leviathan*, 11–13, 16, 19, 22, 189–90, 200; to Smith's *Elegiac Sonnets*, 108–11, 114, 121, 219; Wordsworth's, 152, 156, 177–78, 232
Frye, Northrop, 216
Fumerton, Patricia, 124, 221
Furniss, Tom, 62, 211
Fuseli, Henri, 71, 75, 109

Gainsborough, Thomas: *Mrs. Siddons*, 15–16
Galleries: ancestral, 1–4, 31, 44, 56–58, 107, 150, 191; of characters, 109, 201; national, 31–32, 74–87, 105, 126–27, 183–93; parliamentary, 10, 45, 198; private, 1–4, 44, 59, 75, 85, 127; public, 4–5, 10, 12, 13, 29, 33, 43–44, 74–87, 91, 103–4, 109, 183, 191; textual, 4, 8, 19, 24–27, 31–32, 105, 126–27, 190–93, 200–201, 203, 208. *See also* British Institution; Country house(s); Macklin's Poets' Gallery; Madame Tussaud's Wax Museum; National Portrait Gallery (London); Royal Academy; Shakespeare Gallery; Society of Arts; *and under* Canon; Character(s); Coleridge; Dickens; Engraving
Galperin, William, 29, 202, 230–31
Garrick, David, 77, 84, 90–91, 96, 216
Gender, 142, 160; and academic hierarchy, 49, 63; and classical allusion, 71–72; and disinterestedness, 32, 63. *See also* Femininity; Homosociality; Masculinity

Genius, 8, 48; and Hazlitt, 142, 144, 225; and melancholy, 117, 220; and reproducibility, 43, 80, 135–36, 159–63; as romantic ideal, 142, 144, 170; Wordsworth and, 150–52, 159–63, 166, 168, 170, 175, 178, 181. *See also* Absorption
Genre, hierarchies of, 7, 23–26, 34–38, 63, 104, 106–7, 108, 134, 136, 216. *See also* Aesthetics, academic; Distinction, generic
George III, 11, 18–19, 79, 90–91, 216
George IV, 11, 20, 22, 25, 35, 36, 73
Gidal, Eric, 225
Gigante, Denise, 228
Gigantism, 140, 145, 170–71, 173, 177, 186, 222, 226. *See also* Scale; *and under* Miniature(s)
Gilfillan, George, 162, 176, 178
Gill, Stephen, 158, 170, 177, 180, 229
Gillies, Margaret, 163, 166, 168. *See also* Wordsworth, Mary, portrait of
Gillray, James, 11, 18–19, 53–54, 102–3; *The French Invasion; or John Bull, bombarding the Bum-Boats*, 18–19; *The Monster broke loose*, 102–3; *Notorious Characters*, 54; *Temperance enjoying a Frugal Meal*, 11; *Two Pair of Portraits*, 53–54
Gilpin, Sawry, 99
Godwin, William: *Cloudesly*, 145–46, 148
Goethe, Johann Wolfgang von, 113
Gombrich, E. H., 48
Granger, James, 24, 29
Gray, Thomas, 96, 126
Guillory, John, 96, 133

Hagstrum, Jean, 88, 221
Hamilton, William: paintings for the Shakespeare Gallery, 91, 93, 94, 95, 96, 100–101, 103
Harries, Elizabeth W., 219
Hastings, Warren, 47
Hawley, Judith, 221
Haydon, Benjamin Robert, 170–80; on Elgin Marbles, 143–45, 226; *Wordsworth on Helvellyn*, 168, 170–71, 177–80
Haygarth, William, 144
Hayley, William: *Epistle to Admiral Keppel*, 69
Hayter, George (Sir): *The House of Commons, 1833*, 183–90
Hazlitt, William, 24, 32, 50, 57, 67–68, 85, 87, 169, 187, 200; and aesthetics of particularity, 16, 29, 31, 140–44; on Elgin Marbles, 140–44, 148, 225; on genius, 142, 144, 225; Hogarth's influence on, 31, 142–44; on portrait practice, 60, 136; on the self, 41, 43; on Titian, 29, 41
Heath, Charles, 176
Heffernan, James A. W., 40, 205
Hemans, Felicia: "To My Own Portrait," 42–43; on Wordsworth, 151, 160, 168
Hemingway, Andrew, 200, 225–26
Hemm, J. P.: *Portraits of the Royal Family in Penmanship*, 19–22
Henry VIII, 24, 85, 163–64
Heringman, Noah, 225–26
Hilliard, Nicholas, 6
History, 8, 10, 40, 173, 183; of art, 76, 103, 158, 185; and biography, 24–26, 50, 190; literary, 105–7; and narrative, 52, 62, 85–86; and national identity, 24, 26–31, 48, 85–86, 87, 104, 127, 129; personified, 62, 65; private, 25, 42, 133, 179, 201; as romance, 85–86, 87, 104; teaching of, 25–26. *See also* History painting; *and under* Authority; Burke; Character(s); Theatricality
History painting, 5–6, 23–24, 34, 38, 44, 49, 62–63, 75–78, 80–82, 84–87, 91–92, 96, 104, 107, 133–35, 169, 216; cultural authority of, 23, 50, 216; and display, 133; downsized, 76, 85; English school of, 89, 103; engravings of, 77, 80, 82; high cost of, 76, 133; and masculinity, 50, 81; problems of display, 76; and public virtue, 81. *See also* Aesthetics, academic; Civic humanism; Distinction, generic; *and under* Boydell; Nationalism
Hobbes, Thomas, 66, 189–90; *Leviathan*,

frontispiece to, 11–13, 16, 19, 22, 189–90, 200
Hodges, William: "Antigonus Torn by a Bear," 99, 216
Hogarth, William, 4–5, 14–15, 19, 29, 31, 44, 142–44, 199–200, 225; Barry on, 15; on beauty, 15; "Britophil" campaign of, 14; and Hazlitt, 31, 142–44; legacy, 29, 31, 142–44; rawness of, 15; realism of, 14–15; Rouquet on, 15; and Signboards Exhibition, 5; *Analysis of Beauty*, 14–15; *Heads of Six of Hogarth's Servants*, 14–15
Hogle, Jerrold, 222
Holland, William, 50
Hollander, John, 164
Holt, Elizabeth Basye Gilmore, 45
Homosociality, 67–73, 215
Hoppner, John: *Mrs. Sheridan and her Son*, 26
Horne Tooke, John: *Two Pair of Portraits*, 22, 53
House of Commons, 4, 7, 34, 45, 183–90. *See also* Parliament; Reform Bill; Representation, political; *and under* Hayter; Rowlandson
Humphreys, William: *Who's in Fault? (Nobody) a view off Ushant*, 69–71
Hunt, Bishop C., Jr., 174–75, 231–32
Hunt, Lynn, 61, 210
Hunter, John, 24
Hurst, Richard, 100

Inheritance, 1–4, 6, 23, 31–32, 44, 162, 195; artistic, 15, 96, 131; entailed, 1, 47, 56; literary, 106–7, 125–27, 150, 219; political, 55–57, 58, 59; property, 1, 47, 55–57, 58, 59, 125, 126; matrilinear, 44, 125; spiritual, 71. *See also* Galleries, ancestral; Property; *and under* Burke

James, Henry, 8, 224
Jephson, Robert: *Roman Portraits*, 24–25
Jerdan, William, 31–32
Jerningham, Edward: "The Shakespeare Gallery," 81
Jewsbury, Maria Jane: "A Poet's Home," 160
Johnson, Claudia L., 65, 218
Johnson, Samuel, 24; on portraits, 40; and Reynolds, 48, 206; on the sonnet, 106
Jones, Robert W., 63

Kandl, John, 144
Kay, John: *Hieroglyphic Portrait of Bonaparte*, 16–17
Kearns, Katherine, 148, 222
Keats, John, 8, 10, 39–40, 144–45, 173; "Addressed to Haydon," 144; "Ode on a Grecian Urn," 39–40; "On Seeing the Elgin Marbles," 226
Kelley, Theresa, 38, 199, 204, 222, 234–35
Kemble, John Philip, 87
Keppel, Augustus, Lord, 67–73; Burke's verbal portrait of, 67, 72–73; court-martial of, 67–69, 71; friendship with Burke, 67–69, 72–73; as national icon, 68–69; parodied, 69–71; representations of, 67–71, 73. *See also under* Burke; Hayley; Reynolds
Knight, G. Wilson, 216
Knight, Richard Payne, 142
Kraft, Elizabeth, 208
Kramnick, Isaac, 49–50, 59
Krieger, Murray, 205
Kristeva, Julia, 115
Kriz, K. Dian, 204

Lamb, Charles, 75, 77
Landscape, 10, 19, 34, 71, 98, 175, 178. *See also under* Property
Lavater, John Casper, 39, 205
Lawrence, Thomas, 4, 7, 11, 141
Legitimacy, 11, 58, 88–89, 92–93, 100, 137
Levine, George, 131, 222
Likeness, 24, 105, 119, 127, 178, 191; affective power of, 157; and assessment of portraits, 88, 157; vs. idealization, 57–58, 73, 130–31, 164; imagined, 39, 162; and legitimacy, 88, 92–93, 100; in *The Winter's Tale*, 88, 92–93, 100. *See also* Mimesis

Lippincott, Louise, 76
Literacy, 159, 181
Livy, 19, 65
Locke, John, 11
Lootens, Tricia, 192, 214
Louvre, 41
Lucretia, 63–65, 211–12
Lynch, Deidre, 57, 75, 109, 135, 144, 201, 226

Macklin's Poets' Gallery, 5, 109
Madame Tussaud's Wax Museum, 5, 7
Magnuson, Paul, 141–42
Mallon, Thomas, 192, 235
Malone, Edmond: on Reynolds, 48, 71; on the Shakespeare Gallery, 79
Mandeville, Bernard: *Fable of the Bees*, 13–14, 15
Manent, Pierre, 11
Manet, Edouard: *Olympia*, 228
Manin, Bernard, 189
Manning, Peter, 158
Marie Antoinette: Burke on, 43, 48, 59–65, 71, 210–11; as Lucretia, 63, 65; as "paper queen," 61. *See also under* Burke
Marketplace, cultural, 5, 6, 8, 38, 44–45, 57–58, 75–76, 78–80, 82, 120, 133, 135, 150, 152–53, 158–59, 181. *See also* Consumerism; Copyright; Galleries; Taste; *and under* Portraiture
Markley, Robert, 218
Marshall, Tim, 146, 223
Martini, Pietro, 34; *The Exhibition of the Royal Academy, 1787*, 34–38
Marvell, Andrew, 41
Masculinity, 92, 107, 142–43, 214–15; attenuated, in Burke, 50, 52, 71–73; civic-humanist conception of, 49–50, 63, 65, 229; and English liberty, 56–59, 126; and desire, 61–63, 65; and melancholy, 117; and property, 56–59, 71, 126, 158, 160–61, 229; and sociability, 65–67; Wordsworth's, 154–55, 158, 160–61, 229. *See also* Gender; Homosociality; *and under* History painting
Mason, William, 114
Massing, Michael, 235
Mayhew, Henry, 29, 45
McPherson, C. B., 49
Meadows, Kenny, 45
Melancholy, melancholia, 109–17, 119–26, 168; and allusion, 115; and genius, 220; literariness of, 114; and nationalism, 191–93; personified, 117, 220–21. *See also under* Allusion; Genius; Portraits
Merchant, W. Moelwyn, 76, 78
Middle class, 10, 22, 53, 77, 96, 161; and art patronage, 5, 23–24, 77, 79, 101, 134, 213; character and, 75, 84–85, 109; cultural and economic influence of, 6–7, 22, 38, 77, 90, 101, 213; and Englishness, 11–12, 78; homes of, 80, 104; political representation of, 4, 101, 186; portraiture as, 23, 78, 80–81; readers, 45, 66, 75, 104, 148; social anxiety of, 133–39, 148. *See also* Distinction, class; Social mobility; *and under* Boydell; Consumerism
Miles, William, 72
Mill, John Stuart, 178
Milton, John, 23, 114; Fuseli's Gallery, 109; "Il Penseroso," 117
Mimesis, 5, 42, 48, 88, 100, 123, 166; and dependence, 16, 38, 86, 156, 158; vs. idealization, 39, 57, 60, 158, 163, 190; and realism, 141–42, 146. *See also* Copying; Likeness
Miniature: A Periodical Paper, The, 130
Miniature(s), 25, 35, 38, 42, 50, 81, 88, 107–8, 115, 187; and Austen, 54, 130; as commodity, 38, 135–36; display of, 35–38, 122, 133; Elizabethan, 6, 124, 221–22; in *Frankenstein*, 132–39, 148–49; and generic hierarchy, 35, 107–8, 133, 138; and the gigantic, 140, 171, 173, 176; hanging practices, 35–38, 132–33; metaphorics of, 38, 221–22, 227; on money, 58–59; "monstrous," 139–40, 149; and realism, 130–31, 135, 138, 140, 190; and sensibility, 44, 122–24, 134; and sexuality, 38, 138; and the sonnet, 43, 44, 107–8, 115, 122, 164, 171, 173, 176, 221–22; as toys, 35, 108, 138; as women's property, 124, 125, 130. *See*

also Gigantism; Portraits, miniature; Scale; *and under* Southey
Mitchell, W. J. T., 166, 197, 201–2
Money, 23, 57–59, 73, 75, 103, 120, 135, 161, 195, 209. *See also* Consumerism; Nouveaux riches; *and under* Authority; Property
Monstrosity, 7, 33, 103, 131–32, 133, 139–40, 144, 147, 148–49. *See also* Aesthetics; Beauty; Deformity; *and under* Miniature(s); Realism
Moretti, Franco, 1, 32, 227–28
Morgan, Macnamara, 90, 216
Mortimer, John Hamilton, 109
Motherhood, 89, 119–21, 122–25, 214–15. *See also* Femininity; Pregnancy; *and under* Inheritance; Smith
Moxon, Edward, 152, 154
Museums, 5, 24, 196, 203; and ekphrasis, 40; and prestige, 10. *See also* Galleries

Napoleon Bonaparte, 16–17, 19, 31, 175–76, 200, 222. *See also under* Kay; Wordsworth
Narrative, 204; and Austen, 54, 130; Burke and, 52; and character, 34, 52; desire, 62; providential, 85; and painting, 92–93, 99, 134, 165–66, 180. *See also under* Character(s); History; Novel, the
Nation: allegorized, 11–13, 16–22; as a body, 11–13, 16–22, 29, 60–61; and commerce, 78, 80; and domesticity, 13, 56, 158; English vs. French, 52, 55–59, 61, 72, 73; as imagined community, 3–4, 6, 7, 22–23, 32, 45, 55–56, 183–93; membership in, 19, 26–30, 48, 77–78, 85–86; providential narrative of, as romance, 85–86. *See also* Englishness; Nationalism; Representation, political; *and under* Beauty; Boydell; Galleries; History; Sentimentality; Shakespeare; Wordsworth
National Portrait Gallery (London), 3, 126, 181, 183, 203
Nationalism, 44, 69, 73–74, 77, 78, 80–81, 85–87, 104, 144–45, 190, 192, 203. *See also* Englishness; Nation; *and under* Boydell; Galleries; History; Portraits
Neely, Carol Thomas, 89, 214–15
Neoclassicism, 13, 142, 147–48, 166, 189
New York Times, The, 191–92
Nicol, George, 78, 82
Northcote, James, 47, 75, 76, 86, 103
Nostalgia, 40–41, 43, 215; Burke's, 66–67, 73; for rural scenes, 90; Wordsworth's, 156, 175
Nouveau riche, nouveaux riches, 7–8, 31, 78
Novalis: on Burke, 73
Novel, the, 4, 10–11, 31–34, 38, 45, 54–55, 108, 130–32, 145–49, 163, 227; and anatomy, 145–49; and character, 10, 32, 34, 54–55, 145–48, 208; large scale of, 8, 145, 224; and narrative desire, 62; and *portrait moral*, 43, 55; portraits in, 4, 31–32, 132–39; and realism, 130–32, 145–49; as representative space, 4, 32–33, 45, 54, 145; as resurrectionism, 146–48; and sketching, 54–55; and women, 13. *See also* Character(s); Narrative; Realism

Opie, John, 75, 97; "Leontes Commanding Antigonus" (painting for Shakespeare Gallery), 91–93, 100, 101. *See also under* Coleridge
Orgel, Stephen, 216
Orwell, George, 45
Otway, Thomas, 117–19, 121
Ownership, 10, 124, 167, 230. *See also* Copyright; Property

Paine, Thomas, 22, 52, 209
Parliament, 6–7, 10, 11, 12, 16, 31, 33, 45, 52–53, 66, 80, 142, 145–46, 148, 159–60, 188, 195, 197, 198. *See also* House of Commons; Reform Bill; Representation, political
Pascoe, Judith, 115, 220–21, 228, 233
Paster, Gail Kern, 214–15
Pater, Walter: on Wordsworth, 162–63, 230
Patten, Robert, 199

Paulson, Ronald, 15, 127, 143, 199–200, 214, 225
Payne, E. J., 63
Peel, Robert (Sir), 176, 188
Penshurst, 105–7, 111, 125, 129, 217–18
Perry, Gill, 207
Petrarch, 113–14
Pfau, Thomas, 207
Photography, 31, 45, 174, 193, 201–2, 206. *See also under* Portraits; Realism
Pickersgill, Henry William, 150, 152, 154–58, 176, 180–81, 229. *See also under* Wordsworth
Pinch, Adela, 114, 218, 220–21
Pocock, J. G. A., 211
Pointon, Marcia, 6, 81–82, 119, 201, 207–8
Politics, as art, 45, 53, 56, 183, 186, 203. *See also* Aesthetics, politics of; Nation; Representation, political; *and under* Burke; Reform Bill
Poovey, Mary, 11, 185
Pope, Alexander, 114
Portrait moral, 43, 55
Portrait poems, 10, 41, 43–45, 159, 162–63, 166–68, 180
Portraits: allegorical, 7, 29, 71, 211, 220–21; of authors, 42–43; of characters, 75, 82–85, 109, 201, 214; of children, 82, 119; conversation piece, 24, 56, 127, 153; frontispiece, 11, 16, 22, 26, 108–11, 114, 121, 152, 156, 177–78, 219, 232; of "Melancholy," 117; memorial, 24, 132, 134, 137, 191–93; mental, 39–40; miniature, 6, 35–38, 42, 43, 44, 54, 88, 107–8, 115, 122–25, 130–31, 132–39, 140, 148–49, 171, 176, 187, 190, 221, 227; national, 6–7, 11, 13, 19, 22, 31, 45, 47, 141, 183, 185–86, 188, 190; photographic, 202; poems about, 8, 10, 39–41, 43–45, 121–23, 125, 159, 162–63, 165–68, 171, 173, 175–76, 180; of politicians, 208; self-portraits, 10, 115, 157, 162, 168, 171, 173, 175–77; textual, 45, 190–93, 200–201, 203, 208; theatrical, 84, 210, 220–21; of trees, 8, 127, 129; verbal, 4, 22, 27, 43, 50, 54–55, 59–60, 66, 72, 113, 132, 138, 159–60; working-class, 26–30. *See also* Biography; Miniature(s); *and under* Novel, the; Siddons; Wordsworth
"Portraits of Grief," 191–93, 235; collected, 192; and national sentimentality, 192; as representative space, 191–93
Portraiture: and affect, 38, 40, 157, 192; and biography, 24–26, 61, 71, 119, 129, 144, 177; and consumerism, 49, 78, 84, 85, 86, 104, 133–35; dominates Academy exhibitions, 82; and dress, 7, 26, 48, 49, 186; as epistemology, 25; and generic distinctions, 7, 23–26, 29, 34–38, 44, 49, 75–77, 84, 86, 92, 96, 104, 106–8, 132, 163, 216, 226; and idealization, 8, 24, 29, 38–40, 183, 185; and ideology, 5–8, 197; as middle-class art, 23, 78, 80–81; as mimetic, 39; pedagogical use of, 25; politics of, 23, 53, 132, 157, 159, 181; and sociability, 171, 173; and the sonnet, 43, 44, 107–8, 115, 122, 164, 171, 173, 176, 221–22; and theater, 84, 210, 214; and theatricality of class, 23, 132. *See also* Miniature(s); Portraits; *and under* Boydell; Burke; Coleridge; Hazlitt; Johnson; Likeness; Shakespeare Gallery; Wordsworth
Pregnancy, 89, 214–15; and Siddons, 220; in *The Winter's Tale*, 89. *See also* Femininity; Gender; Motherhood
Pre-Raphaelites, 185, 233
Prestige, 5, 49, 78, 134. *See also under* Museums
Print culture, 8, 10, 16–22, 26–32, 52–53. *See also* Engraving; Printing; Galleries, textual; *and under* Boydell; Burke
Printing: as metaphor, 8, 88–89, 117, 154
Property, 180; and aesthetics, 48–49, 73; and allusion, 48–49; and authorship, 160, 162, 167; common, 4, 48–49, 160; fixed (land) vs. mobile, 6–7, 23, 31, 56–59, 67, 84, 107, 147, 197; and landscape, 10; national, 4, 56–59, 160; and political representation, 6–7, 147, 186, 197; transmission, 56–59, 109, 120–21, 127; women's, 109, 120–21, 127. *See also*

Copyright; Ownership; *and under* Masculinity; Miniature(s)
Propriety, 23, 33, 107, 119–20
Prosopopeia, 165
Pulteney, William, 60

Queen Caroline, 31
Queen Victoria, 187

Ramberg, J. H., 34–35; *The Exhibition of the Royal Academy, 1787*, 34–38
Realism, 13–15, 26–31, 45, 131, 148, 190, 201–2, 206, 222, 228, 234; and Dickens, 32, 45; and Eliot, 130–32, 227; of Elgin Marbles, 131–32, 140–46; and Hogarth, 14–15; and the miniature, 130–31, 135, 138, 140, 190; as monstrous, 145–49; and the novel, 130–32, 145–49. *See also* Aesthetics, of particularity
Redfield, Marc, 198, 203, 235
Reed, Henry, 171–72
Reform Bill (1832), 3, 6, 31, 45, 146–48, 150–52, 156–57, 181, 183, 186, 188–90; as aesthetic, 45, 186, 206; marketing of, 190; practical effects of, 188, 234; and revolution, 188; shortcomings of, 186, 233–34. *See also* Democratization; Representation, political; *and under* Beauty; Hayter; Shelley, Mary
Reid, Christopher, 210–11
Reni, Guido: portrait of Beatrice Cenci, 38
Representation, political, 4–5, 6–7, 10–13, 16–22, 34, 45, 103, 147–48, 185–86, 188–89, 195, 203. *See also* House of Commons; Nation; Parliament; Reform Bill; *and under* Middle class; Property
Representative space, 3, 12–13, 34, 45, 76, 185, 188–89, 193, 195. *See also under* Novel, the; "Portraits of Grief"
Revel, Jacques, 61
Revolution, 65, 73, 100, 217; aesthetic, 131–32, 145, 212; English, 11, 188, 209, 217; fear of, 31, 132, 148; French, 52, 58–61, 65, 71, 159, 212; and Reform, 45, 132, 186, 188; Shakespeare Gallery as, 5, 77, 79, 212. *See also under* Boydell; Burke; Reform Bill
Reynolds, Graham, 108, 133
Reynolds, Joshua (Sir), 3, 4, 185, 191, 225; and allusion, 16, 48–49, 82; Blake on, 13, 16; and Burke, 43, 47–50, 59–60, 61, 67, 71–73, 206; and the central form, 60–61, 141; and civic humanism, 16, 29, 48–50, 60–61, 63, 77, 135; compared with Gainsborough, 15–16; and *Frankenstein*, 44, 148; and idealizing portraiture, 15–16, 26, 60–61, 62–63, 82, 130–31, 141, 146–47; Johnson on, 48, 206; paintings of Keppel, 67–71; politics of, 33–34, 47–50; 60–61, 73, 146–47, 206; and Shakespeare Gallery, 75, 80, 82; *Admiral Viscount Keppel*, 67; *Commodore Augustus Keppel*, 71; *Discourses on Art*, 13, 16, 43, 47–49, 60, 63, 198, 206; "Ironic Discourse," 33–34, 47, 206; *Lady Elizabeth Delmé and her Children*, 127; *Mrs. Robinson as Perdita*, 84; *Puck*, 82, 84–85; *Mrs. Siddons as the Tragic Muse*, 15–16, 115, 117; Three *Ladies adorning a Term of Hymen*, 26. *See also* Aesthetics, academic; *and under* Burke; Canon
Richardson, Jonathan, 6
Richardson, Ruth, 147, 227
Robertson, Andrew, 108
Robinson, Henry Crabb, 154, 171, 173, 180
Romance, 139, 149; history as, 85–86, 87, 104; and national identity, 85–86; Shakespearean, 216–17; of upward mobility, 131. *See also under* Shakespeare; History; Nation
Romney, George, 75, 86, 117
Rosen, Charles, and Henri Zerner, 7
Rossetti, Dante Gabriel, 124
Rothenberg, Jacob, 141
Rouquet, Andre, 15
Rowlandson, Thomas, 15, 26; drawing of House of Commons, 186–89
Royal Academy, 3, 47, 73, 77, 130–31, 136, 141; charges entrance fee, 5, 79; ex-

cludes engravers, 5, 108, 111; hanging practices of, 34–38, 183; prevalence of portraits at, 5–6, 23, 32, 81–82; representations of, 7, 34–38; as representative space, 7, 11, 13, 45, 183; Shakespeare Gallery and, 74, 79, 81–82, 84; Wordsworth's portraits exhibited at, 158, 180. *See also* Aesthetics, academic; Reynolds, *Discourses on Art*
Russell, Gillian, and Clara Tuite, 170
Rydal Mount, 152, 160, 168, 173, 176. *See also* Jewsbury; Wordsworth

Scale, 2, 33, 60, 108, 130–33, 139–40, 170–71, 173, 185, 188, 190, 222, 225–26. *See also* Gigantism; Miniature(s); *and under* Novel, the; Portraiture
Schnapp, Jeffrey, 185, 200
Schor, Esther H., 113, 122, 219–20
Scott, Grant F., 78, 171, 205, 212, 231
Scott, Walter (Sir), 109, 227
Sculpture, 44, 49, 71–72, 88, 91, 100–101, 166; Elgin Marbles, 130–31, 140–41, 143–47
Senior, William, 217–18
Sentimentality, 2–3, 43–44, 49–50, 53, 65–67, 78, 96, 104, 107, 113–14, 132–34, 152, 156–58, 162, 180; heteroerotic, 65; national, 158, 192, 210; politics of, 218–19. *See also under* Burke; Miniature(s); Portraits; "Portraits of Grief"
Sewter, A. C., 170
Shaftesbury, Anthony Ashley Cooper, 3rd Earl of, 14–15, 77, 98
Shakespeare Gallery, 5, 23, 43–44, 74–104, 109, 212, 216; business plan, 78; closing of, 104; Malone on, 79; as nationalist project, 77, 82, 84, 104, 213; origins of, 78; paintings of, slashed, 103; portraiture in, 85; as representative space, 76; reviews of, 85; as revolution in art patronage, 5, 77, 79, 212; vs. Royal Academy, 74, 79, 81–82, 84; treatment of authority in, 91–103. *See also* Boydell; *and under* Hamilton; Opie; Reynolds; West; Wheatley; Wright
Shakespeare, William, 25, 32, 74–104, 109, 114; and illustration, 23–24, 76–77, 82–84, 91–103, 212; as national poet, 75, 78, 214; Jubilee, 214; stage adaptations, 90–91, 216; *Comedy of Errors*, 111; *Coriolanus*, 19; *Cymbeline*, 75; *Henry VIII*, 24, 85, 164; *King Lear*, 75; *Romeo and Juliet*, 75; *The Tempest*, 85; *The Winter's Tale*, 44, 72, 76–77, 82, 85, 86–103, 214–15. *See also* Shakespeare Gallery; *and under* Coleridge; Romance
Shee, Martin Archer: *Rhymes on Art*, 108, 136
Shelley, Mary, 227; economic uncertainty of, 148; and the novel, 131–32, 145–48; oversees publication of husband's work, 227; and Reform, 132, 148, 223; takes drawing lessons, 132; *Frankenstein*, 31, 44, 131–41, 146–49, 222; review of *Cloudesly*, 145–46, 148. *See also under* Miniature(s); Reynolds
Shelley, Percy Bysshe: *The Cenci*, 38, 204; "Defense of Poetry," 227; "Essay On Love," 38, 227; "On the Medusa of Leonardo in the Florentine Gallery," 40; "Ozymandias," 40
Sheridan, Richard Brinsley: *The School for Scandal*, 58
Siddons, Sarah, 87, 115, 117, 210–11, 220; portraits of, 15–16, 115, 117, 211, 221. *See also under* Beach; Gainsborough; Reynolds
Sidney, Algernon, 106, 217–18
Sidney, Philip (Sir), 105–6, 121, 129, 221
Sieyès, Emmanuel, 189
Simpson, David, 235
Siskin, Clifford, 107
Sister arts, 87–88. *See also* Ekphrasis; *and under* Narrative
Sketching, 107, 130, 146, 186, 219; of character, 4, 25, 32, 43, 53–55, 67. *See also under* Character(s); Novel, the
Smith, Adam, 80
Smith, Charlotte: 44, 105, 125; and autobiography, 219; and canon, 126–27; daughter's death, 120, 123; and literary

authority, 115; and marketplace, 221; and matrilinear inheritance, 125; and Otway, 117, 119, 121; premature obituary of, 109; and Sidney's oak, 129; sorrow of, as literary, 109, 114; theatricalization of motherhood, 120. *See also under* Canon; Character(s); Domesticity
— *Elegiac Sonnets*, 44, 105, 125; frontispiece, 108–11, 114–15, 219; prefaces to, 108, 113, 119–20; sonnet 1 ("The partial muse has from my earliest hours"), 105, 113–15, 121; sonnet 3 ("To a Nightingale"), 107, 117, 119, 121; sonnet 4 ("To the Moon"), 105, 111, 115, 121–22; sonnet 8 ("To Spring"), 115; sonnet 12 ("Written on the sea shore"), 115; sonnet 24 ("Supposed to be Written by Werter"), 113; sonnet 26 ("To the River Arun,"), 119; sonnet 29 ("To Miss C—"), 115, 117; sonnet 32 ("To Melancholy"), 117; sonnet 37 ("Sent to the Honorable Mrs. O'Neill"), 107; sonnet 38 ("When welcome slumber sets my spirit free"), 121; sonnet 46 ("Written at Penshurst"), 105–7, 111, 122, 125, 129; sonnet 65 ("To Dr. Parry of Bath"), 107; sonnet 91 ("Reflections on Some Drawings of Plants"), 111, 121–26; sonnet 92 ("Written at Bignor Park, Sussex"), 121–22, 125
Smith, Johanna, 132, 148
Smith, John Thomas, 29
Smollett, Tobias, 33, 34
Sociability, 5, 61, 66–67, 97–98, 170, 180, 204. *See also* Sentimentality; *and under* Ekphrasis; Portraiture
Social body: and art genres, 23, 34–38, 76; clothing and, 59–61; consumerism and, 5, 48, 67; and detail, 16–19, 132, 144, 148; emergence of, as terminology, 11–12; historical transformation of, 10–11, 50, 65, 66, 76; imagined, 3–11, 26–30, 48, 77, 131, 146–47, 131, 188, 191; imagined as inclusive, 4, 13, 16, 26–30, 45; imagined as monstrous, 7, 33, 132, 145–48; imagined as unified, 11, 16–19, 77, 104, 183, 188, 190, 193; ordering of, 34–38; plurality of, 11, 16, 19, 77; portraiture and, 4, 133; realist aesthetics of, 4, 7, 13, 16, 26–30, 33, 45, 131–32, 145–48. *See also* Body; Democratization; Middle class; Nation; Representative space; Working class
Social mobility: and art patronage, 34–38, 77–79; Burke and, 66; and class anxiety, 132–39, 148–49; downward, 125, 135–39; and mobility of artistic genre, 23–24, 49, 73, 78, 132–34; and Reynoldsian portraiture, 49, 73; theatricality and, 7, 23, 26, 49, 73, 85, 132; and *The Winter's Tale*, 90–91, 93, 95. *See also* Distinction, class; Middle class
Society of Arts, 5, 24
Society of Painters in Water Colour, 108
Sokol, B. J., 217
Solkin, David, 98, 197, 211
Sonnet(s), 42, 43, 44, 105–9, 110–11, 113–15, 117, 119–26, 129, 144, 150, 156–57, 163–64, 167–68, 170–80, 221–22. *See also under* Johnson; Miniature(s); Portraiture; Smith; Wordsworth
Southey, Robert: "On My Own Miniature Picture, Taken at Two Years of Age," 42–43
Spacks, Patricia Meyer, 218
Spiller, Michael, 114
Stallybrass, Peter, and Allon White, 12
Stanton, Judith, 221
St Clair, William, 227
Steele, Richard, 2
Steiner, Wendy, 205
Sterrenburg, Lee, 147, 222–23, 227
Stewart, Susan, 176, 191, 226
Stothard, Thomas, 117
Strutt, Jacob: *Sylva Britannica: or Portraits of Forest Trees*, 8, 127, 129
Stubbs, George, 15
Sublime, the, 2, 10, 72, 91, 97–98, 105, 176, 178, 183
Suffering, 62, 120, 123, 133, 172

Swartz, Richard G., 230
Swift, Jonathan: *Gulliver's Travels*, 140

Tagg, John, 31, 202
Talfourd, Thomas Noon, 159–60
Tanner, Tony, 55
Taste, 13–14, 34, 47–49, 52, 62, 75–79, 80–82, 84, 86, 160, 200, 225
Taylor, George (George the Barber), 26–27
Temple, Lancelot, 72
Teskey, Gordon, 22, 235
Thackeray, William Makepeace: *Vanity Fair*, 11
Theatricality, 10, 44, 84–87, 96–97, 108, 111, 115, 117, 119–20, 123–24, 133, 135, 137, 142, 145, 151–52, 158–59, 170, 176, 180–81, 209, 228; of class, 7, 23, 26, 49, 73, 85, 132; of country houses, 106; of domesticity, 167; of history, 85–86; of motherhood, 119–20; of propriety, 119–20. *See also under* Character(s); Portraits; Portraiture
Thomson, Henry, 93, 216
Thompson, E. P., 233–34
Titian, 29, 41
Tourism, 105, 152, 192, 208
Turner, James, 107
Turner, J. M. W., 222
Twain, Mark, 204

Uphaus, Robert W., 206

Van Dyck, 6, 32, 71, 205
Verbal portraits, 4, 22, 27, 43, 50, 54, 55, 59, 60, 72, 113, 132, 138, 159, 160, 207. *See also* Sketching; *and under* Burke; Keppel; Portraits
Vernon, James, 208–9
Vickery, Amanda, 137

Wakley, Thomas, 162
Waller, Edmund, 106, 129
Walpole, Horace, 82, 105, 217
Warton, Thomas, 106
Watercolor painting, 7, 26, 108, 217
Watt, Ian, 11–12, 33, 190
Watt, W. H., 152, 154, 156, 158
Wayne, Don, 106
Wellington, Duke of, 170–76, 180, 188, 232; frequently caricatured, 176; Wordsworth identifies with, 174, 176, 232
Wendorf, Richard, 84, 206
West, Benjamin, 15, 23; and Shakespeare Gallery, 75; *Death of Wolfe* (1776), 77, 212
West, John, 132
Whale, James, 140
Wheatley, Francis, 26, 217: and Shakespeare Gallery, 91, 96–98, 101
Williams, Raymond, 131
Wilson, Richard, 15
Wolcot, John (Peter Pindar), 7, 22
Wolfson, Susan J., 157
Wollstonecraft, Mary, 50, 52, 62
Woloch, Alex, 34
Wood, Gillen D'Arcy, 206
Wordsworth, Christopher, 155, 160, 179
Wordsworth, Dora, 152, 157, 168, 170, 229
Wordsworth, Dorothy, 40, 42, 157, 160
Wordsworth, Mary, 157, 163, 166–68
Wordsworth, William, 7, 29, 32–33, 38–42, 44–45, 107, 113, 150–81; annoyed by printer's errors, 177; Arnold on, 177–78, 180, 232; and the body, 154; Chantrey's bust of, 155; conservatism of, 150, 168; as domestic icon, 151–52, 157–58, 160, 166, 168, 181; identification with Napoleon, 175; identification with Wellington, 174, 176, 232; invites Haydon to Rydal, 177; and Lord Lowther, 218; as national poet, 7, 77, 150–52; offends wife, 168; painted posthumously, 180; Pater on, 162–63, 230; petitions Parliament on copyright, 158; on politics and portraiture, 157, 159, 181; portrait by Pickersgill, 150, 152, 154, 156, 158, 180, 229; and pose of absorption, 158–68; as public poet, 168, 229; and revision, 173; and Rydal, 152, 160, 168, 173, 176; and self-promo-

tion, 24, 85, 152–54, 157; and unauthorized editions, 158; and Victorians, 178, 229–30; sends anonymous letter to *Kendal Mercury* on copyright, 161; strikes whip through ancestral portrait, 150; *Wordsworth on Helvellyn*, 168, 170–71, 177–78, 180, 232; "By Art's bold privilege," 170–77; "Elegiac Stanzas Suggested by a Picture of Peele Castle," 232; "I wandered lonely as a Cloud," 163; "Lines Composed a Few Miles Above Tintern Abbey," 40, 42, 157, 163, 174, 230; "Lines Suggested by a Portrait from the Pencil of F. Stone," 164–66; *Lyrical Ballads*, 29, 150; "Michael," 32, 229; "More may not be by human Art exprest," 166; "Ode: Intimations of Immortality," 175, 216; "Poet to His Grandchild, A" 161; *Poetical Works* (1836), 152, 154, 156–57; *The Prelude*, 7, 29, 33, 113, 163; "Recollection of the Portrait of King Henry Eighth," 163–64; "Sonnet to a Picture by Lucca Giordano in the Museo Borbonico at Naples," 231; "To a Painter," 163–64, 167; "To B. R. Haydon, On Seeing His Picture of Napoleon Buonaparte on the Island of St Helena," 175; "To the Author's Portrait," 156, *See also under* Absorption; Barrett

Working class, 4, 10, 26–30, 45, 86, 90, 96, 136–38, 144, 147–48, 186, 234. *See also* Anatomy Act; Reform Bill; Revolution; *and under* Portraits; Social body

Wright, Joseph: painting for Shakespeare Gallery, 91, 98–100

Zimmerman, Sarah D., 111, 219–20

Zoffany, Johan, 15, 216; *Garrick and Mrs. Pritchard in Macbeth*, 84